Fractured Emerald:
Ireland

FRACTURED EMERALD:
IRELAND

EMILY HAHN

OPEN ROAD
INTEGRATED MEDIA
NEW YORK

Copyright © 1971 by Emily Hahn Boxer

ISBN 978-1-4976-3827-3

This edition published in 2014 by Open Road Integrated Media, Inc.
345 Hudson Street
New York, NY 10014
www.openroadmedia.com

INTRODUCTION

Ireland, one occasionally feels, has suffered as much from her historians as from her oppressors. In the Irish schools, the nation's history is taught as if it were a medieval morality play; Irish newsstands are cluttered with poorly written paperbacks by old patriots, each of whom explains in detail how he wrested Ireland's freedom from England's grasp; and even gifted amateurs (civil servants and barristers who should know better) write as if Ireland's national experience has been the result of one long anti-Hibernian conspiracy.

Fortunately, since the Second World War, a professional counter-point to the amateur intermeddling in Irish historiography has developed. The professional historians have worked quietly and patiently to uncover what *really* happened in the Irish past. Sometimes their results have been acutely embarrassing to blindered nationalists and, often, cherished myths have been exploded. But just as often the professional workers in Irish history have led us to understand the complexity and richness of Irish life which had been hidden previously beneath the cloud of sentimentality.

I am especially happy to introduce Miss Hahn's book because it is based on her reading of the professional historians and, more important, on her personal discussion with many of the same historians. Her book is Irish history for the general reader, but not for the reader who wants to rehear the romantic nonsense he heard from his IRA grandfather. It is an informed, lively, and highly readable book that will be enjoyed by anyone with even the slightest interest in Irish history.

Were I to single out the section that I find most fascinating, it is the author's discussion of medieval Ireland. The Middle Ages in Irish history are incredibly confused. Hibernicized Englishmen, Anglicized Irishmen, and Dublin Castle officials swirled about in a political-social game that appears to have had no rules and no winners; somehow everyone lost. Miss Hahn has delineated the patterns beneath the confusion without simplifying to the point of distortion.

Most readers will, I imagine, be interested in the material on the nineteenth and twentieth centuries because of its proximity to our own times and because of the interest in the development of modern Irish nationalism. Herein is food for thought about the nature of nationalism in general, for the Irish nationalist revolution was the first of the wars of national liberation that have become so prevalent in our times. Ireland seems almost to have been the template for the now familiar revolutionary pattern: national revolution against an external oppressor, followed by civil war, culminating in a long period of domestic repression. Inevitably, I am reminded of the comment of a former student who, after sitting through a full year of lectures on Irish history, commented, bewildered, after the last class: "Sir—all that history for *this?!*"

Still, and all, Ireland's story is a good story and this version is well worth reading.

Donald H. Akenson
Associate Professor of History
Queen's University
Kingston, Ontario
Canada

FOREWORD

It was Easter 1916. Rebellion had broken out in Dublin, and no news got through to London until Max Aitken—the future Lord Beaver-brook—managed to reach Tim Healy, who was in Dublin, on the telephone. Healy, Irish M.P., was to be the first governor-general of the Irish Free State. Beaverbrook has recorded the conversation:

"Is there a rebellion?" asked Aitken.

"There is," said Healy.

"When did it break out?"

"When Strongbow invaded Ireland."

"When will it end?"

"When Cromwell gets out of Hell!"

"This conversation in one sense summarizes Irish history, 1169-1922."
                              -Rev. F. X. Martin, O.S.A.

CHAPTER

1

IRELAND'S story, if not unique, is exceptional. Through centuries of being conquered, occupied, cruelly used, fought over, and exploited, she has retained her individuality and has never lost sight of her goal, freedom from the invader. She has gone her own way, which coincides with no other. How is one to account for this long feat of endurance? Not by citing the peculiarities of race: the original settlers of Ireland were the same men who populated Britain and northern Europe. The answer probably lies in her geographical position—close to Britain yet detached, in the cold north where the population has always had to struggle for survival. The Irish are tough, or they would not be there.

Geologists think it was something like eight to ten thousand years ago when rising waters isolated Eire from the great land mass of the European continent, at an earlier date than the separation of Britain, too, from the mainland. Britain's western coastline curves over and around Ireland, protectingly or threateningly depending on one's political point of view. The water dividing these two islands is 120 miles across at its widest, but in the North Channel there is one place where the passage is only 25 miles wide. Studying the map, any jigsaw-puzzle addict's fingers will itch to move the two pieces of land together because they seem to fit so well, but if history teaches us anything it is that such a reunion would be—as the doctors have it—contraindicated.

Travel by water was slow and perilous at the time of Christ: on the far side of Britain from the Continent Ireland was cut off from the rest of the known world. New ideas and developments in Europe were a long time arriving if they got to Ireland at all, and they were usually weakened by that time, or otherwise altered for the worse. The Roman invasion, however, was completely absorbed by Britain en route, the Romans never passing beyond Pembrokeshire, let alone the Irish Sea. When Caesar landed on British soil the other island was still considered and dismissed as a dangerous outland of forest and mountain and bog, full of wild beasts and wilder men.

The background of these wild men is vague to us. There may have been humans in Ireland even before the waters rose and separated the countries, but the first people who left signs of occupation were Neolithic tribes who evidently came from southern and eastern Europe by way of Britain or perhaps Brittany. They were Picts, of the same race that lived in Britain, who could domesticate animals and pasture them. They built houses of woven lath and clay, cut down trees and grew crops on the clearings, made pottery, and spun wool. Their most lasting achievements were stonework buildings—great tombs and monuments and certain structures that may have been temples. Many of these stone edifices have survived. In the Boyne Valley, at New-grange, is a splendidly preserved burial mound with patterns chiseled on the inside walls, regular circles and whorls like those found in Britain. Most Picts cremated their dead and buried the ashes in mass graves. This was done at Newgrange, but individual burials too have been found in smaller graves. Also, the living buried possessions with certain of the dead people—pots, tools, and beads.

Later, probably after 2000 B.C., a different people came into Ireland, bringing techniques unknown to the earlier settlers. They were the Early Bronze Age men, who dug copper and tin and smelted the metal to make the alloy called bronze. Bronze Age pins, buckles and other jewelry have survived in large numbers, with bronze spearheads and knives and swords, and have been dug up by modern man. Then these prehistoric miners found gold, mainly in the Wicklow Mountains. They developed a new technique to work the malleable stuff and produced exceedingly beautiful objects—golden collars, torques, bracelets, rings, and brooches. Raw Irish gold left the country in ingots which were traded in continental Europe and Asia Minor, and the traders brought home objects from those far-off lands. Some of these, too, have been exhumed.

After a.d. 600 yet another wave of migrants came into Ireland, bringing an end to the Bronze Age. These Celts, or Gaels, were offshoots of the iron-using people who had overrun Britain and the Continent. Bronze Age metalworkers had brought weaponry up to a high standard and equipped their warriors with efficient short-bladed swords and leather bronze-studded shields, but even they couldn't stand up to the new iron weapons, and the Celts vanquished the Picts. They became the new overlords of Ireland.

In such telescoped form, eighty or a hundred centuries of Irish prehistory can be made to sound tidy. Bronze Age pushes out Stone Age, to be dislodged in turn by Iron Age, as in a gigantic game of musical chairs, but events do not really arrange themselves in such obligingly neat form. The changes took place irregularly, at different times in different places, with long lags. And the defeated races did not disappear from the scene just to make our work easier. They lingered as subservient members of the new order, or, more often, left the areas they favored to take refuge among hills and the thick forests that still covered most of the country. The overlords moved in and lived on the flat plains of central Ireland, where crops grew best and animals could graze easily. To the north and south the island is mountainous, its ranges leveling off toward the center in little hills called drumlins, still fiercely steep but eventually tailing away. The central flat region is a wide band running at a slant on the map, northeast to southwest, coast to coast. In the west these lowlands are boggy, but the eastern half is naturally well drained, a good place for farms and herds. It is the district most thickly studded with remains of prehistoric fortifications.

In Caesar's day the Irish were passing through their Heroic Age. Kings battled kings rather as men today go to work—it was their daily task. The social structure was complex. Small groups were governed by kings, but the kings had their own hierarchies, with high kings over subkings. There were nobles, priests (Druids) of the same social status, freemen of lower status, and unfree men. The Irish had no written language, the Druids keeping the entire store of racial knowledge in their heads. Among the free members of society was an arrangement of fealty that bore little if any relationship to the feudalism of Europe. It was based on livestock. A freeman would borrow breeding cattle from his lord and pay rent on the beasts for a certain period of time, until they had bred enough new animals for him to stock his farm. These payments constituted fealty, and the borrower was expected to serve his lord when called upon to do so, on the battlefield or in other emergencies. When the parent stock was no longer needed he could return the beasts to their owner, such repayment automatically releasing him from fealty to that overlord: usually, however, people preferred to continue as followers of the same man until death ended the connection.

The Irish meaning of the word "king" is also unlike that of neighboring countries, since there were many limits to a king's powers. Usually he could not adjudicate; justice was the preserve of the Druids. He could not appoint his successor, nor was it taken for granted that his son would automatically inherit, for the Druids had declared that such matters were settled by the *darb-fine,* a special law of succession. The royal family group must elect the new tanist, or king, from a precisely defined circle comprising not only the late king's sons but his brothers, his father's brothers, his grandfather's brothers, and even —assuming they were still alive—his great-grandfather's brothers, with the children of all these relatives. This would seem to give the electors a wide choice, but the prize was usually passed back and forth between the two main branches of the family. To avoid quarrels and bloodshed, the election of the tanist was usually held well before the existing incumbent died, though even with such precautions there were quarrels. As the method applied also to non-royal families and their inheritances, we can see why genealogies were so important to the Irish, and why the Druid genealogist needed a trustworthy, retentive memory.

When Christianity pushed out Druidism, the legal powers of the priests passed to a new class, the brehons, who inherited something of the Druids' supernatural aura as well. The Druids had been masters of magic, and when newly converted kings had to give up the comfort and promise of spells they must have felt sadly insecure. We have little information on that lost magic, the Church having effectively erased most of it from the records, but "Druid mist," which could be called up to befuddle the enemy in battle, is still remembered in legend.

Until the ninth century and the era of the Norsemen there were no towns or cities in all Ireland. In that pastoral country, people's lives were arranged about their cattle. They grew crops with which to feed the animals, and in the summer they drove the beasts to where the grain was growing, though they reserved some of it in dry form for winter needs. During those summer months in the fields they camped out in *buaile,* or booleys; the rest of the year they lived in little rural or family groups, complete with domestics and farmhands, in self-sufficient homesteads often called raths. These were ring-forts of a sort, much of a pattern though they varied in size and strength. An earthen rampart, usually circular and always topped by a wooden stockade, surrounded the land on which stood the owner's house-nothing grand, made of mud and lath or timber—and outhouses for his slaves, farm gear, and perhaps a few animals, dogs and horses. Cattle were kept outside the stockade. Everyone lived in this fashion, though prosperous men advertised their wealth with luxurious furnishings and kings had two ramparts rather than one. A poor freeman's house was far inferior, but the actual land was no problem, since in all Ireland there were at most half a million people. This townless existence seems isolated, but the ancient Irish were not really secluded, for they attended periodic meetings, get-togethers for business and pleasure where everyone could meet friends, settle disputes, arrange loans of cattle, dance, race horses, and take part in contests of skill or strength, with the high king, or ardri, presiding over all. These meetings, even after Christianity arrived, always took place on an ancient burial ground, for which reason some people think they derived from pagan funeral games. Our country fairs and church bazaars may have a similar source.

The oldest Irish epic that can be traced deals with the story of a warrior queen, Maeve of Connacht, said to have lived about the time Christ was born, who made war on Cuchulain, of the great kingdom of Ulster, to get possession of the magic bull of Cooley. Two centuries later the epics tell of two high kings who held power over all the other Irish rulers: Conn of the Hundred Fights controlled most of the fertile center of the island and Eoghan More ruled the south. After many inconclusive battles the two agreed to divide the country, each on his side of a line running from today's Dublin to Galway. Eoghan More's descendants were the Eoghanachts. Their kingdom included Munster and Clare, with the hill of Cashel for center and capital. Conn's descendants, the Dal Cuinn, vigorously expanded their central territory all the way to the west coast, taking in land from Leinster and Ulster. Of his breed the greatest was Niall of the Nine Hostages, whose people the Ui Neills ventured even farther, across the North Channel by way of the Hebrides to Britain. In those wild outlands they made themselves at home, some tending their beasts, others voyaging back and forth for trade or piracy from Antrim to

Argyll or Kirkcudbright. Alba was their name for the new country, but as Irish Celts were known as Scots (*Scottici*), this adopted land, in the course of time, was called Scotland.

In 306 the southern half of Britain was a thriving Roman colony ruled by Constantius, Augustus of the Western Empire. That year he was in England with his son Constantine, and when he died Constantine succeeded to the tide, but was dissatisfied with it. He was an ambitious man. In 312 he invaded Italy to make war on the Emperor for the greatest rank of all.

The Christians were then a suppressed minority. Constantine was favorably disposed toward the new faith nevertheless: a racing man would say that he felt a hunch about it. His imagination was stirred by the thought of Jesus, so much so that before he rode into the decisive battle for the Empire against his enemy Maxentius, he ordered his soldiers to paint on their shields the Greek-character monogram of Christ, chi rho or X P. Riding with his men toward the Milvian bridge outside Rome, he saw a cross of light high in the sky over the sun. The omen proved true. That afternoon at the bridge, Maxentius was killed in battle and Constantine the Greek became ruler of the Roman Empire.

It is impossible to exaggerate the effect of his conversion on subsequent world history. Now the Church was honored, not persecuted, and free of the litigation that had so hampered it. Constantine's subjects followed his example until within a century Roman Britain was probably more Christian than pagan. But Roman power there was fading. There was no dramatic or sudden abandonment of the colony, only a measured withdrawal: the legions slid away like a slowly ebbing tide, with soldiers embarking in greater and greater numbers on the homeward-bound ships. They left a few British trained to fight the Roman way, but as the disciplined troops who had policed the country disappeared, Celtic raiders, long intimidated, grew more audacious. Some made forays from Scotland across the ruined Wall of

Hadrian, more arrived in ships from Ireland. Ireland's patron saint Patrick was born at this time, while his native Britain was still Roman in tradition and law, when educated people spoke in Latin and the new Christian faith had taken root and flourished. But the great days of the Empire were over, and Rome ceased to be bulwark and protector of Britain.

When I was a child in St. Louis, our Irish cook used to tell me that Patrick was the first Christian ever to go to Ireland, and that he converted all the Irish. She sincerely believed this, but it is likely she was mistaken. I say likely because one can't absolutely refute her statements (or any others about the subject) with chapter and verse: little is known of Patrick's life. The legends accrued around his name are many and bewilderingly contradictory. But a lot of research has been done since our cook's day, and I am particularly grateful for a recent publication, *Saint Patrick: His Origins and Career,* by the Reverend Professor R. P. C. Hanson. For instance, the author convinces with his argument that the saint was born not before 388 and not after 408. It may seem a small point, but no point concerning Patrick is small-it is too rare for that. Some people even doubt that he existed at all: one man recently referred to him as the Paul Bunyan of Ireland, but this is carrying caution too far. Patrick existed. It is not his fault that he has been accredited with many fatuous-sounding miracles, for he himself seems never to have claimed credit for even one. Of his actual writings only two examples have been preserved, and both have been sifted over and over for meanings other than the obvious. His Latin style was awkward in the extreme, though at that time the writings of other scholars were polished and beautifully balanced. The British Pelagius, whose well-known heresy shocked and angered the Church, was one of Patrick's contemporaries. He was an accomplished scholar; Patrick was not. Nevertheless it was Patrick who went on that important mission to Ireland. The explanation for this puzzling combination of facts lies in a painful but very important adventure of his early youth. He tells us that he was the son of a comfortably fixed man, a decurion or alderman who seems also to have been a deacon—he may have taken the latter office to save himself from taxes. The family lived in a country villa, just where is unclear. At fifteen the boy was probably learning his lessons like other boys of his class, acquiring Latin as one of the refinements no gentleman could afford to be without, but for everyday purposes he spoke the dialect of the country. He says he paid little attention then to religious matters. At fifteen or sixteen he was kidnapped by sea raiders and carried off, with many fellow captives, to Ireland, and there sold into slavery.

For six years Patrick was a swineherd somewhere in Ireland. As to where, many have guessed, but Patrick has given few if any clues. Hanson thinks it might have been in county Mayo on the west coast, for Patrick mentions "the wood of Foclut," and there is a place of similar name near Killala in Mayo. In his loneliness the young exile found comfort in prayer. "Before I was humiliated I was like a stone lying in the deep mire; and He that is mighty came and in His mercy lifted me up, and raised me aloft, and placed me on top of the wall...." One night in his sleep a voice told him it was time to escape. Patrick succeeded in getting away and finally, after many dangers, made his way back to England and his family. There the episode might have ended, even though Patrick's education had been ruthlessly interrupted. But he could not forget Ireland. He thought about his days of servitude until—"And there it was that I saw in the vision of the night a man coming as if from Ireland whose name was Victoricus with countless letters and he gave me one of them and I read the beginning of a letter that contained 'The cry of the Irish,' and when I began to think that at that very moment I heard the cry of those who were by the wood of Foclut which is near the Western sea, and this is what they cried out as if with one mouth, 'We beseech you, holy boy, to come and again walk among us,' and I was greatly pricked at the heart and I was not able to read further and so I woke up" (p. 207).

Patrick made up his mind to enter the Church, doubtless

with the intention of returning to Ireland to share his faith
with his friends. There are theories that he did his training
in Gaul, but Professor Hanson argues that if he had, his
Latin would have improved, and all too obviously it didn't.
Furthermore, he writes that he wishes he had been able
to visit various holy places on the Continent. Presumably,
then, he wasn't able. After ordination he returned to Ireland.
One naturally assumes he was sent by the Pope. Not so,
says Professor Hanson: instead, he must have gone under
orders from the Church of Britain, for Pope Celestine had
very recently sent another bishop to Ireland, a man named
Palladius, and His Holiness would hardly have duplicated
officers thus, even though Palladius' name does disappear
almost immediately. Besides, Patrick was almost certainly
a monk (an interesting fact in itself, since in his time
monasticism was a new idea) and Pope Celestine did not
like monks as bishops. "It is inconceivable that he should
have sent one as a bishop to Ireland. Even if Patrick was not
a monk, he did encourage monks..." (p. 195).

I think we can discount our cook's statement that Patrick
was a pioneer among heathen who had never heard of Christ.
The traders from Gaul and Britain who visited Ireland were
nearly all Christian, and the Irish knew them long before
Patrick came. Ludwig Bieler *(Ireland, Harbinger of the
Middle Ages,* p. 15) quotes a curious poem circulated by the
Druids even before Patrick was born:

> Adze-head will come,
> Across the bald-headed sea,
> Hollow-headed his mantle,
> Bent-head his staff,
> His table facing east,
> His people, chanting, answer;
> Amen, Amen.

Unless we believe that Druids really had the magic power
of second sight we must conclude that someone among them
had seen a foreign bishop with miter, chasuble, and crozier,

celebrating mass, or that someone who had witnessed a mass in Gaul brought the word to the Druids, who, sensing that Christianity threatened them, resisted with mockery.

Patrick was bishop in Ireland from about 425 until his death in 460. Most of that time he probably worked from Armagh, his main successes being among the poor and humble, though at least once he refers to aristocratic converts: he rejoiced to see, he said, that "the sons of the Irish and the daughters of their kings are monks and brides of Christ."

"No rhetoric enhances the effect of his circumambulatory and painfully awkward utterances," the professor sums up. "But no rhetoric stands in the way of his conveying his real sentiments to the reader....There is no barrier between him and his reader. He is one of the most honest men who ever wrote Latin, perhaps the most honest of all who ever wrote Christian Latin" (pp. 206-7).

The Irish adopted monastic life with such enthusiasm that soon the conventional ecclesiastical system of bishops and sees simply did not work any more. Within a century and a half after Patrick, the monasteries had taken from the prelates a large part of their congregations, who as monks and nuns retired from the world. There would have been too many bishops in any case. According to Roman usage each kingdom was entitled to a prelate, a rule that worked well enough in Gaul where kingdoms were of considerable size, but Ireland was divided into smaller areas, 150 *tuatha*—kingdoms—and that meant 150 bishops, most of whom had little to do. Many had no sees. The surplus were attached to monasteries for want of something better, and as over each monastery an abbot ruled, the attached bishop was answerable to this comparatively humble official. The Venerable Bede, two centuries later, still found this unusual arrangement worth mentioning, observing of Iona that it was "always wont to have an abbot that is a priest to be the ruler, to whose law both the whole district and also the bishops themselves ought, after an unaccustomed order, to be subject."

Armagh itself after a.d. 500 became a monastic community with both abbot and bishop. The pattern was so familiar to the world that later popes who wanted to communicate with the Church of Ireland, instead of writing to bishops as traditionally they would have done, applied as a matter of course directly to the great abbots. Also, a new fashion developed among Irish kings who adopted Christianity. It is true that during Patrick's time he had little success with these aristocrats, but many later did take the step of conversion and went to the other extreme, moving outright into monasteries with their entire households and endowing the foundations with their worldly goods. Thus the king did not really undergo all that much of a change: he simply exchanged his temporal throne for an abbot's seat or arranged that some trusty relative become abbot as his deputy. The selected monastery became a family monopoly, the same group remaining in control for generations. It did not occur to anyone to disapprove of these arrangements, which were quite openly arrived at.

The first Irish monasteries were places of retreat pure and simple, where people of a religious bent could leave the world behind to concentrate on spiritual matters. But early in the sixth century this concept changed, and the alteration had incalculable effects. It started when Finnian, a scholar who had studied in Wales, founded at Clonard in Meath a house where classes were held and a novice could learn to read and write Latin, using a stylus on a wax tablet. In this manner the Irish for the first time had an alphabet. Before, the only written records in Ireland were in the ogam script, a clumsy code of long and short lines cut across the edges of stone or wooden slabs, employed mainly for funerary inscriptions and so limited as to be almost useless otherwise. As we have seen, Ireland's culture in all branches that entailed language—history, genealogy, all tradition— had been locked up in the minds and memories of a few savants. Now, monks and even laymen could use the flexible Latin alphabet, and they soon realized that letters could be employed equally well for writing Irish. The key was in their hands, and literature was born. More and more monastic schools appeared, until the country was dotted with great communities of monks and students, each with its own workmen and provisioners and artists and libraries as well as the monks and abbots. Workmen of the type that had been itinerant—tinkers, tanners, and the rest—settled down and lived there because employment was steady, and the schools have been described as the nearest things to cities that the Irish possessed.

One who shared in this rich inheritance was St. Columba, or Columcille (Colum of the Cell). Born in Donegal in 521 of a northern Ui Neill family, he was an ardent scholar and poet whose life was dramatically altered by what has been called the first copyright lawsuit in history, when he lost his temper over a book. As the story goes, Columcille was visiting a scholar named Finnian of Moville when he borrowed one of his bibliophile host's most prized possessions, a psalter, and copied it out secretly, late at night, in Finnian's own church. Finnian found out and was furious. He demanded that Columcille hand over the copy, but Columcille refused, arguing that he had stolen nothing, that Finnian's book was not damaged, and that in any case sacred texts were in the public domain, or words to that effect. The quarrel raged until it was taken to the high king, Dermot-mac Cerr-beil, to settle. Dermot gave the decision to Finnian, supporting his judgment with a somewhat dubious analogy: "To every cow her calf, to every book its copy."

Columcille cursed Dermot. The quarrel was not settled, but spread further and further until Columcille's grand Ui Neill connections came into it, brandishing their weapons. There was a battle between the high king and the Ui Neill, and Dermot lost. But on the heels of Columcille's triumph came the reckoning: according to legend an angel appeared to him and rebuked him for the harm he had done, telling him that to do penance he must go into exile. In fact Columcille did go into exile, to the Hebridean island of Iona, and there he founded his most renowned monastery-school. He had already created various houses in Ireland, including

Durrow and Derry, but the monastery in the Hebrides was
the most considerable. Beautifully named Iona is a rocky,
sandy scrap of land only a few miles across, which lies off
the coast of Argyllshire within view of Mull and Skye. In
pagan days it was a resort of Druids, who left traces of their
rites in runic inscriptions; otherwise only a few fishermen
inhabited it. Columba and his companions arrived in 563
and set to work on a house that was to endure for nearly
three centuries and send out missionaries to far-distant
points where they founded daughter houses. The terms
of the saint's exile seem to have been fairly lenient, for he
visited Ireland now and then, but it was on Iona that he died
in 597.

In general plan the monastery was like those of Ireland,
but unusually large. The customary earthen rampart and
wooden stockade surrounded, among other buildings,
separate cells—huts like wickiups, made of interlaced twigs
and clay, to house small groups of monks, with the abbot's
cell standing a little apart. There was a church, small like
most Irish churches of the period. There were a cemetery, a
refectory with kitchen, a workshop and forge, a guesthouse,
and a scriptorium or library that was no doubt very well
stocked: St. Columcille would have seen to that. Outside
the ramparts were the farmlands and their buildings. The
manual labor was done by "working brethren," who farmed,
cooked, cleaned, tanned, worked in metal, and milled flour,
under the direction of an abbot's deputy. The monks enjoyed
fishing, and of course fish was the chief supply of food
on Iona: in Adomnan's *Life of Columba* the writer, who
lived on Iona in the founder's day, speaks enthusiastically
of catching fish. Naturally the brothers, as islanders, were
great sailors as well, and they kept a considerable fleet of
various kinds of boats.

But this was only one side of the monastery's existence.
Men especially skillful in calligraphy, who bore the honored
title of "scribe," spent most of their time copying sacred
texts, while those talented in painting were trusted with the
decoration of the texts. The earlier work of the Book of

Kells, now at Trinity College, Dublin, was done on Iona. Adomnan describes the daily existence of the monastery: "governed by the principles of perfect mutual love, common property without exception, and strict obedience....Chastity, humility, and the mortification of body and will, being essential parts of monastic life, were practiced rigorously. The obligation of silence was not enforced as strictly as elsewhere, but the monks were not allowed to indulge in idle talk" (Bieler, p. 40). Everyone fasted every day, but rules were sometimes relaxed, as in the presence of visitors. Like other Irish monks the Ionans sometimes went in for further mortification of the body and will: they used corporal punishment, hitting the offender's hands with leather straps.

I have said that Columcille was a poet, which means that he was not only a versifier, but had actually been to school under a *fili,* or official poet. These *filid* were of much higher rank than the bards: they were learned men who claimed that their works were inspired. In pre-Christian days they had been closely associated with the Druids: some scholars think they were Druids themselves. Now that they had the Celtic script they were able to write their works, a practice on which certain churchmen looked with disfavor, for they suspected the *filid* of being insincerely Christian, secretly retaining the pagan faith and even, possibly, indulging in Druidical rites. It was also said in criticism of the *filid* that they had an inflated idea of their own worth, and a poet who sang after dinner in some noble's house expected too large a present afterward. Columcille did not agree with these complaints. At a convention in Ireland, at Drum Caett, he forestalled an anti-*fili* movement to banish all poets. As an alternative he suggested that every king in the land employ his own *fili,* who would live in the royal household as a kind of laureate. The suggestion found favor, and the poets were saved. Thereafter they possessed new dignity and pride of place, and formed a caste as respectable as that of the brehons.

For years they dedicated poems to Columba, and

Adomnan records that whenever a *fill* visited Iona he sang
after dinner.

Columba had saved the elite of Irish literature, and was
indirectly responsible at the same time for the bards, inferior
poets like minstrels or troubadours, who strolled the
country and paused now and then at the houses of patrons.
Such a man used to sing flatteringly of his patron's wealth,
ancestry, and personal glory, and if—as often happened—
the patron happened to be carrying on a feud at the time, it
was considered tactful for the minstrel to work him up in
song. Often the patron, fired with wine and inspired by this
singing, went straight out to settle his quarrel then and there.
Some lords used bards expressly to inspirit their fighting men,
much as present-day football coaches ginger up their teams
with pep talks. In years to come the Normans detested this
practice among the Irish, as did the English. Time after time
the invaders passed laws against Irish harpists and bards,
without effect.

The Romans planted Christianity in Britain, but when they
departed they left many Britons still pagan. As Ireland was
the more Christianized of the two islands, the Irish Church
began sending missions to Britain. Rome, observing this
shifting of power from her chosen center, took steps to cancel
Irish influence in England. Pope Gregory I, well-known
to school children for his statement about the fair-haired
English slave boys—"Not Angles, but angels!"—in 597 sent
a Benedictine, Augustine, as head of a mission to Britain's
south coast, and Augustine became the first Archbishop of
Canterbury. Some of his men moved up to Anglo-Saxon
Northumbria, where, as the Romans had heard, the Irish
Church maintained a firm hold over the ruling family. Why
this Irish predominance in such a far-off region? Because
the king, Edwin, had sent his nearest of kin, two young
nephews, to be educated at the monastery of Iona, where
they naturally grew up Irish-speaking Christians. Edwin
was killed in 633 fighting the pagan Mercian, king of Penda;
and Oswald and Oswy, the nephews, were recalled, the

elder Oswald assuming the crown. With them came a group
of Ionan monks to found a monastery on Lindisfarne, Holy
Island. Nine years later Oswald too was killed by Penda,
and Oswy became king. He vowed to endow a second
monastery if God permitted him to kill the family enemy. He
did kill Penda, and in 658 the new settlement was founded
at Streaneshalch—Whitby—in Yorkshire.

In the meantime the Roman mission from Canterbury
had been busy downgrading the Irishmen from Iona.
Certain ecclesiastical customs observed by the Irish seemed
laughably out of date to the Romans and Gauls, for Ireland
had been out of touch with Rome for nearly two centuries.
The Roman emissaries made the most of this, and found
a ready audience among the younger Northumbrian
priests who wanted the British Church to align herself
with Rome rather than Ireland. It was decided that certain
pressing matters connected with the subject be settled in
open discussion at a council, or synod, at the new Whitby
monastery in 659, with King Oswy in the chair.

There were two main quarrels. One concerned the
correct tonsure for men of the Church: the Irish favored the
so-called Celtic style, shaving off all the hair in front but
leaving untouched that which grew in back, whereas the
well-dressed Roman churchman wore his hair in the fashion
we have seen in pictures, shaved all round save for a fringe
that represented the crown of thorns. The difference may
seem trivial, but hairstyles were to be a sore point between
the Irish and the English for centuries, and the Whitby
discussion was only the opening shot of a long, weary war.
Technically the Roman tonsurites won the argument, but the
Celtic hairdo was not abandoned. No Irish prelate worthy
of the name would have surrendered.

Now the assembly turned to a far more complicated
matter, the Easter question. The Church had decreed that
Easter should always be on a Sunday, celebrated at the same
time all over the world, but it soon became evident that when
it is one time in Rome it is quite another at some distance to
the east or west. Astronomers had tried manipulating dates

here and there on the map so that Easter Sunday could be reconciled with these facts, but every year the world went astray from simultaneity. Various time cycles too were tried out and for a time seemed to work. One cycle of 84 years was approved for a while, and Ireland among other countries adopted it. Iona and Armagh were still using it at the time of the Whitby council, though Rome had long since found it unsatisfactory and recommended a 522-year cycle in its place. It was explained to the Irish that almost the whole Christian world now went along with Rome, and that they alone, with the Eastern Church, were out of step (with the British Church as well, of course, for they followed Iona). Even King Oswy's household was feeling the strain. As a loyal Iona alumnus he used the Irish Easter, but his wife, spiritually guided by a chaplain from Kent, did what her chaplain told her to do about Easter and observed the Roman date. As a result, the spring season at the palace could be very awkward, and never more so than in 651, when Queen Eanfleda determinedly fasted for Palm Sunday on the same day King Oswy was celebrating Easter.

Many a dignitary lost his temper during the Easter discussion at Whitby. Colman, abbot of Lindisfarne, as spokesman for his Church attempted to explain why Ionans kept things as they were. In reply Wilfrid, the passionate, ambitious young abbot of Ripon, leader of the stylish pro-Gaul faction, bitterly demanded, "Though your fathers were holy, do you think that their small number in a corner of the remotest island is to be preferred to the Church of Christ? Would you put your Columba before the Prince of Apostles...?" which was to say St. Peter, patron of the Church in Rome.

Colman stood up bravely to this attack, but Oswy was shaken. If he had to choose between Peter and Columba, he felt, there could be no hesitation. He lined up on Peter's side and the Roman date for Easter, and thus settled the fate of the British Church for the following nine centuries, until Henry VIII broke with Rome.

Next year saw Wilfrid rewarded; he became Archbishop

of York. But the Church of Armagh and Iona, unmoved by the loss of Britain, did not budge. Her abbots, monks, and laity continued in the old way, celebrating Easter according to the eighty-four-year cycle, and on that remotest island remained firm for the next half century. It was 716 and Wilfrid, after a stormy life, had been seven years in his grave before first Iona, then Armagh capitulated. Nobody, not even Rome, was ever going to find it easy to order the Irish around.

CHAPTER

2

WHEN the synod was over, most Irish monks in Northumbria left England. Colman took the Lindisfarne contingent, including thirty sympathetic English monks, to Ireland, where they founded a new monastery on Innisboffin off Galway, but a majority of others moved on to foreign countries. There was already a fashion among Irish monks for going abroad, so that those now leaving England need merely join one or another party. A few pilgrims went west to Iceland, but most chose Gaul; some even went on to the Holy Land. These pious odysseys were undertaken for various reasons. Exile was sometimes imposed by abbots as a penance, but there were many non-penitent clerics as well who wanted to see the world, or felt personally impelled to carry out some mission. Columbanus was one of the latter. Late in the sixth century, long before the synod of Whitby, he crossed the Channel to France and founded monasteries at Luxeuil (Vosges), Annegray, and Fontaines in Burgundy, then went to Italy and founded Bobbio. Such houses served as hostels for other *peregrini* who came after him.

The pilgrimage movement was important to Ireland and to the rest of the Christian world. It was a time of growth in intellectual spheres, when scholars in one country found stimulation and fertilization from those of other nations, and the wandering monks carried knowledge from country to country. Until well into the ninth century they did so, studying or teaching wherever they went and often carrying with them specimens of the beautiful books made in their monasteries at home. When the owners died, in Italy or Flanders or Middle Europe or France, the books remained to become the cherished property of foreign houses. The scholarship of the Scots was recognized and honored wherever they went. The seventh and eighth centuries especially witnessed a flowering of Irish culture, and the characteristic Irish script of the scholar-monks became familiar in many far-off corners of the world.

A few books that were not carried out of Ireland survived great dangers and are still with us. Perhaps the outstanding one is the volume now called the Book of Kells, possibly still in the making at Iona's monastery when Vikings first sacked the island in 795. Much of the monastery's wealth was looted at that time, but the raiders returned twice more in the following eleven years. In 806 on the third occasion they killed sixty-eight monks, and Cellach, the abbot, decided that the rest of them must leave. They took such of the treasure as was left—relics of St. Columcille and the Book—and went to Ireland, to Kells in Meath, where land was given them and they built a new house with a church. For two centuries the Book was left in peace and possibly it was then that the rest of it was written and illuminated. It was splendidly bound with gold and jewels. In 1007, because of the gold and jewels, it was stolen from the church by a thief who pulled off the cover and discarded the manuscript. Three months later it was found not far from the church, buried in a shallow grave of turf.

Today the Book of Kells is on view at Trinity in Dublin, where we can look our fill at its drawings and illuminations of cavorting animals that twine themselves about elaborate gilded initials or stalk across the bottom of the page or simply sit, delightfully vivid, wholly "modern." Conventionalized saints in carefully draped folds and curled whiskers stand or sit stiffly, weighed down by brilliant clothes, against backgrounds of miniature churches. Occasionally script and pictures melt together like those of Chinese calligraphy-paintings.

Some monks traveled in groups of twelve to represent the twelve apostles. "They left a monastery like Bangor or Clonmacnois or Armagh and usually crossed first to Britain. Unless they intended to settle there, they made quickly for one of the Kentish ports such as Richborough, and sailed across the Channel to Quentovic or Boulogne or Wissant. Here they joined merchants on the way to Aachen or rowed up one of the great continental rivers, the Seine or the Meuse or the Rhine, in their frail coracles. There was plenty of hunger and suffering on the journey" (*Irish Cultural Influence in Europe,* government brochure). But many enjoyed the adventure, like John Scottus Eriugena, whose name literally means "John Irishman born in Ireland." A ninth-century scholar, he was for some years head of the French King Charles the Bald's palace school. Once at a rollicking party at court when John Scottus sat across the table from the king, Charles made a pun that is none the worse today for being eleven centuries old. Besides, it translates perfectly. He asked John, "Quid distat inter sottum et Scottum?"—"What's the difference between a sot and a Scot?" To which the monk smartly replied, "Tabula tantum"—"Only a table."

In one respect members of the continental orders found it impossible to feel kinship with such cheerful birds of passage—the harsh penances imposed by Irish abbots shocked them. It has been mentioned that Irish monks were quite casual about administering or receiving corporal punishment, and this is strange, for in Irish temporal law there are very few cases of beatings visited on malefactors. Perhaps the Druidic code inherited by the brehons represented a gentler viewpoint than Celtic Christianity's, but whatever the reason, Irish monks were really hard on each other and themselves, and it was a tendency that strengthened with time. The earliest known penitential cited by Bieler is attributed to "Vinnian," most likely Finnian of Clonard, and it is not extreme: a cleric who has committed the sin of fornication or murder in his heart, but not in deed, can be "helped" by the penance of living half a year on bread and water and a full year without wine and meat. A cleric or woman who by the practice of magic has led anyone astray shall do penance for six years, three on an allowance of bread and water. These punishments, one would say, are unpleasant but not actively painful. It is when Bieler comes to the Monks' Rule of St. Columban that we find things tightening up. Take the following:

"Of Mortification:... Thus him who has not waited for grace at table and has not responded Amen, it is ordained to correct with six blows. Likewise him who has spoken while eating, unless because of the wants of another brother, it is ordained to correct with six blows....If he has called anything his own, with six blows. Let him who has cut the table with a knife be corrected with ten blows." A monk working in the kitchen who dropped an inordinate amount of food or drink on the floor was to do penance "with a long pardon in church by prostrating himself without moving any limb while they sing twelve psalms at the twelfth hour." For coughing during a psalm or biting the Communion cup, six blows sufficed, but "He who forgets to make the oblation right until they go to Mass, with a hundred blows."

The rules stiffen even more by the time of the Culdees, the reformed monks who first appear late in the eighth century. In their Table of Commutations, among other passages equally extreme, is this: "A commutation for rescuing a soul out of hell: three hundred and sixty-five Paters and three hundred and sixty-five genuflections and three hundred and sixty-five blows of the scourge every day for a year, and a fast every month—this rescues a soul out of hell." Dr. Bieler further comments, "The habit... of reciting the entire Psalter while standing in icy water is reported in the Lives of so many Irish saints that we must assume it to have been a custom actually practised," and he adds that later centuries were evidently shocked at such excess of zeal, since one copyist wrote a marginal note on a severe penance thus prescribed; "Hard art thou, O Penitential!" Because of scandalized talk among their contemporaries abroad over such excesses, the *peregrini,* if not their brothers at home, eventually dropped the more extreme penances—though in view of the Celtic temperament it is safe to assume that this change was a long time coming about.

The Church has left plenty of records, but what of the laity, who made up the greater part of the Irish population, even when monasticism was at its height? Though their daily lives were not so closely documented, details can be made out from the epics that found their way into writing during and after the sixth century. Much is myth in these tales, which like Homer's are heroic stories of kings, but from Homer one gathers a good deal of knowledge about contemporary everyday life and the same is true of old Irish stories. We must remind ourselves now and then that Ireland was thinly populated and people knew each other better because there were fewer of them to know. Even the nobleman, who was probably much like a prosperous farmer of today, was acquainted with most of his neighbors, though his social peers—the other aristocrats and the professional elite such as brehons and *filid*—were few. The class immediately beneath him were less splendid freemen who borrowed his lordship's breeding stock, and farmers in descending order. Then came a hiatus, on the other side of which was the unfree, a category including slaves, workmen, and the lower grades of entertainer.

It was not an inalterably fixed pattern, for status depended on skill as well as possession. Even an unfree man, if he learned a skilled trade and became a smith, a physician, or a harper, was reclassified as a freeman and permitted to own land—for every freeman was a landowner. To qualify as an aristocrat a man had to own land of a certain minimum value, measured—since the Irish didn't have coined money —in units of cattle or women, carefully defined. The lowest unit, or "set," represented a female heifer. A milch cow was worth two sets, and a female slave or cumal equaled six sets or three milch cows. An aristocrat's land had to be worth at least twenty-one cumals (*The Course of Irish History*, Ed. Martin and Moody, Cork, 1967, p. 51). In the brehon code, as in sumptuary laws of later days, are detailed lists of the property the ownership of which was incumbent on members of society who wished to retain their status. Among other things, the Irish aristocrat had to possess a vat for brewing ale, iron pots, a kneading trough, wooden mugs, a bath, candlesticks, knives for cutting rushes, ropes, ax, adz, wooden shears, whetstone, billhook, a vessel of milk and another of ale, a kiln, a barn, a mill or the share of one, a house at least twenty-seven feet long, an outhouse of seventeen feet, pigsty, pen for calves, sheep pen, at least twenty cows and two bulls, six oxen, pigs, sheep, saddle horse with enameled bridle, and sixteen bushels of seed in the ground. (It is not explained who checked up on these things.) The house owner and his wife must have four suits of clothes apiece. Trousers were worn only by the lower classes: More important people, male and female, dressed much alike in large cloaks over shirts and tunics, held in place by brooches. Yet the touchstone of a man's standing was less in all this household equipment than in his "honor price," a figure on which much else was based—damages in lawsuits, the limit of value in any contract he might make, and the *eraic,* or blood money that must be paid by one family group to another if a member of the first killed a member of the second. As a substitute for blood vengeance the *eraic* was a good thing because it removed the danger of lasting, wasteful feuds, but sixteenth-century English found it revolting.

Brehon laws also dealt with fosterage, the custom of handing over one's child to another family to be reared, which was done to cement relations between groups, or to give a nobleman's son a closer knowledge of the people he would someday rule.

There is no evidence of violent disruption of the Irish way of life before the ninth century, but the gradual spreading out of the people, especially those of the prolific and hardy race of Ui Neill, inevitably led to forgetfulness and neglect of some of the old customs. Especially for those who settled in Alba it was hard to take seriously the claims of family loyalty, and the old custom of tanism was often disregarded —though not forgotten: victims of usurpation remembered them as they brooded over their wrongs. Yet the wars of succession were not as bad as they sound. Battles were not catastrophic clashes, only straggling fights between small groups of men who chased each other through the countryside, now and then meeting by prearrangement for a day's battle, or in the same amiable manner taking a day off. The Vikings were to change all that.

As has been said, Iona had her first experience of the Vikings in 795, and a harsh one it was. Other islanders too suffered from the sea raiders, years before the mainland had reason to fear them, the early parties being too small for more ambitious campaigns. "Viking," which means sea pirate, is a label applied to all three Scandinavian peoples, Norwegian, Swedish, and Danish, after they took permanently to the sea. They seem to have developed suddenly. In earlier days most Scandinavians had lived quietly within their own countries, farming and herding a little, fishing extensively, and becoming expert in the art of sailing. They were past masters in carpentry and excellent shipwrights. Presumably their countries became too crowded. At any rate they took to setting out in small parties of two or three ships at a time in search of more land, each nation making for the nearest territory. The Danes attacked England and Germany; the Swedes went to Russia; the Norwegians made for Ireland, but took the long way round. Their first colonizers landed on Iceland and settled down to an existence much like that of home. They next drove on west, to Greenland and possibly North America. Some found the Shetlands and Orkneys and stayed there. It was years before they concentrated on the islands off Ireland, but they got there in the end. Wherever any of these Scandinavians encountered people they fought them, usually conquering them and taking their property; it must have dawned on them fairly soon that this was a stimulating, profitable life, much more fun than farming or fishing. Their appetite for robbery became voracious. The lovely long ships skimmed over the sea, wind in their bright patterned sails, with gilded carved prows that looked appropriately like birds of prey. Helmeted, carrying glittering shields and axes, faces decorated with long flaxen beards and pale hair hanging down in matted locks, the Norsemen must have been terrifying.

Soon they learned the northern sea routes and waterways, and moved about the ocean with as much certainty as that of landsmen on solid ground. Merchants who plied the Great Silk Road that used to run into China would put up caravanserais along the way where they could rest and refresh themselves, meet their friends, and perhaps do a little trading. In the same way the Vikings at strategic places along their waterways built sea towns, each half fortress, with a long reach of water safely enclosed for their ships, and above it on the land, surrounded by ramparts, an area of little houses clustering about a wooden lookout tower. Such fortressed villages removed the arduous necessity of returning home between raids for supplies and contacts. Here shipmasters met each other by appointments that might have been made months ahead of time. Here provisions could be stored. In time, shops were set up for the women and children, pirates more and more often bringing their families with them on their freebooting expeditions. Here, most important of all, large fleets could gather and set out on forays. The mainland Irish felt the effect of this development in 837 for the first time, when such a fleet arrived off the mouth of the Liffey on the east coast and Norsemen came ashore to build a ship's wall, or *longphort*. They then constructed on shore the town that would one day be Dublin, Ireland's first city.

At this point the natives were not unduly alarmed, because there were not many to see what was going on. But soon the first of the Vikings, Thorgest, or Turgesius as he is called in the annals, advanced into the country. To the marvel of everyone who saw it he sailed his ship straight in and upriver to the inland lakes, for Viking craft were of shallow draft and could go almost anywhere that was wet. Thorgest anchored wherever he liked and sacked the rich monasteries of the neighborhood, the choicest being Armagh: he not only looted Armagh and drove out the monks, but set himself up, mockingly, as the monastery's new abbot. Tired of this game, he moved on to pillage the Shannon settlements. His robber-sailors came back again and again to plunder Clonmacnoise, and the same rough humor that had led him to assume the title of abbot now caused him to hand over Clonmacnoise to his wife Ota, who presided at the altar as a heathen priestess and sometimes in that role gave out oracles. After what must have been a very long eight years for the Irish, Thorgest was killed by a king of Meath, but more Norsemen had by this time settled in to stay. They looked on Ireland as their colony, and reinforcements arrived from Norway to move in with them.

However, time has a trick of altering such situations. The pirates' children, growing up in Ireland, fraternized with the Irish, and the new-generation natives did not resent the Norsemen as strongly as their fathers did. Norsemen married Irishwomen and some Irish kings took Norse brides. Heathen Norwegians became Christian, or their children did. Thus, though peace cannot be said to have reigned over the nation, the character of the wars changed: instead of battles between Irish on one side and Norsemen on the other, it was more often a case of one mixed group of Norse and Irish allies against another, similarly polyglot.

Dublin grew fuller and fuller until its walls could accommodate no more residents. The overflow settled in the country nearby, the Norse community spreading north and south in a narrow band along the coast. Ultimately their chief declared that Dublin should be rated as a kingdom as well as a city, the kingdom of the Ostmen (Eastmen), and this was accepted by the people. In later days when the Ostmen had to relinquish control of Dublin, they asked for, and got, a piece of land north of the Liffey on which to build their houses. It was called *villa Ostmannorum,* Ostmantown, which became Oxmantown. Dublin has grown around it, but it is still there.

The flood of immigrants from Norway stopped for a while late in the ninth century, and their ships were no longer seen on rivers and lakes in Ireland. The descendants of Niall were still pre-eminent in much of the north; in Munster the outstanding dynasty was also as it had long been, the Eoghanachts of Cashel, who were nominally in possession of Leinster as well. Suddenly, in 914, the Norse menace flared up again: a new contingent of Norwegians sailed a fleet into Waterford Harbor on the southern coast. As at Dublin they installed a fort settlement and used it as a base for large-scale incursions, this time into Munster. Once more, if from a different direction, the invaders moved into the Shannon, and the unfortunate monks and abbots had to watch the sacking of their monasteries. The Norsemen built another town in the west at Limerick, and followed it up with a fourth at Wexford across the island and around the corner, as it were, from Waterford. Ireland was becoming ringed with alien strongholds, but the Eoghanachts of Cashel could not offer effective resistance because they were plagued by internal dissension.

In East Clare, a rocky, barren country, the local people, the Dal Cais, resented the fact that their overlords the Eoghanachts did not protect them from the rapacious Norsemen, and their own King Mahon, when he came to the throne in 964, immediately set about mending matters. With his younger brother Brian Boroime, usually known to us as Brian Boru, he led an army against the Eoghanachts and drove them out of Cashel, Mahon assuming the tide of king there as well. Next the brothers moved on the Norse town of Limerick, from which they drove the leader and sacked the settlement. Twelve years later the evicted Norseman returned and killed Mahon, in 976, but the brilliant Brian became king of Cashel in his brother's stead and began taking control, piece by piece, of all Munster. For the first time the south was becoming unified.

A parallel movement was going on in the north at the

same time under the king of Meath, young Malachy. In 980 he defeated Dublin's Ostmen at the battle of Tara and took over the throne of that ancient hill town. Like Brian he next moved on the nearest Viking town, Dublin in his case: his troops occupied it in 981. Dublin's downfall, like that of Limerick, marked the beginning of the decline of Norse power in Ireland, but the Ostmen, having become part of the national fabric, remained. In fact the ancient Irish seem to have been devoid of race prejudice except in times of war. For example we have Olaf, chief of Dublin, who though an Ostman was also Christian and had married the beautiful Irish princess Gormflath of Leinster, who bore him a son, Sitric. Olaf fled to Scotland when Dublin fell, and Malachy put Sitric in his place as chief. Malachy had fallen in love with Gormflath, and when news came of Olaf's death, he himself married her.

Then Brian Boru sent a message to the northern king. It was not a challenge to battle, for Brian saw no advantage in a long, grinding war if he could attain his ends peacefully. He merely suggested a meeting and a consultation. Malachy, knowing that he was sure to lose any war with Brian, concurred, and at the meeting the two kings agreed to divide Ireland officially, and go on much as they were, though Dublin was now to pay tribute to Brian rather than Malachy.

Brian Boru was more than an excellent general; he was a statesman and in important ways he changed Ireland forever. For one thing he weakened the influence of the cumbersome laws of succession. Like Mahon before him he usurped his throne and set an example, so that afterward kingship often passed from father to son in the continental way, which was an advantage. So was his work in pulling together and consolidating the country, so that unification became an ideal for Irish leaders. He also had deep religious convictions, and brought back hope to the monastic foundations that had suffered cruelly at the hands of the Vikings. Twice he paid special visits to St. Patrick's see of Armagh. On the second occasion he made a gold offering to the church and confirmed to the see ecclesiastical supremacy over all Ireland.

He met his fate—though admittedly at a ripe old age—through the agency of a woman, none other than the renowned Gormflath, who had been cast out by Malachy after seventeen years of marriage. It should be mentioned that brehon law permitted such laxity, and that foreigners in Ireland were still being scandalized, generations later, by what a sixteenth-century priest called "divorcements at pleasure." Gormflath's brother Maelmorda, king of Leinster, had a grievance of his own, having been ousted by Brian Boru, and brother and sister conspired with Gormflath's son Sitric, chief of Dublin, to rise against the hero of the south. In 999 Brian marched from his home in Thomond to put down the revolt. Having quickly sent the insurgents packing, he entered Dublin, where for the first time he saw Gormflath. Though now sixty years old, he fell in love with that amazing princess, married her, and was persuaded by the bride to let Sitric return to his chieftainship and give Leinster back to Maelmorda.

In 1002 Brian brought matters to a head and forced Malachy to yield to his superior strength and acknowledge him as "Emperor of the Irish." A few years later his passion for Gormflath cooled, and like Malachy he set her aside. Again the princess raged and vowed to have revenge, and again she called on her brother and son to come to her aid. Again they did so. Sitric appealed to his Norse kinsmen who were settled in the Scottish isles, and they agreed to join him in an effort to overthrow Brian Boru. The most powerful noble among them was Sigurd the Stout, Earl of Orkney; Sitric promised him all of Ireland, and Gormflath for his wife, if he could rid the country of Brian.

It was 1014 when the Emperor of the Irish led his army for the last time from Thomond, northeast to meet the enemy. He was now too old and infirm to do any active fighting, but he planned the formation in which his troops were drawn up on the battlefield, near Clontarf, north of Dublin, at the coast. Malachy and his men backed his army, and Brian stationed himself in a tent to the rear of the lines, to direct affairs.

The Ostmen from Dublin and their allies of the islands fought so well at first that nobody could shift them until Murchad, one of Brian's sons, attacked fiercely and broke their lines. Sigurd the Stout was killed, and after him Maelmorda. This deprived the rebels of important leaders, and panic struck them. Murchad too lost his life, but Maelmorda's men retreated, making with Sitric's troops for the sheltering walls of Dublin. The Norsemen from the isles fled in disarray, hurrying toward the coast where their ships were drawn up. Suddenly they found themselves cut off by the high tide, and in the swirling waters many were caught and drowned. One of the island men, Brodir, stumbling by chance in his flight on Brian's tent, found the old man alone. Brodir paused long enough to kill him, and ran on.

CHAPTER

3

MOST great men in dying leave a void, and Brian Boru was no exception. A son, Taig, tried to fill it, but it was all he could do to hang on to the throne of Cashel. As for Malachy, he too was an old man, and he died in 1022. It was almost as if Ireland had never been united. She reverted to form and became a conglomerate of seven large kingdoms, called Ulidia, Aileach (or Ulster), Oriel, Connacht, Meath, Munster, and Leinster. There had always been small kingdoms, or sub-kingdoms, in Ireland, and there still were, about a hundred in all. For years thereafter the heads of the large countries tried to do as Brian and Malachy had done, grasping power over their neighbors and uniting the whole country's strength, but no real high king emerged. The aspirants fought, they won battles and lost battles and kept things at a gentle boil, but none reached an impregnable position. There were so many turns and turns about that the annalists found themselves forced to coin a new title, "king with opposition," for kings who almost but not quite succeeded in controlling the seven restive countries at once.

Side by side with these struggles was a conflict in and about the Irish Church. The spirit of reform had already overtaken Rome and the churches of Gaul and Britain. Now it was Ireland's turn. In most of her regions the monastic system still prevailed, the only exceptions being the churches of the Norse towns. The Dublin Ostmen especially favored the Roman diocesan system since they had never experienced any other, their religious foundations being those of the Benedictine and Augustinian orders. Now, however, in the other regions too the idea spread that all was not well in the monasteries, that the abbots had for too long a time enjoyed prosperity and unquestioned power, and had grown slack. Hereditary succession was still commonplace: Armagh, for example, had been the sinecure of one family for 150 years. There was also talk of scandalous conditions among the laity. Shaking their heads, reformists declared that the people were neglecting their prayers, that they resented paying tithes, and had ceased to respect the Church to such an extent that footpads would as soon rob a monk or nun as anyone else. In addition, laxity prevailed in lay marriage customs. Concubinage was generally accepted, and brehon law still applied. Suddenly it seemed deplorable that so many of the abbots were married men, though this circumstance was not really out of the way: in England there were married clergy until the end of the eleventh century, when Anselm, Archbishop of Canterbury, introduced changes in canon law according to the code of Rome. A more disturbing fact, no doubt, was that many abbots were not in holy orders. On this point too Armagh was a bad example: of all the abbots there, seven of them since the house was founded, *none* had been ordained.

From England came word about all this. Lanfranc, first Archbishop of Canterbury to hold office under the Normans, wrote to various Irish kings suggesting a cleansing of the Irish Church and a general tightening up. The Irish Church's initial reaction was, as we might expect, resentful and defiant, but after a time the clergy complied. There was no other choice. The most bigoted abbot knew that Ireland had outgrown the monastic system, and reappraisal began. The then high king of the south presented to the Church the great Rock of Cashel for an archbishop's seat. Callach, the controversial married abbot of Armagh, took holy orders and was consecrated as bishop—presumably having left his wife—and soon became first archbishop and primate of the Irish Church. At a national synod held in 1110 it was resolved to introduce the diocesan system into Ireland, for which the country was to be divided into twenty-four sees. Of course all this was very complicated: it was not to be completed for another forty years, during which there was much correspondence between Ireland and Rome, and papal legates traveled back and forth many times.

In Ireland only the Norse towns ignored the reform movement; their bishops did not consider themselves a part of the Irish Church anyway, but looked toward Canterbury for spiritual leadership. Dublin sent her bishops all the way to the English city for consecration, and so did Waterford and Limerick, so Anselm felt justified in claiming primacy for the English Church over "all the British Isles" including Ireland. Only in 1152, when at the synod of Kells the Irish Church brought forward evidence that it was now purified and regularized, with a uniform liturgy and organized dioceses, did the Ostmen surrender. They did it reluctandy, however, and the development did not please the contemporary Archbishop of Canterbury, Theobald. Because of it he may have been instigator of the notorious bull *Laudabiliter*.

There used to be much argument about this letter, certain scholars arguing that it was a forgery, but the dispute died away about thirty years ago. Those who thought it a forgery made the point that the original document has never been found in the Vatican archives, but if it has been lost it would not be the only one, and other arguments have been countered neatly by the Reverend J. F. O'Doherty, D.D., in 1933 ("Rome and the Anglo-Norman Invasion of Ireland": *Irish Ecclesiastical Record,* Vol. 42, pp. 131-45). Briefly, this is the story:

In 1154, when Henry II of England acceded to the throne, an Englishman named Nicholas Breakspear became Pope Adrian IV, first and only man of his nationality to occupy that exalted position. In the following year Henry sent an embassy to Rome, one member of which was Theobald's secretary John of Salisbury, a close friend of Adrian and a man of great honesty. John brought back to Henry from the Pope the disputed letter, or bull *Laudabiliter*, so called because of its opening word, and the gist is found in this passage: "Laudably and profitably doth your Majesty contemplate spreading the glory of your name on earth and laying up for yourself the reward of eternal happiness in heaven, in that, as becomes a catholic priest, you purpose to enlarge the boundaries of the Church, restraining the downward course of vice, correcting evil customs, and planting virtue, and for the increase of the Christian religion, you shall enter that island and execute whatsoever may tend to the honour of God and the welfare of the land... provided always that the rights of the churches remain whole and inviolate, and saving to the blessed Peter and the Holy Roman Church the annual tribute of one penny from every House."

"It is to be noted," says Father O'Doherty, "that the brief contains no 'grant of sovereignty' nor 'any intention of ceremonial investiture.' The Pope regards himself (by reason of the Donation of Constantine) as the sovereign lord of Ireland and all islands, and the *Laudabiliter* does not contain any transfer of this sovereign dominion, so that the Pope would remain the lord of Ireland even after Henry had carried out his proposed invasion and ecclesiastical reform in that island." So, though Henry was permitted, even encouraged, to occupy Ireland in order to reform that "rude, ignorant, vicious" people, he was not given ownership. It is a distinction that was overlooked, as was possibly the intention. John of Salisbury himself overlooked it in his *Metalogicon*, published in 1159. Adrian had recently died and John laments the loss of his friend, thinking back: "It was at my request that he granted to the illustrious King of the English, Henry II, the hereditary possession of Ireland, as his still extant letters attest; for all islands are reputed to belong by long-established right to the Church of Rome."

The charges against the Irish of ignorance and evil are not easily explained, coming as they do from Rome, where papal secretaries had presumably been receiving regular reports of reform and progress from Irish churchmen. Perhaps Theobald had made the most of the ammunition furnished by the Ostmen bishops, who were resentful at having been forced back into the Irish Church. Another possible source of adverse criticism is Malachy, Archbishop of Armagh in succession to Callach. As papal legate, Malachy set out for Rome in the 1140s on business that concerned the as yet incomplete reorganization of the Irish Church. On the way he stopped at Clairvaux to visit St. Bernard. (He was greatly impressed by what he saw there of the Cistercian Order, so much so that when he got back to Ireland he prevailed on the king of Oriel to donate land for a Cistercian abbey, Mellifont.) At Clairvaux Malachy in his enthusiasm may well have talked freely to the sympathetic Bernard of his problems in Ireland and the wicked, obstructive habits of certain unreformed prelates. Gossip of this sort would have been forwarded by Bernard to Rome, where, combined with Theobald's reports, it could well add up to a prejudiced attitude which Adrian inherited.

In any case the *Laudabiliter* was shelved for the time being. Henry was busy with other projects nearer home.

By 1152 the Irish clergy had taken warning and mended their ways, but the kings continued in their old feckless manner, quarreling, allying, breaking pledges, realigning, and making war most of the time. Of all these Irish chieftains the king of Connacht, Turlough O'Connor, was the most able: he alone went a long way toward unifying the country, and when he claimed the title of high king of Ireland the boast was not quite ridiculous, though Murtough MacLochlainn of Ailech and his ally Dermot MacMurrough of Leinster disputed it. Dermot MacMurrough was a strong, good-looking man, "tall of stature and of stout build," according to the chronicler Gerald de Barry (Gerald of Wales), who met him later. "A man of warlike spirit and a brave one in his nation, with a voice hoarse from frequent shouting in the din of battle." So far so good, but Dermot had one of the outstanding talents of all time for making himself unpopular, and Gerald noted that too: "One who preferred to be feared rather than loved... obnoxious to his own people and an object of hatred to strangers. His hand was against every man, and every man's hand was against him."

Gerald did not overstate the case. To keep his throne Dermot had fought his vassals to a standstill—the king of Ossory, the Norse kings of Dublin and Waterford, and the chiefs of northern Leinster. He had taken the Leinster chiefs prisoner and blinded or killed seventeen of them. It was said that in his youth he sacked the abbey of Kildare and raped the abbess, but none of these crimes had such momentous results as his elopement in 1152 with Dervorgilla, wife of the king of Breifne. Put that way it sounds romantic and pretty, but the facts are not: Dervorgilla was no tender young damsel but a charmer of forty-five who proposed the affair to the forty-two-year-old Dermot. He obligingly carried her off on horseback in the traditional way, and kept her for quite a year before sending her back to her husband, Tiernan O'Rourke. Tiernan appealed to Turlough O'Connor for justice, and the king decreed that Dermot must pay the wronged husband damages of one hundred ounces of gold, but for years Dermot ignored the obligation. History has not recorded the dialogue between husband and wife when Dervorgilla came home, but we know that Tiernan O'Rourke, nursing his hatred, waited for his chance of revenge against her lover.

In 1156 Turlough O'Connor died and his son Rory, succeeding, naturally plunged immediately into the same old unfinished war with Murtough MacLochlainn, his stanchest ally now being Tiernan O'Rourke. Ten years later Murtough's people, their patience at an end, rebelled and killed their chief, and Dermot MacMurrough, left alone and hotly pressed, retired to his palace of Ferns near Wexford. Tiernan O'Rourke followed his enemy into Leinster, close on his heels. The avenger's cause proved a popular one. Those chiefs of Leinster who survived joined him, as did the heads of the Norse towns and the king of Ossory, all thirsting for a chance at Dermot. They reached Ferns and looted it, pulling down most of its fine stone walls, but Dermot managed to escape, and with his daughter Eva and a few retainers took ship to Bristol.

Everyone in Ireland has heard the story of how the villain Dermot MacMurrough betrayed his country by inviting the Normans to come and take it. For eight centuries his name has been cursed for this, so perhaps it is too late to ask if it really was all his doing, yet when we look at the facts his total responsibility does seem open to question. There were certain circumstances. There was the Anglo-Norman, or rather the Welsh-Norman character. Above all there was the *Laudabiliter* letter, waiting as it were in Henry's pocket. It might reasonably be argued that all Dermot did was remind the English king of its presence.

The Normans who lived in Wales and were destined to invade Ireland were much like their ancestors who had accompanied William from Normandy; a mixture of aristocrat and bandit, tough, acquisitive, and a law unto themselves. They lived in Wales because their fathers, having aided Henry I in a campaign to get back the north of England regions from Malcolm of Scotland, were rewarded with a license to take such estates in Wales as they could, and keep them if they could. The Welsh had given the barons a stiff fight, but that was over. At first the invaders maintained the upper hand with superior weapons and ruthlessness, but later they triumphed by being so adaptable—a euphemism for being willing to cohabit with the Welsh. The Welsh proved themselves equally willing. Their princess Nesta, or Nest, whom Curtis calls the queen bee of the Norman-Welsh swarm, bore children to Henry I, and Stephen the constable of Cardigan, *and* her legal husband Gerald of Windsor, thus founding the families of— among others—the FitzGeralds, the FitzHenrys, the Barrys, and the Carews. It would be difficult to find a more adaptable woman. By Dermot's time these Anglo-Welsh-Normans were as hardy a crowd as ever lived by force of arms. Their followers were ethnically

various: Normans, Welsh, and Flemings, these last having
settled in Wales after finishing terms in the king's military
service.

In spite of their mixed ancestry the barons of twelfth-
century Britain retained the code of feudalism in which their
Norman forefathers had been reared, a code that was to
give rise to much perplexity, not to mention outrage, among
their Celtic hosts in the years to come. A Gaul's debt to his
lord was something far more complicated than Irish fealty.
An Irish freeman's loyalty depended on whether or not he
held a lord's cattle on lease, and it expired with the life of
either partner in the bargain. In Gaul, however, people were
bound to be loyal to the king as a national duty, and bound
to military service automatically and not because of special
land tenure or anything else. Holding land from the king
was of course possible, but it did not govern the underlying
code. Moreover, *everything* belonged to the king or lord.
Says Guizot, "Thus in England the national peace is the
king's peace; the state domain—the folkland—is *terra regis*.
The township has become the lord's manor, the township
waste the lord's waste, the township court the lord's court"
(Encyclopaedia Britannica, 9th Edition, Vol. IX, p. 121).

When Norman met Celt, such a wide discrepancy in
attitude was fated to lead to lifelong misunderstanding and
a sense of deep indignation.

Dermot's first objective was Henry II, and when the monarch
proved to be absent in France the Irish king followed until
he ran his quarry to ground in Aquitaine, where Henry was
tending the vast properties that had been his wife's dowry.
Dermot's proposition is given by Gerald de Barry, who was
there: "Your liege-man I shall come henceforth all the days
of my life on condition that you be my helper, so that I do
not lose everything."

Henry listened and recollected Adrian's grant. The Irish
project did not seem urgent enough to tempt him personally,
but he had no objections if any of his barons felt like taking
it on and doing the work for him, and he gave Dermot

an open letter to this effect. The Irish king went back to Britain to recruit. England disappointed him, all the barons there being busy and content to stay where they were, but in Wales, where he went next, things went better. There he found a number of lords dissatisfied with their chances of advancement at home, willing to try new adventure in Ireland. As the outstanding among these Dermot carefully selected Richard FitzGilbert de Clare, second earl of Pembroke and Striguil, nicknamed—like his father before him—Strongbow. Gerald calls Strongbow "a man whose past was brighter than his prospects, whose blood was better than his brains, and whose claims of succession were larger than his land in possession." Because this man had supported the claim of Stephen, Henry's rival aspirant, to the throne of England, he was out of favor at court. Henry had taken land Strongbow considered his own and given it to a Fitz-Gilbert cousin. A powerful neighbor kept taking bites out of the remaining estate, and on top of everything else, Strongbow's wife had recently died. He was tired of Wales and more than ready for a change, but of course he did not tell Dermot MacMurrough this: he haggled over terms until Dermot promised that if Strongbow would lead an army of Norman volunteers into Ireland, he should have Princess Eva's hand in marriage and succession to Dermot's throne of Leinster.

Dermot waited only to see preparations well in train before in 1167 he returned to Ireland, bringing with him one of the younger barons and a few troops. With this help he repossessed Ferns and held it, even though O'Connor and O'Rourke, as soon as they heard he was back, descended on him and forced him to disgorge the hundred ounces of gold he had been owing to Dervorgilla's husband for fifteen years. After that he simply waited and did nothing except rebuild his palace, until May 1169. Then the first large detachment of Normans arrived from Wales and disembarked, horses and all, at Bannow Bay, on the south coast near Wexford. They came as a complete, shattering surprise to the Irish, and—though Dermot must have prepared the invaders somewhat—Gerald's record shows that the surprise was not all on one side. He describes the natives in lofty terms, but he is thorough. A rude people, he calls them, living on animal produce, little advanced from the pastoral stage. While shunning the labor of agriculture, he says, they are not attracted by the refinements, and dislike the restraint, of town life. Most of their land is rough pasture, little is cultivated and less sown, though the land is naturally fertile. They have few fruit trees. Yews are plentiful, often planted in ancient cemeteries, and there are many firs. They don't bother much to make the linen and woolen cloth they wear. "Sunk in sloth, they think the height of luxury is to have no work to do, and what they most dearly prize is the enjoyment of liberty" (G. H. Orpen, *Ireland Under the Normans,* England, 1911, Vol. II, p. 136).

On the other hand, Gerald admits that the Irish are highly skilled in music, especially with two instruments, the cithara or harp, and the tympanus, a sort of psaltery with brass strings, played with a plectrum. He is enthusiastic, too, over the illuminations he has seen in a book of the Gospels. The children he describes as being left almost entirely to nature, growing up with tall, handsome figures and regular features, but, he adds, the Irish have a barbarous fashion of beards and clothes, which with their ignorance marks their uncivilized state. They are "slightly clad" in woolen clothing that is black or drab, the color of their sheep. Close-fitting patchwork hoods extend over their shoulders and down to the elbows, and under it they wear a *phalanga* rather than a mantle, with woolen trews usually dyed some color. An Irishman rides without saddle, boots, or spurs, urging on the horse with a crooked stick; the reins serve as bit and bridle. He wears no armor in war. He carries a short spear, a pair of javelins, and a large battle-ax "well wrought and tempered" which is borrowed from the Ostmen. When these fail he throws "hand-stones" more dexterously than any other nation.

We can imagine what it must have been like for such men when they were faced by mounted knights wearing coats of mail, helmets, and steel gorgets, the like of which had never been seen in the country, carrying shields and long lances. The Vikings too had worn armor and carried shields, but that had been a long time ago in a different generation: the Vikings had been forgotten. As if the Norman knights were not redoubtable enough, they had in their train Flemish foot soldiers with crossbows, weapons altogether new to the Irish, who depended on fleetness of foot and agility in battle, who wore linen tunics instead of chain mail, and fought on foot. The discrepancy was as great as that between Iron Age and Stone Age man.

The new Norman forces numbered six hundred, and when joined by Dermot and his men, their army was a thousand strong. Together they made for the seaport town of Wexford. When the Ostmen came out to give battle, the engagement did not last long; they were soon driven back. Within twenty-four hours the town had surrendered and the Norman invasion was on.

Word of all this, naturally, soon reached Rory O'Connor. As usual he summoned Tiernan O'Rourke, and they hurried back to Ferns to attack Dermot once again. The crafty king of Leinster kept the truth hidden and battled them in the ordinary straggling fashion of the Irish. No Normans were seen in the neighborhood, and after one or two token fights Dermot consented amiably enough to parley. His enemies proposed slightly easier terms for a new peace and he smoothly agreed. All he wanted, he said, was to rule Leinster in peace; he would not insist on retaining control of Dublin, and he promised not to use the Normans in future. O'Connor and O'Rourke, satisfied, withdrew from Ferns and did not even suggest continuing to Wexford. Their armies were hardly out of sight before Dermot was sending urgent word to Strongbow in Wales, telling him the time was at hand.

Strongbow set sail at once. A small advance party entrenched themselves on a Wexford beach and acted as decoy. Soon, with Irish allies, they were beating off a large host of Norsemen from Waterford. By the time Strongbow

had disembarked, his men were ready for an assault on
Waterford, and they easily took the town. There Strongbow
was married to Eva, and then he went on with his father-in-
law Dermot to conquer Dublin. O'Connor and O'Rourke,
realerted, got there first in an attempt to save the city, but
they found that the Ostman chief Asgall was overready, in
their opinion, to surrender, and they quit in disgust. Asgall
did surrender quite promptly when the Normans arrived,
then escaped. In September 1170 the Normans occupied
Dublin.

The first surprise was over, but the Irish were still puzzled
by many Norman habits—their plan of campaign, for
instance. In Irish wars the walled Norse towns were not
considered of much importance, but the Normans had a
tradition of warfare from behind the walls of castles and
fortresses and keeps, and their first act after victory in
open country was to put up castles for defense. They had
left behind them a Wales heavily studded with such edifices,
and they were to do the same to the Irish landscape. In the
meantime they instinctively turned to the fort-cities of the
Norsemen.

Dermot MacMurrough was jubilant, seeing nothing now
in his way to becoming high king of Ireland. It was true that
Rory O'Connor was planning all-out assault on Dublin, but
Dermot had no fear of Rory now that the Normans were
on his own side. Suddenly, early in the summer of 1171, he
fell gravely ill at Ferns, and Strongbow arrived only in time
to see him die. Now the Norman was king of Leinster, and
he started back to Dublin in that capacity, but his career
was nearly cut short at its beginning when he ran into an
army of a thousand Norsemen who had been collected by
Asgall from Norway, Man, and the Hebrides. Fortunately
for Strongbow they did not realize who he was, and he
escaped by the skin of his teeth. The Norsemen were going
straight from the beaches to Dublin, where they launched
an attack on the gates, but in spite of their heavy armor
they could not withstand the charge of a party of mounted
Norman knights. Breaking ranks, they rushed back to their

ships, leaving Asgall in Norman hands. He was promptly decapitated in the castle's main hall.

The next challenge came from O'Connor and O'Rourke in alliance with a kinsman of the late Dermot, whose unpopularity seems to have prevailed even among his family. The Gaelic idea of a siege was more relaxed than the Norse. The army simply sat down outside the castle, making camp in what is now Phoenix Park, and waited for hunger to force the inhabitants to surrender. While waiting, O'Connor sent in an offer to leave Strongbow in undisputed possession of Leinster if the Norman would agree to recognize O'Connor's high kingship and send his compatriots back to Wales. Strongbow refused, possibly absent-mindedly since he was engaged at the same time in refusing another proposition far more urgent—a suggestion made repeatedly, in different forms, by his young Norman lieutenants, that they forget their vows of loyalty to King Henry and strike out on their own in Ireland, gathering private kingdoms. Strongbow was against this idea. It was all very well to sit idle in a besieged castle, dreaming dreams of glory, but he knew that Henry would soon be coming to Ireland in person to see how rich the prize might be that had been won by his barons, and no king ever had a keener nose for treason.

To cure his men's restiveness the leader eventually picked two of the young barons to help him lead six hundred men out of the castle. By a roundabout route, quietly, they made their way to Rory's camp in the park and caught the high king and his men bathing in the Liffey. Nobody was on guard and the Irish were completely taken by surprise. Naked, they scattered, Rory among them. When at last the high king was at a safe distance and clothed, he faced the fact that the Normans had come to stay and he had better learn to live with them.

Henry's expected arrival took place in the autumn of 1171. It was barely a year since Becket had been murdered, and relations between the English king and Pope Alexander were still under strain, but Henry did not have to take the risk of using Adrian's *Laudabiliter* paper: nobody he met in Ireland disputed his authority. Wherever he went he was acclaimed. Of course he had brought a large army with him, but it wasn't needed. He visited Cashel and summoned there a synod of the Irish clergy, where there was much discussion between bishops of their flocks' backwardness, and the members agreed to have an annual council of the same sort from that time on. Henry sent a report of all this to Alexander as a peace offering, and ultimately the Pope in reply sent Henry another privilege authorizing him to rule the people of Ireland—once again described as ignorant of the rudiments of faith—and "mold" them into conformity with the usages of the Church of England.

The king confirmed Strongbow's right to hold Leinster as his vassal. For himself he took Dublin, Waterford, and Wexford, with king-sized areas of land along the coast adjoining Dublin and Waterford. At Waterford he held a court and accepted the homage of several kings, and many more came to pledge vassalage to him at Dublin, where he spent the winter. All the Irish kings were now accounted for except Rory O'Connor and the chiefs of the north country, and Rory submitted in 1175, signing the treaty of Windsor, in which he recognized Henry as his overlord and promised to collect annual tribute from all Ireland for the Crown. For his part, Henry agreed to accept Rory as high king of all areas unconquered by the Normans.

All this treaty making and easy surrender represented a misunderstanding on the part of Rory O'Connor and the other kings. They thought Henry would be satisfied to reign in name only, *in absentia;* they expected him to behave like an Irish high king and leave them alone as long as he collected his tributes. The treaty of Windsor broke down for two reasons, says the Reverend Dr. Frank X. Martin: "Rory was ardri [high king] in name only: he found it hard to enforce authority even in his own territory in Connacht," while Henry couldn't prevent the Norman barons from seizing more land, as they persistently did. Henry made himself grants of large areas without consulting Rory or the other Irish kings *(The Course of Irish History,* pp.

134-35). In feudal England this sort of behavior was the king's undisputed right. All land titles depended on him: he was "Dominus Terrae," the supreme landlord. This was a conception unknown in Irish law and alien to the Irish mind, and the kings were stunned when Henry coolly handed over the kingdom of Meath, a huge tract of land including today's Meath, Westmeath, Cavan, and Longford, to the Norman Hugh de Lacy. The entire royal family of O'Melaghlin was unseated in one moment, by one signature. And this was only the first of a whole series of shocks. Leinster's throne was felt by the Irish to be an exception; Strongbow had come by it fairly according to their Irish standards, but none of the other baron-landowners could claim as much.

Alexander III had not yet received Henry's peacemaking letter and report when he sent a letter of his own to the king, threatening him with an interdict because of the murder of Thomas à Becket. Henry immediately went home. He had been in Ireland only six months, but that was long enough for him to acquire a firm grip on his new possessions that was not to relax during his lifetime, even though he never returned.

CHAPTER

4

WHEN Henry II handed over Meath to Hugh de Lacy he was, of course, not actuated by simple generosity. He was playing his usual game of checks and balances, dividing to rule: he saw De Lacy in Meath as a makeweight for Strongbow in Leinster. Each baron would keep an eye on the other. But the next Norman who became an Irish chief played outside the rules and for himself only. This was John de Courcy, a dashing young man from Somerset who had not taken Strongbow's "no" for an answer during the siege of Dublin. He chafed at the feudal custom that kept him in vassalage to the king, and refused to apply for the usual "speculative grant" from the throne when in 1177 the urge came strongly upon him to go out and get a kingdom. He simply rounded up a few hundred restless types in Dublin and marched at their head into Ulster, where the terrain then as always had a reputation for difficulty in warfare. They drove the king of Ulidia out of his capital, Downpatrick. The king went for help to a friend, the king of Aileach, and with their combined armies, two bishops, and some holy relics, the allies mounted a counterattack on De Courcy's forces, but De Courcy came out of this engagement even more firmly the victor.

Having done it all without debt to Henry, the Norman felt himself entitled to take the position of undisputed prince of the country, and for almost thirty years he maintained his rule in complete independence. In true Norman fashion he covered the land with casdes and manors wherever he needed an outpost or watchtower, preserving the property and keeping the peace. In these respects, Hugh de Lacy and the other landowning barons behaved in similar fashion: such garrisons and buildings were the Norman hallmark. Until about 1210 they made their castles of wood and earth, rather like very elaborate Irish raths. In the center was the motte or mote, a high, steep, flat-topped mound on which stood a wooden palisade with boltholes, topped in its turn by a wooden tower. This edifice was surrounded by a wide ditch and the ditch was ringed by a wider space in which stood the soldiers' quarters and the workshops. In later days such a space was called the bailey. For run-of-the-mill wooden castles, one earth-and-palisade fence around the whole estate was considered sufficient protection, but if the chief thought the place needed even more he would put a second ditch and palisade around the first one. The result was a formidable defense, and when in the next century such castles were built of stone, they were even more difficult to capture.

Once built, the castles and manors were occupied by the barons' officers and men who had come with them from Wales, but these classes were not enough to maintain the economy. What was needed was the common Irish serf, *betagh* as he was called in Gaelic, who had fled when his king was defeated and now stayed hidden. The Normans lured such people back to the land, tempting and pacifying them, until most of the peasants had returned to their old fields and pastures. There they found that life was not so different, once the change in lordship was accepted. Nevertheless the land did seem altered, for the men of the Normans' garrisons, realizing that they were in Ireland for life, behaved accordingly and settled down. As they dropped out of active service they took land of their own as part payment, on which they built houses. They found wives among the native women, but for the most part they didn't adopt native ways, but tended to live in communities grouped around the local castle. Among these clusters of dwelling places something developed that was new to Ireland, a fashion of selling services or goods in one place instead of peddling them from one country house to the next. Soon tanners, chandlers, and blacksmiths lived among the settlers; the millers, of course, had always lived with their mills, and now these were built conveniently close to the castles. As time went on new religious orders appeared, introduced and encouraged by the Normans to set up abbeys near the houses, or at least churches. So Ireland's inland towns grew up—Trim, Drogheda, Carrickfergus, Dromore, New Ross, Kilkenny, and hundreds more, peopled for the most part by foreigners. "The Gaelic Irish never took kindly to the towns, and for this reason the roll-calls of the towns list names which were almost invariably Norse, Norman, Welsh, and English—Le Decer, Lawless, Keppok, Golding, Forster, Newton, Bodenham, Holywood, and the like, but you will rarely find the Os and the Macs among them" (The Course of Irish History, p. 140).

Like any father, Henry II wanted to provide for all his children. John, the youngest and his favorite, was known as "Lackland" because he had no territory, and he seemed likely to be out of luck without some special provision. Henry decided that Ireland would answer the purpose very nicely. In his judgment, John at the age of seventeen, in 1185, was old enough to take on responsibility. Though Henry had not been back to Ireland, he kept himself informed of what went on there. He did this with all his possessions; he had a wary nature, always watching for signs of rebellion or intrigue. That year, for example, he was displeased by the latest reports on his justiciar (viceroy) Hugh de Lacy of Meath. De Lacy's first wife died and he took an Irish bride, Rose, daughter of Rory O'Connor. Henry was sure De Lacy planned to inherit the high kingship from O'Connor, after which he might feel strong enough to defy Henry. One had to think of everything, according to Henry's philosophy, and it was time to show De Lacy that he was under surveillance. The justiciar was dismissed from his post, and Henry bestowed on Prince John the title Dominus Hiberniae—Lord of Ireland—and sent him across the water to become familiar with his property.

John disembarked at Waterford in April 1185, accompanied by a royal army and three youths of his own age. They marched to Dublin, where John held court and received homage from Irish nobles. These worthies, dressed in a style strange to the English arrivals, with long beards, struck the lordlings as comical. When they spoke French—the speech of the English aristocracy—they pronounced it badly. The whole ceremony seemed funny to John and his friends. They roared with laughter and openly made fun of the Irish gentlemen; they even tweaked some of the beards. The Irish went away, gravely offended, to complain of the matter.

No doubt Irishmen around the court knew by this time what to expect of English royalty. John appropriated much land for himself and generously handed out estates to his friends. For William de Burgo he cut into Munster, which until now had been untouched, but for once the royal gift did not bring instant despair to some Irish family. This land was in the domain of Donal More O'Brien, and De Burgo announced that he would not try to take it over until Donal More died. In 1193 the Norman carried his peaceful policy further by marrying Donal More's daughter, so the land would remain with the O'Briens in any case. Few dispossessed Irish got off so lightly.

After the gifts had been bestowed the young lord of Ireland found little more to do. He presented land to Limerick's cathedral, and proved himself a true Norman by building some castles, but in December he returned to England, having spent eight months in Ireland. "In this brief period, he had driven the Irish into open opposition, alienated the sympathy of the Anglo-Norman colony, dissipated the treasure entrusted to him, and frittered away his army to no purpose. He had shown no capacity, either to govern with prudence or to fight with success" (Orpen, *Ireland Under the Normans*, Vol. 2, p. 105). It was a severe comment which John doubtless merited, but he was only seventeen, and his careless attitude toward Ireland, as toward most things, changed later.

Irish affairs simmered down for a time. There were still battles at the borders of new states, but overall the country became more peaceful than it had been for decades, and the *betaghs* could not have found much difference in their lives. There was still a master-man relationship; only the identity of the masters had changed. But the Irish chiefs suffered and could find no place in the new system. Rory O'Connor, left alone because he had submitted early, faded away and died in a monastery in 1198. Dervorgilla too died in sanctity, at Mellifont Abbey in 1193. She was eighty-five.

The lands that remained unconquered made up about half Ireland's area in 1195, and belonged chiefly to kings in the west who had resisted the barons. Kerry and the territory north of it had not even been attempted. In the conquered regions—though the fact could hardly have comforted those Irish kings who had lost their thrones—the country had by this time begun to assimilate her conquerors. The Normans' children grew up, as the expression had it, more Gael than Gaul; in any case many of them were half Irish, like the daughter of Eva and Strongbow, who married William Marshal in 1189. Hugh de Lacy had his Rose of Connacht, William de Burgo the daughter of Donal More O'Brien, whose sons could justly claim descent from Brian Bom himself, and there were many other intermarriages, though John de Courcy, as if to prove once more that he was different, married no Irish girl but Affreca, daughter of Godred, the Norse king of Man. Such assimilation might not have proceeded so rapidly if Henry II had sent more parties of Normans from Britain after the first invaders, but he refrained from doing this because the feudal lords of Ireland were already too powerful for his peace of mind.

It will be recalled that he gave Hugh de Lacy the great country of Meath on purpose to hold down Strongbow and prevent his becoming too strong, but the plan had gone wrong. Strongbow died and Leinster temporarily reverted to the king of England, while De Lacy, with no competition, flourished. Fortunately for Henry's neurosis, however, De Lacy was suddenly removed from the scene, murdered by an Irishman, and Meath too reverted to the Crown. Henry himself died in 1189, and was spared the spectacle of William de Burgo's rise to power after Donal More died in 1194. The way was now open for the Norman son-in-law and other barons who had stayed their hands as long as the Irish king lingered. With Philip de Braose, De Burgo now occupied Limerick, and set about building the usual castles in which to place trusty henchmen.

Richard I, the Lion-Hearted, succeeded to the throne and immediately went off to the Continent. Always preoccupied with crusades, he found time to visit England only twice in the ten years of his reign, and very likely spared no thought whatever for Ireland, his younger brother's lordship. He died in 1199, leaving no direct heir. John was now Henry's only surviving son, but an older brother, Geoffrey, had left a child, a twelve-year-old boy, Arthur duke of Brittany, and for a time Richard looked on this boy as his heir. He had later changed his mind in favor of John, but the French still claimed that Arthur was the rightful heir. He was French in his sympathies and had been brought up in France, and their eagerness to attain influence through his succession is comprehensible. John was crowned king, but the French still clamored for Arthur. Anjou acknowledged him as king and Philip of France received his homage, until at last King John found it necessary to take certain steps. It was done quietly, but when in 1203 the boy was murdered there was little doubt who had instigated the deed.

The murder strained relations between the king and some of his barons who felt more French than English. Even some Anglicized Normans did not approve, and among them

was William Marshal, Strongbow's son-in-law and heir—
or at any rate his heir if John would confirm him chief of
Leinster. Marshal was no green youth; he had disapproved
of earlier kings as well. Born in 1140, he had now served
three monarchs of the English line and would live to be
regent for a fourth. As a small child he was a hostage in
King Stephen's household. As a man he had been completely
trusted by Henry II even though he demurred when Becket
was murdered. He had served Richard throughout his reign,
and afterward had declared for John. True to the feudal
code, in spite of his distress when Arthur was killed he
remained a dutiful Marshal, for there could be no break
initiated by a liege between liege and lord. In 1207 his long
wait was rewarded and John confirmed him in possession of
Strongbow's country and title, as first earl of Pembroke and
Striguil of the Marshal line, and lord of Leinster.

For years people have execrated the memory of King
John. Textbooks refer to his defeat over Magna Carta as a
proper punishment for evil-doing, and it is true that he was
no paragon of virtue, but he was no worse than Henry II,
and in some ways might be considered a good deal better. At
this period of his reign his actions regarding Ireland indicate
that the ill-mannered boy had turned out better than anyone
had had a right to expect. Though he was king of England
with many holdings in France, he did not forget he was
lord of Ireland as well, and his first measures there were
well-considered and constructive. They were needed, for
Ireland languished for want of reform, and even the Anglo-
Irish, as the Normans were called, were inconvenienced. "A
Dublin government scarcely existed, there was a fortress
in Dublin under a constable, there was a royal deputy and
royal demesnes, but no coinage, courts, or administration
of State. So far as a Council of State existed, it was the body
of baronial tenants-in-chief themselves. The real strength
of the colony lay in the feudal element whose 'conquered'
lands covered half the island" (Edmund Curtis, A History
of Ireland, pp. 67-68).

John's program of reconstruction covered the years 1200-

8 and comprised the minting and circulation of coins, the beginning of Dublin Castle (a portion of which still stands, built into more modern fabric), and the introduction of the law of England. Trial by jury for criminal and land cases (though only for freeholders) had existed for some time in England, and now it was to be introduced into Ireland. Unfortunately for the free Gaels this new rule of law, advantageous as it was for the Anglo-Irish, was of no benefit to them. On the contrary, it dealt a deathblow to their status, since if the Normans were to admit the claims of the many Irish against those who had taken their lands by force, the Normans themselves would be in trouble. The only way out for them was to change the position of the victims from free to unfree, so the cases might not be brought. This was done, reducing the free tenants to the level of *betaghs,* so that the word "hibernicus" became a general term for villein or serf. To protect themselves still further the Normans saw to it in 1214 that this "writ of villeins and fugitives" was rendered retroactive to 1170, thus giving the new landlords power to claim and "recover" the new-made serfs, while laws protecting freeholders from unjust dispossession were inoperative for the period preceding 1199. The year 1204 brought a decree that no one could be sued for taking the goods or even the life of an Irishman until after Michaelmas 1205. Harsh though it was, the wording of this decree offered the hint of hope: might it not be read to imply that an Irishman with a grievance could sue *after* Michaelmas 1205? No; events proved that it didn't mean that.

Nevertheless King John's attitude toward the native Irish did relax somewhat. At the beginning of his reign he behaved like an insensitive conqueror: he gave his cousin Meilor FitzHenry, the justiciar, a large slice of the country of Kerry, hitherto untouched, and made a number of smaller grants of Irish property. But soon he was beset by the same kind of doubts that had plagued his father. He grew suspicious of his barons, especially those in Ireland because he couldn't keep an eye on them. It seemed prudent to cut one or another down to size every so often, and for a start he concentrated on the defiant, independent John de Courcy of Ulster. De Courcy was said to have spoken indignantly of Arthur's death, so FitzHenry, acting on orders from the king, summoned him to Dublin to give an account of himself. De Courcy refused to come, and John in 1205 announced that Hugh de Lacy, son of the late founder of the house of Meath, had been created earl of Ulster. De Lacy and FitzHenry then attacked the aging De Courcy, defeated him, and put him into prison for a while. After his release he left Ireland to spend the rest of his life in France.

John struck another blow at the barons' feudal authority by granting Connacht not to a Norman but to Rory O'Connor's heir Cathal, and he followed this act in 1210 by handing over Thomond to another Irishman of the royal line, Donough O'Brien. Already he was regretting that he had bestowed Ulster on young Hugh de Lacy, for the De Lacys needed only the slightest encouragement to become overween-ingly ambitious, and Hugh had combined forces with his brother Walter of Meath and William de Braose, lord of Limerick, to defy him. John hated to waste time on Irish affairs, embroiled as he was in quarrels with France, but he was determined to crush this rebellion in person. He came back to Ireland in June 1210, landing with a large army at Waterford, where, by appointment, he met Cathal O'Connor and Donough O'Brien with their forces. Within a few weeks the combined armies had driven De Braose and the De Lacys out of the island. The king stayed on in Dublin for a time to see that the processes of government were being improved according to his orders. The conquered territories were divided into counties, each with a sheriff and court, and John also appointed a new justiciar, John de Gray, bishop of Norwich—the first episcopal viceroy in Ireland and the first not chosen from among the great Irish landowners. The king then departed, reasonably confident that things were in order at last.

Events justified his confidence when he quarreled with Pope Innocent III over the choice of the next archbishop of Canterbury. Innocent's riposte was swift and telling: in

1213 he declared the Crown of England forfeit and offered it to Philip Augustus of France, who started preparing a huge army just across the English Channel. An invasion seemed imminent, and King John called on all his barons, including those in Ireland, to come to England's defense. In response, five hundred Irish Normans, led by William Marshal, crossed the sea to stand guard at Dover—not that they loved John, but the action was in accordance with their feudal code. In the end John made peace with the Pope, but his influence over the barons, which had been waning before the crisis, now sank to its nadir. The English barons combined and acted quickly to demand rights that the king had long withheld; in 1215 came the famous scene at Runnymede when he was forced to sign the Magna Carta. Crushed by this defeat, King John died in the following year.

The heir, Henry III, was only nine years old when he came to the throne, and William Marshal became regent. As such he was able to cancel out some of John's harsher strictures against the Irish Normans, which included the confiscation of his own lands. He died in 1219 and was replaced by another official with Irish interests, Hubert de Burgo. Under Marshal and Hubert the rebels who had been chased out by John dared to return. Many barons resumed the old ways, expanding their territorial limits at the expense of the Gaels, until only Hugh de Lacy was still unreconciled with the Crown. In 1223 he returned from the Crusades determined on revenge and the repossession of Ulster. In Meath he collected some sympathetic local lords and they went on the warpath. Ravaging the country as they went, they approached Dublin and frightened Archbishop Henry, the justiciar, into paying them off. Henry was succeeded by William Marshal the Younger in 1224, and Marshal fought back against Hugh de Lacy, but in the end the latter got his lands back after all.

Rebellions and readjustments did not interfere with Dublin's routine, where the government developed along the lines laid down by John. By the time Henry III attained his majority Dublin Castle sheltered a chancellor, a treasurer, and a number of justices for the assize courts. Seven counties were included in the conquered land, their outlines roughly approximating those of the kingdoms they replaced: Cork, Limerick, Waterford, Kerry, Tipperary, Connacht, and Oriel. Dublin had a parliament made up of bishops, abbots, and lay peers, which could be summoned by the justiciar whenever he thought it advisable. The country was being managed by the Anglo-Normans— at last—in fairly orderly fashion. It has been said that among their sins against Ireland was one of omission, because the Normans never followed the fundamental principles of colonization. This is true, and it is also explicable. At the beginning of the conquest nobody concerned thought in terms of colonies. The invasion with its subsequent scramble for prizes was in no way a national act of war, but a private arrangement between Henry and the barons, comparable to such speculative ventures as Isabella's with Columbus, or Elizabeth's with Raleigh. It cannot be equated, for example, with William's conquest of England, which was, as it were, official and involved two major powers. Strongbow's was a freebooting expedition. That many of his barons wanted to cut their feudal ties with the English king indicates that they were lawless and impetuous even by Norman standards, and with such beginnings the wonder is not that law and order should have been slow in coming, but that within the space of two generations it came at all, even in limited form. For this coming, however much it goes against the grain, we must in justice thank King John.

CHAPTER

5

WHEN Henry III took personal control of his affairs in 1232 the regency with its strong Irish bias was abolished, but much of what the regents had done for their relatives and friends survived their terms of office. Hubert de Burgo, for example, in 1227 had conferred on his kinsman Richard de Burgo the lordship of Connacht, thus scrapping John's promise to Cathal O'Connor that the Irish king and his heirs should rule the country in perpetuity. In 1235 a large number of other barons joined Richard in driving out the incumbent Irish ruler, Felim O'Connor, from nearly all Connacht, which they then divided among themselves. Felim was left with the poor regions of Roscommon and Leitrim. One of the baronial company, Maurice FitzGerald, moved north and staked out claims in fresh territory, founding the town of Sligo and subduing Tyrconnel. But he died in 1257, and an Irish chief, Goffraidh O'Donnell, won back Sligo and Tyrconnel.

Henry III never found the time to visit his other island personally, and eventually conferred the lordship of Ireland on his son Edward, but he could not forbear to meddle with it afterward nevertheless. Always money-hungry, he squeezed the Irish for revenue to bestow on the Pope, and in 1250 he directed the archbishops of Ireland to preach the cause of the Crusades. Letters from Innocent IV granting boons to those who contributed were published throughout the country. But on the whole Henry's long reign, especially from the Norman-Irish point of view, was dull. The barons of Ireland seemed lazier than their fathers, perhaps because they had more territory than they could safely manage; the invasion and dismemberment of Connacht was their last big venture. However, even then peace did not prevail in Ireland: there were still many small forays, or run-of-the-mill encroachments, and during these flare-ups it began to be apparent that the Gaels were at last fighting back effectively. The development came in time to put off for a little more the inevitably complete occupation of Ireland, the Gaels owing their success to a new element in the country, the *galloglach* or gallowglass, the "Norse soldier" or Hebridean mercenary. These Hebridean warriors were tall, fair, strong men of mixed Norse and Irish descent who wore armor and fought with long-handled axes fiercely enough to frighten even the Normans. One of the Tyrconnel O'Donnells introduced them into Ireland when in Scotland he married the sister of the gallowglass leader Mac-Sweeney and brought home not only a bride but a brother-in-law and all his men. The first time Normans met them on the battlefield was in 1258, when the Normans were soundly defeated. After this the mercenaries became the most sought-after soldiers in Ireland. There was a noteworthy battle at Callan near Kenmare in 1261, at which Irish beat off Normans who were trying to occupy the southern countries of Desmond and Decies, killing the leader FitzThomas with his son, driving off the enemy, and putting an end to the Norman conquest of southwest Ireland. In 1270 gallowglasses helped to turn the tide against Normans who tried to take over the remaining Connacht countries of Roscommon and Leitrim. The invaders were ignominiously run off the field.

Perhaps because of this breathing space the Irish began to evince a new concept of self-protection, often behaving rather like a nation united against threats from outside. For instance, in 1258 Brian O'Neill of Ulster resurrected an old custom by declaring himself high king of Ireland—nothing fresh in itself, but he also persuaded two other chiefs to agree and recognize his claim. That was as far as it went, because a fourth king refused to fall in with the idea, and Brian O'Neill was killed soon afterward. Still, it had represented a step toward unification. Five years later, in 1263, a few Irish kings sought another sort of unity when they applied to Haakon, king of Norway, who happened to be in the Scottish isles in quest of tribute, to adopt their cause as a sort of high king and lead them against the English, but Haakon was not interested.

In 1276 the most powerful and aristocratic of the native Irish sent a request to Edward I, who had succeeded Henry in 1272, asking him to change the English law and make them equal to the Anglo-Irish in the courts. They even offered to pay eight thousand marks for this privilege. It was not that they liked the law, Curtis comments, for some of its penalties seemed dreadful to a people whose own law rarely punished by death or mutilation. But as long as they were conquered it would be better than nothing. (The rank and file of the Irish if they had been asked would probably have declared in favor of brehon law.) Edward took no action for three years, then he referred the question to a parliament of Anglo-Irish barons, who naturally shelved it. It was not until 1302 that the English king commanded a great council in London that a grant of English law be made to all Irishmen who demanded it. For Edward, at war with France, needed more money from Ireland than he was getting, though his officials had already imposed export duty on Irish wool, hide, and leather. He had sent a new justiciar to Dublin in 1295, the English John de Wogan, with orders to squeeze the country in every way possible, for money and men. Still unsatisfied, in 1304 he claimed suzerainty over Scotland as well, whereupon the Scottish chiefs rose against him. One of these was the earl of Carrick, better known to us as Robert the Bruce, who in time was to play a part in Ireland too.

Wogan must have been startled by the Irish scene and its effect on his compatriots. Some of the feudal barons, especially those living a long way out in the marches, had long since gone native: they spoke fluent Gaelic by choice and wore their hair long in the Irish style called the glib. Many lords had picked up from the natives the custom of fosterage, sending their sons to be reared in Irish families. As we saw with Wales, the Normans had always been ready to adopt native ways, and in Ireland this behavior paid off, since it was easier to pacify and rule people with whom one had much in common. In the wild western country, for instance, the so-called Red Earl, Richard de Burgo, managed very well the difficult task of governing both Connacht and Ulster because he was popular with the people: he had O'Brien blood and talked Gaelic, so they considered him one of themselves. In Dublin, however, as in the other settled lands near the coast, the English regarded such fraternizing sourly, declaring it treasonable.

In 1297 Wogan summoned a parliament with a difference. Up to a point it resembled the rudimentary assemblies Dublin had seen since King John's time, with justiciar and ministers, prelates, and lords, but Wogan added something novel by summoning also two knights and the sheriff or seneschal from each of the eleven counties and five liberties of the settled lands. It was a more representative conclave, though even so no Irishman except the odd prelate or abbot had a place among these deputies and magnates, and all transactions were, as usual, in French or English. It seems natural that some of the first laws enacted by this body should have been aimed at the Hibernicized Anglo-Irish, like the one stipulating that any "degenerate English" who persisted in wearing long hair in the glib must become Irishmen in law—which meant, more accurately, Irishmen without the law. At a larger parliament held in Kilkenny in 1310, in which representatives from shires and towns were included, a harsher discriminatory law was passed that "no mere Irishman shall be received into a religious order among the English in the land of peace." This law was revoked at once when the English Archbishop of Armagh appealed to the king against it, and I mention it only for its use of two interesting phrases: "mere Irishman," meaning a native with no civil rights, and "land of peace," i.e. the "obedient shires" or true English land, as distinct from the "march lands" of the feudal lords and the "land of war" or unconquered territory.

That hairstyle, the glib, that so angered the die-hards was not a simple matter of unshorn tresses. One lock of hair in the back was permitted to grow and was brushed up and forward, over the head, then down to the eyebrows. The fashion remained in favor in spite of the law against it. Two centuries later Edmund Spenser was still criticizing bitterly "the wearing of mantles and long glibbes, which is a thicke curled bush of hairs, hanging down over their eyes, and monstrously disguising them." He adds that these hairdos were fit masks for a thief.

The Irish were naturally quick to return such lavish compliments, calling the settlers English stammerers, tongue-tied strangers, and dumb foreigners. In Spenser's era Shane O'Neill of Ulster, asked why he did not speak English, demanded wrathfully if it was compatible with his honor "to writhe his mouth in chattering English."

The Crown approved of Wogan, who was skillful in extracting money and men from Ireland. For the latter commodity he was especially indebted to the Red Earl of Ulster, and must soon have conquered his early feelings of distrust for that peer, since De Burgo had perfected an ingenious way of getting troops from his Ulster chiefs. He allowed them to pay their tribute in men instead of money at the rate of one man one pound.

As the months passed, the English ventured farther north. When Edward in 1304 incurred the hostility of the Scots lords, they cast about for a king of their own. Robert the Bruce was eligible, but so were half a dozen others, and he hesitated at first to press his claim: the Bruces owned lands in England as well as Galloway. That year, however, the

Bruce's father died, and Robert decided to forget the family's
ancient loyalty to the Crown of England and take his chances
as king of an independent Scotland. His adherents agreeing,
at Scone in 1306 he had himself crowned King Robert I.
Edward quickly took a cruel revenge. Robert himself was
out of reach, but the English king captured Robert's wife,
sister, and daughter, took them to England, and maltreated
them, while the Bruce's brother-in-law and three of his
brothers were executed.

Edward I died in 1307 and the crown passed to his son
Edward II, but it was a stormy succession because the court
barons objected to the new king's overfervent friendship
with a good-looking youth named Piers Gaveston. In 1312
the lords rebelled and put Gaveston to death. What with all
this, Edward II neglected the war north of the border, and
Robert Bruce used his chances to win for himself a kingdom
to go with his new crown. He fought against the Scots lords
who opposed him with such vigor that in 1310, at a general
council at Dundee, he was recognized by all his compatriots
who mattered as king of the Scots. For the next two years
he worked at eradicating the English from the forts they
held near the border, and by 1313 had made such progress
that he took to raiding England itself, and Edward II felt
impelled to stop this activity. He gathered all the English
soldiers and Irish troops within reach, collected an immense
army, and set out to the north. On June 24, 1314, Robert
Bruce and his forces met the English army at Bannockburn
and the English were thoroughly routed.

Across the water the Irish watched these developments
with wonder and pride, feeling that Robert was their own
boy. And to some extent they were right. His father was
Norman, but his mother was descended from the Gaelic
kings of Alba, and he had married the daughter of the
earl of Ulster. The mere Irish and Anglo-Irish were agreed
about him, for the feudal barons too were dissatisfied with
Edward II. So many claimed kinship with the hero who had
beaten the king of England that the situation gave Robert
Bruce a new idea. He was faced with the classic problem

of the victor—the upkeep of a great army now idle and unnecessary. There was also the question of his remaining brother Edward Bruce: nearly as good a general as Robert himself, Edward now had nothing to do and was getting restless. Robert thought that the solution to all this might be a campaign in Ireland, under the leadership of Edward, to free the country from the English.

In May 1315 Edward Bruce sailed into Larne Harbor with an army of six thousand men, and there was met by two Irish chiefs and their armies, eager to join forces with him. The campaign started well and continued to flourish for a year, with the Scots triumphing over all resistance, but their pitiless methods soon alienated many Irish, as when at Ardee they burned down a church full of people. However, many others welcomed them and were jubilant at their success. The De Lacys became their allies, others submitted whether or not they approved, and on May Day 1316, having taken over all the north but Carrickfergus, Edward Bruce had himself crowned king of Ireland at Dundalk, then continued his campaign. Wherever he went, the sympathizers seemed to outnumber the badly trained local troops who tried in vain to hold him back. Some who welcomed him were Irish clergy, eager to entertain men they looked on as deliverers. Edward was confident of a general Irish uprising in his support, and thought it bound to happen soon.

The Scots army's first major setback took place in Connacht, where their ally Felim O'Connor, after making a magnificent fight against the English at Athenry, was defeated and killed. Edward abandoned Connacht for a time and turned back to besiege Carrickfergus, occupying it in the early autumn. In Ulster he was safe, but he had a temperamental resistance to remaining cooped up, and he might have plunged into rash action if it had not been for the arrival of Robert, come over to see how things were going. Together the redoubtable brothers moved again into the field of Connacht and Meath and this time conquered the defenders, but they left the twice-ravaged land in a terrible state, with no crops standing, no stock, and so little to eat that in some districts, according to a much disputed tale, the famished people resorted to cannibalism.

Early in 1317 the Scots marched to Dublin, but the audacious attempt failed and after a short siege the Bruces retired once more to the north. Meantime the earl of Ulster was clapped into Dublin prison on suspicion of complicity with his Bruce in-laws.

Even the casual Edward II now began to view the proceedings in Ireland with alarm. He bribed some of the Anglo-Irish nobles to keep them from turning against him, and appointed as his new lieutenant for Ireland Roger Mortimer of Wigmore. Mortimer had not won favor with the barons when first he came to Ireland because they looked on him as an outsider even though he was related to the Marshals and the De Lacys and owned much Irish land. Now, however, they were glad to see him. He landed at Youghal on April 7, 1317, with fresh forces, and immediately hurried in pursuit of the Bruces.

The Scots, leaders and men alike, were feeling discouraged. Rations were more and more of a problem, and that general rising they had so confidently expected kept evading them. Robert heard that there was disquiet along the English border, and in May he went home, while Edward composed himself to wait again in Ulster. There at least he could count on the De Lacys.

Mortimer went to Dublin—where he managed to extricate the Red Earl from prison—and sent a message summoning the De Lacys to surrender. They killed the messenger and defied the sender. Then Mortimer, who had been invested with extensive powers, proclaimed them felons and confiscated their lands. Through the summer of 1318 Edward Bruce stayed quietly in Ulster waiting for reinforcements from Scotland. When they had not arrived by October 14 he could not control his impatience any longer, and emerged, in company with all the De Lacys, to fight an Anglo-Irish army under John de Bermingham, near Dundalk. Undermanned and ill-supplied, his troops could not stand against the enemy and most of their leaders were killed. Hugh and Walter de Lacy with a few others escaped, but Edward Bruce himself lost his life on the field, and John de Bermingham carried his head to the king.

Thus England won the war in Ireland, but it was a near thing, and the king's policy makers knew that a little relaxation of tension was desirable for the sake of peace. As a sop, Mortimer in 1320 was instructed to remind the Dublin parliament that all the Irish except the *betaghs* were to be admitted to English law. Furthermore, some of the barons of the marches were commanded to restore certain territories to the royal Irish families who had been robbed of them. The Irish fringe around the English-settled land of peace grew wider, and the settlers retired little by little toward the coast and its fortified towns. A number of march lords, fearing for the future, abandoned their property altogether and made their homes in England and France, where they felt safer.

Edward Bruce's adventure, which had promised so much to the Gaelic Irish, left behind only new graves and ruined farms. The Irish wanted no more of such treatment, but there was a lesson in the period 1315-18 that they would not forget: a prince had come from abroad to be their champion, and together they nearly succeeded in getting rid of the English.

Relations between King Edward and the barons of England deteriorated, if that were possible. The defeat at Bannockburn was held bitterly against him, and now he had installed new favorites, the foreign Despensers, father and son, who like Gaveston held a dangerous amount of influence over him. In 1321 Parliament sent the Despensers into exile, and war followed between king and lords. This time Edward won, and the barons fled to Paris, Mortimer among them. The exiles were still there in 1325 when Edward's queen, Isabella of France, visited Paris and met them again. Isabella had no sympathy with her husband's actions. She became Mortimer's mistress, and joined the group in a conspiracy. They all sailed to England, where they landed near Bristol and captured the port, then moved on London. They caught and executed the Despensers, and put Edward II into prison. Parliament deposed the king in 1327, and soon afterward he was murdered at Berkeley Castle in a singularly brutal fashion. The prince of Wales, now Edward III, was only fifteen, so Mortimer and Isabella ruled the country as regents. Once again the Anglo-Irish could boast a friend at court: Mortimer made Maurice FitzThomas earl of Desmond, raised James Butler to the rank of earl of Ormond, and himself took the title of earl of March. But as soon as Edward III attained maturity he put a stop to all this. Like Hamlet he resented his mother's sins and the man for whom she sinned. He allied himself with some of the barons and overthrew the regents, and the earl of March was executed.

Edward III was disappointed with the revenue produced by the government of Ireland; besides, he felt that the political situation there was unsound. Many of the great families had died out or abandoned their Irish property. The few barons who remained all held enormous estates, and the king suspected it was only a matter of time before one of them felt strong enough to crown himself king of Ireland. He decided once again to introduce his ancestors' game of balancing lords against each other. Already the Anglo-Irish were ignoring his father's directions to extend English law to the Gaels, and he knew they would continue to do so unless they were forced to submit. Edward therefore dispatched Sir Anthony Lucy to serve as justiciar and see to it that his father's commands were obeyed. Lucy carried other unpopular orders as well: all the juicy grants that had been bestowed by Mortimer on his Anglo-Irish friends were to be "resumed," or taken back by the Crown. Twenty-four great lords, chronically absent from their Irish estates, were peremptorily commanded to return, or at least to make sure their lands were garrisoned. This made the erring barons very indignant, but because they thought Lucy of no importance they continued to ignore the king's orders.

The situation had the effect of combining Anglo-Irish with Gaelic Irish in a common resentment against England, which grew into what might be called a new colonial spirit. In fact, the barons were about to repudiate Edward, England, and all when Lucy was recalled. Instead, they turned to another matter—their tenantry, members of which were growing rebellious against their traditional masters. William de Burgo, earl of Ulster, was murdered by his people in 1329, and his widow fled to England with their only child, Elizabeth. The fortunes of this family were important to Ireland. While the little heiress grew up in England the Gaelic chiefs who in earlier days had been kings in Ulster moved back and occupied their old estates. Elizabeth was also heiress to Connacht, and here too the property was preempted during her absence, but this time the culprits were her cousins, two members of a junior branch of the Burgo family. Because it was to their advantage to follow the Gaelic law of inheritance, which stipulates male succession, they did so and divided the land between them. Ulick Burke—as the name of Burgo had now become —took that part of Elizabeth's land that lay in county Galway, and Edmund Burke settled on the Mayo land. A sprig of a third branch, which styled itself the De Burghs, helped himself to land in Limerick and Tipperary though all of it, according to Norman law, was Elizabeth's. Thus time brought Ireland her revenges, and the Burkes, behaving like Gaelic chiefs, scampered to occupy the land they said had been stolen from themselves. Often by that time the two races were so blended that it was impossible, without inside knowledge, to tell them apart. The Gaelic Irish rendered confusion thicker by adopting Norman customs. They took over Norman-built castles to use as strongholds; they adopted Norman-style armor and imitated Norman codes of courtesy. And, of course, they continued to intermarry with Normans.

More and more chiefs moved back into east and central Ulster to subdivide it, claiming ancestral rights to the property they now occupied, while the descendants of De Courcy's people moved out and went to settle at the coast.

There they lived like native Irish, having long since adopted Gaelic names. The same thing, though on a smaller scale, was happening in other regions, until in 1341 the lords of Desmond and Kildare wrote to the king complaining that a third of the country had been "lost" to the native Irish in this way. The whole situation, they said, was due to English-born justiciars who couldn't be expected to understand what course of action was needed. Possibly the letter impressed Edward III: at any rate in 1344 a new viceroy arrived with orders to reform Ireland. This was Sir Ralf d'Ufford, who might be said to have a vested interest in his mission, because he had married William de Burgo's widow. He brought the lady along to prove it, and immediately went into Ulster to redeem her property and acquire the title for himself. He did not succeed. What was worse, the attempt further offended the touchy Anglo-Irish lords, who blamed him in writing for being "an invader of the rights of the clerics and of the lay, rich and poor, a robber of goods under the colour of good, the defrauder of many evils on the native-born, the poor only excepted, in which things he was led by the counsel of his wife." This attitude exasperated the English D'Ufford, to say nothing of the English king. When the earl of Desmond called another assembly to marshal new complaints the viceroy promptly marched to Callan and imprisoned him, at the same time putting to death three of Desmond's people for oppressing the Irish.

The Anglo-Irish would probably have been less captious if the king had ever found the time to visit Ireland in person, but Edward, like many of his predecessors, had more absorbing interests. He was still carrying on spasmodic war with Scotland, and had become embroiled in a quarrel with France over a question of succession. (The Hundred Years' War, as it was later called, started in 1338.) Yet, in spite of Irish grumbling, the country was comparatively prosperous at the time. Churches and schools benefited, and a university was founded at Dublin. It did not last long, but the idea took root, though serious scholars in Ireland still had to go abroad, like the ancient *peregrini*. Then came the dreaded

Black Death, which before arriving in Ireland in the winter of 1348-49 had scourged the Continent, killing more than a third of the population. The plague spread most quickly in large towns, so that the people of Anglo-Irish Dublin and Drogheda were nearly all victims, whereas country people escaped comparatively lightly. Friar Clyn, a Franciscan of Kilkenny, kept a journal during that time. In Kilkenny, he reported, no house and scarcely any household escaped with the loss of only one member: more often the whole family died. He believed that the end of the world was at hand, and for him it was. "Among the dead expecting death's coming, I have set these deeds down in writing, truthfully as I have heard them and tested them; and lest the writing should perish with the writer and the work fail with the worker, I leave parchment to carry on the word, if perchance any man survives or any of the race of Adam may be able to escape this pestilence and continue the work I have begun." It was Friar Clyn's last entry.

After the plague the Anglo-Irish lost heart, and their numbers dwindled further as people departed for England or the Continent. Many of these had held lands near the border, and as they moved out the Irish steadily moved in on manor and field, taking back their territory, while the land of peace grew smaller and smaller, huddling close to the coast. In 1350 Sir Thomas Rokeby arrived as viceroy to counteract this defeatist movement. As he patrolled the borders of the shireland with his army to see for himself how much the colony had shrunk, he realized that the situation could not be redeemed by force of arms and he did not try to drive out any resettled Irish chiefs, but suggested to three of them who were living in the hills near the Dublin border that they make treaties with him and simply stay where they were. They agreed. This was the first official recognition of Irish captaincies made by an Englishman, but afterward it was often imitated, up to the end of the sixteenth century. Of these three Irishmen, Curtis notes wryly, two bore old Ostman names of families who had become lords along the slopes of the Dublin mountains and turned themselves into Irish septs, or clans.

Elizabeth de Burgo, grown to womanhood, married Lionel, duke of Clarence, who was Edward III's second son, and in 1361 the king sent him to Ireland as lord lieutenant. A royal prince seemed a good deal better to the colony than the men formerly appointed to the post, and Lionel was made very welcome, but the sixty-four absentee landlords who reluctantly accompanied him must have been glum. Lionel brought an unusually large army, for he meant to try, as Ralf d'Ufford had done before him, to repossess Ulster and Connacht in the name of his wife. To begin with he decided to drive back the native Irish who had moved into Wicklow, and called on the Anglo-Irish to help him in the operation, but if the barons had changed at all since D'Ufford's day it was to grow less tractable. Nobody came forward and the opposition was loud: Lionel noted that it was headed by that stormy petrel the earl of Kildare. He and his troops went alone, therefore, to do the job, and he met with far more success in Leinster than his critics had thought possible, capturing the slippery Irish king Art MacMurrough and even recovering some territory in Cork. Now he felt ready for Ulster. Still without help, he went on the warpath there and again was successful, holding back the septs and reclaiming a part, at least, of Elizabeth's land. But it was hard, monotonous campaigning, and the Dublin lords remained aloof. At the end of five years Lionel had had enough of Ireland. He was tired, and deeply envied his older brother Edward, the Black Prince, who was making a great name for himself in France while Lionel was stuck, as he felt, in the backwater of Ireland. Deciding that his wife's lands, even if he got control of all of them and could hold on, were not worth the sacrifice of his youth, he set about winding up affairs and called a parliament to Kilkenny in 1366. At this meeting the assembly formulated the famous Statutes of Kilkenny—thirty-five acts framed to discourage the Anglo-Irish tendency toward Hibernicization.

The preamble states that the English when they conquered

Ireland had used the English language, way of riding, and clothes, and in all were governed by English law. But times had changed: "Now many English of the said land, forsaking the English language, fashion, mode of riding, laws and usages, live and govern themselves according to the manners, fashions, and language of the Irish enemies, and have also made divers marriages and alliances between themselves and the Irish enemies aforesaid, whereby the said land and the liege people thereof, the English language, the allegiance due to our lord the king, and the English laws there, are put in subjection and decayed." Of course this is a translation: we would not be able to read the original. The English language, a mixture of Anglo-Saxon and French, had long been changing, with or without the help of the Irish, into the tongue of Chaucer. (Incidentally, Lionel's wife Elizabeth was of Gaelic as well as Norman descent.) The document continues: in order to set things right a number of new laws were now introduced. From that time on the English were forbidden to make fosterage, marriage, or gossipred (the relations between godparent and godchild) with the Irish; to use brehon law or, as the document calls it, the law of the marches; to entertain Irish minstrels, poets, or storytellers; to sell horses or armor to Irish people, or food in time of war. Those Irish who lived within the boundaries of the English land ("among the English") must speak English, use English names, practice with the bow, and ride with the saddle, not bareback. There was much more of the same sort.

At that date the land of peace, shireland, English land, the Pale-all these names were applied—consisted of Louth, Trim, Dublin, Kildare, Kilkenny, Wexford, Waterford, and Tipperary; about a third of Ireland's area. The lawmakers realized that things had gone too far with the so-called degenerate English of the marches for any hope of reform. They lived like independent kinglets, never paying homage or dues to the Crown. They got special treatment in the Statutes and were officially permitted to do what they had long done anyway: keep Irish troops and live generally like captains of nations. No more attempt was made to force obedience to English law in the marches, the only Gaelic Irish to whom it applied being those who lived in the English land or who were given grants or charters of emancipation. Curtis points out that this arrangement did not include the many Irish chieftains and kings who had moved back into abandoned territory. English law did not apply to them, though they were left undisturbed at that time. The Norman titles were still valid, and years and years later, many such settlers learned that according to the Statutes of Kilkenny they and their people, though they might have lived on that land for generations, had no rights in it.

Through the Statutes the true dilemma of the Irish became clear to them for the first time. Until then important Irish kings had been protected by English law, even when there was no written promise of such protection. (Some, of course, actually held treaties.) Now, it appeared, they had no rights whatever. Since they were no longer subjects of the English king they were not even freemen; they couldn't hold land or live in the Pale or go to court to redress grievances. The Statutes described them as the king's Irish enemies. Yet no Irishmen protested when these laws became public, because they did not appreciate the full significance of the legislation. Neither did the English. One hundred and thirty years later, Poynings' parliament was forced by the sheer pressure of conditions to drop from the books the acts dealing with the Irish language and fashions of horsemanship, for the people had continued to ignore them all that time.

After the assembly Lionel got his wish and escaped at last from Ireland, not realizing that he had failed at Kilkenny to halt the forward movement of the Irish chiefs. The feudal lords did not want to halt it. They had business relationships with many chiefs through whom they procured foot soldiers and mercenaries, and they had no desire to cut off such advantages. In defiance of Lionel's attitude many barons became even more Irish, if possible, than they had been before, and those who did not dare to behave like freethinkers found it advisable to leave the country. In 1368 King Edward paused in his war with France to introduce into Ireland a new act that repeated in stronger terms than ever his commands against absentees, but the king's attention could not long be diverted. The French war was not going well for England, and he decided not to throw good money after bad in Ireland. In 1369 a new viceroy, Sir William de Windsor, was sent over with orders to hold on if possible, but not to instigate trouble. Unfortunately for Windsor he arrived on the heels of a successful foray by Brian O'Brien of Thomond into the earl of Desmond's domain. O'Brien had not only trespassed, as the Anglo-Irish said indignantly; he had taken the earl prisoner and then gone on to occupy Limerick, where he still was. The Pale buzzed. Windsor ransomed the noble captive, but the situation remained critical; rumor said that the Irish kings of Munster, Connacht, and Leinster were allied in plans to overrun the Pale itself. It was hardly a tactful moment for the viceroy's news, but he had no choice but to give it. The settlement could be saved, he said, if the Pale's residents would meet the cost of the operation. He estimated it at about £5000.

Forgetting their fears, the settlers haggled. They could not possibly muster such a sum, they protested, especially in a year. That year was long past before they appealed directly to King Edward, over Windsor's head, and Edward replied that Dublin parliament should send to England a deputation of sixty delegates to present their case. The settlers sent the delegates, but declared at the same time that they were not bound to do so, and their compliance should not serve as a precedent. Clearly the colonial spirit was now full-grown and flourishing. Windsor was recalled and the Anglo-Irish were glad to be rid of him, but they had hoped to see him severely punished, and when it became evident that he would not be, the delegates in London tried to impeach him. They failed, but they tried. It all left in the Anglo-Irish mind a conviction that they could perhaps take better care of themselves than the king's men could.

In the meantime the Irish kept moving back, taking up more land.

Edward died in 1377, having outlived his three elder sons. Three other princes survived, the eldest being John of Gaunt, duke of Lancaster. John expected to succeed his father, and his sense of grievance was acute when all the brothers were passed over in favor of the Black Prince's eleven-year-old son Richard, but he accepted the post of co-regent with another of the uncles. In 1380 the regents agreed that the English of the Pale were in grave danger of being completely overwhelmed by the Irish, and they selected a new, dynamic viceroy, Edmund Mortimer, third earl of March. Mortimer made a good beginning as a general, driving the Irish from his lands of Leix, but he died at Cork only eighteen months after taking office, and by 1389, when Richard II was old enough to assume his duties, Ulster, Connacht, and Westmeath had all slipped completely under Irish control, as had most of Leinster, while Wexford, Carlow, and Kildare were hard pressed. With all this, only the Pale settlers clamored for relief; the march lords, inured and adapted to the Irish way of life, did not care. Even those few among them who still observed English customs and spoke the English language were self-sufficient, and wanted no help from the shrinking land of peace. The Absentee Acts had had little effect; most lords who left Ireland insisted on staying away and were quite resigned to losing their Irish property. Such defections strengthened those who remained behind, for though they were now fewer in number they were correspondingly more powerful. An attenuated barony ruled the conquered lands. Connacht, at least where the O'Connors did not hold sway, supported two branches of Burkes. The Kildare earldom spread as far as the Butler estates in Carlow, and the Butler land was bounded on the other side, miles away, by that of the Desmonds. An Irish clan, the O'Kennedys, had taken possession of some of the land formerly held by the earls of Ormond, but the Ormonds still held much territory in south Tipperary and Kilkenny even before James, the third earl, in 1391 received another great tract that had belonged to the Despensers.

So the barons were all right, even though Leinster by the end of the century was completely in Irish hands.

CHAPTER

6

ART Oge MacMurrough, greatest of the native kings of Leinster, was born to be a national hero. A big, handsome man, he came of a family well-known and feared in the Pale: two of his forebears were so dangerous that the Dublin government willingly paid each of them eighty marks a year just to stay away from the shireland. When the second one died, the colony heaved a sigh of relief and stopped the remittance, a prudent act that annoyed Art MacMurrough. He immediately rallied other Leinster chieftains and with their help ravaged the English land until the payments were resumed. He was much respected by the *urraghs,* or smaller chieftains: they looked up to him as if he were an ardri of ancient days. Only two other kings, O'Neill of Ulster and O'Connor of Connacht, had such status; the three names still evoked the old glory.

In 1390 Art MacMurrough, having managed to occupy most of Carlow, married a Kildare woman of the governing class—Elizabeth Calfe, heiress to the barony of Norragh. Such matches were by now quite frequent, but Art had taken his wife in ignorance of a Kilkenny statute that forbade him, as a mere Irishman, to own his English wife's estate. When he discovered the facts he flew into a rage and set off on a fresh tour of destruction, burning and pillaging in Kildare, Wexford, and Carlow, until his exploits came to the attention of England's young monarch, Richard II. Richard, in an unusually receptive frame of mind—England was at peace with France for the first time in years, and also had a truce with Scotland—studied the reports from Ireland. He concluded that the situation was quite simple to understand: clearly, the man responsible for most of the trouble on the other island was this Art MacMurrough. If they got rid of him, all would be well.

The settlers, as usual, were clamoring for a royal personage to come on over and see conditions for himself. Richard gave them the surprise of their lives by accepting the invitation. He arrived in 1394 at the head of the largest army anyone had yet brought to Ireland, and immediately the word was circulated that he was there in Dublin, the king of England himself, ready and willing to talk things over with the Irish kings. The response, especially from those of the north, was prompt: for some days Richard held audience with them, thought things over, and wrote letters home embodying his observations. He said solemnly that there were three sorts of people in Ireland: the wild Irish who were the enemy, the quiet or obedient English of the shires, and the Irish rebels, as he called the lords of the marches. He also called them "the middle nation," since they stood, he explained, between Dublin and the enemy. Without their help Ireland could never be reconquered, so they were of the greatest importance. This being so, said Richard, their tendency to become more and more Irish must be checked, but he did not stipulate how it should be done.

When not indulging in theory, Richard seems to have enjoyed his visit, helped as he was by two excellent interpreters. One was the earl of Ormond, who no doubt should not have been able to speak the Irish tongue so well, but whose knowledge of it did come in very handy. The other was Henry Christede, the king's own squire; as a boy he had been captured by the Irish and brought up by them as an Irishman. The interpreters prevailed on the reluctant chiefs to accept and wear the fine English-style suits presented to them by the king, of linen and silk with fur trimming. Ill at ease in these garments, which they put on only after much persuasion, the kings partook of royal banquets, and were puzzled by so much pomp and circumstance. But they were pleasant to talk with, and very easy and ready with their pledges. The four most important chiefs led the others in promising to move out of the lands they had recently taken, retaining only such territories as they and their fathers had held all along, outside the conquered areas, in return for which they were given Richard's word for the ownerships they proposed to keep. New boundaries of the Pale were mapped in their presence, and they were agreeable to all of the alterations.

After this diplomatic triumph Richard was ready to receive homage from the rebel English. They had been invited to come in with the kings and receive the royal pardon for their sins, but very few responded, and after a short wait Richard let it go. Last came the matter of Art MacMurrough, which he had deliberately allowed to remain in abeyance until all other business was finished. It would not be seemly, he decided, for the king of England himself to make war on a small king, so he handed the matter over to Earl Marshal, lord of Carlow. In the event the earl had little difficulty—the lesser chieftains of Leinster had been persuaded to join their northern colleagues in paying homage to Richard, and Art, left on his own, had no choice but to surrender. Soon he too was making his obeisance to the king of England, promising to vacate the captured lands of Leinster and thereafter fight on Richard's side when called upon to do so. In return he was given that barony of Norragh—which, he must have reflected, was his by right in any case—and the assurance that his eighty-mark annuity would be his for the rest of his life.

Richard returned to England in May 1395, well pleased with what had been done, and the Irish too were pleased, since their titles to their own lands had been confirmed by the king of England in person. But they had no intention of implementing the promises they had made. Not one, Art MacMurrough or any other, did that. They felt that in dealing with such an august personage as Richard the form of the pledge was all that mattered. Ireland had gone through generations of experience of gifts bestowed by the English and then taken away, of promises forgotten when the kingly givers died, or even before, and everything was a matter of expediency. One's word of honor did not mean much to the Irish kings. They said that Art MacMurrough had been trapped; that he had gone to "the king's house" in good faith because he was invited, and had been detained as a prisoner until he gave the required promises. Nor could they take seriously their right to sit in parliament. Richard had scarcely sailed away before Art MacMurrough and the other Leinster chiefs were refusing to move out of their recently gained territory. They may have been really surprised that the English expected it.

Richard had left behind when he went the young Roger Mortimer, earl of March, to be his lord lieutenant. Roger was the son of Edmund who had died at Cork and Philippa, Lionel's daughter. Thus his grandfather was a royal prince, and as Richard II was childless and much attached to the youth, his advisers decided that young Roger would do to fill the place of heir apparent. So it was arranged. Soon Roger, like Edmund before him, was seeking to recover by force of arms the lordships of Leix and Ulster. He was an attractive man of great courage —too much, for he went into battle one day clad like an Irish soldier in a linen tunic without armor, and for his rashness was killed. When he heard the news, Richard flew into a rage and immediately revoked Art MacMurrough's grant of Norragh. But this was not revenge enough to suit him, and he came again to Ireland in 1399, to punish the chieftain further. This time Art was impossible to find, and it proved a bad time for the king to have left his throne unguarded. Not long before, he had banished his cousin Henry Bolingbroke, the son of John of Gaunt, who in time became duke of Lancaster. While Richard was hunting Art MacMurrough in vain through the Irish forest

Henry returned to England, and in Richard's absence found it easy to capture the throne. Richard, returning empty-handed, arrived just in time to be thrown into prison, after which the barons formally deposed him and bestowed on Lancaster the title of Henry IV, king of England. Richard's death and the manner of it were kept secret and even today the details are unproven, but it is generally accepted that he was quietly murdered in 1400. Henry gave back to Art MacMurrough once again that much disputed barony of Norragh, but Art had lost interest: he allowed the grant to lapse, and like Richard's other Irish reforms it disappeared.

For the space of the following reigns the revival of Gaelic strength proceeded with little interference from England. Henry IV and Henry V were anxiously occupied with keeping their thrones and trying to annex France. Neither of them bothered about Ireland except to appoint lieutenants when necessary. The Irish kings had things much their own way at this time, and under their repeated onslaughts the Pale grew smaller and smaller. Even the settlers tended more and more to use the Irish language and abandon English, possibly because their numbers were so diminished with many of the "common English" and their clerics departing. From the middle nations came a corresponding stream, also eastward bound, of tenants on the way out because they no longer trusted in their feudal lords' power to protect them. The English who remained resented the homeland for neglecting them, but still hoped for better times.

In 1422 Henry V died, leaving a son of nine months—Henry VI. By the terms of the treaty of Troyes the infant king of England also became king of France, but French nobles contested his claim and the long war dragged on. Henry's regents, two of his uncles, chose a new viceroy for Ireland—a second Edmund Mortimer, grandson of the Edmund who died at Cork and son of the late Roger. This Mortimer, being an aristocrat of royal descent, was happily welcomed by the Gaelic as well as the Anglo-Irish, but he died only two years later of the plague, and would

hardly deserve mention if he had not been uncle to Richard
duke of York, his heir, for Richard's mother was Edmund's
sister Anne, duchess of Cambridge. During Edmund's short
tour of duty in Dublin he received homage from five Ulster
chiefs— since he was earl of Ulster as well as March—and
these men were still in the city when he died. Cannily, the
new justiciar, Talbot, wouldn't let them leave until they had
confirmed their submission all over again in another round
of ceremonies. Thus the leader of the Ulster delegation,
Eoghan O'Neill, acknowledged the thirteen-year-old
Richard as earl of Ulster. In all, the boy was undisputed
holder of a number of titles, being lord of the Irish lands
of Ulster, Trim, Leix, and Connacht, also the marches of
Wales and the duchy of York. His uncle Edmund, without so
many of these honorifics, could if he wished have claimed a
better right to the throne than had the baby Henry VI, but
he never pressed his claim. Richard, in whom two English
dukedoms were combined, was even more eligible, but in
the early days, like Edmund, he did nothing about it.

During the following decade voices were heard asking
that the throne of England pay more attention to the
neglected colony across the Irish Sea. Among the archives
of the Irish parliament there is a request sent to Henry VI in
1435 to consider "How that his land of Ireland is well nigh
destroyed and inhabited with his enemies and rebels, in so
much that there is not left in the nether parts of the counties
of Dublin, Meath, Louth and Kildare that join together, out
of the subjection of the said enemies and rebels a scarce
thirty miles in length and twenty in breadth, whereas a man
may surely ride or go to the said counties to answer the
king's writ and do his commandments." A poem published
a year later carries the same warning message under the title
"Libelle of Englische polyce":

> Nowe here beware and hertly take entente,
> As we woll answere at the last jugemente,
> To kepen Irelond, that it be not loste,
> For it is a boterasse and a poste

Undre England and Wales is another,
God forbede but sche were other brothere,
Of one ligeaunce dewe until the kynge.
(*The Course of Irish History*, pp. 158-59).

Complaints often heard from the people were that they were taxed more heavily than they could stand, being required to lodge and feed troops and also their horses. (They had to put up the great man of the district as well once or twice a year.) The theory was that the troops and horses were there for the people's protection and that the custom was therefore just, but soldiers ate and drank a lot, and demanded pocket money over and above their living expenses. This custom of quartering soldiers on the people was called "coyne," and the keep for the horses—stabling and grain—was "livery." Coyne and livery are mentioned time and again in the annals, never with affection.

Another form of taxation was the so-called "black rent," a euphemism for payments settlers had to make to Irish chiefs so that the latter would not attack and loot their property. We would call it blackmail, or protection money. What with coyne and livery for their own troops and black rent for their enemies, the unfortunate English had much to complain of. A far better portion seems to have been that of the great lords of the middle nations, who by now were an accepted, intrinsic feature of the Irish scene. Outstanding among them was Gerald, third earl of Desmond, who died late in the fourteenth century. Powerful, wealthy, and generous, "Gerald the Rhymer" was well-known for his love of Irish poetry, and often wrote it as well as reading that of others. So much for the Statutes of Kilkenny. When he died the control of the southern marches was divided between two houses of the Geraldines (as the descendants of Gerald of Windsor were called), the Butler family that ruled Ormond and the FitzGeralds of Desmond and Kildare. Even at the end of the century the earls themselves had not started to marry among the Irish, but the practice had become common among the junior branches. Such alliances proved useful, and later generations of earls themselves followed the example, while all, earls and cadets alike, continued without interruption the old custom of fostering their children with Irish families. So much, again, for Kilkenny. Gaelic and Norman lords shared so many customs and tastes—Irish language, brehon law, patronage of bards, feeling for local independence—that they could be distinguished only by their names and lineage. In Curtis's words, the barons built up "whole 'counties' twenty or thirty miles square, in which they ruled partly like feudal seigneurs and partly like Gaelic kings" (p. 136).

In 1449 Richard, duke of York, was thirty-seven, a tall, good-looking man who had done his tour of duty in France—a task that was *de rigueur* at court. He was beginning to feel the itch of ambition, probably because the king had not yet produced a direct heir. The king's advisers thought him better out of the country and appointed him lieutenant of Ireland. In July he arrived in Dublin with his wife Cicely Neville, "the Rose of Raby." The Irish were delighted with a viceroy of such good breeding. Chieftain after chieftain made his submission, and Richard's peaceful progress through the country was punctuated by triumphs. When in October Cicely bore a son who would one day be duke of Clarence, the people adopted the baby as their particular prince. A year passed, then Richard heard that his most powerful enemy at court had died. In 1450 he therefore took his family back to England, leaving many faithful friends behind. He found Henry VI in great trouble, for the war with France had gone steadily against him and England had lost almost all her territory across the Channel. In 1453, when Aquitaine was taken by the enemy, the king's mind gave way under the strain and he was declared by his physicians unfit to govern. Unfortunately for Richard's hopes of the crown Henry's wife Margaret of Anjou gave birth just then to their first and only son, Edward. But Richard swallowed his chagrin and professed himself happy to serve as protector of the realm with Margaret as long as the king was incapacitated. Only two men were in his confidence: his elder son Edward, earl of March, and his nephew Richard, earl of Warwick.

The protector and his co-regent Margaret soon quarreled, and when in 1454 Henry VI recovered, the queen told him about it. An open break followed, and the Wars of the Roses were under way. A battle at Ludlow in 1459 went against the Yorkists, and Richard sailed to Ireland, where all the Irish lords save the Lancastrian Butlers of Ormond were delighted to welcome him back. They declared themselves enthusiastic Yorkists and proposed to declare their duke the king of Ireland. Richard, after bigger game, had to exert all his tact to avoid the honor, and even then they achieved the next best thing: they summoned a parliament to Drogheda in February 1460, at which they proclaimed independence for Ireland and named Richard the chief governor of the country—the first instance of Home Rule in Irish history. Soon, however, Richard found a welcome excuse to get away from these embarrassing honors. His son and nephew had successfully invaded England, and Warwick had actually taken Henry VI prisoner at the battle of Northampton. The duke of York immediately sailed from Ireland, accompanied by the flower of Irish nobility and their troops. They rode in triumph into London and forced Parliament to acknowledge that Richard, not Henry's son Edward, was heir to the throne. Then the Yorkists permitted Henry to go free. Now things happened fast. The Lancastrians refused to admit defeat and continued to challenge the enemy, until on the last day of 1460 Richard and his Irish allies met the Lancastrians at Wakefield, not far from Richard's castle of York. There many Yorkists were slain, Richard among them. His head, mockingly adorned with a paper crown, was stuck up on the castle walls for the world to see. His son immediately marched on London and deposed Henry, and in 1461 he himself was crowned King Edward IV. Not long afterward the Lancastrians submitted and accepted him.

Though Ireland mourned deeply for Richard, the enthronement of his son was popular there and the great Irish loyalty to the cause of York did not waver. The Wars of the Roses had cost the cream of Anglo-Irish nobility: in Ulster so many lords never came back that the native kings found it easy to recover their land. But the colonists had got their first taste of self-reliance through Richard, and for that if nothing else they would always love him.

It will be recalled that the Butlers had been odd man out. In fact, James, fifth earl of Ormond, was killed fighting for the Lancastrian cause at Towton, but his brother Sir John Butler, who also fought, survived, and came home to Ireland, where he carried on the Lancastrian batde, enlisting relatives and other adherents in Kilkenny and Clonmel to such good effect that soon a little War of Roses was raging in Ireland. Finally, at Pilltown near Carrick-on-Suir, it was doused by Thomas, earl of Desmond, a loyal Yorkist. In 1463 Edward IV made Desmond chief governor of Ireland as successor to Richard, and many of the old laws against intercourse between native Irish and the settlers in towns outside of the Pale—Cork, Waterford, Limerick, and Youghal— were abandoned. Life in these communities had long been hazardous and, at the least, unpleasant for the inhabitants, who, while looking on themselves as English, were cut off from any others of their kind, and were forbidden by the Statutes of Kilkenny to have anything to do with the Gaelic Irish who surrounded the towns. These Irish still showed no desire to live in the towns themselves. When conditions were unsettled outside the town limits it was impossible for the citizens even to send representatives to parliament. There was no doubt in the new governor's mind that they would be the better for less segregation. A typical Anglo-Irish lord of the best kind, Thomas of Desmond had never subscribed to the policy of segregation. Like his kinsman Gerald he had a taste for reading and writing Irish poetry, and he was fond of books: one of the first objects he looted after the battle of Pilltown was the Psalter of Cashel. Having founded a college at Youghal, he became more ambitious and tried to create a university at Drogheda. Not the least of Ireland's needs, he felt, was such an institution: the country that until the ninth century led all the nations of Christendom in scholarship ought to have at least one center of learning in the fifteenth. There had been a time, until 1422, when a number of both Gaelic and Anglo-Irish students attended Oxford and Cambridge in England. But fellow students had complained that Irish living together in large numbers sooner or later got noisy and violent and there was no handling them. Accordingly, the universities imposed a quota system on Irishmen, and decreed that those admitted must be scattered around among non-compatriots: exclusively Irish halls of residence were banned. Much to Desmond's disappointment his Drogheda project was opposed and came to nothing.

Nevertheless he was a powerful noble and he made no secret of it, but moved through the Dublin streets like a general, surrounded by gallowglasses. Such ostentation and his openly Gaelic sympathies turned the Pale settlers against Thomas. Led by the bishop of Meath they did their utmost to discredit him, laying against him the charge of extorting coyne and livery for his enemy. Such quarrels between the settlers and the lords of the march were common. To the settlers it was outrageous that a man so Gaelic in his ways as Thomas should be their governor, and no service he paid to the Yorkist cause could make him acceptable. They complained and agitated until Edward in 1467 sent an English replacement, Sir John Tibetot, earl of Worcester, commonly called Tiptoft.

Tiptoft had served as constable in England. Though a man of culture he had been so harsh in that post, condemning to death so many Lancastrians, that he was known as The Butcher. He came to Ireland with orders to end Home Rule agitation and demonstrate the power of the throne by any methods necessary. In the course of the year he summoned two parliaments, first to Dublin and then to Drogheda. At Drogheda he delivered a smashing blow. At first he brought up routine pieces of business, but on February 4, 1468, just as everyone felt lulled, an act was passed attainting the earls of Desmond and Kildare and Sir Edward Plunkett of "horrible treason and felonies," as well as alliance and fosterage with the Irish enemies by giving them horses,

harnesses, and arms. These charges came as a thunderbolt
to everyone except the English of the Pale: the three men
were great heroes. Both earls were there at the parliament, so
Desmond was easily apprehended and imprisoned, though
Kildare somehow escaped to England. Within ten days,
before he had a chance to appeal, Thomas, earl of Desmond,
had been beheaded at Drogheda. But Kildare managed to
get a reversal of his sentence and his life was spared.

The execution did immense harm to King Edward's
prestige in Ireland. Thomas's son James quickly rallied the
Munster Geraldines, leading them to raid Meath and with
it the king's own land of Trim, and he vowed never again
to attend a king's parliament or enter any of the king's
walled towns as long as Edward reigned. Becoming even
more Gaelic than his father, he married Margaret, daughter
of Taig O'Brien, who was one of Ireland's most rebellious
kings. James was the first earl of Desmond to make an Irish
marriage.

Tiptoft returned to England at the end of 1468, just in time
to be caught in the revolution that sent Edward IV fleeing
to Holland for safety. Edward survived to be reinstated, but
Tiptoft was caught and killed, and this news brought grim
satisfaction to many in Ireland.

The star of the house of Kildare was now in the ascendant.
In 1471 Thomas, the seventh earl, was elected justiciar by
the Irish parliament in straightforward defiance of London
and the law. Furthermore, the same body elected his son
Gerald, usually known as Garret More, the Great Earl,
when Thomas died in 1477. By means of a special act of
parliament in 1480 Garret More aided and abetted the
marriage of his sister Eleanor to Conn More, son of the lord
of Tyrone. Naturally these independent acts of the Kildares
were marked and disapproved of by Edward IV, but he
could hardly go to war over them just then, nor did he wish
to. Instead, in 1478, after hearing of Garret More's election,
he sent over his own justiciar, Henry Lord Grey, but Garret
More refused to relinquish the great seal which had always

been the governor's badge of office, and when Grey had another one made, nobody in Dublin paid any attention to it. So Grey gave up and went back to England, and in 1482 King Edward too gave up and confirmed Garret More in office as his deputy.

What happened to the English royal family thereafter is well-known. Edward died in 1483, leaving two young sons. The eldest was fifteen: he became King Edward V, but with his young brother he soon disappeared, and neither of the Princes of the Tower was ever seen again. Their uncle Richard of Gloucester, who had acted so briefly as regent, now took the title of Richard III. He was killed at Bosworth in 1483, and with him died the rule of the house of York.

CHAPTER
7

THE new king of England, Henry VII, was the first Tudor to sit on the throne. Though the London Parliament had considered his claim good enough to elect him, Yorkists on both sides of the water were bitter at the choice. They were not placated when in 1486 he married Elizabeth, daughter of Edward IV, though the match united the White Rose and the Red, and in Ireland the lords felt strong enough to take a hand in the matter. After all, Garret More had been acknowledged the king's deputy governor, and his parliament was virtually running the country without aid from England: why shouldn't they pick out a king who suited them, and replace Henry? Garret More seriously considered three possibilities among the young Yorkists. He was still hesitating between them early in 1487 when there arrived in Dublin a ten-year-old boy called Lambert Simnel, in the care of an English priest. The priest said that the child was really Edward of Warwick, the son of George of Clarence, who was that baby born in Ireland to Richard, duke of York, and the Rose of Raby—he who had been hailed as Ireland's own prince. If little Lambert Simnel was really George's son... The story was too tempting to reject. With much rejoicing and excitement the Yorkist lords, along with a number of clerics, swallowed it whole. Margaret, duchess of Flanders and sister of Edward IV, helped along the cause of her young "kinsman" by sending two thousand German mercenaries who arrived at the beginning of May. In Dublin, on May 24, the boy was crowned Edward VI of England and Ireland.

Nearly the whole country believed he was truly their king. Even the Butlers, though they rejected his claim, accepted his identity as the duke of Clarence's son. Events moved swiftly. In June an army of German and Anglo-Irish under the earl of Lincoln sailed over to England to claim the country for "Edward VI," and met Henry's forces at Stoke in Lincolnshire. They were badly defeated. Lincoln, among many others including one of Garret More's brothers, was killed on the field. But even in those harsh times a boy of ten could not seriously be accused of treason, and the life of Lambert Simnel was spared. He was put to work as a scullery boy in the royal kitchens, and there he remained for the rest of his life. One wonders if they talked much belowstairs of his adventures as king of England.

Naturally Henry VII was not pleased with the incident, but there was little he could do to Garret More without more violence than he was prepared just then to use. Still firmly entrenched as viceroy, the earl swaggered about Dublin and the countryside more boldly than before the Simnel episode. He had lately learned how to use gunpowder, and he liked it: it was effective in local wars.

Then in 1491 the Yorkists of Ireland saw another chance to unseat the Lancastrian: a French-speaking youth of seventeen, traveling with one attendant, landed at Cork and declared that he was the duke of York, that younger son of Edward IV who had disappeared from the Tower in 1483. Henry's adherents protested that the youth was nobody but Perkin Warbeck from Tournai, a Flemish commoner, and offered proof of their statement, but a large number of very important personages preferred to believe the young man, and rushed to support him. Among these Garret More was not in evidence, for he had learned his lesson, but his lack of enthusiasm did not matter, since the self-styled duke of York was backed by Emperor Maximilian of the Holy Roman Empire, the king of France, and the king of Scotland. The puppet was well guarded: his string-pullers were careful not to give a chance of a pot shot to some Lancastrian assassin, but soon removed him from Ireland. He was next heard from in France. Ireland didn't see him again until 1497. Ultimately, after many unsuccessful attempts to substantiate his claim, Perkin Warbeck was apprehended by Henry's troops, imprisoned in the Tower, and executed in 1499.

This was too much for Henry VII: he decided that Ireland must be firmly gripped and washed clean of intrigue once and for all. It was not so much the pretenders, he felt, as the island's strategic position that made her dangerous: some ambitious continental monarch, sooner or later, would try to use her as a steppingstone to the conquest of England. The first move in such a cleansing campaign, obviously, was the ousting of Kildare as viceroy, and this was at last done, with the king's own lieutenant Sir Edward Poynings put in his place. Poy-nings arrived in Dublin in October 1494 with an army of only one thousand, but they were picked men, and without resistance they dislodged from office the Home Rule officials, replacing them with Englishmen. Then the new lieutenant summoned a parliament at Drogheda to outlaw all Home Rule legislation. It opened December 1, 1494.

Garret More played a waiting game. "Do not attempt anything against the deputy that you would not attempt against me myself," he wrote to a northern chief, "for he is a better man than I am, but enter into peace with him and give him your son as surety."

The parliament was carefully packed, and things went smoothly for Poynings. The first consideration being to get Kildare out of the way, the assembly promptly attainted the earl of treason and sent him to the Tower of London. Next came the act known as "Poynings' Law," stipulating that parliament was to meet in Ireland from that time on only when royal permission had been granted and after the king and council in England had been informed of and had approved the measures it was proposed to enact. For the rest: border dwellers between the Pale's four counties and the rest of Ireland were required to build a double ditch six feet high (or deep) to repel Gaelic invaders, and the castles of Dublin, Trim, Athlone, Wicklow, Greencastle, and Car-rickfergus—the main fortresses of Ireland—must be guarded by English-born constables.

Parliament also re-enacted the Statutes of Kilkenny, with one significant omission: it was no longer against the law to learn or talk Irish. Other Irish styles were still banned, though such action seems not to have been effective: "... no person or persons, the king's subjects within this land... shall be shorn or shaven above the ears, or use the wearing of hair upon their heads, like unto long locks called 'glibes,' or have or use any hair growing upon their upper lip, called or named a 'crommeal.'..." Nor must people wear mantles, coat, or hood made after the Irish fashion, said the assembly, though it seemed evident that anyone who did *not* dress in one Irish fashion or another would have appeared very odd. Perhaps what the legislators had in mind was the costume of the poor, particularly those who lived in the bogs or mountains: they went bareheaded, their naked bodies covered only by the Irish cloak. More prosperous men wore wide yellow tunics of linen dyed with saffron or urine, pleated with wide yellow sleeves, under mantles of frieze (a coarse piled woolen cloth) or some other material and over the tights called trews. On their heads were conical caps like dunce caps of frieze. Women wore bright embroidered skirts tucked up at the hem, and folded linen hoods—though even among the richer classes the ladies when they took their ease seem not to have been too particular about covering their bodies. English visitors always complained of the dirtiness of the Irish as they have complained through the centuries about most of the peoples of the earth, innocently and ignorantly, as if they themselves were more clean and hygienic than the rest of the contemporary world, but the statutes make no mention of housing. Probably the status quo was taken for granted. Laborers, hinds, and peasants sheltered in primitive conditions, some in poor tumble-down huts of clay and wattles and some out of doors in the fields. In both cases they were usually accompanied by the beasts they tended, especially when they were spending the summer months in the booleys, when their cattle shared their roofs, such as they were. The Irish gentry occupied comparatively elaborate houses of several stories, built to be watchtowers as well as villas—the tower houses mentioned in writings of the time. The style was adopted from the Normans.

Garret More did not have to languish long in durance. His dossier when examined showed nothing against him, and he was pronounced innocent of forming treasonable alliance with the Ulster chiefs. In 1496 by order of Henry VII he was released from the Tower of London and restored to his viceroyalty. Even then he seems not to have accepted the fact that the Wars of the Roses were indeed over, and he never desisted from plotting and hoping for a Yorkist revival, but he was cunning, and avoided being implicated. Ostensibly he devoted himself to local wars. He had what was probably his greatest domestic triumph in 1504, warring against the Clanrickards, who were led by Kildare's own son-in-law Ulick Burke. Ulick had usurped the crown of the royal town of Galway, and this was admittedly bad, but what seemed far worse to Kildare was that the usurper wasn't treating Kildare's daughter well. When Garret More wanted to he could organize a huge army, and this time he had more troops than ever, but so did the Clanrickards. The forces met and settled matters at Cnoc Tuagh—"Knocktoe,"—on August 19, 1504. After a hard fight Kildare came out the victor.

Still playing the loyal viceroy, he now allied secretly with the younger O'Donnell, Hugh Oge, who inherited from his late father Red Hugh the vast lands of Tyrconnel, Sligo, Fermanagh, and Leitrim. Planning a Yorkist revival, the chiefs based their hopes on two surviving nephews of Richard of York—Edmund and Richard de la Pole. Secretly, Kildare and Hugh Oge tried to bring about an anti-English union between Scotland and Ireland, but 1513 brought failure to the project, for in that year James IV, king of Scots, was killed at Flodden Field. Soon afterward Garret More himself died of a wound he got fighting the O'Mores of Leix, a death that spelled the end, in characteristic style, of a rule that had lasted forty years. Hugh Oge was knighted in London at the court of the young Henry VIII, but the conspiracy lived on and on, until Richard de la Pole died in battle years later, in Italy, The Yorkist dream was one of the most tenacious in Anglo-Irish history.

Henry VIII had succeeded in 1509 when Ireland was still enjoying a period of tranquillity. Though Garret More certainly played favorites, the Irish felt that they knew where they were with him, and they at least were comparatively quiet. Intermarriage between Gael and Anglo-Irish was now common, in the ruling classes as in the lower orders, and Irish education gained ground. Kildare built a college at Maynooth, the same place where his castle housed his splendid library, and Sir Piers Butler, always bitterly jealous of the Kildares, promptly followed by founding a school in Kilkenny. The Geraldines were popular, even with some of those English who lived in the Pale (though most settlers would never trust a march lord), and the death of Garret More did not presage much of a change: his son Garret Oge moved smoothly into the post of viceroy, and in most respects he was like his father. But change was on the way nevertheless, from outside.

In London Wolsey made it his business to keep the young king worried about Ireland, saying that he should be getting far more money out of the island. When Garret More died he talked more forcefully than ever, drawing pictures of the great lords of the marches with their spacious estates and strong castles, happily collecting tax-free rents the year round and able to summon up armies at will. Wolsey reminded Henry that past kings of England had spent a lot of money on Ireland, but, he demanded, had the Crown ever reaped a commensurate return? His most telling point, however, was the familiar one that Ireland was a natural landing place for European monarchs with designs on England. Henry pondered all this. Moreover, pro-Tudor settlers in Ireland were writing letters to England. Most of these came from the seaport towns, where feeling had always run especially high against the middle nations: they were full of complaints about black rents and Garret Oge's levying of coyne and livery. The viceroy maintained a full army, they said, of gallowglasses and kerns (foot soldiers), and all the lords were carrying Irish arms instead of the honest English weapons specified in the Statutes of Kilkenny. These men lived openly according to Irish law and spoke the Irish tongue. In sum, said the settlers, they were even more degenerate than they had been in earlier days, and outside the Pale no fewer than ninety English "captains" and Irish chiefs lived like robber kings, completely independent and each with his army.

Henry VIII and the court felt a strong urge to do something about Ireland, but were unsure as to what. Then in 1519 Garret Oge, like his father before him, was summoned to London and lodged in the Tower, and Henry sent the earl of Surrey with orders to reform Ireland *at once:* the unfortunate man was also commanded to unify and Anglicize the Irish Church. Either commission alone would have been far too much for him, as the earl soon discovered and reported to London: he had brought with him only a small army, but the conquest of Ireland would call for at least six thousand troops and a vast amount of ammunition. And even if he could reduce the land, he said, what then? It would not remain reduced unless it was thoroughly settled with loyal English subjects—the "plantation" method—and the offending Irish were forced to move out.

The question of the Church was shelved once Surrey had seen the whole situation, but reports in the Roman archives fill in the gaps. The clergy had long since been forced to give up any attempt to minister to Pale and unconquered lands alike, though such a program had been planned from early days. For example, the important archdiocese of Armagh was divided between the settlers of the southern Pale and the Gaelic Irish of the north. This was a hopeless arrangement, and the archbishop no longer tried to minister to the Gaelic Irish: he didn't even live in Armagh, but in Louth. English bishops, sent out to Gaelic Irish dioceses, discovered on arrival that they couldn't understand anybody, and after short, frustrating periods they usually went home to England. The once proud Clonmacnoise and Armagh cathedrals were in ruins; at Armagh even the walls had nearly disappeared. One altar remained in the open air, and on this mass was celebrated very infrequently by the one priest who remained. According to an observer, in the Irish countryside no English or Irish archbishop, bishop, abbot, prior, parson, vicar, or anyone else who could preach was to be found —always excepting the mendicant friars. These men alone, Franciscans, Dominicans, and Augustinians, kept Christianity alive in Ireland.

Surrey's report with its talk of troops, armaments, plantation, and money—above all money—frightened the prudent Henry. Wolsey or no Wolsey, he postponed any idea of chastising Ireland, recalled Surrey, and set free Garret Oge.

Years passed, and the king's relations with Rome became strained when he wanted to divorce Catherine of Aragon and marry Anne Boleyn. The Pope flatly refused to give his permission for annulment or divorce, so Henry cut off communication and set up his own Church, independent and separate. The Reformation had begun. Henry married Anne Boleyn, but he was sensitive to the cries of outrage that resounded from the countries of Europe and the strident protests of the begging friars of Ireland—for this time religious controversy lined up Ireland on the side of Rome and Gaul.

Henry was very angry with the Irish for daring to criticize his actions. In 1534 he summoned Garret Oge once again to London, so the earl left his eldest son Thomas, Lord Offaly, to take care of things while he was away. The twenty-one-year-old Offaly was known as Silken Thomas because his armed followers wore silk fringe on their helmets. He was an excitable type, even hysterical. Hearing a rumor that his father had been executed, he got himself stirred up in the time-honored way by the martial chanting of his harper, then led his fringed army at a gallop into Dublin, where he irrupted into the council chamber, flung down the sword of state entrusted to him by Garret Oge, and at the top of his voice declared war on the king of England. (Garret Oge was alive all the time in the Tower of London.) A small, sharp revolt followed, and the English Archbishop Alen, trying to escape, was killed. Silken Thomas had intended to take Dublin, but he failed. Retiring to the Kildare stronghold in Maynooth, he appealed loudly to the Emperor of the Holy Roman Empire and the Pope to declare King Henry a heretic—but he himself, already excommunicated for the death of Alen, was in no position to call names.

For once Henry, in his fury, did not stop to count the cost, but immediately sent Sir William Skeffington with a large army to Ireland. Silken Thomas was proclaimed a traitor and "the Curse of the Church" was visited on him; this was so dreadful, it is said, that when poor old Garret Oge heard it in the Tower he fell dead of shock. Offaly remained at Maynooth with a garrison of one hundred, until Skeffington arrived in March 1535, bringing the new heavy artillery with which the English battered the castle walls. They were not designed to withstand such treatment and the occupants, or the third of them who were left, surrendered at the end of a week. Offaly himself had escaped by this time; the others, who laid down their arms unconditionally, were immediately cut down to the last man. This treachery was extremely shocking to the Irish. They could not be described as a mild or kind-hearted people, but they were not accustomed to slaughter on such a large scale or in such circumstances. The incident was never forgotten, living in history as "the pardon of Maynooth," which is to say the epitome of treachery.

That August, Silken Thomas gave himself up and was sent to the Tower, where he spent miserable month after month with five Fitz-Gerald uncles. In February 1537 he was executed at Tyburn, as were the uncles. Henry was determined to wipe out all the Kildares.

For generations after this the rulers of England insisted that viceroys in Ireland be English, but Henry's early fury simmered down after a time. He remained inflexible in his resolution to settle the island and bring it to heel, but large-scale military adventure cost a good deal, and Henry was thrifty. He decided instead to abolish by peaceful means what he considered the most troublesome element in the country: Gaelicism. Even now, he reflected, in spite of three centuries of Norman invasion, the Gaelic Irish lived according to their own traditions, institutions, laws, and language. They lived side by side with the English settlers—at least, only the march lords separated them—but they were still two different nations. Henry was determined to erase the Gaelic Irish's marks of difference and force them to join with the English in every respect. Of course this meant reforming their religion in accordance with the Protestantism he had introduced into England, and it was a proposition bound to turn the lords, who were confirmed Roman Catholics, even more violently against his country. At first, however, it seemed feasible in spite of the difficulties, for there seemed some Irish—though, to be sure, they were Anglo-Irish— ready to help. Sir Piers Butler, earl of Ossory and Ormond, was one of these. Happy with the destruction of the house of Kildare, he promised to oppose Rome's jurisdiction as strongly as the king could wish so long as he might rule Kilkenny, Tipperary, and Waterford. The Butlers became Protestants, and some of the others followed their example, but a plan of action was still necessary to reform the whole country as quickly as possible. Henry's Lord Privy Seal Thomas Cromwell, working with the Irish council, outlined a program, and when it was ready, in 1536, they called to Dublin a "reform parliament" to embody their resolutions in law.

For a while all went well at the parliament. It was a small, hand-picked assembly that was expected to give no trouble.

The members quickly passed the usual acts that came up in even[7] important parliament at the beginning of a season: black rent to be abolished, intermarriage and fosterage with the Irish banned, and so on. But as soon as the assembly came to grips with the religious program there was strong opposition. The Anglo-Irish prelates and clerics stubbornly refused to pass acts calling for the dissolution of abbeys or the transference of Church revenues to the Crown, and when it came to the Supremacy—Henry's assumption, as ruler of England, of the title "Supreme Head on Earth of the Church of England"—they were scandalized, and dug their heels in. They did the same at Henry's changing the law of the land to exclude his daughter Mary (by the discarded Catherine of Aragon) from inheriting the crown. Henry had to write a threatening letter to the Dublin parliament before the members allowed these innovations through.

Even after that, reform was never successful in Ireland. Laws might be passed—and were; the religious houses with the Pale and the royal towns were dissolved, but inwardly the Irish never submitted. Their resolution was stiffened by those priests outside reform's zone of influence. In Ulster they preached daily to their flocks that every man "must fight against our sovereign lord the king's majesty" (Thomas Lynch of Galway, State Papers, Henry VIII, Ireland, iii. 141), saying that if he died in the struggle his soul would go to Heaven, "as the souls of SS Peter, Paul and others, who suffered death and martyrdom for God's sake." Inevitably in the Irish mind Protestantism appeared to be merely another aspect of English oppression. An Irishman might be intimidated into accepting the new religion, but his secret allegiance to his own Church became the more fervent for this necessity. The dissolution and robbing of the abbeys outraged him, especially when he saw that the lands went to make rich Protestants richer. He was not converted, but shocked and disgusted by the burning of sacred relics, and when St. Patrick's crozier, which the people called "the staff of Christ," was consigned to the flames in a Dublin street, the most lukewarm Irish Catholic felt his faith strengthened.

However vigilant, the reform's officials could not police the whole country, and bishops came in from Rome to replace those who had been taken over by the Church of England.

At such times men often resort to dreams. The Anglo-Irish, called "Old English" to distinguish them from the Protestant arrivals now flooding the country, were in trouble. Gone was the charmed life of the past, when a lord of the marches lived like an Irish king and was never troubled by royal tax collectors. Henry was as determined to tame these privileged beings as he was to bring the common Irish to heel, and under unsympathetic English justiciars they felt the pinch sorely, all those who, unlike the Butlers, were not Protestant or pro-Tudor. They entertained dreams of returning to the old happy way of things, centered around a child—Gerald, ten-year-old half brother of Silken Thomas. When Henry was busy eradicating his older relatives this child, suffering from smallpox and too small to attract attention, was packed into a hamper and whisked into hiding in Offaly. He rapidly became the darling and hope of those who had loved and admired the Geraldines. Around the forlorn scrap of humanity was formed the "Geraldine League," the members of which were sworn to restore his house to power. In 1541 they smuggled him out of the country and took him to Rome and Florence, where young Gerald readily adapted himself to his surroundings. In later days, when he came into his inheritance and returned to Ireland as earl of Kildare, he never seemed at home. We will come upon him again.

Thinking over his campaign to Anglicize Ireland, Henry decided that the country should no longer be a lordship. She must henceforth be known as a kingdom, and he himself would be king of England and Ireland. The move seemed advisable on several counts, among which was that it would settle once and for all a stubborn belief, still held by the common Irish, that the Pope was king of Ireland. The necessary formalities immediately proceeded. In Dublin, the councilor's speech proclaiming Henry king of Ireland had to be translated into Irish for the benefit of the peers, many of whom could not have understood it otherwise. On this somewhat unpromising note, Anglicization was launched. It was carried on from there by the king's troops, not in all-out assault à la Skeffington but by roving bands of soldiers who moved doggedly through the country subduing one stubborn chief after another. Though it was not completely effective, the method did meet with a certain amount of success: by the time Henry died in 1547 England could claim sovereignty over half of Ireland, and forty important lords, both Gaelic and Anglo-Irish, had sworn allegiance to the Crown. The outstanding Irish magnate among these had been Conn O'Neill of Ulster, "The O'Neill," who in 1542 had surrendered that proud title for the king's, becoming earl of Tyrone. Other lords who accepted English titles included the Old English Burkes of Connacht. In return, the Crown expected more than mere fealty: it demanded integration. "The outlying Old English magnates were made to come into appreciably closer relations with the Dublin government, to admit judges on circuit, and even sometimes to pay taxes, while the growing influence of Irish practices and customs on their lands was curbed though not terminated....There, too, the break with Rome was carried through: monasteries were suppressed and their possessions often handed to local magnates to keep them well disposed" (David Beers Quinn, *The Elizabethans and the Irish*, pps. 2-3). Then a few settlers—the New English—were introduced into the country and presented with confiscated Church lands or property that had been taken from the FitzGerald family when Brian O'Connor of Offaly, Thomas's brother-in-law and a leading spirit of the Geraldine League, rebelled and was banished for his pains. This was a profitable banishment for the Crown, yielding as it did a pretext for acquiring all of Offaly and Leix.

Yet, even when all these changes are taken into account, it must be admitted that Henry VIII and his agents failed to achieve what had been his intention—the thorough reform, political as well as religious, of Ireland. The king never sent enough troops to complete the job. Ireland's revenue, in spite of all, continued to disappoint, and Henry was not one to be attracted to missionary work for its own sake.

Two short reigns followed his: that of his small son Edward VI (1547-53) and Mary (1553-58). Edward's regents did nothing much about Ireland save to cope with a Catholic resurgence on the Pale's western border. As a fanatically unreformed Catholic, Queen Mary could not have expected any similar trouble, but she got it: a flare-up in Ireland when she appointed a number of English—though irreproachably Catholic—bishops to benefices in Ireland, rather than Irish prelates. This was quickly damped down, and many processes of her father's abhorred reform were halted and reversed under her rule, but when all was said and done she was an English queen even though she married Philip II of Spain, and the conquest continued. The earl of Sussex was sent to Ireland as her deputy to oversee the anti-reform reform, but also to "plant" the confiscated counties of Leix and Offaly in the midlands. Plantation in this sense means sweeping land clear of such population as lives there and replacing the people with others who are members of or appointed by the ruling caste. Ireland had undergone a somewhat similar operation during the Norman conquest, but Norman evictions were on a far smaller scale than the Tudor plantations, which involved whole kingdoms at a time. Much trickery had to be employed before the way lay open for plantation: each kingdom must be confiscated with a show of legality. This done, it was cleared of its Irish owners of all classes, king or kern, who were sent packing with whatever they could carry, and who, in return for their good pastures and farmlands, were fobbed off with wretchedly poor lands in the west of Ireland. When the truth dawned on the Irish lords who found themselves thus dispossessed, they raised such a storm that the program had to be delayed while they were "pacified," and the operation was hardly under way by 1558 when the queen died. It was under the long rule of forty-five years of the next sovereign, Elizabeth, that plantation reached its heyday and the Irish problem was created.

CHAPTER

8

IT has been said that England learned the business of empire building in and from Ireland, and that the colonization of that country served as a dress rehearsal for her later ventures in lands much further away. The trouble with Ireland, from the English point of view, was that colonies are expected to pay dividends, and Ireland didn't. Before Elizabeth and her ministers could hope for profits from their unruly neighbor, certain affairs must be put in order. One at least was political. It was suspected, and with reason, that some of the Irish nobles were in touch with Spain, plotting against England. The English really didn't know much about Ireland. "For English contemporaries the entry into sixteenth-century Ireland was an entry into a world as strange as the Indies were to Columbus," writes Sean O'Faolain in *The Great O'Neill* (p. 5), and he describes with scorn some of the maps consulted by Elizabethans, one dated 1574 bearing the legend that Lough Erne was created by a rising of the waters that smothered the people who farmed on that spot because they committed "filthy abominable acts with beasts," omitting all indication of the rocky headlands of the country, and labeling the Aran Islands as places where no corpses can putrefy. A map of

1609 shows lakes of enormous size, and Lough Conn two counties away from where it should be. The best, of 1610, depicts forests and mountains haphazard, and not one road. O'Faolain admits, however, that the English knew all there was to know about the coastal towns in which they traded. But whether they welcomed the information or not the English learned something from the soldiers who roamed the Irish countryside and came home to tell of it, while the royal court got an occasional picturesque glimpse into the world of the Irish great when some chieftain or lord arrived in London to receive his accolade and new title at the ruler's hands. Such a visit by Sean O'Neill of Ulster in 1562 created quite a stir. Sean claimed the title of earl of Tyrone, though his father Conn had named Sean's elder brother Matthew as his heir, because, Sean maintained, Matthew—admittedly an illegitimate child —was not really Conn's son at all. Sean had made doubly sure of inheriting, however, by murdering Matthew. He was a powerful lord in Ulster, and the only result of one English attempt to subdue him had been the murder of Matthew's eldest son. To save the life of the next son, Hugh, baron of Dungannon, the queen's lieutenant Sir Henry Sidney picked up the little boy and took him to England, where he was raised in Sidney's household and in the house of the earl of Leicester. It was a custom of the times: such protégés were educated in the hope that they would play their part for the empire at some future date. In the meantime Sean had continued to lord it in Ulster, though another kinsman, Turloch Luineach O'Neill, complained that *he* was the rightful head of the house. As lord of Tyrone, recognized or unrecognized, Sean O'Neill was a little out of the ordinary run, dissatisfied with life as his father Conn had lived it. Conn, the first earl, behaved like any lord of his times. O'Faolain rather lyrically describes a typical day's work for such a man, setting out on some long ride through his demesnes. He must see each of his *urraghs*, or lieges, at least twice a year and make sure of his lawful dues of "oats and oatmeal, butter, and hogs, and mutton, and rents." He moved with a retinue of swordsmen and horsemen, lawyers, chroniclers, and poets from one woodland camp, or booley, to another, where he dismounted. Food was laid out by his host's people on great stone slabs or beaten fern, or if it was raining in a wooden shed. The host's orator recited a poem of welcome, accompanied by the harper, who strummed a simple accompaniment. A friar said grace. After the meal the chief and host would sit at ease discussing crops, cattle, rents, and raids....Idyllic, but for Sean insufficient. He was ambitious: at one stage of his career he actually contemplated marrying Mary, Queen of Scots.

When Elizabeth at last summoned him to that audience in London —for since she could not crush him she determined to treat with him— he borrowed thousands of crowns from her with which to make the journey. A tall, good-looking man, he brought with him a bodyguard of tall, good-looking gallowglasses and—of course—his own poet. His demeanor was so haughty that the courtiers called him Sean the Proud —"O'Neill the Great, cousin to St. Patrick, friend to the Queen of England, and enemy to all the world besides," they said spitefully. But they were impressed. Elizabeth herself was impressed by the tall, handsome Irishman who was so sure of himself. There seems to have been no misgiving in him, no suspicion that he might be detained in England indefinitely, as sometimes happened with refractory Irish lords, and he was right not to fear. When he took his leave of London five months after his arrival it was with the knowledge that he had been accepted as lord of Tyrone, though the title of earl was still unsettled. He had made a good-will gesture of his own: in return for the court's hospitality, said Sean, lordly as ever, he would clear the Glens of Antrim of "the Scots."

This was a rash promise and referred to a problem of long standing. The Glens of Antrim were the least accessible portion of the notoriously inaccessible north, in which were settled Scots from Britain and the islands who had remained secure there for over a century and a half. Naturally their numbers increased, and a further augmentation began about fifty years before Sean visited London when new arrivals came from the Hebrides, rugged characters like their kinsmen the gallowglasses and equally good at fighting. The immigration continued steadily until at least ten thousand of these Redshanks, as the Irish called them, stood ready in the Glens, under their leader James Mac-Donnell, to hire out to local chiefs willing to pay for their services. The English rightly considered the Redshank colony a threat to themselves. In Queen Mary's reign when the earl of Sussex was her deputy in Ireland he was under orders to rid the land of the Antrim Scots, and he actually mounted a campaign to oust them, but it failed as Sussex had failed to quell Sean O'Neill in the latter's pre-London days. After O'Neill came back from his audience with Elizabeth there was no holding him.

"Lucifer himself was never puffed up with more pride and ambition than O'Neill is," wrote Sir Henry Sidney feelingly. "... He is the only strong man in Ireland. His country was never so rich or inhabited, and he armeth and weaponeth all the peasants of the country, the first that ever did so of an Irishman." According to Curtis, Sean was ready to acknowledge the sovereignty of the queen, but was firmly opposed to the introduction of English law into Ulster. "He was proud of his descent from the Earl of Kildare, which thus gave him friends in the Pale, for by this time, though the law made a distinction between the Irish and the Old English, in fact through intermarriage the Butlers, Burkes, Desmonds, O'Neills and other great families were of mixed blood" (pp. 185-86). This was a circumstance too often forgotten by the New English, but it is not surprising that they should have forgotten it when Irish lords like Sean O'Neill could themselves ignore it when it proved inconvenient. On one occasion Sean said to some government envoys—and one can feel the sincerity of his speech —"I care not to be an earl unless that I am better and higher than an earl, for I am in blood and power better than the best of them, and will give place to none but my cousin of Kildare for that he is of mine house. My ancestors were kings of Ulster and Ulster is mine and shall be mine."

Splendid   or   megalomaniac?   Both,   perhaps.   There

are many anecdotes about this cruel, passionate, tricky, overweening lord of Tyrone, but the most sensational is the glimpse afforded by David Mathew in *The Celtic Peoples and Renaissance Europe,* when Sean had beaten the O'Donnells of Tyrconnel in the west of Ulster and had also won a triumph over the Antrim Scots. "James and Sorley [MacDonnell] were his prisoners of state, taking the place of Calvagh O'Donnell, whom he had for three years exhibited in chains as an indisputable evidence of his power.... He had dissolved his first marriage with a MacDonnell of Cantyre and was now living with the Dowager Countess of Argyll, who was the wife of his former captive, O'Donnell.... There was in Shane O'Neill nothing of that 'civility,' which marked the later generations of his house, and there can have been few greater burdens than the constant company of such a man. In the morning when he woke from his stupor... was the best time to approach him, for his mind was then clear" (p. 123). According to Sidney it was in the morning that he dictated business letters and generally showed good judgment, "but in the afternoon, when the wine is in, then unfoldeth he himself, *in vino Veritas*... he would order Lady Argyll to be brought to him out of that dungeon where it was his pride to keep her in fetters. It was a satisfaction to O'Neill, who boasted that he spoke no tongue save the Gaelic, to wound the O'Don-nell so deep in his pride by keeping for his pleasures the Lady of Tyrconnell and Argyll, reputed Very sober, wyse and no less sotell, beying not unlearned in the Latun tong (speakyng) good French and, as is said, some lytell Italyon.'" And yet, adds Mathew, gossip had it that this refined lady had betrayed her husband to O'Neill in order to become Sean's mistress.

For five years after the London visit O'Neill devoted himself either to independent and violent action or political intrigues centered around Mary, Queen of Scots, and he could not have been surprised when in 1567 he was proclaimed a traitor. At least the proclamation released him from his promise to drive the Redshanks out of Antrim, and he made peaceful overtures to them. These were not well received, the Scots finding it impossible to forgive and forget the indignities he had heaped on their leaders, but Sean's attention was soon distracted from Antrim by the news that his archenemy Calvagh O'Donnell of Tyrconnel was dead. Concluding that Tyrconnel was therefore ripe for the plucking, the lord of Tyrone hurried westward to do battle. But Tyrconnel's resistance was strong and fierce, and Sean lost the main part of his army. Fleeing, he sought safety at Cushendun with the MacDonnells, and they murdered him.

Turloch Luineach O'Neill was given little time to marshal his forces of men and persuasion in an effort to take over Ulster. The English did not permit such things to happen. For years they had been grooming the young baron Hugh O'Neill, and now the time seemed ripe to use him, so they sent him back to Ireland in 1568 to take possession of his castle of Dungannon. At eighteen, very much the young Englishman—though his hair and beard were red—he behaved as such and aided the queen's forces against risings of Irishmen in the south. As a mere baron Hugh was of small account, useful only for putting a spoke now and then in Turloch's wheel. Certainly nobody would have thought him a serious rival for the lands and title of lord of Tyrone. The Elizabethan ministers were glad to think that at least one loyal lord had now been placed in troublesome Ulster. Though an English president was supposed to be ruling each county, the court could hardly feel secure about the north.

Indeed, not even the other counties of Ireland were thoroughly pacified. There was trouble in the south, and it was stirred up once again by Geraldines, this time the southern branch of the family. Gerald FitzGerald, fifteenth earl of Desmond and heir to nearly all of Munster, did not look in the least like a great rebel. He was a puny man, nearly a cripple. For practical reasons he married his widowed cousin, the countess of Ormond, who was much older than he but brought to the wedding the benefits of connection with a powerful family as well as the more doubtful gift of five stepsons, five strapping Butlers about the same age as the bridegroom. Observers in London decided that a man with such vast estates should be encouraged in sentiments of loyalty to the Crown, and in 1562 he was summoned in the usual way to appear before the throne and render an accounting. There he was presented with an "agreement" as it was called, a list of promises he was urged to fulfill, to pay feudal dues to Elizabeth and rid his country of Irish customs. This last item had continued to fret the English more and more sorely until now such manners and habits appeared downright sinister to Her Majesty's officials. According to the document Gerald assented to (for he had no choice but to promise) he must not permit "idle men of loose demeanour" such as rhymers, bards, and dice players to travel within Munster, and such lords as did allow them must be fined. "And as those rhymers by their ditties and rhymes, made for divers lords and gentlemen in Ireland, in commendation and high praise of extortion, rebellion, rape, rapine, and other injustice, encourage those lords rather to follow those vices than to abandon them," the lords and gentlemen must not pay for these verses: if they did they would be fined double the amount paid. The Elizabethans also worried a good deal about other wanderers such as gamblers and jesters, because they spread news, some of which might bring aid and comfort to the wrong hearts. Outright paranoia imbues the official reports written by Edmund Spenser, who came to Ireland in 1580 to be secretary to the deputy lord, Grey de Wilton. The poet simply could not abide footloose Irishmen of any description. He even disapproved of the age-old system of transhumance, the pasturing of cattle in fresh grazing grounds during the summer months. Camps where the cattle watchers lived at such times, he pointed out, were in remote woods far from towns, and naturally attracted outlaws and tramps. Moreover, "the people who live thus in these booleys grow thereby the more barbarous and live more licentiously than they could in towns" (David Beers Quinn, *The Elizabethans and the Irish*, Ithaca, 1966, pp. 55-56). But it is his contemporary Stanyhurst, himself a member of an Old English family, who sums up the matter:

"A conquest draweth, or at the leastwise ought to draw, to it three things, to wit law, apparel and language. For where the country is subdued, there the inhabitants ought to be ruled by the same law that the conqueror is governed (by), to wear the same fashion of attire wherewith the victor is vested, and to speak the same language that the vanquisher parleth. And if any of these three lack, doubtless the conquest limpeth" (Ibid., pp. 56-57).

Like many Irish lords before and after him, Gerald of Desmond bowed to the inevitable and pledged himself to make over his people in a form nearer the Elizabethan ideal, and like the pledges of those others his were not fulfilled. Along with the Statutes of Kilkenny and tens of dozens more, the rules were ignored by the people of Munster, who went on wearing their Irish clothes, speaking their Irish language, and governing themselves according to their own law.

On the east and north boundary of Gerald's territory was the land of his stepson Thomas, earl of Ormond. Ormond's family, the Butlers, and the FitzGeralds, in spite of their intermarriage, still retained a certain amount of the ancient enmity in their feelings about each other. Thomas was on excellent terms with Queen Elizabeth. A model magnate for Ireland, he was Protestant and very powerful, with holdings that only his stepfather's exceeded in acreage. Thomas and Gerald came to blows in 1565 over a boundary dispute in Tipperary. It was a routine quarrel at the start, the kind of fight that was a country-life pastime like cattle raiding, not a life-and-death affair. But there was a sharp clash, some deaths did result, and Elizabeth, who had set out determinedly to pacify Ireland, was not amused. She summoned both earls to London and sorted out the affair. For the favorite Ormond all went well and he was soon at liberty, but Gerald did not escape so easily. He was "honorably confined" in Southwark as the guest of Sir Warham St. Leger, and there he remained for years, vainly pleading for leave to depart. Elizabeth did not like Desmond, but his detention was due to practical considerations as well as spite. He had to buy his way out, and when at last he was allowed to go home, in 1573, he was considerably poorer than when he arrived.

In the last analysis that long imprisonment was not good for the queen either. Gerald would have been willing and able to keep order in Munster, whereas during his absence one of his cousins, Captain James Fitzmaurice FitzGerald, rallied the Geraldines and instituted rebellions in Munster and beyond—those same disturbances in which Hugh O'Neill of Tyrone fought on the English side. The English presidents of Munster and Connacht were not able to quell such risings. James Fitzmaurice's resistance to the English was rooted in religion as well as a mere desire to avenge the FitzGeralds, but many of his most ardent supporters were men with material interests at stake—those chiefs who had just discovered that according to English law their lands were not theirs after all. What had happened was this: almost overnight the newly "pacified" country swarmed with English adventurers, mostly from Devon and Somerset, looking to make their fortunes out of Ireland. Among them were Humphrey Gilbert, his young half brother Walter Raleigh, and a Sir Peter Carew. "Theirs was the ideology of the typical sixteenth-century soldier and wandering privateer," says O'Faolain, "blooded on the coasts of Barbary and in the wars of France, as indifferent to the lives of any number of natives as ignorant of their ways, but at the same time sufficiently informed... to look for courdy sanction and a guarantee of title before embarking on their adventures" (p. 55). In England these men had been advised not to grab things crudely, but to start their confiscating with tact, preferably in the county Cork region where Desmond had given up much land as part of his ransom. But Carew was precipitate, pressing what he said were his hereditary claims to the choicer half of the Cork territory, where a Carew ancestor had briefly lived before being driven out by the Irish. However, this land was held by two Butlers, brothers of the earl of Ormond. Butlers had been in Cork since feudal times—it was a classic case of Old English pitted against New. One of the brothers, Sir Edmund Butler, already predisposed to this action because he was Catholic, was enraged by Carew's claim and threw in his lot with Fitzmaurice and the rebels, saying, "I do not make war against the queen but against those who banish Ireland and mean conquest,"

The militant Catholics like Fitzmaurice were further encouraged by an announcement from the Pope. Elizabeth had failed, said His Holiness, after many years' forbearance on the part of the Church, to return to the ancient religion, and so she was now deposed, while the captive Mary, Queen of Scots, was named the true sovereign of the kingdom. Of course merely saying this did not make it true as far as the real world was concerned, but to the Irish the Pope's word was enough.

The fortunes of war swung back and forth, with England holding a slight advantage because of her new artillery, until James Fitzmaurice resolved to get help if possible from Spain. After the Reformation, and more than ever after the marriage of Queen Mary and Philip II, cordial if secret relations had been maintained between Spain and Ireland. Many Irish priests had slipped out of their country to take refuge in Spanish academies and schools, and Spanish priests and prelates, in spite of the dangers they had to run, often visited Ireland. In 1571 Elizabeth's deputy complained in a letter to London that Ireland was overrun with "Spanish spies and vermin." So Fitzmaurice wrote to Philip asking for ships and men, and when the Spanish monarch put him off he went to southern Europe to press his case in person. For several years Philip kept him dangling at the court, neither promising nor refusing outright, and without his restless urging the Irish at home tended to subside. Even Ulster was quiet. Only Connacht preoccupied the deputy, Sir Henry Sidney. The biggest man of that county was Richard Burke, earl of Clanrickarde, who said that he had accepted the new religion from England, but his two sons, Ulick and John, were another matter, being violently anti-English and often anti-Protestant—"vague in religion, by turns Henrican and Papal, moody and fierce," to quote David Mathew (*The Celtic Peoples and Renaissance Europe,* London and New

York, 1933, p. 183). While their father was away in London
they revolted against the president of Connacht. Burkes came
from near and far to join them, and so did the redoubtable
woman Grania O'Malley, queen of Clare Island and Clew
Bay, who commanded a large fleet of galleys. With all
this help the earl's sons resisted the English for four years
until 1576, when they surrendered and Sidney took them
to Dublin. There they made the customary agreements and
signed the usual pledges. But on their return to Connacht,
in sight of the castle of Athlone (occupied by English forces)
"they shook off their English clothes in the Shannon and
resumed Irish dress" (Curtis, p. 196). Later they attacked
Athenry and burned down most of the town including the
church where their mother was buried. Someone reminded
Ulick of this circumstance, and he "blasphemously swore
that if she were alive and in it he would burn the church
and her too rather than any English churl should inhabit or
fortify there" (Ibid.).

Such gestures must have disturbed the deputy, but he
could not have been surprised, for he had already noted
during a tour of Connacht and Clare that few of the Old
English of those parts spoke the English language at all,
and their English—or, rather, Norman—names had been
dropped; though the owners were acquainted with those
original labels they never used them. Sidney persuaded the
MacMorrises, for example, to admit that they had been
known as Prendergast in the old days, and the Costellos
knew that their ancestors were called De Angelo, but there,
evidently, the matter ended.

It should have been a heartwarming and dramatic occasion
when Gerald FitzGerald, earl of Desmond, came back at
last from London. In fact it was a disappointment for his
Geraldine relatives who had loyally rallied to the call of
James Fitzmaurice. Possibly Gerald's brothers had forgotten,
when they emotionally agreed not to rest until they had
him with them again, that he was an odd-looking little
man who might truthfully be called a weakling, and it

was undeniable that his thanks for their efforts were only pallid and lukewarm. Fresh from the grip of Elizabeth's officials, Gerald wanted nothing so much as peace. He was not attracted by the intrigue, rebelliousness, and generally bustling undercover activity he was expected to take charge of. For nearly six years he managed to put off any action. Then in July 1579 Fitzmaurice came back from Spain bringing with him a bit of token help from Philip: a few soldiers and many promises. Also accompanying him were two Englishmen, Dr. Nicholas Sanders the papal legate and Allen, a Jesuit, as well as the Spaniard Oviedo, sent by the Pope as emissary to the troops.

Fitzmaurice, full of characteristic vigor and hope, sent out word to all his followers that the struggle of which these men were forerunners was for the Catholic religion, a fight for the cross of Christ and His Holiness's banner, "courage and stoutness for the defense of His Faith and in the world to come life everlasting." Desmond could feel neither courage nor stoutness of heart. We can imagine the bitterness of his thoughts as he heard these words and thought back on his years in exile among the hatefully strong English of whose real power his cousin James Fitzmaurice had no inkling. Danger also lay in the fact that his brothers, Sir John and Sir James, were wholeheartedly committed to Fitzmaurice's cause. Sure enough, within a few weeks the younger men took drastic action. One night while the sheriff of Cork and the provost marshal of Munster lay asleep in an inn bedroom in Tralee, they marched in and killed both men.

One thing at least was clear to Gerald—he was doomed no matter what he did. If Fitzmaurice's followers met defeat, he himself would be compromised and lose everything he still possessed, but if Fitzmaurice won Gerald would still lose, for he would be deposed. He couldn't fight Fitzmaurice because his men would never consent to obey him. Then for a little time fate seemed to be averted, when James Fitzmaurice, only a month after his return, was killed skirmishing with the Burkes in Limerick. Gerald used his reprieve as best he could, anxiously trying to stay on the right side of the English. He is accused of having betrayed a priest and his party to the officials. But no matter what he did the English liked him less and less, and through it all Dr. Sanders stood at his elbow, exhorting and urging him to join his brothers on the side of righteousness in the holy war, and to return to the Church he had so long neglected. In the end, that is what he did.

Vicious fighting followed. In the notorious campaign of 1580 an English army under Ormond and another general marched straight through Munster, killing everyone they met no matter what age or sex, and burning all buildings. Desmond with his wife and Sanders escaped for that time and wrote urgently to Philip for more soldiers-eight thousand men with six months' worth of ammunition and provisions. Philip responded vaguely, with chilly politeness. Then Elizabeth offered a general pardon, but the spirit of the earl of Desmond was wonderfully stiffened by desperation, and he did not rise to the bait. He was a transformed man. When a relative of his accepted the offer, the man's lands were attacked and spoiled and his cattle killed by Gerald's men. So the war went on until, as the annals say, "The lowing of a cow or the voice of a ploughman was not to be heard from Dingle to the Rock of Cashel." Sanders died in the forest. On the Dingle peninsula, in the winter of 1583, Gerald was taking refuge with three followers when they were attacked by a band of countryfolk, recently beaten in a cattle raid, who were determined to have revenge on any strangers. Let O'Faolain describe the last scene: "A Kelly or O'Kelly struck at [Gerald] and almost cut off his arm. The old man revealed his identity crying out, 'I am the Earl of Desmond, spare my life.' Moriarty took him on his back, but he was bleeding to death, so in the woods they finished him, and cut off his head" (p. 83).

So Munster's rebellions were over at last, and the way lay open for Devon's and Somerset's gallants to swarm over the desolated region, seeking their fortunes in plantation. Of the country's five million acres, a tenth were declared liable to confiscation: in the end not half of this, though it was the choicest land, was disposed of, and it is noticeable that though the queen's regulations declared that the new settlers must be English, religion was not mentioned. Clearly it was feared that there would not be enough Protestant applications to make the project pay. Each chief grant, or "seigniory," was of an area above four thousand and below twelve thousand acres, and no "undertaker" or chief grantee could hold more than one seigniory, though this rule was easy to get round by faulty measuring or simple bribery: Sir Walter Raleigh thus cornered forty thousand acres for himself. The undertaker paid quit-rent to the Crown. For a time these developers were very busy scurrying around their estates dividing them up for the expected flood of settlers, but after a few years they had to admit that the plan had failed. People simply didn't or wouldn't come to devastated Munster. It seemed that undertakers, even those as ambitious and enterprising as Raleigh, would have no lasting effect on the countryside. Raleigh himself finally gave up after various experiments, which included planting some of his land with a new species of vegetable. These roots, or tubers, had been sent to him by a group of colonists in North America, out there on another of his schemes—for Raleigh always had many irons in the fire. They were odd-looking objects, lumpy and without symmetry; potatoes, they were called. He put them in the ground according to the colonists' written directions, and they seemed to flourish. But no matter what methods he and the other undertakers used to tempt settlers, the plantation in general did not do well, and Elizabeth, after waiting in vain for her money, lost interest in it. In the end all that remained of the great Munster design was a small—a very small—number of new settlers who had struck root, and an increasing crop of potatoes. As late as 1588 not so much as a hundredth of the county had been reinhabited.

This failure did not turn the English, Elizabeth least of all, against the general idea of plantation in Ireland. The fact that it had not worked out in the south was due, thought the Elizabethans, to special circumstances: Ulster appeared far more promising. Sir Humphrey Gilbert had suggested various alternative methods, and some advantages in planting the northern county were immediately evident. The most legally inclined adviser could not insist that England must prove her right to that region, as had been necessary in Munster, since the queen through her Mortimer ancestors was already countess of Ulster. The movement began in 1573, the year of Desmond's return, when Elizabeth sent Essex to plant a large portion of Ulster. This was more or less the county long ago carved out by De Courcy and then called Ulidea. In Essex's time it was Antrim and Down, and was considered Crown property though it had long been occupied by the Clandeboy O'Neills and, of course, the Antrim Scots. Both native factions leaped to the defense of their properties, and Essex, though he didn't succeed in getting a permanent foothold, did considerable damage for a time. He captured Hugh O'Neill's father-in-law Sir Brian MacPhelim O'Neill and took him, with his wife and followers, to Dublin, where all of them were executed. The English forces also cornered a number of the MacDonnell Scots, mostly old women and children, who had taken refuge on Rathlin Island, a scrap of land that lies off the northernmost part of the coast, and slaughtered every one of them.

In spite of all this, Hugh O'Neill continued to keep his copybook clean and carefully remained aloof. The noisiest O'Neill was Turloch, helping to keep up the rebellion of the Burkes in Connacht and encouraging the Antrim Scots with material reinforcements. Unwittingly he thus did service to his kinsman and rival Hugh, drawing off English attention from the young baron: Ulster was believed to be safely divided between Hugh, Turloch, and Henry Bagenal. Hugh O'Neill also resisted all blandishments to join in a conspiracy of Irish lords— "the Lords of the Pale"—to throw off English rule. This was a remarkably inept performance inspired by Viscount Baltinglas under the so-called leadership of Gerald, earl of Kildare, chiefly interesting because Gerald was that same FitzGerald who had been smuggled out of danger during his half brother Silken Thomas's rebellion, when he was ten years old. Back from Florence, he assumed his place. But he was an indecisive character and the plot soon fell to pieces. It showed Hugh O'Neill's prudence that when the conspirators were counted he was not among them.

He bided his time. Not until 1585 did he present to parliament his carefully worded petition for the title earl of Tyrone and the lands that went with it—those taken over by Sean years ago when he killed Hugh's father Matthew. Nobody in parliament could call the request unreasonable: Hugh had been loyal to the queen, had done his utmost for the Crown, and seemed the perfect prototype of Anglicized, indoctrinated Irish lord. Certainly he deserved better than the barony of Dungannon. There was news, too, that the O'Neill clansmen had elected him tanist, making him next in line to Turloch as The O'Neill, the proudest title an Irishman could wear even though, or because, the English disapproved of it. The colonists granted the request. Even noisy Turloch showed willingness to share out, and leased much of his land—"a vast territory" says O'Faolain—to the new earl for several years. In the end, Tyrone never returned them, and Turloch died before he could do much about it.

One inexperienced in Elizabethan ways might think the way now clear for Hugh O'Neill through life, but he knew that anyone whom the gods and Queen Elizabeth elevated was in constant danger of falling. From the day in 1587 when he went to London to assume his title ceremoniously, the earl of Tyrone never made a move or sent a message that was not reported to headquarters. He was constantly surrounded by spies. The deputy Sir John Perrot so often summoned Hugh to Dublin to explain away circumstances of one sort or another, even the most trivial, that the earl protested by letter: "... Withal I humbly beseech your Lordship not to send for me to Dublin upon every information of my back friends." He grew more and more indignant, felt more and more beleaguered, until sometimes during his interviews with Perrot he would burst into tears.

All that time, under all that surveillance, he was building up a strong army, and nobody caught him at it. Lords in

O'Neill's position were strictly forbidden to maintain garrisons of more than a stipulated number of men: O'Neill obeyed the rules, and his troops at any one time were well within the numerical limits. But he built an army nevertheless, in a marvelously simple way: he would train one group thoroughly and then, when he was sure they would remember, would send them back to the land and train a new lot, so that after a while all men of military age in his county had been drilled in the arts of war. He bought stores of ammunition and smuggled in more. He never relaxed in his aim. Archbishop Lombard of Armagh, who knew him well, says: "Whenever he used to go out hunting or fowling, or on some other exercise of business, he even arranged that some guns should be carried by his company, and seized an opportunity of chatting familiarly with any of the people he met in the district, and used to ask them sundry questions as to their lives and habits... and when they replied that they knew nothing except spears, and bows, and arrows and other such primitive weapons of their fathers, he would produce a gun and having briefly explained its use bid them try if they could manage it. He would praise anyone handy and give him a piece of money and sometimes would bestow the weapon itself."

In 1587, the year Hugh O'Neill was recognized by Queen Elizabeth as earl of Tyrone, the queen came to a decision that affected Ireland indirectly. For years she had held her kinswoman Mary Stuart, Queen of Scots, in captivity. It was rather like keeping a time bomb on the premises, for Mary bred conspiracies as naturally as she breathed: many a young gallant had dreamed of delivering her from prison and setting her on the throne of Scotland and England, with himself living happily ever after as her husband the king. A number of these plots had been averted, but there was always another—as there was in 1587, ripening in the fertile brain of Philip II's illegitimate son Don Juan of Austria. Yet, in spite of the danger, Elizabeth had insisted on keeping her royal captive alive, since Mary was a valuable card to play in the game of international intrigue. However, the clamor of Elizabeth's councilors now grew too strong for her, and she reluctantly signed the death warrant. The Scots queen died at Fotheringhay on February 8.

Word of the execution sped swiftly through Europe to the ears of Philip of Spain. Relations between this king and Elizabeth were already nearly at their nadir: years had gone by since the two monarchs had briefly considered marrying in order to combine their countries, and England was now aiding the Protestant Netherlands in their struggle to throw off Spanish rule, whereas Philip was in alliance with England's Catholic enemies. Francis Drake prowled waters claimed by Spain and took prizes like the pirate he was. The news of the beheading of Mary of Scotland precipitated a rupture between the two countries, with the Catholic kings all urging Philip to act before England became too powerful, and at last the vacillating king of Spain gave orders to prepare a fleet with which to attack Elizabeth's country. In all the chief harbor cities of Spain and Portugal there was frantic activity. It was first thought possible to send this huge "armada" or battle fleet on its journey within the year, but such prompt preparation was beyond the capacity of the officials concerned, and much of the important work was brutally interrupted by Francis Drake—the building of the huge fleet was an open secret in England. Drake sailed down to Cadiz Bay and attacked the ships that lay there at anchor in the harbor, wreaking havoc before he found it wise to depart. The foray gave him the idea of a more ambitious project, to lead far more of the queen's ships down to the Iberian peninsula and dispatch the "invincible Armada" before it even got started. But Elizabeth was hard to persuade, and while they argued the winter passed. It was high summer in 1588 before the queen, after changing her mind a dozen times, consented to action of the sort. In July Lord Howard of Effingham, as the lord admiral commanding Drake and Hawkins as vice-admirals, set sail to deal with the Armada. They had no word as to whether or not it had set out, but halfway through the Bay of Biscay they encountered contrary winds and had to return to Plymouth Harbor. It was a summer of freakish weather. In fact, the Spanish fleet, under the command of the duke of Medina-Sidonia, had set out at about the same time. Medina-Sidonia was to get into the Channel if possible before alarming the English, and there at Dunkirk meet with the duke of Parma, who was in charge of Philip's forces in the Netherlands and who was supposed to contribute provisions, ammunition, and small ships when needed. Late on July 29 word came to Drake at Plymouth Hoe that one of their captains, scouting the mouth of the Channel, had sighted Spanish ships off the Scilly Isles.

The defeat of the 130-strong Armada by an English fleet of 80 ships (and terrible weather) was more or less accomplished by the end of August 5, though for a fortnight more there was activity. A heavy storm blew many of the Spanish ships far off course and wrecked them on the Irish coast, where people had heard the big guns and had been able to watch, wondering, as ships sailed past in flight. It was from Ireland that Philip got the first news of Spain's losses. Possibly the greatest tragedy of the whole affair was that of the Spaniards who saved themselves by swimming or drifting to Ireland's shores only to be caught there and immediately killed. Many had their brains knocked out, Gerald Mattingly (*The Defeat of the Spanish Armada*) says, as they lay exhausted on the beaches where they had managed to drag themselves. Others were "slaughtered like wild beasts by parties of soldiers or reluctantly handed over by their Irish hosts to English executioners" (p. 386). The deputy, Sir William FitzGerald, took this harsh line because he had only two thousand English soldiers to depend on, and in Ireland, where the people's temper was always uncertain, the Armada's arrival had filled the settlers' hearts with terror. Bingham, president of Connacht and always a hard man, announced that anyone who sheltered a castaway would be considered a traitor. Later, he boasted that his brother had killed seven hundred or eight hundred. Yet here and there, in spite of danger, Irish dared to show kindness to the castaways. The Burkes of Mayo were of this number, and so was Sir Brian O'Rourke of Leitrim, who sheltered, fed, and outfitted a thousand men. For this crime Bingham drove him out of Ireland. He went to Scotland, where James VI caught him and handed him over to Elizabeth, and he was executed at last in London.

Ulster was another place where castaways were kindly treated. Black Hugh O'Donnell of Tyrconnel took in a large number of men who had been wrecked on the rocky Donegal coast, and with the connivance of Tyrone, his closest friend, sent them on to safety in Scotland. Inevitably the news came to the attention of the English, and they did not like it.

The Armada incident gave rise to two persistent stories concerning Ireland which Mattingly for one scathingly dismisses as myths: that the Spaniards who came ashore were murdered by the Irish for their clothes, arms, and jewelry— he says this story was put about by the English almost from the Armada year—and that black eyes and hair, aquiline profiles, and swarthy cheeks among the Irish are evidence of the blood of the Spaniards who came ashore from the Armada ships and stayed. "Not infrequently the wild Irish did relieve their unbidden guests of their valuables," says Mattingly (p. 386). "Perhaps, now and then, a throat was cut. But there is only one recorded instance of the killing of Spanish castaways by Irish not directly in English pay, and it aroused general disapprobation." It was far more usual for the Irish to shelter the Spaniards, feed them, and help them get away, the historian insists. As for the persistence of "Spanish" features among the Irish, he continues, there simply weren't that many Spaniards who remained. "Perhaps here and there some castaway found a roof and a wife in a friendly village, but not enough, surely, to have any effect on the look of the people as a whole."

CHAPTER

9

HUGH O'Neill, earl of Tyrone, fascinates historians because of apparent inconsistencies in the nature of the man who came nearest, until modern days, to driving the English out of Ireland. What puzzles many is his transformation from the wellborn, well-educated Protestant youth of the sixteenth century, too aristocratic for his own good, into a redoubtable Catholic leader of tough Irish fighters, who came to be known—and in no jocular spirit—as king of Ireland. But most people *are* inconsistent. O'Neill's temperament was capable of swinging between violent extremes, especially when his pride was injured. The English often injured Irish pride, and when they got on Tyrone's nerves his reaction was swift and sometimes involuntary. This was probably the reason for his attitude on that occasion when he and Black Hugh O'Donnell of Tyrconnel helped Spanish castaways to escape. In 1587, the English, determined to chastise Black Hugh for his defiant attitude, had kidnapped his favorite son Red Hugh and imprisoned him in Dublin Castle as pledge for his father's good behavior. Parents and household mourned the young man bitterly, and when Black Hugh had the Spanish prisoners in his hands, he thought of bartering some of them for his son. However, the very mention of such a plan sent Tyrone into a great passion: he would have none of it. Now the earl was like most other contemporary chiefs in lacking the fine chivalric sense of honor that this reaction implies, and we must suppose that the strain of constant espionage and criticism trickling in from Dublin was fraying his nerves.

A year or so later he was exasperated to the utmost degree by a new spy, Hugh Gaveloch O'Neill. This man, the son of Tyrone's hated Uncle Sean by Lady Argyll, sent information to the deputy Sir John Perrot to the effect that the earl was plotting with one of the MacDonnells of Antrim, basing his conclusion on various things he had seen when Angus MacDonnell visited Dungannon Castle for a merry drinking party. Hugh Gaveloch said that in the morning he had seen with his own eyes how MacDonnell, taking his leave, gave some Scotch plaids to Tyrone's men, and Tyrone presented MacDonnell with seven horses: it was all very sinister. Perrot communicated severely with Tyrone, who was beside himself with rage. Then one of his friends happened to catch Hugh Gaveloch and sold him to Tyrone: the informer was immediately hanged. Himself he had not done it, said Tyrone, when, inevitably, he was summoned to Dublin to explain, but, he continued, certainly he had instigated the hanging: anyone would have done so. Indeed, he insisted on going to London again to explain things, which was a dangerous thing to do. Yet, though he was coolly treated there, he got out again unscathed after pleading self-defense to the Privy Council. He also promised to make his people wear English dress and cut their hair, to spread his sphere of influence in the Crown's behalf, and stop taking black rents. He was always promising this.

It was 1591, and English attention was fixed on the north. Elsewhere in Ireland everything was under control. Those Irish and Old English who had stood out against them were dead, in exile, or had been quieted with a mixture of threats and bribes, but the northerners stood safe behind their natural allies, the lakes, mountains, and deep forests that were strung along as if by design from coast to coast. Above the line, Irish and Scot visited each other at will and did a brisk trade in war material. In Ulster the old Gaelic customs serenely survived, much to English annoyance: poets chanted martial songs just as poets had done for generations past, and ethics were governed by brehon law. The New English told each other—and London—that this must stop: they appointed sheriffs to posts in the north against the time the places should be available, and planned to "shire" the land.

In the north most men held themselves ready against the English push, but Tyrone took time out for his third marriage. Unaccountably, he had fixed his fancy on an English girl, completely unsuitable—not because she was twenty to his forty-one, such matters counting little, but because she was Mabel Bagenal, daughter of the Sir Nicholas who in his time had held Down and Leith for the queen and was one of Hugh O'Neill's most effective antagonists. Mabel's brother Henry, now queen's marshal like his father before him, furiously opposed the idea of alliance between his sister and any Gaelic lord, least of all Tyrone, but Mabel was as eager as her suitor, and an elopement was arranged in the accepted romantic pattern, with O'Neill carrying her off as if by force. The affair caused a tremendous hubbub. A couple in their position should have asked for royal consent to the match, and Henry Bagenal contested the legality of the wedding, but in time the matter simmered down. In any case it would have been forgotten in the excitement of news from Tyrconnel, just after Christmas, that Red Hugh O'Donnell had escaped from Dublin Castle.

He had broken out with two other prisoners who were sons of Sean O'Neill. In the savagely cold winter that year the men had a terrible passage through the mountains. One of the O'Neills froze to death, but Red Hugh got home safe, though permanently crippled from frostbite. The people rejoiced. His father Black Hugh, to celebrate on a proper scale, retired and handed over to him the proud title of The O'Donnell. "It was the last 'enkinging' and Hugh was to be the last of the old Gaelic kings," says Curtis; but Tyrone too, when his cousin Turloch died in 1595, assumed the style of

The O'Neill (though English law did not permit him to bear it) because he knew that The O'Neill wielded more power than the earl of Tyrone would have over Ulstermen, and by that time he needed all the strength he could command.

The year 1591 had seen the loss to the Irish of the county of Monaghan, lying below Fermanagh between the northern fastnesses of Ulster and pacified Connacht. The English had executed Monaghan's chief MacMahon and put various tame leaders in his place, then shired the county so that the way was left open to Fermanagh. Within Fermanagh's borders was the eastern coast of Lough Erne, affording one of the few passes through which an army could get into Ulster, and the English came very near to controlling that crucial approach not once but several times within the following two years. Hugh Maguire, chief of Fermanagh, held them back as best he could with the guerrilla tactics at which the Irish excelled, but he was losing the war when his liege lord Hugh O'Donnell came to his aid, a brother of Tyrone's at his side. In August 1594 the combined Irish forces beat back the enemy at Enniskillen.

Hugh O'Neill then made his position even clearer. He himself joined the Irish side and defeated Henry Bagenal on the battlefield at Clontibret. Immediately, of course, he was proclaimed a traitor in London. The northern Irish, definitely on the offensive, moved forward. Red Hugh went south into Connacht to reclaim land that had formerly belonged to the O'Donnells, and with Hugh Maguire signed appeals to Rome and Spain for help in the name of the ancient faith: this, they said, was a holy war like that of James Fitzmaurice.

The settlers were stunned. They could do nothing at first, because, owing to the queen's parsimony, their forces were down to a minimum. In 1595 they proposed a parley and their Irish foes agreed. In October the two sides met to arrange a peace, and at the meeting Tyrone wept, embarrassing everybody but impressing some. Thereafter until the end of the year there was a lull. In January 1596 Tyrone—now dry-eyed—presented his terms: liberty of conscience, the removal of English garrisons, and county administration for the north. When the proposals were submitted to the queen she accepted everything but the clause dealing with liberty of conscience. Even with this reservation the Irish ultimately consented to make peace, which was declared in April. Naturally the declaration was immediately followed by a scramble on both sides to build up military strength. English soldiers and equipment were hastily shipped across the sea, while Tyrone for his part wrote to the Irish leaders of the south, urging them to join him for the sake of Christ's religion. At the same time he sent off to Philip II a request for six thousand men and suggested that the archduke of Austria come along with them, to be crowned king of England when everything was sorted out.

It is typical of the rambling nature of Elizabethan war that 1592, which sounds so bloody in the annals, was also the year when Trinity College, the University of Dublin, was peacefully founded in the capital city. Chartered by the queen and endowed by outstanding families of the Pale, Trinity was—of course—Protestant: nevertheless it was for a time open to students of all denominations.

In May 1597 the English, having built up their army to seven thousand, decided to start again and bring the peace to an end with a three-pronged attack on Ulster. This failing altogether, another truce was hastily arranged. But Elizabeth was growing more and more angry with her deputy and soldiers; something had to be done to crush O'Neill once and for all, she said, and in June 1598 the truce ended. The English had regained possession of Portmore, but the garrison of the fort appeared to be in danger, and the deputy, Lord Brough, sent an enormous portion of the English army—more than four thousand men—under Sir Henry Bagenal to defend it. On August 15 Tyrone and Red Hugh intercepted them at the Yellow Ford on the Blackwater River, and in the battle that ensued something between fifteen hundred and two thousand English were killed, including Bagenal himself. For the Irish this was the high point of the war: the victory set off that general rising that had long been England's nightmare. Everywhere people plucked up heart and threw in their lot with Hugh O'Neill, so that for a time he could have claimed, with truth, an army of thirty thousand. Following up his advantage he sent two of his best generals into Munster. They arrived in October to find the Irish uproariously happy, though some of the Old English did not join in the rejoicing, and for a short time Munster's plantation was completely eradicated. If any doubts of Tyrone's success still persisted they were wiped out by the reaction of the non-English world outside. Suddenly Ireland was being discussed in foreign courts. James VI of Scotland, for example, who had always been overawed by Queen Elizabeth until he dared not call his soul his own—though he was believed to be a Catholic in his secret heart—now hinted that his country and Ireland might enjoy amicable relations as soon as the queen was dead. (Elizabeth was sixty-five, and it seemed fairly obvious that James would succeed her.) These overtures were at least morally encouraging, though without practical value. More important were the promises made by Philip II to send help. To be sure, he then died, but his son Philip III readily repeated the assurances.

Tyrone knew, however, that these fair promises rested on mistaken assumptions of his strength versus that of the English, and as to this comparison he entertained no illusions. If the English—when the English—brought to bear their full might on his poorly armed people, the story would be different. That is, it would be different unless some outside occurrence such as considerable help from Spain or the death of Queen Elizabeth changed the course of events. The latter would be preferable. In the hurry and scurry of installing her successor it was unlikely that the English would find the time or resources to gather together the largest army ever amassed merely to subdue Ireland. So Tyrone played for time, and when in 1599 Elizabeth sent over her favorite Essex as lord lieutenant, the Irish leader harried the English forces and did his best to wear them down slowly.

In fact Essex did not do at all badly against these tactics, but Elizabeth was impatient with him for failing to conquer the archtraitor himself in one swoop. She wrote repeatedly to this effect, rebuking Essex and telling him to drive straight to Ulster: "Your two months journey hath never brought in a capital rebel against whom it hath been worthy to have adventured a thousand men....Full well do we know that you would have long since scorned to have allowed it for any great matter in others, to have taken an Irish hold from a rabble of rogues, with such force as you had, and with the help of the cannon, which was always able in Ireland to make its passage where it pleased....Whereunto we will add one thing that doth more displease us than any charge or expense that happens, which is, that it must be the Queen of England's fortune (who hath held down the greatest enemy she had) to make a base bush-kerne be accounted so famous a rebel as to be a person against whom so many thousands of foot and horse, besides the force of all that nobility of that kingdom must be thought too little to be employed." Repeatedly she commanded him to move north, but Essex, who may have felt that he was in a better position to judge the field, ignored the orders or gave excuses for not obeying them.

In August Tyrone sent him a message suggesting a secret parley, and Essex was glad to agree. The two met more than once, and what was said at the meetings has never been discovered except that a truce was arranged and was to last until the end of 1599. Among the theories firmly believed in certain circles was that Tyrone promised Essex the throne of Ireland if the Englishman would come over to his side. However, at the news of the truce Elizabeth peremptorily sent for Essex, listened with mounting anger to his report, and sent him to the Tower. He emerged only to be beheaded on February 25, 1601.

The post of deputy was now conferred on Lord Mountjoy, an experienced military man who went to Dublin that same February. His method of attack was quite different, and the campaign that followed was of the kind Tyrone

had reason to fear—an orderly, inflexible destruction of
the country's crops, marching step by step with military
conquests until The O'Neill at last had to gather his forces
and retreat to Ulster. He stayed there, hemmed in, while
the English worked by word of mouth to soften up his
lieutenants, playing on their ambitions and tempting them
with promises of advancement. Tyrone whiled away the
time with hopeful plans, for he knew that Spanish ships
and men were on the way from Philip III. However, the new
king of Spain proved to be very much like his father, and the
fleet on which so much depended turned out to be only a
handful of vessels that carried four thousand men under the
command of Don Juan d'Aquila, a conceited commander
whose judgment proved woefully bad. He brought his ships
into the harbor of Kinsale near Cork, in a region firmly held
by the English, instead of sailing around to the west or north
where Tyrone's forces could easily have joined with his. To
meet them the northerners made a tremendous march from
north to south, severely taxing their strength but managing
to get through the English lines at the end, where they
met the Spaniards and prepared for battle. It took place
on December 24, 1601— a struggle on which everything
depended, when the country could have been won by and for
the Irish. Instead all was lost to them. Some say D'Aquila's
faulty estimate of the situation was responsible, but most
attribute the failure to Red Hugh's impatience, for he forced
Tyrone's hand and led him to start the attack too soon. In
any case the Irish were completely routed. O'Donnell fled
to Spain, humbled and heartbroken, and died in Salamanca
shortly afterward, possibly of poison. O'Neill retreated
once again to Dungannon, though it, like all his domain,
was now overrun. The scorched-earth tactics of the English
had left all Ireland in the grip of famine, and once-proud
Ulster, too, had to suffer. For a year and more Hugh
O'Neill lived like a fugitive near his castle, fleeing from one
hiding place to another in the forest, vainly trying to rally
enough companions in arms to rise up and try again. Many
of these old companions had succumbed to the enemy's

blandishments when they were promised a share of Tyrone's honors and wealth, and they avoided their old chief. At last The O'Neill swallowed his pride and sent word that he would surrender. He met Mountjoy at Mellifont on March 28, 1603, and submitted in humble words, renouncing claim to the tide The O'Neill, promising to break off with the king of Spain and never again to make alliance with a foreign power, renouncing authority over his *urraghs,* and resigning all lands and lordships.

At the time O'Neill did not know—and Mountjoy did not tell him —that Queen Elizabeth had died on the twenty-fourth, four days earlier, or his submission would have been far less humble. When in Dublin he learned at last of her death, he wept with rage, but even at that moment he had to be cautious. Asked why he wept, he said his tears were of grief for the dear queen.

He was given back his earldom and his grandfather Conn's lands, as well as the fealty of some unimportant *urraghs,* but the Crown retained his profitable fisheries, as they did those of Rory O'Donnell, heir to Red Hugh. Rory was allowed the title earl of Tyrconnel, but lost Inishowen and the fort of Ballyshannon. In short, though the façade had been restored, life in Ulster, and indeed in all Ireland, was now permanently altered. In Curtis's words, the settlement of this rebellion, finishing what was begun with the extinction of Desmond twenty years earlier, brought to an end Gaelic and feudal Ireland. "There were to be no more 'lords of counties' and 'captains of their nation,' no wide territory in which the poets, Brehons, and chroniclers could practise freely of their art….Now the country from end to end was disarmed and save for foreign aid could not be armed again….English landlordism took the place of the older tenures of Brehon and semi-feudal law" (pp. 219-20).

For Hugh O'Neill and Rory O'Donnell especially, living in Ireland was now a shabby business. Four years after the submission, finding themselves beset with threats and in danger of being charged with conspiracy, they gave up trying. With ninety-seven companions who could be trusted and who felt the same way, on September 3, 1607, they sailed for the Continent in the famous "flight of the earls." O'Donnell died in exile not long afterward; Tyrone lived on, quietly and sadly, in Rome. He went blind, and finally, in 1616, he died there.

In *The Elizabethans and the Irish* Professor Quinn studies the English of that period and the light in which they, in turn, studied the natives of their first colony. Now and then in the writings of the officials and military men one can see some reason or motivation for their presence in Ireland—apart, that is, from the obvious search for power and fortune. It seems clear, for example, that among the policy makers were some who genuinely feared that Spain might use the island as a steppingstone toward conquest of England herself. There was also religious zeal, though this could not compare with that of the later conquerors, Cromwell's army. But imperialism is a complicated urge, and imperialists, like war makers generally, can always find convincing reasons for their actions. What interests Professor Quinn is the side result of this situation, the impression made on the conquerors by the conquered. The English attitude was compounded of suspicion, perplexity, and condescension, with condescension uppermost. These people! we hear them saying—brave, one admits, good-natured once they have been tamed, but incapable of telling the truth, and hopelessly dirty. The Elizabethan English were convinced that everyone but themselves was dirty and immoral. The Irish appeared offensive because they chased their lice unabashed (in fact they were probably wood ticks rather than lice) and didn't know how to prepare decent English food. An English traveler named Barnaby Rich complained that the country people ate oatcakes instead of sensible wheat or rye bread. Barnaby Rich did not like oatcakes, which, he said, were flat and hard, and cindery because of the way the Irish cleaned the grain. Fynes Moryson, another Englishman who visited Ireland, was equally disapproving of the diet, partly because "the... wild Irish do not thresh their oats but burn them from the straw," and he was shocked at the way the Irish ground corn in their ancient querns: "At Cork I have seen with these eyes young maids, stark naked, grinding of corn with certain stones to make cakes thereof... striking off into the tub of meal such reliques thereof as stuck on their belly, thighs, and more unseemly parts" (Quinn, p. 63).

Even of this unappetizing oatmeal the Irish ate surprisingly little. A Bohemian baron told Moryson that in Ulster, for eight days after landing, he found no bread, not so much as an oatcake, until he reached Dungannon Castle and stayed for a while with Tyrone. In fact, Quinn comments, the Irish were pastoral people, not agricultural, and their diet reflected this circumstance. According to Fynes Moryson they drank a lot of milk, which they warmed by dropping hot stones into it or mixing it with beef broth. They made much butter, which they ate mixed with oatmeal. They often "let" blood from their cows in the manner of East Africa's pastoral Masai tribesmen, mixing the coagulated stuff with butter and eating it as a jelly, but the mainstay of their diet was meat, often eaten raw as well as roasted or boiled— and without bread. They didn't care for cooked vegetables, but ate herbs, watercress, mushrooms, and "shamroots" or shamrocks. (Incidentally, Professor Quinn holds that the ancient shamrock was not a species of clover, the yellow trefoil people think it is, but a sort of wood sorrel).

Not only were the Irish considered dirty, with peculiar and un-English eating habits, but they were condemned as immoral as well-immodest and given to carelessness in their clothing. Even when young girls weren't grinding corn in shameless nakedness, they were perfectly capable of wandering about like the older women, wrapped in nothing but their mantles. That Bohemian nobleman who visited Ulster and couldn't find any bread told Moryson an astonishing story as to the Irish nakedness: "He coming to the house of Ocane [i.e. Donnell O'Cahan, who was lord of part of modern county Londonderry], a great lord among them, was met at the door with sixteen women, all naked, excepting their loose mantles, whereof eight or ten were very fair and two seemed very Nymphs. With which strange sight his eyes being dazzled, they led him into the house, and there sitting down by the fire, with crossed legs like tailors, and so low as could not but offend chaste eyes, desired him to sit down with them. Soon after, Ocane, the Lord of the County, came in all naked except a loose mantle and shoes, which he put off as soon as he came in, and, entertaining the Baron after his best manner in Latin tongue, desired him to put off his apparel, which he thought to be a burden to him, and sit naked by the fire with this naked company. But the Baron, when he came to himself, after some astonishment at this strange sight, professed that he was so inflamed therewith as for shame he durst not put off his apparel" (Quinn, pp. 71-72).

A woodcut by an Englishman dated about 1575 depicts an Irish lord dining in open air, "in the fern." In detail but not in spirit it is like O'Faolain's description of a booley visited by Conn O'Neill. There is the lord with his lady and several guests, seated at an oblong board which lies close to or on the ground, the diners on cushions of straw or fern leaves. The lord's wife on his right wears her hair in a roll and is wrapped in a mantle. Standing before him on the other side of the table is a bard, attitudinizing as he recites or chants to the accompaniment of the bearded harpist, crouching on the ground close by. A friar stands behind the lord blessing the food, which is served in the simplest possible way with only one tankard and three wooden platters on the board. One of these platters, in front of the host, holds a lump of meat and he is preparing to cut it with his short sword. On the ground a skinny dog gnaws a bone. There are two scenes of the same action yet of progression: in the first two men are slaughtering a calf, while nearby the same men are stewing the same animal in its own skin, slung like a hammock between props over a fire. Over on the other side of the picture, close to the table, two men are defecating. There they are, says the picture silently: the savage Irish with their disgusting habits.

English visitors were severe about other Irish characteristics as well —idleness (Fynes Moryson thought they should work hard in the fields like honest English peasantry, and not merely loll about while their animals grazed), lack of inventive faculty (they used manpower at the plow, each man hanging onto the tail of his horse), carelessness of marriage vows, and a fondness for barbaric customs at funerals, when the deceased's family and friends "make a monstrous cry, with shrieking, howling, and clamping of hands, in like sort they follow the dead body at the burial...." Spenser for one considered keening altogether heathenish.

On the other side of the medal, the English admitted, the Irish were a remarkably good-looking people, with "wonderful soft skin." They excelled in nimbleness and flexibility. They were remarkably brave and hardy. And they made a drink called usquebaugh, or whisky, that was fit for the gods.

CHAPTER

10

A S the son of Lord Darnley and Mary Stuart, James VI of Scotland— "that vile Scot, the minion-kissing king," he was called by a later poet—was descended from the royal line on both sides, which made him the natural successor to Elizabeth. Without delay he was crowned King James I of England, Scotland, and Ireland. We have seen that the Catholics in Ireland believed that James too was Catholic but for political reasons had concealed his religion, and now the people of the towns reacted promptly. It was typical of these inhabitants, who had always been spoiled, in a manner of speaking, to assume that, because the towns had not been implicated in rebellion, they still retained certain privileges, the "liberties" as they were called, sacrificed by the countryfolk. In 1603, soon after the coronation, the people of Cork, Waterford, and Kilkenny simply took back their churches and celebrated mass in them. Mountjoy would not have it; he swooped down with his men, and the citizens were trounced. Indeed, if James did want to help the Irish Catholics—as some of them continued stubbornly to believe—his hands were tied, for in 1606 the Gunpowder Plot was discovered, and many hitherto tolerant English Protestants became hysterically anti-papist.

Though Mountjoy had done his duty regarding the open masses of the towns, he did not approve of this harsh treatment of Irish Catholics. He wrote about it after he left Ireland—he was replaced in 1604 by Sir Arthur Chichester—warning the English not to institute another Reformation, and his words were to some extent heeded. Not that religious persecution ceased, but it took another form. In pacified, supine Ireland, Catholics were discriminated against and made to pay heavily for immunity. There was the oath of Supremacy, which could always be used to keep a Catholic out of office or from the practice of law, and the recusancy fines, but at this period the greatest burden was borne by landowners who were driven out in the cause of plantation. Few in Ulster escaped. The chieftains who had helped to prepare the accusation of conspiracy against Tyrone and Tyrconnel, that which sent the earls into exile, had done so in the confident belief that they would receive as reward permission to keep their own estates from the Crown's greedy grasp. Too late they found that treachery had profited them nothing, for their vanished lords' domains, the entire counties, including their own property, were taken over. The English were eager to get on with the shiring of the north, and on one pretext or another soon confiscated Donegal, Derry, Armagh, Cavan, and Fermanagh, from all of which areas they ordered the Irish out. In May 1609 half a million acres of the land were thrown open to settlers, on an arrangement not unlike that of Munster's plantation but better thought out. This time the authorities set up three ranks, or classes, of would-be settlers. The first rank was made up of English and Scots only, and with the second rank, mostly Scots, they had their pick of the land. To qualify for place in either of these select companies an applicant had to take the Supremacy oath. The third and lowest rank, of "natives," did not have to take the oath, but they paid more rent for inferior land.

Second-rank settlers were permitted—at a price—to take Irish tenants, but no Irish could live on first-rank land. In all respects this policy was harsh, and Chichester for one was opposed to it, but greed overran all objections, and plantation went ahead according to this pattern.

At least that was the intention. In practice the arrangements were not so rigid. To say, as many have done, that the Irish were driven en masse out of their land to the hills and bogs (says Curtis) is rhetorical exaggeration, and he goes on to argue a case for the plantation makers, declaring that not absolutely *all* Irish were expelled from their ancestral acres. There were several hundred native freeholders (in rank three) who got grants; there were also native grantees from earlier days for whom the Crown had confirmed their rights, so they were untouchable. Thus what with one or the other among the Irish aristocracy some O'Donnells remained, as did quite a few O'Neills. Brian Maguire got his father's estate intact and became baron of Enniskillen. Magennis of Iveagh was lucky enough to have his whole country granted back to him—he became Viscount Iveagh. And so on. Still, more than these were forced out, and fate had not finished playing tricks on the survivors.

The lot of the poorer Irish was often less harsh than the aristocracy's. In theory they were all ordered to get out, but after a little time it became evident that the settlers could not in fact do without them, and they were tempted back much as their forerunners had been first ejected and then recalled by the Norman invaders. One of the new factors in the plantation of Ulster was that the City of London's twelve companies obtained a huge grant, practically all the north half of county Derry, with rich forest and fishery resources, on which they pledged themselves to build a stated number of towns and to admit only English and Scottish tenants. But not enough English and Scots came forward to take the available places, and the company managers discovered that the native Irishman was a better tenant anyway, working industriously on his own small holding and willingly paying a good rent. The Irish were also better laborers than most new arrivals, so the settlers ignored the original rules and thousands of Irish tenants settled on City of London land. If it had not been for them the London Corporation would

probably have found it impossible to pull through the
first lean years of plantation, but at last, a few at first and
then a greater number of Scottish Lowlanders made their
appearance, and so did New English settlers. Between them
they changed the face of Ulster, cutting down the trees and
carving out neat little farms from what had been grazing
country. There is a 1622 plan of a plantation village on
Lough Neagh that was built by the Salters' Company, county
Londonderry: it could as well be a textbook blueprint for any
English village, laid out in neat straight rows of timbered
houses and complete with fortress and church.

The church, of course, would be a Protestant one, and if
Scots predominated in the village, as seems likely, it would be
Presbyterian. Nevertheless the Irish continued to be Catholic.
There were no more public masses like those put down by
Mountjoy, but the strictures against their worshiping were
more or less forgotten except by the occasional bigot. The
new settlers had other things on their minds. "The situation
was chaotic. The English settlers, whatever they made it
look like by law and on paper, held what they had taken by
force, or the threat of force. The Irish, defeated in the wars,
did not consider the matter closed. Certainly there would be
rebellion again; in the meantime they raided and robbed the
settlers whenever possible. Their religion, though in theory
prohibited by English law, was generally and openly practised
since no Deputy in his right senses could risk suppressing it.
It was as strong among the 'old English' landowners and
among the small but important middle class—lawyers and
merchants who on the whole supported law and order—as
among the so-called 'wild Irish' and their chiefs" (C. V.
Wedgwood, *Thomas Wentworth*, pp. 128-29).

"The government took it for granted," says Aidan Clarke,
"that [the Old English] were disloyal, and suspected that the
chief among them were in constant communication with
England's enemies on the continent. In many cases, the
government was right" *(Course of Irish History,* p. 193).
But religion rather than politics, he adds, was the real tie
between Ireland and the Continent. Rome had undertaken a

campaign to recover the ground lost during the Reformation. To strengthen the Catholic Church in Ireland she appointed bishops to sees that had long been vacant and recruited members for religious houses—especially the Franciscan: an Irish Franciscan, Father Luke Wadding, was very active in Rome. Most important of all, the Romans arranged educational facilities abroad for young Irishmen wanting to enter the priesthood. Of course all this had to be under cover and out of Protestant sight, but "a steady stream of young men crossed to the continent, to enter one or other of the twenty Irish colleges which prepared them for the Irish mission....And this intimate and continuous contact with continental Catholicism was the lifeline of the faith in Ireland" (Ibid., p. 193). Thus it was inevitable that the educated Irish Catholic should exhibit a distinctively French, or Spanish, or Italian coloration in his thinking, since such youths were not permitted to study in English schools: to do so would entail taking the oath of Supremacy.

Ties with Europe were not confined to the educated classes in Ireland. Boys who liked army life naturally wanted to avoid service under the English, so they slipped away to the Continent and joined foreign forces there, as forerunners of the "Wild Geese." In due course, many countries could boast that their best officers were Irish. As with mercenaries everywhere, the loyalties of such men were adaptable: they had to be.

In such surreptitious ways many members of the middle classes were accommodated. It was the Old English aristocrat who was caught in the middle, unable to hold office or practice law or teach school or take university degrees save on sufferance and always under the disability of the Supremacy-oath threat. This was worse than the recusancy fines. Many were blackmailed and none were free of fear. In 1617 matters were taken out of the hands of some of the great families, tenants in chief of the Crown, when the king established a court of wards, which included the deputy and chancellor and took over the affairs—and the education— of minor sons of the family heads. Invariably the court pocketed a healthy portion of the estate at the same time, but that is by the way. The boys were educated at Trinity or in England, in Protestant schools, where they were under constant pressure to adopt the religion of the English, and anyone who knows what it is to be odd man out at school can understand why many of them gave in. James Butler, later earl and then duke of Ormond, was educated at Lambeth and became, says Curtis, the first *convinced* Protestant in his family, for the Ormond who was Elizabeth's favorite had been Protestant merely for diplomatic reasons, as was—for a time —Hugh O'Neill. Other peers of native stock went the way of the new Ormond—the earls of Kildare, Barrymore, Thomond, and Inchiquin. But some went the other way. By the time Charles I came to the throne, surprisingly enough, the Bagenals were Catholic.

While Ulster was being shired and transformed, an earlier battlefield of plantation, Munster, was undergoing a transformation of her own. At last the county that had produced the earl of Desmond and defeated the Elizabethan planters was tamed, becoming an English, Protestant province, a change that was due in large part to one man— Richard Boyle, earl of Cork. Curtis calls him "the outstanding example of the new magnate type that had supplanted the lords and chiefs of Ireland" (*History of Ireland*, p. 237). Boyle, born in England, arrived in Ireland in 1588 with no money at all. But he must have collected a little, and that little was enough to start him off when he found Sir Walter Raleigh's vast properties in Munster neglected and running to seed. Raleigh, in disgrace and ruined, had forgotten all about his early plans to colonize Ireland. Boyle bought up the lot, of (it will be remembered) immense acreage, for £1000, adding marginal lands that cost practically nothing. (Among them was the College of Youghal: Boyle was to hear a good deal about that years later.) On this great expanse he built towns and developed the industries of iron smelting and linen weaving, and profited so greatly that in 1620 he became earl of Cork. He was a prototype of the bullying political boss, the ward heeler. In business, no doubt, he was a buccaneer. But one of his many sons, Robert, discovered Boyle's law, and was a bright star of the Royal Society.

In England the fast-growing Protestant sect called Puritans were always on the watch for signs of "toleration" in the king and his ministers. James may or may not have wanted to be tolerant, but in many other ways he would not pretend to agree with popular opinion. He did not share the English phobia against Spain, but believed that Philip III would be a better ally than enemy, and behaved accordingly. In 1620 his son-in-law Frederick, the Elector Palatine, became embroiled in war against the Emperor of the Holy Roman Empire because he accepted the crown of Protestant Bohemia, which was in rebellion. Ferdinand, the Emperor, was the cousin of Philip and also his brother-in-law. The English were all for making war on Spain as well as Ferdinand for the sake of their popular princess Elizabeth, now queen of Bohemia, but King James dragged his feet. During the next two years the Commons objected more than once to the king's method of getting money out of Catholics: he exempted them from penal laws if they paid up—and the members were even more hostile, of course, when they got wind of James's project to marry his son Charles, the prince of Wales, to the Spanish infanta. James was angered by this criticism, and in effect told the House to mind its own business. He persisted in his attempt to make a match between Charles and the Spanish princess, not only for the sake of cementing friendly relations with Spain but because the girl would bring a huge dowry, and he was badly in need of money. (The Stuarts were always badly in need of money.) In 1622 he sent Charles, along with his favorite, Buckingham, to Madrid to consolidate arrangements. But there things did not go well for Anglo-Hispanic relations. No marriage took place, Charles came back furious and humiliated, and Buckingham urged James to make war on Spain forthwith. James did not, but after his death in 1625, when the prince became Charles I, such a war seemed far more likely, and

Charles's attitude toward the papist nation left nothing for the anti-Catholics of England to desire. On the occasion of his marriage to the French princess Henrietta Maria, the king readily promised the people never to extend toleration to Roman Catholics even though he was marrying one.

He now found out, however, that even the most rabid anti-Catholics are not necessarily openhanded when it comes to crusades. James might have got money for a war with Spain, but Charles found the Commons very reluctant to vote him funds for the same purpose, and he decided to look elsewhere. Inevitably, his eye lit on Ireland. The paradox of making a Catholic nation pay for an anti-Catholic war did not trouble him. He knew that the Old English, along with the native Irish landowners and the professional classes, wanted nothing so much as peace and security. As Catholics, no matter how loyal they professed themselves to be, they were constantly at the mercy of the New English. They still possessed considerable wealth but it was a constant struggle to hold onto it, since the New English could always raise the cry of No Popery. As for the professional classes, "their right to hold office, to practise at the bar, to sit or vote in Parliament (all of which things, in fact, they did) could always be called in question" (C. V. Wedgwood, *Thomas Wentworth*, p. 130). The remedy for all their ills, it seemed to Charles, was obvious. He would simply sell security to the rich Old English and Irish Catholics. In 1628 the Catholics of Ireland agreed, in return for privileges called "the Graces," to pay over a period of the following three years the huge sum of £120,000. Most important of these privileges were a guarantee that sixty years' possession of land amounted to legal tenure, and that Catholics would be permitted to hold office without taking the oath of Supremacy. These two Graces were the cause of most of the protest that followed, when the New English realized how severely such leniency would affect their well-being.

Charles I had his war and it did not turn out well for England. Then, of course, he regretted his bargain and looked around for a way to get out of it. Fulfillment of his promises was postponed again and again. There would have been far more disillusionment among the Irish had they not been Catholic and aristocratic. As Catholics they respected the conservative order, and as aristocrats they had a vested interest in maintaining authority. Besides, it was not always so bad: conditions in individual cases were often ameliorated. Charles himself occasionally turned a blind eye to this or that infraction of the law, and his officials ignored things as well, mainly because they could do nothing else. At that time, for example, there were thirty "mass houses" in Dublin, illegal but undisturbed.

Then the deputy Lord Falkland was recalled, and in his place as viceroy came Thomas Wentworth, viscount from Yorkshire. This ambitious, capable, and curiously unattractive man had an overwhelming ideal, to add to the power of the monarchy and thus impose a beautiful pattern of order on society. In conversation and correspondence with his good friend Archbishop Laud, Wentworth often used the word "thorough," which both summed up his philosophy and described his methods in dealing with Irish questions. He made up his mind at the beginning that Ireland could be made to yield far more revenue than she was doing, through trade and manufacture—"naturally of a kind not to compete with England," says Dame Veronica Wedgwood dryly. He aimed, always, to consolidate the king's authority. He intended to weaken the power of the magnates, and to bring the people —wild Irish, tame Irish, Old and New English alike—into "a state of suitable docility." He showed all the beliefs and prejudices of Englishmen of his epoch, the biographer observes, seeing in ancient Irish civilization nothing good. "It was to him self-evident that the wild Irish would be better men, more pleasing to God and happier in their lives, if they gave up their savage ways, learnt more sensible and profitable methods of tilling the land, were grouped into villages and towns, apprenticed to trades, and turned as fast as possible into clean, industrious Protestants" (Wedgwood, *Thomas Wentworth,* pp. 130-31). But he was efficient and hard-working, and whatever one may think of his aims, he achieved many of them against tremendous odds. Dublin depressed him at first. He wrote of streets and countryside so boggy that he couldn't even take a walk, let alone go shooting, but by the time he left, seven years later, either the city had changed or Sir Thomas had learned to love it as it was. On the other hand, Dublin never learned to love Sir Thomas.

Early in his tour of duty he had to deal with the king's Graces. Charles's debt to the Catholics had now been outstanding for several years, the Old English having made their final payment long since. Of course the money was gone, and the king was more than ever averse to keeping his promises: indeed, it is exceedingly doubtful if the anti-Catholics of England would have countenanced his doing so. Wentworth had other reasons for disapproving of the Graces, for if the important clause was honored and sixty-year ownership was confirmed, the holdings of the New English could not be expanded. The deputy was full of a plan to plant Connacht, and this plantation would be impossible if a lot of Irish and Old English landowners stood in his way. Wentworth outlined his strategy and then, with the king's approval, called together a parliament for the spring months of 1634. During the intervening time he worked hard to pack the assembly so that he could be sure of getting a Protestant majority, but the resulting numbers disappointed him, and he put off the question of the Graces until parliament's next session in the autumn of that year. In the meantime, however, he persuaded the members to contribute a further sum of money by hinting that such subsidies would help the cause of the Graces when the time came. Not until November did he make public his decisions about the king's pledges. They came like a slap in the face to the Old English, for he coolly declared that he was jettisoning the two chief clauses relating to land titles and toleration of Catholics practicing law or holding office. For land ownership, he said that sixty years' possession was not sufficient to give an owner valid title. However, he reminded parliament, he had already set up a Commission for Defective Titles, and each grant could be examined there, under his own viceregal eye. As for toleration, here too each case could be judged on its own merits, and the decision would depend on the deputy's discretion. The deputy could always suspend a Catholic lawyer or officeholder by requiring him to take the oath of Supremacy. In short, the Irish Catholics were exactly where they had been before, save that they were the poorer by £120,000 plus the subsidies they had voted that spring, and were now certain to lose Connacht as well.

The strength of the members' protests surprised Wentworth. There could be no question of the Catholics' winning any remission through protesting, but he was irked nevertheless. He was willfully blind to the fact that their grievances were very real, and put down their opposition to the influence of friars and Jesuits, to their own "insolent forwardness," and other faults of temperament. "A bigoted Protestant, he felt, at best, contempt, and at worst a real hatred, for the Papists, and took a sour pleasure in retailing their quarrels, their delinquencies, or even their poverty... Catholicism was, for him, with his Calvinist and Elizabethan background, the religion of traitors and rebels. 'So long as this Kingdom continues Popish they are not a people for the Crown of England to be confident of,' he wrote. The statement was, of course, true, so long as the Crown of England continued a policy of taking away their land to give it to Protestant strangers" (Wedgwood, *Thomas Wentworth*, p. 158).

What made the deputy something particular even among bigots was that he did not really favor Protestants either— beyond, that is, generally facilitating their conquest of Ireland by confiscation. His foremost aim was to strengthen and enrich the Crown, and nothing, no great name or powerful interest apart from the Crown's, was permitted to stand in his way. He quite realized that English Protestants could outdo Irish Catholics when it came to sharp dealing and grasping ways: this was natural because it was much easier for them to indulge such propensies: knowing it, he showed no caution in dealing with such malefactors. He was merciless. Even Protestant landowners and planters were required to present their grants for review, and Wentworth was quick to spot cases where they had evaded tax. Not only did he make them disgorge, but often raised their rents as well. One of the most flagrant wrongdoers in this respect was the mighty earl of Cork, whose fortune and rise depended in large part on the Munster lands he acquired at the beginning of his career. Wentworth was easily able to trace evidence that in the original purchase Boyle had grabbed too much land. An outstanding example was the College of Youghal, originally a charitable foundation for the sick. It was a mistake for Boyle to have taken the college, because in so doing he contravened a law against dealing in Church property. In the years that had passed since the purchase, when Lord Cork had every reason for supposing it was all forgotten, he had settled the college on one of his close relatives as a marriage settlement. The marriage involved, as the other partner, a connection of Wentworth's, and Cork naturally supposed that the deputy would be willing to overlook the whole affair for that reason if for no other, but he misjudged his man. Nothing of the sort would have deflected Wentworth, and he continued pressing until the whole matter was taken to England for adjudication. Judgment went against the earl and he had to give up the college and pay a penalty of £15,000. With expenses and other losses contingent on the case, Cork's encounter with Wentworth proved exceedingly costly. "God forgive the Lord Deputy," he wrote in his diary. Later he changed the entry to "God never forgive the Lord Deputy."

Another instance of Wentworth's tactless zeal was the quarrel he picked with the mighty London Corporation over its settlement in Deny. There the merchants had bypassed the law in many ways, until Wentworth caught up with them. The Corporation had to pay heavily —£70,000 fine and confiscation by the Crown of the profitable customs of Coleraine and Derry. In the end they were squeezed out from Ireland altogether, and the names of another body of men were added to the now formidable list of the deputy's enemies in high places. Thorough Sir Thomas also turned his withering, probing eye on the Scots Presbyterian Church of Ulster, and made the churchmen pay taxes which, he claimed, they had attempted to evade.

As if to prove that absolutely nothing was sacred, he attacked the original towns through their ancient liberties, and forced the corporations to open their doors to new industry. In the end, of course, this was a good thing for Ireland, but the towns did not like it. He also built up mercantile shipping, for which he had to sweep the nearby sea clear of pirates, and this too, one must admit, was good. He encouraged the linen industry, investing much of his own money in it— Wentworth was never above profiting personally from his work. Curtis says approvingly, "In an account of his office to the King in 1636 he could rightly claim that he had endowed the Church, wiped out the Irish debt, given the Crown a surplus of £50,000, and raised an army to keep the peace between parties" (*History of Ireland,* p. 242), and C. V. Wedgwood points out that once he had assured himself of the interests of the Crown and the Protestant settlers, he really did try to get justice for the poor and a measure of economic consideration for Ireland.

Nevertheless, he had not forgotten his plans for Connacht, and now he took an important step toward achieving their fruition. He confiscated a quarter of all Catholic-owned land in that country, and now saw the project as including Clare as well as Connacht. He had embarked on the next step when he found himself opposed in county Galway by elderly Richard de Burgh, earl of Clanrickarde. Clanrickarde was obstinate, Wentworth inflexible, and the whole business of plantation was held up. Suddenly the old earl died. This should have left the coast clear, but to Wentworth's annoyance the new earl, Clan-rickarde's heir, popped up and carried on the struggle. It all took valuable time, and the deputy chafed. Besides, he was faced by another difficulty—a strange shortage of settlers of the type he wanted for his plantation. In fact it was Wentworth himself who was responsible for this shortage. In earlier days the most energetic settlers of Ireland had been Puritans, because they felt that to colonize Ireland was to combat popery. But Puritans were also opposed to Wentworth's main aim, the centralization of the Crown's power, and as long as he was lord deputy of Ireland they would not go there. Instead, the most able and hard-working among them were now sailing to America, to build an "austere, sober and vigorous civilization in New England" (Curtis, pp. 173-74).

In England, friction mounted between the king and his subjects. Like his father, Charles did not like parliaments and seldom called them, thus annoying everyone. There was other trouble too: through Laud's agency he altered the Church service, and this stirred up the Protestants, especially the increasing number of Calvinists, for any tampering with the Church awoke their alarm at the threat of popery. Then the king infuriated the Puritans by refusing to ban shooting and dancing on Sundays—he didn't like Puritans—and in 1637 he outdid himself when, in a passion for tidiness, he tried to impose a new prayer book and various other Anglican forms of worship on the Scottish Presbyterians. The gesture had explosive effects. There was rioting in Edinburgh, and afterward the Scots did not calm down: on February 28, 1638, a number of their leaders met and signed the "National Covenant" to defend their Church. Afterward the Scots who opposed Charles in the quarrel were known as Covenanters.

Wentworth was fully aware of the dangers to the king's authority in this situation, not only in England but on his own island. There, Ulster was again the chief threat, with her hundreds of Scots settlers stirred up in sympathy with their kinsmen at home. The Covenant was circulating among them, and agents were collecting signatures. In addition, the minute the Irish of the north heard of the Scots' troubles they contributed their share of rebellious activity. Nevertheless the deputy set to work building up an Irish army in case the king should ever have need of it. The

work went slowly, for his recruiting agents were plagued by
a sudden increase of Frenchmen bound on the same errand,
who tempted prospective cannon fodder with better offers.
But by the following year, 1639, Wentworth's Irish army of
nine thousand men was in good shape.

He kept writing to the king, outlining the strategy he
thought should be followed. Above all, he said, Charles
should put off actual hostilities as long as possible. The
Irish army ought to be mustered on the Ulster coast, as
near as possible to the danger area, or even used to garrison
northern towns such as Dumbarton, so that the Scots could
not steal a march on England. But the letters went unheeded
while the king floundered on in his usual fashion, listening
to too many advisers and showing no judgment or decision.
It was still early spring in 1639 when they heard that the
Covenanters had done just what Wentworth feared, and
themselves occupied Dumbarton. Then, belatedly, Charles
pretended to give in, and to gain time signed the pacification
of Berwick. Within the fortnight he also wrote to Wentworth
and asked him to come over and help, for even Charles I
could not be blind now to the hostility of his own people.
Many of them were in sympathy with the Scots, and many
others, though they were not Calvinist, resented the war.
They refused him funds. The City of London itself fobbed
him off with the ridiculous sum of £5000.

Wentworth naturally departed immediately, confiding
the affairs of Ireland to two of his trusted lieutenants. (One
of their tasks was to carry on with the administration of a
non-resistance oath, taken by the Scots of the north: it was
known to them as "the Black Oath," and heartily hated.)
Dame Veronica Wedgwood comments that the problem
seemed to him much simpler than it was, as merely a matter
of civil rebellion against authority. "He did not understand
the religious issue as such. To him ceremonies were 'things
purely and simply indifferent.' He used those prescribed
by Archbishop Laud because it was the royal desire that he
should, not because he believed in them for themselves. If he,
with his anti-Popish fervour and his Calvinist upbringing,

was not offended by them, why should lesser men presume to raise their voices?" (Wedgwood, *Thomas Wentworth*, p. 269). Wentworth made a major miscalculation because he remained convinced that the "ancient animosity" of the English toward the Scots would be stronger when it came to war than the Puritan dislike of ceremonies or the resentment of the king's government that was binding them together. For the moment, however, his arrival and advice gave Charles more assurance. The king had already repudiated the pacification of Berwick. Now he sent peremptory messages to the Scottish parliament and refused to give audience to two covenanting peers who came to talk matters over with him. Wentworth was always at his elbow, and the Covenanters were sure that he was responsible for the change.

At New Year's 1640 the deputy's dearest ambition was gratified when the king at last conferred on him the earldom of Strafford, and he was also lifted in rank to that of lord lieutenant of Ireland. When he returned to Dublin in March—delayed on the way by painful gout and various other disabilities—it was to preside from that height over the parliament summoned by the new deputy, Wandesford. Under Strafford's eye the mixed group of Catholics and Protestants ignored their knowledge of how unpopular the war was in the countryside, and meekly voted the large sum of £180,000 to meet the expenses of hostilities.

The English Parliament—the "Short Parliament"—which met in April, was the first one in what Calvinists called "The Eleven Years of Tyranny." Strafford's return was delayed by a sharp attack of dysentery, and he could not take his new place in the House of Lords until April 23, by which time the other members of Parliament were locked in acrimonious debate over the subsidies—£850,000—wanted by the king. During these disputes word came that hostilities in the north had begun again, with the king's men in Edinburgh Castle and the Covenanters in the town firing at each other. Still Lords and Commons haggled. It seemed dangerously likely that the Commons leaders would bring up the religious grievances in Scotland along with their own, an eventuality which the king's advisers thought must be avoided at all costs: "If the sympathy between Puritan England and Covenanting Scotland was, so to speak, officially endorsed in Parliament it would be virtually impossible for the King to go on with his war" (Wedgwood, p. 285). Strafford tried to dissuade Charles from applying the Stuart cure-all—dissolution of Parliament—to the situation, but he had to give in, and the assembly was dissolved on May 5, 1640.

For some time England had been discussing finances with Philip IV of Spain. For their war in the Netherlands, the Spaniards wanted English warships to convoy their transports up the Channel, and they were ready to pay heavily for this service. It seemed to Charles and Strafford a most fortunate way out of their difficulties, but within a few months the project had to be abandoned, since the Dutch threatened that they would go to war with England otherwise. That summer Strafford was so ill that he was thought to be dying. Though by the middle of July he had recovered to some extent and was back at work, the reports of his illness had had an immediate effect on Ireland. The Irish Commons had voted £180,000 and made it possible to raise a nine thousand-man army not for love of Strafford or the king but because they were afraid to refuse. Now it seemed possible that they had backed the wrong horse. "Strafford overthrown or Strafford dead would be equally useless to those in the Irish Commons who were thinking of their own incomes and careers" (Ibid., p. 291). And Strafford could not at that moment go over to Ireland to mend his fences because the earl of Northumberland, general of the king's forces in the north, suddenly fell ill just at the moment Lord Conway in Newcastle wrote that he could not hold out for a week against the twenty thousand Scots who were on their way to attack his garrison.

In spite of being so ill and weak that he had to be carried on a litter, Strafford went north to do what he could. But the royal troops could or would not fight effectively against the Scots, who had crossed the border into England. On the twenty-ninth of August they occupied Newcastle. Charles was forced to call a "council of peers" to negotiate with them. At a meeting at Ripon the peers had to accept the *fait accompli,* leaving the Scots in possession of Northumberland and Durham and promising to pay their army until the next English Parliament met. The moment this "Long Parliament" opened, on November 3, eager members of the Irish parliament got in touch with the English members with the object of getting Strafford. The Long Parliament was more than willing to co-operate, and a whole set of complaints arrived shortly afterward, accusing Strafford of treason. He had plotted, it was said, to bring over a large army from Ireland and overthrow the government. The Irish in their confidence had already disbanded that army and removed from the hands of the deputy all the extra powers accrued during Wentworth's reign.

The trial, which ran from March 22 to April 10, 1641, would have resulted in Strafford's discharge if there had been no interference, for he defended himself brilliantly, but his opponents took steps to keep this from happening by changing the impeachment at the last minute to a bill of attainder—an "antiquated and terrible machinery for putting Strafford to death" (Ibid., p. 357). Charles refused at first to lend his signature. The usually feeble king actually stood firm in the face of threats against his office and family, until Strafford implored him not to take such a risk. Then Charles surrendered, and on the morning of May 12 Thomas Wentworth, shorn of honors and fortune, was publicly beheaded on Tower Hill.

CHAPTER

11

IT had been futile of Strafford to hope—if he ever really
did—that the sacrifice of his life would help the monarch.
That summer one power after another was stripped from
Charles I, while the Commons in its dour way reveled
in the changes. A member wrote joyfully to a friend that
reformation was "going on as hot as toast." The king's
ministers disappeared; either they ran away or they were
killed, and the members of Parliament insisted as one of
their first reforms that thenceforth the assembly *must* be
called every three years at the very least: there were to be no
more long periods of voiceless "tyranny." In his extremity
Charles thought of Ireland, and belatedly tried to salvage
some part of the loyalty existing there. To placate the Old
English and Irish, he dropped the idea of planting Connacht
and Clare and the Commission for Defective Tides. The
Graces were confirmed, and he proposed in addition a bill
to confirm those disputed sixty-year titles, but in spite of
such good things the inhabitants of Ireland, including many
of the New English, did not feel safe, and, considering
the source of the largesse, they did not rejoice either. The
king found it easy to make such promises, but even easier
to forget them if they became inconvenient. It seemed to

his subjects in Ireland that if he really wanted to win their affection he would do better to permit the Irish parliament to be reformed along the lines followed by the English. But they were not like the English: they had no way of forcing the king to agree to this, and the idea was soon dropped.

Besides, though Charles had become friendly, the Irish and Old English knew that the changes in England did not bode well for their own country. The English Parliament that held so much new power in its hands was made up for the most part of Calvinists as anti-Catholic as their friends the Scots Presbyterians. Between the Scots and the English Puritans, Ireland's ancient religion bade fair to be in more danger than ever, and to make matters worse the new deputy was not to be, as they had hoped, the popular though Protestant Ormonde, an Irishman who knew his country's ways. Instead Charles placed in the post the weakling earl of Leicester, and Leicester stayed away from Dublin, leaving things to two Puritan lord justices. Following their natural inclinations, these officials did their worst for the Catholics, among other things stopping the bill the king had ordered prepared that was to confirm the Graces. It looked as if the gloomiest prophecies of the Irish Catholics were justified. But with Strafford, the hated Wentworth, gone forever, the people of Ireland felt that there might be a way out, after all, and soon the whole country, led by the Irish of Ulster, rose in rebellion.

The two chiefs among the rebels bore names that must have sounded ominously reminiscent to English ears— Rory O'More and Sir Phelim O'Neill. According to their plans, everything should have started at the same moment on October 23, a number of small insurrections in the north coinciding with the seizure in Dublin of the Castle, but the Castle venture never even got off the ground; too many people had to be told the secret, and one of them got drunk and betrayed his companions a day ahead of time. In Ulster, however, everything went smoothly. Under O'Neill, the Irish attacked one plantation outpost after another and killed many of the settlers. The account of their cruelties and murders was bad enough in truth: then on its way to London it became exaggerated, as these things do, until it arrived in so horrific a version that the rebellion soon bore the name of "the Great Massacre." The Puritans were appalled. They never forgot that first impression, and told each other with great sincerity that they had been right all along about the papists. It was the English story of the Great Massacre that moved Oliver Cromwell to behave as he did later, when he reached Ireland as a conquering general.

Yet even at their most recalcitrant the rebels, sustained though they were by encouragement from the many Irish abroad and determined as they were to gain their ends, did not include among these ends or in their demands complete independence from England and the Crown. Their imagination does not seem to have been able to compass such a giant step. What they wanted, they declared, was something less, "the rights of Ireland as a Catholic kingdom with a viceroy acceptable to native feeling, [i.e., a Catholic] Parliament set free from the shackles of Poynings' law, and full civil and religious rights for the Catholic population" (Curtis, *History of Ireland*, p. 243).

In November Rory O'More led a rebel Irish army against government troops at Julianstown near Drogheda. This was the rebels' first taste of genuine warfare, but they acquitted themselves well and beat back the English until the latter sought refuge in Drogheda garrison: many of their number had already done the same and were staying out of danger in the garrisons of Derry, Bandon, and Cork. O'More kept Drogheda under siege while holding conversations with the leaders of the Old English, doing his best to persuade them to join the Irish. It was difficult, for the Old English, who had an ingrained habit of full loyalty to England as well as the Crown, had first to be convinced that a man *could* rebel against English troops and still remain royalist. But in the end most of them accepted O'More's arguments and took their place in what was beginning to be known as the Catholic Army. The rebellion flourished in its growth, spreading through Munster.

In England, meanwhile, the Commons were faced with a ticklish problem, for if they raised an army to suppress the rebellion—and it was inconceivable that they should not—and it was put under the king's command in the traditional way, he might very well use it by turning it against themselves. Finally they adopted an expedient suggested by Pym and did not put the king in charge. Instead, the commanders were men approved by Parliament. These forces were called the New Model Army—a fitting name for a completely new arrangement. To raise money for this army, Parliament declared the estates of the rebel leaders confiscated and offered for sale to "Adventurers." Also, the unfortunate king had to agree to an "Adventurers Act" which forbade him to pardon rebels from that time on.

Charles was not sitting down under all these indignities, but there was little he could do. He made a visit to Scotland to rally support, but the reaction was very muted, and small wonder, for the Scots now felt far more friendly toward his enemies then toward him. When the Commons in their turn solicited help from the Scots, on the grounds that the northerners should help to save their kinsmen in Ulster, the appeal had an immediate effect, and in April 1642 a large Scottish army under the command of General Munroe landed at Carrickfergus, where it was joyfully welcomed by the Ulster Scots: many of these, in fact, joined up on the spot. It was soon evident to Munroe, however, that there was at the moment little to do, for by the end of the month the rebellion seemed practically over and most of the Ulster insurgents had been pushed back into their home country.

London, in fact, seemed more turbulent than Dublin, for the reformists in the English Commons, having reorganized the army and restored a firm hand in Ireland, were turning their attention to the cause nearest their hearts, the rebuilding of the Church of England. For a start they proposed abolishing the bishoprics and throwing out the Book of Common Prayer. One of the most active members in the movement was Oliver Cromwell, M.P. for Cambridge who that year was appointed captain of parliamentary horse. This forceful man was a member of the family of the Thomas Cromwell who as vicar-general to King Henry VIII had carried out the Act of Supremacy and begun the suppression of the monasteries and confiscation of their property in 1536, more than a century earlier. The new seventeenth-century proposals to get rid of the bishops and the prayer book were too much for the House of Lords: the peers objected, and King Charles, encouraged by this support, dared to resist the reformists. But the Commons easily got the people on their side, stirring up latent fears (which they themselves shared) with a scare story of an impending papist rising in England that would lead to scenes of carnage to rival the Great Irish Massacre. A mob thronged the streets, obediently shouting, "No Popery! No bishops!" and the Commons promptly impeached thirteen bishops all at once. Charles I became alarmed for his wife, for he was convinced that the Commons meant to impeach her next. In a rage, he tried to get ahead of them by impeaching a number of their leaders. As a king, however, he could not legally do this, and the matter was taken out of his control in any case because the threatened men simply disappeared.

Things had now reached so critical a stage that war was seen as inevitable. The king sent Henrietta Maria to the Continent where she would be out of danger and could rally support. Then he retired to York to carry on a correspondence, usually angry, with Parliament in London. Deliberately the Parliamentarians now sent to him the famous Nineteen Propositions, fully aware of the fact that this paper amounted to unbearable provocation, suggesting as it did a new constitution for England that provided Parliament with supreme power in all areas, including the upbringing and education of the royal children. The king promptly rejected the Propositions, as they had known he would, and the Parliamentarians prepared for war, which was declared August 22, 1642.

All these developments deeply affected the situation in Ireland. The Irish parliament that met in Dublin that same month had suffered a drastic change, as only Protestants

were now allowed to participate. King Charles appointed
Ormonde as his lord lieutenant, and the marquis naturally
became head of the Protestant royalists in the country. Since
all Catholics were excluded from parliament, the Irish and Old
English formed their own group, the Catholic Confederacy,
at Kilkenny in October, and this too was royalist. Their
motto was "Ireland united for God, king and country,"
and the aims of the Confederacy, anxiously declared on
every occasion, remained much the same as those of its
forerunners—liberty of conscience, government by Catholic
officials, restitution of lands that had been confiscated on
religious grounds, liberty of trade with the Empire, and
repeal of Poynings' Law so that the Irish parliament might
be independent. During the early days of the rebellion the
Catholic leaders, realizing that they needed experienced
soldiers, had sent out a call for help that was forwarded
throughout the widespread brotherhood of Irishmen abroad.
Of the many foreign-trained soldiers who responded, the
Catholics were particularly happy to welcome two military
stars who had served their apprenticeship in the Spanish
forces: the Spanish army was generally acknowledged to
be the best training school of all. One of these men was
Owen Roe O'Neill, nephew of Tyrone of proud memory:
the other, General Preston, was a member of an Old English
family. They brought with them arms, money, and messages
of encouragement from foreign well-wishers, among them
Richelieu.

"For seven years thereafter the situation was extremely
confused" {Course of Irish History, p. 200). In saying this,
Aiden Clarke can hardly be disputed. During that time there
were two civil wars in England, because hostilities were
interrupted when the king was captured. Many changes
took place before the period was over. The Scots and
Parliamentarians came together in 1643 to sign the Solemn
League and Covenant, then fell out; the Parliamentarians
themselves split forces and Oliver Cromwell headed the
splinter party, the Independents. Parliament quarreled with
its New Model Army. The Scots entered a secret alliance

with Charles I. The Irish picture is scarcely less complicated: there were two armies of royalist sympathies there, king's and Confederacy's, while against both—for a time—were the Scots under Munroe and the troops of the English Parliamentarians. Inconclusive fighting took place all over the map. Even a truly brilliant victory won by Owen Roe O'Neill against the Parliamentarians at Benburb on the Blackwater, in 1646, did nothing to settle the war. The Catholic Confederacy had long been showing signs of strain between the Irish and the Old English who belonged to it, for they were held together only by their religious faith. Otherwise they were wide apart. Politically the Old English were conservative, with the sentiments of the landowners most of them were. On their own they would have made up their quarrel for less reward than the Irish had set their hearts on. The Old English had always found it possible to live their lives without full official recognition of their Catholicism, and they knew something the Irish would never admit; that confiscated lands could not in most cases be recovered, and it was hopeless to speak of such readjustments. But they would not persuade their Irish partners to lower their sights.

Now and then in the course of the wars King Charles attempted to avail himself of support from Ireland. In 1645 he sent an English Catholic peer on a secret mission to the Confederacy, to promise recognition of their religion and the restoration of confiscated churches if in exchange they would send ten thousand men to join him in England, but when this arrangement was discovered and exposed he felt it wise to deny all knowledge of the proposition. However, during the following year he fell into worse straits, and became willing to make such offers publicly. In the "Ormonde Peace," so-called because the lord lieutenant was the king's messenger, Charles promised to waive the Supremacy oath, repeal religious penalties, and confirm all land titles from 1628 if the Catholics would help him. By that time, however, even the stanchest royalist was bound to ask himself whether the king had it in his power to keep such promises, or any promises at all. Nor was it in the Confederacy's power to send him the help he required. Nevertheless many Old English would have agreed to the Ormonde Peace if they had not been deterred by the presence of the papal nuncio Rinuccini. This official had been sent by Rome to Kilkenny in 1645, his errand being to stiffen Catholic resistance. Though never openly anti-monarchy, Rinuccini was strongly opposed to the Peace and to the sentiment expressed by Colonel Walter Bagenal when he said, "We shall certainly be overwhelmed if we do not support the king." Those who continued to insist on acceptance were excommunicated by their priests, and in the face of such a telling argument the offer was at last refused.

Which was just as well, considering that before the matter was settled any offer made by King Charles I had become purely academic. Cromwell and his Independents controlled the English Parliament by the end of 1646, and the king, cornered on the Isle of Wight, was practically incommunicado. Ormonde in Dublin, hearing that a Roundhead army was on its way to Ireland to tidy up matters and force his surrender, chose to let the town go without resistance. Better to surrender to English rebels, he said philosophically, than to Irish rebels. He handed over the sword of state and departed, but though the Confederacy recognized the advisability of occupying the town, and sent troops to head off the approaching Roundhead troops, they failed miserably.

A fantastic scramble now followed, with all the embattled parties seeking fresh positions and alliances. Those who found themselves on the same side in the cause of monarchy were an odd combination, the Scots, the English who opposed the Independents, the Ulster settlers, many New English, Ormonde, and most of the Catholic Confederates. But it was Cromwell who held the king: Cromwell and only Cromwell could decide his fate. The Roundhead chief tried for months to find a way of handling his unwilling protege, until at last the king's repeated refusals to give up any of his powers—God-given powers, as he sincerely believed— forced Cromwell to the irretrievable step of regicide. This decision was more shocking than most of us today can realize. The Independents' leader faced tremendous opposition in his own ranks as well as from royalists, but in spite of everything he declared that the king must stand his trial. To almost everyone such treatment of a king was nothing less than blasphemous. Charles ruled by divine right and could not be treated like an ordinary mortal—certainly not like a common criminal. But Cromwell was determined. To deal with Charles I any more, he said flatly, was to meddle with an accursed thing—and Cromwell controlled Parliament.

In December 1648 the formalities were arranged through a "Rump Parliament," a gathering of a very few members after the others had been got rid of, deliberately, on technicalities, a process known as "purging." This select body, on a vote of twenty-six to twenty, set up a high court of justice to try Charles I for various crimes he was alleged to have committed. The king faced the court for the first time on January 20, 1649, and the accusations were read out to him. He refused to reply or to plead, since the king, he said, could not be tried by any superior jurisdiction on earth. After a week of these inconclusive exchanges he was sentenced to death, but only with the greatest difficulty did Cromwell manage to collect enough signatures to the death warrant to afford it the proper appearance of legality. However, he got them at last, and King Charles I was beheaded on January 30.

While most of Europe was aghast at what was considered the contravention of natural law, the royalists of England and Ireland transferred their allegiance to the victim's son, nineteen-year-old Charles II, who withdrew to Jersey for safety, and there waited to see what might now happen. It was hoped that his champions in Ireland would be able to come to the rescue. The marquis of Ormonde was there, rallying the disparate royalists in an effort to rid Dublin of the Parliamentarian troops, but their commander, Colonel Michael Jones, was just as capable as he had been when he defeated the Old English attempt to keep him out of the town. He administered a severe beating to his attackers, and after such a failure Ormonde could not hold his people together. They fell apart into their original groupings.

Cromwell and his party followed up the execution of Charles I with a new form of government, abolishing the monarchy and the House of Lords. England was no longer a kingdom, they announced, but a commonwealth, or free state. The work of government was done by a council of state—forty-one members, elected annually—while lawmaking was left with the easily controlled Rump Parliament. Whatever called, this arrangement was actually government by gang; with the power vested in the hands of a few military men and such civilians as they approved. There was discontent in England, in the army and the civilian world as well, and disappointment and suspicion abroad. The Scottish Covenanters, shocked by the way the Independents had turned on the Presbyterians of England, made advances to the young king, Charles II. After all, he was a Scot; he was descended from Mary Stuart and Darnley. They promised to support him and help to reinstate him if in return he would promise to support their religion. Charles II did not want to give a flat yes or no. He had no temperamental affinity with the Covenanters; it would be far more to his taste if the royalists in Ireland, or friends of the Stuarts on the Continent, could help him, but he needed friends wherever he found them, and could not afford the luxury of offending the long-faced Scots. He waited hopefully for better news from Ireland, but August brought no comfort from that direction, when it was learned that Cromwell, at the head of a seasoned army of twenty thousand, was in Dublin, bent on recovering the kingdom for the new English republic, and on exacting revenge for the Great Massacre of Ulster. Passionately zealous in his religion, he held the whole body of Irish Catholics—the papists, as he always called them—responsible for the Ulster murders. By September 3 he had taken his army up to Drogheda, which was garrisoned by men of the Confederacy, and besieged the town. The inhabitants refused to surrender, whereupon Cromwell's men assaulted and overwhelmed their stronghold, killing nearly all the people—thirty-five hundred of them, men and women alike. According to the rules of war, as some historians have observed, this action was justified, because Drogheda's garrison had made the besiegers assault the town instead of surrendering on demand. Nevertheless the massacre shocked even the English, especially when Cromwell repeated it in Wexford, where he next went. After these two examples, townspeople everywhere were quick to surrender to the invaders.

Where Cromwell did not go he sent his officers, so that before winter overtook them the English had subdued Munster and Ulster as well as Leinster. The people were in terror, but many did not dare to give in even now, for they were convinced that under these cruel ravagers the future would be even worse for themselves and all other Catholics than the dreadful present. It was true that Cromwell usually advocated liberty of conscience—indeed, his was the first official recommendation of this reform—but he excluded Roman Catholicism. "I meddle not with any man's conscience," he proclaimed in Ireland, "but as for liberty to exercise the mass, I must tell you that where the Parliament of England has power, that will not be allowed."

In March 1650 he captured Kilkenny, seat of the Confederacy where those who did not surrender escaped to the western regions, but two months later came disturbing news of the Scots and the move they were planning, to restore Charles II to the throne of England. Cromwell felt impelled to return to London, leaving his son-in-law Ireton in charge, but Irish resistance continued for another two years, and the battles and ensuing punishment remained savage in the true Cromwell tradition. "Thus Cromwell's name continued to be associated in Irish minds with starvation as well as slaughter," says Dr. Ashley, "and no later concessions made by English governments in the way of free trade or representation at Westminster could ever wipe his awful curse from the memories of Irishmen" (*England in the Seventeenth Century*, p. 94). In the same unbending fashion the English regarded the Irish throughout the wars

of 1649-52 as the men who had carried out the Great
Massacre of 1641. "Nothing could smooth away, hide, or
bury the bitterness of those years which has helped to shape
Irish history ever since." Aidan Clarke says the same: "The
indiscriminate inhumanity with which [Cromwell's] revenge
was exacted... became indelibly impressed upon the folk
memory of the Irish" *(Course of Irish History,* p. 202).
Modern tourists comment on the Irish tendency to attribute
to the heavy hand of Cromwell every ruined building in
sight, from a ninth-century round tower to a burned-out
barn dating from 1945, but the genuine ruins are there too.
"Of the lot of them, Cromwell was the worst, to my way
of thinking," a Wexford farmer recently said to the writer.
"He *spoiled* so much."

As a formal war the rebellion came to an end in May 1652 on
the day Galway surrendered, but a large number of armed
men still held out in isolated pockets. These, an estimated
thirty thousand in number, surrendered in their turn when
the English leaders sent them the message that they would be
free to go abroad if they preferred that to being imprisoned.
It was not to the advantage of Cromwell's government to kill
or otherwise punish so many, but it *was* useful to get them
out of the country, and the men were glad to go. Ireland was
left with a very low population, about half a million at most.
    The day of reckoning for the others arrived. The leaders,
those who today would be called war criminals, were tried
at Dublin and fifty-two of them sentenced to death—a figure
which, by the standards of the time, was moderate. One who
died on the block was Sir Phelim O'Neill, another Sir Walter
Bagenal, but Rory O'More was already dead and so beyond
the power of the court to condemn. Then came the turn of
the landed gentry, who were sorted out into two lots, those
guilty of participation in the rebellion and all the others. The
guilty lost their estates and property rights. The innocent
were supposed to keep theirs, at least some of it, but it soon
became apparent that the victors, heavily in debt as they
were to the "Adventurers" who had lent them money and

the soldiers and officers who had fought for them for little pay, would need all the good land available from innocent people as well as guilty. No matter: such matters were easily arranged in a conquered country, by transplantation. The authorities set aside the two countries of Connacht and Clare, which had so often been threatened by Strafford with plantation but had escaped at the last moment. On these they settled the innocent landowners, with acreage that approximated the lands that had been taken away from them. The other twenty-six counties were now free and became the property of the English government, and they were used to pay off creditors. This Act of Settlement was known as the Cromwellian settlement. It left the poor, those who owned property of less than ten pounds' value, untouched, with a general pardon.

It was a gigantic task to move so many transplanted landowners with their households, transport them across the country, and put them down on their new lands. Eleven million acres were involved. Only a Hitler would attempt it today. But it was done: by the end of 1655 it had all been accomplished, and the rest of the country was mapped and distributed. In this "elaborate confiscation," as Curtis calls it, the government took over the towns as well, and all Church property, which was disestablished. Cromwell's policy of toleration was extended to all Protestants. Most soldiers who were paid off with small allotments sold their land and went back to England, but the officers and investors, who fared better, settled down contentedly on their broad acres. They were not even faced with a labor problem—the poor people remained and went on working on the land. Dr. Clarke points out that the Cromwellian settlement was not so much a plantation as "a transference of the sources of wealth and power from catholics to protestants. What it created was not a protestant community, but a protestant upper class" *(Course of Irish History,* p. 203).

Cromwell's hurried return to England was due to a crisis of conscience on the part of the Commonwealth commander in chief, Fairfax, which in turn was due to recent developments in Scotland. There, young King Charles II, having given up hopes of more assistance from congenial allies, was listening to the blandishments of the Covenanters, and General Fairfax was in a strange state of mind about the situation. Ever since the beheading of Charles I he had suffered doubts and remorse about regicide, and it seemed plain that the Commonwealth army would soon be fighting the Covenanters. Fairfax felt that he could not be a party to such a war, because—as he reminded Cromwell when they met—he too had signed the Solemn League and Covenant: all of them had signed it.

On June 23 King Charles took the last step and himself swore to the Covenant. With the Scots preparing at top speed for the approaching hostilities, Cromwell realized that it was no time to indulge in soul-searching with his old friend Fairfax. Fortunately, he himself was a brilliant officer and tactician, as he had proved at Marston Moor and other battles. On June 26, therefore, Cromwell was appointed captain general and commander in chief of all Commonwealth forces, and Fairfax retired. During the autumn, under Cromwell's command the army defeated the Scots at Dunbar, and a year later repeated the exploit at another big battle at Worcester.

By this time Cromwell had become England's mainstay— in a manner of speaking he *was* England, and like most strong men he brooked no opposition. In theory Parliament, which had appointed him, had authority over him: in practice, Cromwell grew less and less inclined to admit this. Someone has said that he could not get on with parliaments and he could not get on without them. But he proved that he could get on very well without them when in April 1653, exasperated by the Rump Parliament, he expelled it, and in December a council of officers, assembled to function in the vacuum, appointed him "Lord Protector of the Commonwealth of England, Scotland and Ireland." Cromwell died comparatively young—he was not sixty— on September 3, 1658, but the effect of his protectorship on Ireland was to outlast him by many years. Under it she had become a recognized member of the Protectorate, permitted—indeed, required—to send thirty members to the English Parliament. At first, of course, these members were all Protestants, but when Cromwell died the Catholic aristocracy in their banishment naturally felt a stirring of hope that their lot might now change for the better.

It is the nature of dictators to die without leaving political heirs. Cromwell had tried to provide for the future of the Protectorate and his sons together. He named his elder son Richard as the next ruler of England, while the younger Henry was left in charge of Ireland, where he had already presided for several years, but neither of these Cromwells was strong enough to hold out. The strongest force was the army, and it was the military leaders who took control when all else had failed. Looking around for a figurehead, they decided that there was, after all, a certain advantage in monarchy. If the Commonwealth could be provided with a constitutional king, with religious liberty for all except Roman Catholics guaranteed to the people, the whole problem would be solved. And if they did select such a king, it had better be King Charles II. People looked on him with the special awe they had felt for his father. Even dyed-in-the-wool Puritans could not help entertaining a certain sentiment about the son of Charles I, as witness General Fairfax. A good deal, naturally, would depend upon Charles II's attitude to such a suggestion, but the military party decided to try the experiment.

Since his failure with the Scots royalists the young King had been eking out a difficult existence as a poor relation in one continental court after another. He was delighted to have the offer of his throne again, on almost any terms. And so on May 14, 1660, it was proclaimed in Dublin that Charles II, king of England, Scotland, and Ireland, was back on his throne, the monarchy having been restored. The Irish and the Old English rejoiced to hear that the whirligig of time had gone full circle: they were confident that their troubles would soon be over. Surely the royalists would now reap

their reward and regain what was rightfully theirs. In every
sense of the word it would be a restoration. They did not at
first appreciate the drastic change that had been undergone
by the monarchy during the past few years. The king had
not the powers his father had enjoyed, and though no doubt
he would have liked to redistribute Ireland's lands once
again in favor of his loyal Catholic subjects, he could not.
He was governed by Cromwell's successors, the Protestants
of England, and one of the terms of the Restoration was that
the Adventurers Act of 1642 should be upheld. However,
Charles's troubled life had taught him diplomacy if nothing
else, and in the early days of reinstatement he promised
good things to all.

The first step in unscrambling the situation was to
decide who were deserving and who were not. "Innocent
Protestants" who had been uprooted and transplanted
were given back their lands without argument, but the
Catholics were divided between "innocent" and "guilty."
The innocents were those who for no fault of their own had
been transplanted: among the guilty, however, were counted
all who had joined the Confederacy or had otherwise borne
arms against English troops before the Ormonde Peace, even
though they had never verbally relinquished allegiance to the
Crown. The king set up a court of claims to investigate the
alleged wrongs of many Catholics and restore their lands to
those found innocent: though it may seem surprising, there
were enough of these, in spite of all restrictions, to constitute
a big problem of accommodation: what was to be done with
all the Cromwellians now to be dislodged in their turn?
Legally they were entitled to other lands of similar value. In
fact such lands did not exist. In the end it was decreed that
the Cromwellians, or most of them, had to give up a third
of the land they held, which was then given to Catholics:
this partial solution was suggested by Ormonde, once again
lord lieutenant, who was now a duke. When everything was
settled, only one fifth of Irish land was owned by Catholics,
a third as much as they had held before the civil wars.

Incomplete as the work of recompense was, Protestants

were strongly opposed to it, and in 1667 the court of claims was closed down, after a sitting that had lasted three years. Those whose claims were not yet cleared, about three thousand of them, had to give up hope, though some had strong cases, and the Ulster Irish, of course, fared worst. Even among those lucky enough to win their cases were many who found it unable to get hold of their property after all. Disillusioned and embittered, the ruined men became outlaws who lived in the hills or forest and preyed on English settlers, often on land that had once been theirs. Such an outlaw was called in Gaelic *toraidhe,* or tory—in English, pursuer. After a time the word, by natural association, was applied to any armed royalist or Catholic, and finally it was—and is— used for a member of the Conservative party of England.

CHAPTER

12

IT was Henry VIII who created the first deep schism between the Church of England and her parent in Rome, but the rift widened immensely during the reign of his daughter Elizabeth, after the Pope announced that she was deposed. Naturally Elizabeth never considered herself ousted from the monarchy. Nor did the majority of her subjects believe that she was no longer queen—and their opinion, after all, was what mattered in the end. The Pope's bombshell, therefore, made no noise in Protestant ears, but it did cause trouble for His Holiness's followers in England; inevitably, Protestants maintained that anyone who believed in the Pope's power to make or break earthly kings was a traitor to his own country. Those who placed the greatest emphasis on this argument were the Puritans, who held that Roman Catholics must not enjoy religious toleration. Soon most of the other Protestants agreed with them.

To counteract this unwelcome development the Roman Catholics of England and Ireland, in the reign of Charles I and during the succeeding interregnum, had done their utmost to convince the Protestants of their loyal sentiments for king and country, but they made little headway against prejudice, and with the Puritan take-over in London their cause seemed lost. Then, unexpectedly, the rebellion of the dissidents in Ireland gave them a chance to prove their claims through the royalist Catholic Confederacy. They had an added incentive to fight well for the Stuarts. Now, with the monarchy restored, they were hopeful of collecting their reward, and once more they presented a request for religious toleration.

If Charles II had possessed the power to do so he would have granted the request, but he had not, and to obtain toleration through popular demand or consent was out of the question. Nor could it be got by parliamentary methods, since few of the members of Parliament were Catholic. Regardless of their real numerical superiority in Ireland— they made up about 75 per cent of the population—the Catholics were to all intents and purposes a minority. The situation was particularly hard on their clergy, for whom no provision was made. Officials of the Established Church were supplied with livings and other expenses and maintenence through the tithes that were paid by all alike, whatever their true religious leanings, but Irish priests had to be supported by a variety of makeshifts: voluntary contributions from their congregations (already taxed on behalf of the Established Church), or funds smuggled into the country from Catholics of the Continent. On such rations few grew fat. The contrast between the churches became particularly vivid with the re-establishment of the Church of Ireland a few months after the Restoration, when a whole set of new Anglican bishops and archbishops were consecrated and took control once more of Irish sees.

Like Charles, Ormonde was not opposed to toleration. Indeed, he sought a way to grant relief to the Catholics. It seemed to him that difficulties might be wiped out if the Catholics would acknowledge the authority of the state and deny the right of the Pope to depose a temporal king. Knowing Ireland as he did, Ormonde must have doubted that the Catholics themselves would accept such proposals, but there were moderates as well as extremists among them, and it seemed worth trying. Accordingly two priests who were in sympathy with the idea drew up a "Remonstrance" that covered Ormonde's two points. It started out with the declaration that all princes and governors are God's lieutenants—a blameless statement that could not be contested by the most touchy—and that the king's power in civil and temporal affairs was supreme. This, again, was indisputable. But the document went on to say that the king's power bound all his subjects, and no foreign power could release them from that allegiance. It was on this, the crux of the matter, that the Remonstrance ran into trouble and finally failed: 21 peers and 164 important laymen accepted the whole paper, but out of 2000 priests only 70 could be found willing to sign it. Once more toleration, legally speaking, became a dead issue, but in practice most people most of the time proved to be more accommodating than the law implied. Most Catholics who swore temporal loyalty were not molested, and the penal measures were seldom enforced, as long as Charles II reigned. He could hardly be called a stout champion for the rights of the Catholics or of any other body, for that matter; still, where he could temper the wind to Catholics, he did so, until the pursuing mutter of Protestant discontent caught up with him.

Thus, apart from the injustices the country inherited from the Cromwellian land settlement and the failure of the Remonstrance that Ormonde inspired, Ireland under Charles II did not do too badly. Statistics indicate that she was even reasonably prosperous: twenty-five years after the Restoration her population had risen to two million. The restrictions placed on Irish trade did not have the deleterious effect intended by English rivals. The English landowners and farmers feared competition, so they insisted on banning Irish cattle and dairy products from England. But these were sold instead on the Continent and found a ready market— Irish beef and butter were soon much in demand in Europe, and the foundations were laid for a profitable commerce that was to go on for generations. The law applying to Irish wool was the exact opposite—it could be sold *only* in England, but that too proved to be no hardship, but an advantage. All the wool was taken every year, the English buying as much as they could get. The only one of the restrictive practices that did go hard with some of the Irish was the Navigation Act of 1663. This was the second act of the same name, the first having been favorable to Irish interests in that Irish ships had a fair share of Empire trade. According to the 1663 act, however, these Irish ships could no longer carry goods directly to and from English colonies; everything in the way of colonial goods had to be sent or obtained through England, and for Irish manufacturers and merchants the regulations put finis to hopes of a fleet for Empire trade. As it happened, most of these manufacturers and merchants were Protestants—Catholics were usually excluded from their towns and corporations, which owed their existence and prosperity to other Protestants such as Richard Boyle, earl of Cork, and Thomas Wentworth, earl of Strafford. But the manufacturers and traders were penalized nevertheless, as Irishmen, and they resented it.

In 1670 two Irish archbishops, Oliver Plunkett of Armagh and Peter Talbot of Dublin, asked King Charles to reopen consideration of the land settlement and to make it easier for Catholics to live and work in Irish towns and corporations, from which they had long been barred. The prelates took this action because it seemed to them that popular opinion in England was softening toward Ireland, and the king—with his ministers—agreed that the attempt might be successful. Charles's cousin Prince Rupert was therefore made head of a commission to examine once again the claims of Irish dispossessed gentry, while the new lord lieutenant, Lord Essex, was bidden to examine and change the exclusionist rules maintained by the townships. Rupert's commission during its short existence did bring relief to a number of people, and Essex's reforms, mild though they were, provided that a Catholic wishing to hold office in a town or join a guild or company need not thereafter take the oath of Supremacy, if the lord lieutenant should agree to waive it: the applicant might take an oath of temporal allegiance instead, and—of course—at the same time repudiate the Pope's power to depose sovereigns. The improvement was slight, since the Catholic was still at the lord lieutenant's mercy and the lord lieutenant was himself dependent on the rich and powerful Protestants who ran the towns. Nevertheless the change gave to a considerable number of men the chance to get into towns and corporations hitherto closed to them.

The archbishops had judged the mood of the times correctly; there was no outcry from Protestants in Ireland or England over these mild alterations. There would have been much more noise if people had fully realized what the king was up to with his brother-in-law Louis XIV, king of France. Because England had been trounced and humiliated in her war with Holland, Charles turned to Louis for help, and had just concluded the secret treaty of Dover with the French king, according to which France was to help Charles against the enemy. Louis promised to provide French money and armed men as soon as Charles should decide that the time was ripe to announce his conversion to Roman Catholicism, for the English monarch also pledged himself to bring the whole nation into the Church with him, and there was bound to be violent public resistance if he tried to do so. In the event, Charles never did make that inflammatory announcement: there is much doubt if he ever really intended to do so. Why, then, did he sign the treaty? Was the whole thing an opportunistic trick to get help out of Louis during the next Anglo-Dutch war? Still, the king of England seems to have been sincerely Catholic in his sympathies. His brother James, duke of York, who had been openly converted, claimed later that Charles confided to him his own intention of joining the Church, and when Charles lay dying he sent for a priest and made certain of dying in the faith. But that was later, and whether he meant at this time to force the nation along with him remains a question. He kept the secret carefully. Alone he could not sign a treaty, so four ministers signed with him; of whom two were Catholic, and the other two, like Charles, were to take extreme unction on their deathbeds. No other minister was told of the ceremony.

Early in 1672 the king issued a Declaration of Indulgence that suspended all penal laws against both Nonconformists and Roman Catholics, hoping that the inclusion of Protestant dissidents would balance in the public mind the favor he was showing Catholics. In March he attacked the Dutch in the opening move of the third Anglo-Dutch war, but Louis XIV disappointed him by sending the promised help slowly, and the English couldn't hold on to their advantage. London's Parliament had not been consulted as to this new war— it was not in session at the beginning—and the members disapproved. Nor did they like the king's Indulgence in spite of its inclusion of Nonconformists. In 1673 the members had a chance to register their disapproval: the three years' vacation was over and Parliament *was* sitting. When Charles issued a second Indulgence they promptly refused to vote funds for the war, and held out until both Indulgences were canceled. The king had to give in to this and other demands of the same nature. Prince Rupert's commission was withdrawn. Certain improvements in the Catholic lot, however, were sustained: those who had penetrated into the towns and corporations remained there—always on sufferance, of course, but it was progress nevertheless, especially since the towns themselves were becoming worthy to live in. During his tour of duty Essex developed and enlarged Dublin until Wentworth would not have recognized her. The dreary mud flats were gone, there were new bridges over the Liffey, and with her population of sixty thousand Dublin was the second largest city in the British Isles.

At best it was a disadvantage to be Catholic under a Protestant English government, even when the king was secretly sympathetic to the Roman Church, but all the trouble the Irish Catholics had encountered earlier faded out and was forgotten in 1678, when Titus Oates made his appearance in London. Oates was only twenty-eight years old, but had already passed through two careers. He was an Anglican clergyman before he was expelled from his naval chaplaincy for misbehavior, and then he was a member of a Jesuit college at Saint-Omer until the Jesuits in their turn expelled him for similar reasons. He claimed to hold a doctorate from the University of Salamanca, but the claim was bogus. He had a friend Israel Tonge, a London rector, who did hold a doctorate from Oxford. Tonge, who possessed a genuine phobia about Roman Catholics, was galvanized when Titus Oates showed him a set of exceedingly popish documents purporting to be letters between Don John of Austria and the confessor to Louis XIV. These forged letters concerned a Jesuit plot to kill King Charles, massacre thousands of Protestants, and place the duke of York on the throne of a Catholic England. Tonge rushed into action and insisted that the documents be shown to the king and his ministers. Soon everybody in town knew about the Popish Plot. It was a gullible age and the English were already uneasy and suspicious —perhaps the still secret treaty of Dover was sending out waves of disturbance. Protestants grew hysterical over Oates's allegations of conspiracy, and sinister occurrences became the rule. The mysterious death of a London magistrate, though he was probably a suicide, was declared murder, and three men were executed for having committed it for some unnamed Irish priest. Charles's wife, the Catholic Catherine of Braganza, employed a secretary and a doctor who were her coreligionists. Both were imprisoned. Parliament summoned Archbishop Plunkett to London; later, after being closely questioned, he was executed. His colleague Archbishop Talbot died in prison.

Ormonde had gone out to Ireland again as lord lieutenant in 1677. Now he was directed to banish the clergy from the country and disarm all other Catholics, but Ormonde was an Irishman though a Protestant, and his sympathies were with his compatriots. He managed to defer drastic action until the first fever in England had died down, but the worst effects of the scare lingered, and injustice prevailed for a space of time. Many Catholic peers in England were impeached and ultimately executed. Catholics were excluded from both houses of Parliament. Standing before the bar of the House of

Commons Titus Oates accused the queen herself of treason, and the House immediately demanded that Catherine get out of Whitehall. Parliament also declared that the duke of York must leave the country. Here Charles put a temporary stop to proceedings, Stuart fashion, by dissolving the assembly. But when it met again in May 1679, Shaftesbury, leader of the Opposition, was ready and waiting with a bill that would have excluded Charles's Catholic brother James, duke of York, from the succession, replacing him as heir—if the king should die without issue— with the Protestant next of kin in the following generation. This Exclusion Bill passed two of the required three readings before Charles stopped its progress by again dissolving Parliament. Even the royal Stuarts could not go on forever flouting the public's demand, and after another delay James had to go into exile, though he didn't stay there long: Charles finally won out over the exclusionists, and immediately recalled his brother.

In 1685 Charles died, and the duke of York became James II of England. The moment so long dreaded by Protestants was now upon them, with an openly Catholic king on the throne, while in Ireland there was discreet rejoicing among Catholics. Surely, they felt, James would give them relief by altering if not revoking the land settlement, and recognizing their Church. But things were not as simple as all that. James felt that his hands were tied by his high office; that he had to uphold the English system even though it included the Cromwellian settlement and the supremacy of the Established Church. The worried Protestants of Ireland were assured that he intended to protect their interests, and he named his Protestant brother-in-law Clarendon as his first lord lieutenant. But the situation was artificial at best, and soon English-Irish relations began to show signs of strain. One of James's oldest and most trusted friends was Richard Talbot, brother of the victimized Archbishop of Dublin. Soon after the king mounted the throne he elevated Talbot to the rank of earl, then duke, of Tyrconnel and put him in charge of the Irish army. Tyrconnel did not even pretend to spare Protestant feelings, but ignored Clarendon—who in any case had no power over the military—and began replacing Protestant offleers with Catholics as fast as he could. The Talbots were an Old English family, and Tyrconnel, characteristically, felt no more kinship with the Gaelic Irish than any other Englishman would have done, but he was passionately loyal to the Roman Catholic Church, and saw no need for delay in reforming its position in Ireland. He scrapped the oath of Supremacy and planned to reconstitute Parliament with many more Catholic members, so that the land settlement might be revised if not repealed outright. Above all, he felt that the Irish army must be Catholic; after all, it must support the king when necessary. Clarendon objected strongly to Tyrconnel's actions, but nobody heeded him. The lord lieutenant himself had to admit Catholics to office in the civil branches of government and law, until two thirds of the judges in Ireland were Catholic, as were most of the sheriffs. Much to Clarendon's relief he was recalled early in 1687, and Tyrconnel took his place. All these changes naturally alarmed the Protestants of Ireland until they fell into panic. Many sold their lands and other holdings at a great loss, and fled to England, leaving empty the towns where they had so lately lorded it.

If at first James needed encouragement from Tyrconnel, his misgivings quickly disappeared when no great trouble seemed to result from the changes. In England, too, it seemed possible to do more for his Church than he had ever hoped for. Parliament and the country remained amiable toward his first tentative changes until his memories of the Exclusion Bill faded. Lacking his brother's sharp intelligence and understanding of human nature, the king began taking public good will for granted. Why should he not? Parliament when he asked for money gave him plenty of it, and everyone seemed determined to co-operate—or almost everyone: there was a bit of trouble during the Monmouth rebellion, but after Monmouth's execution James felt stronger than ever. It was then that he seems to have wondered why his should not be a strong Catholic kingdom like Louis XIV's. Soon he was following the example of Tyrconnel in Ireland, granting army commissions to Catholics. Parliament immediately objected, arguing that such action was illegal, but James did not listen. The members objected even more strenuously to his next project, to repeal the Test Acts, but when voices grew loud James simply prorogued Parliament— for the Stuarts never learned that this did no good in the end. James now began building his Catholic state, putting a co-religionist in charge of the fleet and appointing another master of the ordinance. He installed a Catholic at the head of an Oxford college. He introduced his Jesuit adviser into the Privy Council. In 1687 he published a Declaration of Indulgence declaring that a king could dispense with all statute law in order to secure liberty of conscience for everyone: this Indulgence was extended to Ireland. During the same year he tried to build up a new Parliament that would be more amenable to his ideas.

In April 1688 he published his second Declaration of Indulgence, abolishing the penal laws that were aimed chiefly at Catholics: he directed that this document (also extended to Ireland), be read out in the churches. At this point seven Anglican bishops disputed the king's right to dispense with the laws so summarily. James promptly committed them to the Tower to await trial, and they were still there when the king's second wife, the Catholic Mary of Modena, surprised everyone by giving birth to a boy. Until that day, the king had produced no sons. Of his two daughters by his first wife, the Protestant sister of Clarendon, the elder, Mary, was married to William, Prince of Orange. On Charles II's insistence she had been raised a Protestant, and the public had always felt reassurance in this fact. Now there was a male heir who was the child of Catholics, and Protestants of all denominations groaned to think that the country might well be governed for years to come by Roman Catholic kings. When the bishops were tried, a fortnight after the royal birth, they were acquitted, at which there was open rejoicing in England, and on the same day Parliament invited William of Orange and his wife Mary to be king and queen in place of James. Prudently, James took refuge in France with his wife and baby.

William and Mary accepted the invitation, and Parliament voted them into office February 13, 1689. Scotland naturally threw in her lot with Protestant England against the threat of popery, and Ireland, equally naturally, was for King James the Catholic. Tyrconnel with his Catholic army stood ready to fight for the cause of Rome in Ireland, knowing that he could answer for the whole island, with the exception of Derry and Enniskillen in Ulster. This exception, underestimated at the beginning, was to prove fatal to James's cause; the two towns served as mustering points for such Protestants as did not manage to escape to England, and desperation lent them strength and toughness.

As soon as James heard that his daughter and son-in-law were crowned in London he moved from France to Ireland, disembarking at Kinsale in March. He was accompanied by a few French officers and advisers, and brought with him money and arms supplied by Louis XIV.

It was certainly a religious war, but the participants in the struggle were governed by exceedingly mixed motives. With James, for example, it was not merely a matter of Catholic Ireland versus Protestant England. He was, or still considered himself to be, king of England, Scotland, and Ireland, and had no intention of contributing to Ireland's independence of the other two nations. His brother-in-law Louis's interest was even more complicated: Louis's chief preoccupation was his struggle on the Continent against the League of Augsburg, of which William of Orange was the strong man. As long as William— now William III of England—was kept busy in Ireland, there was no danger that he would bring England into the war against Louis, so the king of France did his best to attract William's attention to Ireland and keep it there. The third principal, Tyrconnel, was interested most of all in achieving a stable Catholic Ireland with or without King James. He and his party, rightly assuming that such a good chance would never come their way again, made pressing demands on James, who was very much at their mercy because he was on Irish soil, dependent on Irish aid.

The Williamite War in Ireland (as the English called it), or the War of the Two Kings (as the Irish called it), started on April 17 when Derry was besieged. Protestants had managed to fortify the town strongly, and it held out until the end of July. In the meantime, in May, James had been prevailed upon to summon to Dublin "the Patriot Parliament," which holds two melancholy records in history, being the last really Irish assembly to convene until 1922, and the last with Catholic members. Of Catholics this parliament was well supplied, Protestants being noticeable chiefly for their absence. Such business as the members transacted is interesting only in the historical sense, for nothing permanent remains of the acts. Old laws were cast aside and new ones formulated with the greatest of ease, in a dreamlike atmosphere, and though none of the new ones were ever put to the test, it must have been a happy time for Tyrconnel while it lasted.

Reversal of the land settlement was quickly followed by a declaration that Williamites were rebels, and Williamite property was accordingly confiscated. Next came liberty of conscience, and after that a matter long wrangled over, the fretful question of tithes, or taxes of one tenth the produce of a man's lands. Until then, tithes for the Established Church had been demanded of everyone regardless of his religious denomination, and—as we have noted—the Catholic clergy depended on private or charitable sources for their incomes. Now parliament settled that Protestant tithes would continue to go to Protestant ministers, the Catholic tithes would go to the Catholic clergy.

James found it useless to attempt any obstruction of these measures, nor could he prevent Parliament's abandonment of English law as it pertained to Irish trade. When the members banned the use of English coal he did not like it, but he did nothing. However, when it came to discarding Poynings' Law as the Irish wished to do, James stuck in his heels and refused to give in to public demand, knowing that if he relinquished that law England would lose her most effective control over Ireland. After a certain amount of wrangling his opponents yielded the point, and James also got his way in leaving the Church of Ireland unmolested.

It was a slow war. The siege of Derry was relieved on August I, and after defeat in one of the biggest battles in Ulster, James's troops abandoned the investment of Enniskillen as well. They retired from the north altogether. Two weeks later, when William's Marshal Schomberg landed at Bangor at the head of a large army, he found no obstacle, and the army settled comfortably in to pass the winter of 1689-90. In March 1690 seven thousand trained soldiers arrived from France to improve the quality of James's army by precept and example, but Louis made this gesture purely as a loan, not a gift, and he insisted on receiving an almost equal number of Irish troops in exchange.

William realized more and more clearly that he was in an awkward position no matter what course he took. As Louis XIV had foreseen, with the Irish war on his hands William could not give his full attention to the far more important struggle on the Continent, even though his own Holland was now endangered. Yet it would be dangerous to devote his full attention to Ireland by going over in person to finish off the war quickly; that meant leaving England open to invasion. At last William took the risk nevertheless, and landed in June at Carrickfergus, bringing with him a large army of foreign mercenaries. Soon he confronted James at Oldbridge on the Boyne, near Drogheda. The famous battle of the Boyne is generally cited as the turning point of the war and the beginning of the Jacobean downfall, not that it settled matters once and for all, but because it was important psychologically. Paradoxically, it signaled the triumph of the League over the defiant king of France, the triumph of Roman Catholicism over rebels, since even though it was Catholic Irish who were put to flight by Protestant William, William was fighting—according to Rome's viewpoint—on the right side, and James was wrong.

With Williamites occupying Dublin and all the rest of

Ireland in the east, observers considered the war over, but a fiery Irish patriot named Patrick Sarsfield, later the earl of Lucan, would not accept the conclusion. He made a stand at Limerick and defended that town so fiercely that William, straining as he was to get back to London, relinquished the struggle for that year and departed. Tyrconnel also departed, for France with Louis's soldiers, whom he was returning. Sarsfield took over his command and carried the war through the following winter. It came to an end finally in the summer of 1691, after the Dutch General Ginkel won a hard battle at Aughrim. Many men were killed on both sides, until Waterford and Galway came to terms with the Dutchman and surrendered.

This left Limerick alone still unconquered. But Sarsfield's sentiments toward the struggle had changed; like many other Irish he had come to realize that he was being a cat's-paw for Louis XIV, and he resented the position. Tyrconnel died suddenly in August, and Sarsfield took command once more, but almost immediately announced that he was willing to talk about surrender with Ginkel. On October 3 the two commanders signed the treaty of Limerick. One of this treaty's terms stipulated that any Irish soldier who wanted to go to France was free to do so, and transport would be provided by the victors. Sarsfield himself elected to go, as did about fourteen thousand others—the first of the "wild geese" of Ireland who flew from their country in greater and greater numbers during the following century. It happened that much of the 1691 transport was provided unexpectedly: just after the treaty was signed a great French fleet arrived off Limerick, loaded with a considerable army—material help at last from Louis, which came too late to be of any use on the field. However, they were in time to carry thousands of Irish soldiers back to France.

"Seldom in history have a few thousand men, departing into exile, represented as these did almost the whole aristocracy, the fighting force, and the hope of a nation," says Curtis *(History of Ireland,* p. 273). Sarsfield and the others who sailed away were motivated chiefly, he observes, by a sense of duty toward the undeserving James: it was a pity, thinks Curtis, that they did not put Ireland first. But it has always been easier for a person than an abstract idea like that of the nation—and the nation was scarcely more than an abstract idea at that time—to attract loyalty.

The terms of surrender accepted by Sarsfield for Limerick appeared tolerable and were much like those for Galway and Waterford. Catholics were to enjoy the same right to worship in private as they had held under Charles II. Officers and soldiers in the garrisons were promised that they could retain their property and the right to practice their peacetime professions, and Sarsfield insisted on a further clause stating that this privilege was to be extended to certain western counties held by the Irish until the end of the war. All in all it seemed a generous agreement, for which the Irish had to thank William's impatience to wind up hostilities on their island. But all did not go smoothly. When the Irish Protestants heard of the terms they were, predictably, indignant at such forbearance, and they set to work immediately to undo as much of the treaty's work as they could. The new Irish parliament was wholly Protestant, so it was easy to alter the original agreement. In the end, the property of those men who had gone to France was confiscated with that of those who had died and many who surrendered before the end of the war. When everything was settled, Catholic ownership of land in Ireland had shrunk to one seventh of the entire area.

James II never again made a serious attempt to regain his throne. He lived quietly, after the fashion of most exiled monarchs, until, having outlived the daughter who supplanted him on the throne, he died at Saint-Germain in 1701. The baby boy whose birth had precipitated the revolution grew up as James Edward, commonly called the Old Pretender. The Pope and Louis XIV recognized him as James III and VIII (of England and Scotland respectively), but this was no help to him in the world of reality, where Protestant England was set against him as firmly as she had been against his father. When William III died in 1702, the English Parliament prudently passed a bill of attainder against James Edward even before the members formally named Mary's younger sister Anne as the next monarch. Anne, it need hardly be said, was as firmly Protestant as Mary had been. Even so, as it became more and more evident that she would die without issue— for her children were weaklings, and none survived—the queen dallied with the idea of naming her half brother as her successor. If only he had not been so firmly, committedly Catholic! As it was, the English would never accept him, Anne knew, and when she died in 1714 her crown passed instead to George, the Elector of Hanover, and his wife Sophia, who was granddaughter of James I.

The Old Pretender tried several times to gain the throne by force of arms, and the English kept a wary eye on these activities. Spain underwrote his last attempt in 1719, but like the others it failed. After that he left the struggle to his elder son Charles Edward, the Young Pretender.

All these strivings and counterstrivings had their effect on Ireland. As long as the Pope recognized a rival claimant to the English throne, Roman Catholics everywhere were suspected of treasonous sentiments. It was like the deposing of Elizabeth all over again: the more stanchly His Holiness championed the cause of Irish and English Catholics, the more suffering he caused the Catholics. It was to be, therefore, a relief to the faithful when the Old Pretender died at last in 1766, and Rome refused to recognize the Young Pretender in his turn as the rightful king of England.

In her study of the Penal Laws, 1691-1760, Mrs. Maureen Wall of University College, Dublin, sketches the background of that period and reminds us of the various ecclesiastical rules and regulations that preceded them. The most noticeable fact about the earlier strictures imposed by the Established Church is that during the seventeenth century they were largely ignored, and those who flouted them usually escaped punishment. The Act of Uniformity of

1560 declared regular attendance at the State (Established)
Church was compulsory for all, including Roman Catholics,
and a penalty of one shilling was to be visited upon each
"recusant"; yet by the end of that century nobody was paying
any attention to the act, and during the following years
no attempt was made to collect the many recusancy fines
that were owing. In general, the Protestants showed little
talent or taste for mission work among Catholics. During
the reigns of Henry VIII and Elizabeth laws were passed
providing that free parochial and diocesan schools be set
up in Ireland for the benefit of all children, specifically to
further the propagation of the Protestant religion and the
English language. But the responsibility of creating and
financing such schools was laid on the bishops and clergy
of the Established Church, and they—not surprisingly—
were markedly reluctant to shoulder such a costly burden.
"Such diocesan schools as were founded, and they were few,
rapidly ceased to be free schools, and since a system of parish
schools for the native population was never provided, little
progress was made either in anglicising or protestantising
by means of schools" (Maureen Wall, *The Penal Laws,*
Dundalk, 1967, p. 3).

Naturally enough, under Charles II nobody was interested
in spreading the true faith. Then James II was driven from
his throne, an act contradicting all that had hitherto been
believed as to the divine right of kings: the authority of the
Established Church was correspondingly weakened. Mrs.
Wall calls to our attention that since 1613 the Church in
Ireland had been governed by its own convocation, which
always met in Dublin during the parliamentary session. But
after the accession of William III it did not meet for some
years, until Anne became queen, and when she died it ceased
again to meet. At last, in 1769, it was called together once
more, but only to preside at its own disestablishment. The
House of Commons was responsible for this development. It
was determined to permit no challenge to its authority: as a
result the conversion of the Irish, which would have entailed
a strengthening of the Church's power, was allowed to go

by the board. In many other ways as well the ministry kept control of the Church. The Crown, usually on English rather than Irish advice, appointed all Irish Protestant bishops, and as a result most of them were Englishmen, not Irishmen. The Irish Protestants naturally resented this development, especially as the choice places usually went to men of strong political and party loyalties rather than to those of deep religious leanings.

Then there was the tithe system, resented not only by Catholics and Dissenters but also by rich landowning members of the Church of Ireland, who did not see why pasture land should be taxed at all. Their stand was of course effectively opposed by the bishops in the House of Lords, so that they could not push through an act of parliament to protect themselves. However, by combining and supporting each other they won so many individual cases at law that to all intents and purposes they won the struggle anyway. Whenever the government wanted to show its power over the clergy it had only to threaten an examination of abuses within the Church system. Church officials knew all too well how vulnerable they were on this point. Mrs. Wall lists a few of the outstanding ones. Plurality—one man holding two or more benefices and being paid for both—was common, as was absenteeism. Many churches had been destroyed in the wars and never rebuilt, and often there was no glebe house for the parson. In parishes with few or no Protestants, the parson often took his salary without ever going near the church, sometimes paying a curate a small salary for doing really necessary jobs. And practically nothing had ever been done about the parish and diocesan schools that had been ordered so long before. Everything considered, it is hardly surprising that the Established Church did not undertake missionary work among the Catholics of Ireland. Money for much-needed schools, churches, and glebe houses, let alone more clergymen, was not to be had from the bishops, certainly not from the House of Commons. The Church convocation of 1711 did outline a plan—which came to nothing—for compulsory education, and an Irish Protestant clergyman, recognizing that the chief obstacle to mission work in Ireland was the language discrepancy, tried to introduce Protestant religious works written in Irish, but he found little support from his colleagues and had to drop the idea. Conversion usually went the other way, especially in isolated communities where a few Protestants lived among many Catholics. Cut off from their co-religionists and clergy the Protestants usually submitted to fate and became Catholics themselves. There was little objection to this in government circles: all the aristocracy was really concerned with was the Protestantizing of such rich landowners as had managed, in spite of the Protestant guardians and Protestant education for their heirs which the law demanded, to keep their Catholic convictions intact. In the end these men usually gave in nevertheless, to save their estates or out of simple loneliness. For the masses, observes Mrs. Wall, "the Irish parliament was content to demonstrate its zeal of the Protestant interest by passing a series of statutes, which, had they been enforced or enforceable, would have extirpated Catholicism in Ireland in a generation" (p. 10). *Had they been enforced or enforceable*—the phrase sums up much of England's government in Ireland. Laws remained in the statute books like threats, swords suspended over the country's head by the thinnest of fiber. The death of a monarch, a quarrel between princes, even a mere change in temperature in London, might in the space of a few minutes affect the fortunes of a hundred ancient Irish houses.

Six years intervened, from the end of the war to 1697, before the treaty of Limerick was ratified, but in 1692 William sent over Lord Sidney as lord lieutenant of Ireland. Sidney's first act was to clear up the composition of the Irish parliament. Members of both the Commons and the Lords were required by a new act to take the customary oath of allegiance, a declaration against Roman doctrines, and the old oath denying the Pope's spiritual supremacy. This law, holding good as it did until 1829, was well calculated to keep all Roman Catholics out of the government, and it did. The "Williamite settlement" followed. Of the property of four thousand attainted landowners, more than one and a half million acres were forfeit to the Crown. William had promised to regain this land for the attainted nobles, and he kept his promise: sixty-five of the richest men unprotected by treaty terms were given back their property. The Protestant members of both parliaments were very angry at this kindness, and retorted by attacking the king's action in giving large tracts of confiscated property to his favorites. One way and another—for much of the monarchy's power had gone with the Stuarts—they managed to reduce his benefactions to the Irish landowners, who dwindled in number from sixty-five to seven. Nevertheless, at the final accounting 400,000 acres had been returned. A million more were sold in the open market. By 1700, Catholic ownership land in Ireland was down to one eighth: within the next few decades even this fraction was to be reduced.

CHAPTER

13

THE Protestants of Ireland had had a bad scare and were determined not to be caught again. James II was gone, it was true, but who could be sure that he would not be smuggled back in? The only way to be safe was to stamp out popery altogether, said the extremists, and to stamp it out one must get rid of the priests. The less extreme favored stamping out by easy stages, arguing that wholesale action would call down retaliatory measures from Spain, France, and the Holy Roman Empire, or Austria. Ireland's Catholic clergy had proved itself tenacious, hanging on all through the years without legal provision for their livings. But if by some other method than starvation they could be eradicated, everyone would have to become Protestant whether he wanted to or not, and the Catholic Church would wither away.

It was out of such simple processes of reasoning that the Dublin parliament, by this time of course exclusively Protestant, evolved the notorious anti-popery acts. The period of the Penal Laws, as history calls them, has become one of the leading scandals in the scandal-filled story of Anglo-Irish relations, and no one has been harsher on the subject than the Protestant Edmund Curtis, who condemns

William III and his sister-in-law Anne quite as severely as he does the legislators who actually drew up the laws. Panic and cruel spirit animated parliament throughout the period, he says, especially when they passed an act that disarmed the so-called papists. "No 'papist' might own a horse worth above five pounds, and no gunsmith might take a Catholic apprentice....Another act made it illegal for Catholics to go for education abroad and forbade them to keep a public school at home. The University of Dublin was already closed to them as regards degrees, fellowships, and scholarships.... William indeed and the noble spirits of England should have vetoed [the parliament's] enactments, but it was much easier to yield to the 'No Popery' spirit in both countries" (A *History of Ireland*, p. 280). The picture is accurate as far as it goes—sweeping generalizations are unavoidable in comprehensive histories. It remains for other writers, who work in smaller areas, to demonstrate that not all non-Catholics in Ireland and England subscribed to the views of the No Popery group. Mrs. Maureen Wall in *The Penal Laws, 1691-1760* shows us that there were dissenters and Dissenters, and that their efforts, combined with the passive resistance of the Catholics themselves, frustrated panic and cruel spirit in the end.

The opening attack in the anti-popery campaign was the Banishment Act of 1697, which called for the expulsion from Ireland of all Catholic bishops and other high ecclesiastical dignitaries—"all papish archbishops, bishops, vicars general, deans, Jesuits, monks, friars and all other regular popish clergy and all Papists exercising ecclesiastical jurisdiction." These were to be out of the country by May 1, 1698, on pain of being transported. Any who returned after transportation would be judged guilty of high treason and punished accordingly, as would persons harboring such ecclesiastics and justices of the peace who spared them. No mention was made in the act of ordinary parish priests, the legislators doubtless being restrained by the thought that a completely wholesale banishment would be in glaring contravention of the treaty of Limerick. Determined anti-papists comforted

themselves for this omission with the reflection that only
bishops could ordain priests, and without new priests the
religion was doomed to die out sooner or later.

King William did not like the act and said so. He
complained that the transportations were making a woeful
impression in those continental countries where it was
important for England to maintain a good name, but he
was no absolute monarch and he could do little, especially
as his own Parliament in England was itself busily forming
anti-popery laws. He could only promise unofficially to
temper the wind where and when he found it possible. His
ministers sought to justify the legislation by claiming that
the Dublin parliament, far from being cruel, was in fact kind
to the Catholic clergy. To prove it they cited the treatment
to which Protestants on the Continent were subjected by
their Catholic masters, who drove them penniless from
their homes and their countries. In contrast to this, said the
ministers, banished Irish ecclesiastics were always given a
bit of money to go on with: no Catholic nation, least of all
the French, could in justice condemn England or Ireland. It
is doubtful if William was really convinced by this specious
argument, though his objections made no difference. The
victimized Protestants of Europe's Catholic countries were a
small group, a minority, but "Ireland was unique in Western
Europe in that the persecuted formed the majority of the
population" (*The Course of Irish History*, p. 218).

The first act was soon followed by another that forbade
any Catholic who did not take the "oath of Abjuration"—
abjuration, that is, of allegiance to James II or his issue—to
practice law. A very few Catholics, exempted from this law,
were the only men left to defend their co-religionists at court.

Naturally James II, far away in safety, lifted up his voice
to protest against these acts, and naturally nobody on the
Protestant side paid attention to him, but the objections of
the Emperor Leopold of Austria were another matter, and
William was worried. In the changeable politics of the time,
Leopold's friendship was likely to matter a good deal to
England, and here he was writing angrily to his ambassador

in London, accusing the Dublin parliament of aiming at the "entire extirpation" of the Catholic religion and contradicting promises that William had made. He added, "Nor will the evil be removed by the plea that the king had to give his sanction, but that he will prevent the laws from being enforced. The king is mortal like other men." Hasty efforts were made by the court to appease the Emperor, with the secretary of state and then the Irish lord chancellor waiting on the envoy to proffer soothing words. They promised that the Act of Banishment would not be enforced down to the last detail. It was true, they admitted, that the regular clergy had to go—they were all Jacobites and could not be permitted to continue to stir up trouble, they argued. But no bishops or other high-ranking dignitaries would be affected, the Catholic religion would not suffer, and the treaty of Limerick would continue to command respect and observance. Leopold was unconvinced: there was nothing here to change his mind.

He knew—everyone knew—that no matter what the diplomats said, the high officials of the Church *were* very much affected. Even before the act of 1697 most Irish sees had been vacated: five prelates, for example, had gone away with James. By the time of the first act only eight bishops remained in all Ireland. Two of these were frightened into leaving before May 1 of the following year, and no doubt they congratulated themselves when they heard that the bishop of Cork, who ignored the deadline, was arrested for it and imprisoned. He would certainly have been transported if William had not interceded. But the king could not continue interceding; he proved his mortality as Leopold had foreseen, dying in 1702. Less than a year after his death the aged bishop of Clonfert was arrested. A large band of Catholics, armed and mounted, rescued him, but he had to remain more or less in hiding until he died.

In the meantime Dublin's parliament, like the opposite body in England, was running into a little trouble with another group than the papists, who were likewise affected by the anti-popery acts. These were Protestant Dissenters,

or Presbyterians, who lived in their greatest numbers in
Ulster, though some smaller Presbyterian communities were
scattered over southern Ireland as well. They had always
complained about the tithes they were forced to pay to the
Established Church: now like the Catholics, subject to these
new laws, they were not allowed to carry arms or own good
horses or hold office in the state and corporations or occupy
seats in parliament—that is, unless they took the Sacrament,
which their religion forbade them to do. They were a
minority and their protests availed them little: they had to
suffer with the Catholics. Even the more tolerant members
of the Established Church never got round to passing the
special legislation necessary for their exemption.

Anne, though she was daughter to James II, was Protestant
to the bone and had always aligned herself firmly with the
house of Orange. After her succession she did demur, though
rather feebly, against the obvious flouting of the treaty of
Limerick. For a time she withheld her assent from the act of
1703, which threatened penalties to any Catholic clergyman
entering England, but in the end she assented to this as to
those that followed. One act that appeared soon afterward
in 1704 surprised the Catholic clergymen remaining in
Ireland with its apparent harmlessness, for it required each
of these priests merely to go to his local court upon or after a
certain date and there register his name, his age, particulars
of his ordination, and a few other details. At the same time
he was to take an oath of loyalty—not the notorious oath
of Abjuration, but a milder one. Other new rules stated
that he could not leave his county on pain of banishment,
nor keep a curate, but these were pinpricks in comparison
with what the priests had expected. There was much relief,
since the act was evidently aimed not at them, but at friars
who had not yet been caught in the net. Registration was in
itself a safeguard, they felt—it gave them a legal status that
had theretofore been lacking. More than a thousand priests
quietly registered themselves. Then they were emboldened
to celebrate mass openly, and their congregations attended

service in chapels that had long been closed. Though the situation as to bishops remained unchanged and there could be no fresh ordinations, the priests did not borrow trouble. The respite was welcome, and something might turn up, they told themselves.

And something did. In 1707, when only two bishops remained in all of Ireland, the Holy See began appointing new ones. Five prelates made their appearance during that year alone. It goes without saying that they had to take care not to be apprehended. Like the parish priests they made no attempt to wear priestly garb—none was seen in Ireland during the whole of the century—and their ordination of new priests, too, was kept very quiet, but it was accomplished.

Good fortune, however, was balanced by bad. The state of the Catholic clergy depended closely upon their Protestant rulers' fluctuating emotions. Leniency was in order when the officials felt secure; but harshness always resulted when the Protestants were worried. In March 1708 news came that James's son the Pretender was on his way to invade Scotland with a French fleet. Presumably every good Catholic rejoiced to think that a Stuart might conquer and rule England once more, but in fact—though the priests would not have put it quite like this—the Pretender had been bad news to Ireland ever since the Pope at his birth had recognized him as "James III." The ruling caste now reacted characteristically and turned their frightened wrath on the priests, ordering that they all be imprisoned immediately. Some clerics actually were caught and locked up, there to remain until the threat receded: the rest, with the help of their parishioners, hid themselves. A new act passed in 1709 indicates that though the Pretender had given up the project the Protestants were still worried. It repeated and strengthened many of the strictures against Catholics that already existed, and stepped up the activity against those clergymen who were not supposed to be in the country at all. Anyone discovering and turning over to the law an unregistered priest was promised a reward of £20, and a bigger prize of £50 was offered for each head of those who exercised ecclesiastical jurisdiction. Most important of all, registered priests were commanded, on pain of banishment, to take the oath of Abjuration—the worst threat yet to the brotherhood, since taking the oath meant abandoning all Catholic loyalties and accepting, with approval, the Protestant-dominated world that Ireland was.

Faced with making such a grave decision, the great majority of priests simply refused to take the oath, and this action saved them. They numbered 1089, of whom 33 gave in, but the recalcitrant 1056 posed a serious problem. Since 1702 England had been engaged in the War of the Spanish Succession, allied with Holland, Austria, and Portugal against Spain and France. To eject more than a thousand priests from Ireland all at once would have called down the wrath of their Catholic allies on the English throne and government, and things were quite awkward enough in that respect—Anne was always receiving questions from the Continent about the treaty of Limerick. The priests were not banished.

Each change in the government of England, from Whig to Tory party and back again, was felt in Ireland. Generally speaking, Tories brought relief, Whigs brought renewed persecution. During the Tory ascendancy of 1710-14 things went fairly easily for the Irish Catholics, but Anne died in 1714, and with George I of Hanover the Whigs returned to power, bringing with them as their usual accompaniment the parrot cry of No Popery. The pressure was increased in 1715 when the Pretender turned up in Scotland to cheer on a new Jacobite rebellion. In Dublin the government resurrected the old anti-popery laws and began to enforce them, which meant among other things that the registered priests were to be banished after all—or, rather, that they had to go into hiding. This state of affairs endured for a year, and then England and France made peace, and the priests reappeared. In fact, in 1716 things improved rather noticeably for the clergy. "The coming and going of Irish priests between Ireland and France was no longer deemed so dangerous, and at times even recruiting for the Irish Brigade went on with the tacit consent of the English Government, although the Irish Parliament did not favor the idea" (Wall, *The Penal Laws*, p. 45. The Irish Brigade was what the eighteenth century called the "wild geese," the officers and men who fled to the Continent after the Jacobite wars. Under the king of France they had made a considerable reputation for themselves, and elsewhere as well these warriors were in great demand. According to an amusing article by Christopher Duffy ["The Wild Geese' in Austria," *History Today*, September 1968], Irishmen gave the army of Imperial Austria thirteen field marshals, two presidents of the High War Council, and dozens of other generals.)

But the game of seesaw was not yet at an end. In 1718 England and Spain went to war again, and inevitably in Ireland voices were lifted in the old cry of No Popery. Protestants spoke worriedly of the Irish Brigade in Spain's army, and repeated the news that the Pretender was in Madrid. Early in 1719 the duke of Ormonde, more at home abroad than he was in Ireland or England, set out from Spain with a fleet to invade Scotland: like the Armada of Elizabethan days the fleet scattered in bad weather. Indeed, it never reached its destination. Then the war ended, the excitement abated, and though No Popery flared up again from time to time, on each occasion there was less fever about it. The end was evident when a bill presented to the Commons in 1719, advocating *branding on the cheek* for every unregistered cleric found in Ireland, was not passed. Another anti-papist bill presented in 1723 also failed to become law, though the Pretender was now a father, thereafter known as the *Old* Pretender. His name seemed to have lost the old black magic.

A few spurts of anti-Catholicism were still to come as accompaniment to the War of the Austrian Succession and the Seven Years' War, but by 1760 it was really quiet. That year was marked by the succession of George III, when few could continue to believe in the bogey of Stuart pretenders, and as Mrs. Wall points out, the king of England was also king of Hanover, where Catholics enjoyed freedom of worship. Why, then, should George and his ministers persecute Catholics in Ireland? For a while, at any rate, life was easier for the priest.

How had the Church survived so many and such savage attacks? The traditional history offered by Catholics is pious: God saved the Church; justice triumphed. But Mrs. Wall offers less supernatural explanations, and they become even more interesting in the light of later periods when Protestants were again outwitted in the same manner. There is a recurring pattern in the story of Ireland.

For one thing (says Mrs. Wall), the Dublin parliament passed the popery acts and made other laws, but it couldn't enforce them: "It had no actual powers. Power was possessed exclusively by 'The Castle,' which controlled the Irish Civil Service and all the country's muscle, such as law officers, army, sheriffs and constables. The Castle was in no way answerable to Parliament. It was controlled directly by the ministry in England, and that ministry alone could enforce the popery laws if it chose to do so. Or could it? Probably not. Enforcement depended on those same mayors, sheriffs, magistrates and constables who were managed by the Castle executive, and they were simply unable to carry out implementation orders. Their offices were undermanned. The constables in Catholic districts, until 1715 at least, were very likely Catholic themselves and would ignore such commands. Each constable held office for a year and was not paid for his official duties, but tried to carry on his regular work at the same time. The expenses of the constabulary were taken care of—theoretically—by taxing the public, who were also expected—usually in vain—to help the constables in carrying out their duties. These duties were multifarious, ranging from 'Affrays and Alehouses' to 'Vagabonds,' and the unpaid constable who tried to meet all these obligations and earn his living at the same time was scarcely likely to be very zealous in harrying Papists. He was more apt to accept bribes to leave them alone. Besides, such roads as existed were bad, "and until the turnpike system was introduced in the second half of the century a large part of the population... were able to live out their lives knowing little of the decrees of government and suffering little interference from its officials" (*Penal Laws,* p. 26).

Most of the public opposed the popery laws—after all, they too were papists—just as they opposed legislation against smuggling and private distilling, and in time-honored manner they worked together to confound the law officers. On the infrequent occasions when some hapless constable actually did take a prisoner he found it hard to confine him, for prisons were crowded and easy to break out of. As if these difficulties were not bad enough, think what problems the constable faced in apprehending priests (who never, it must be remembered, dressed the part) when the latter slipped back into the country, having traveled in smuggling vessels, as part of the cargo along with tobacco and brandy, and being landed like the contraband they were in hidden places, usually somewhere on the wild west coast. As for the outward-bound traffic, it was all very well to talk of transportation, but ship's captains often refused to take penalized priests on board. Lawmen could not, in any case, simply hustle their captives away: any cleric picked up for the first time was entitled to bail before standing his trial, and when he did land in the dock there had to be witnesses against him or the case was dismissed. Naturally most people, fearing reprisals, refused to bear such witness.

During the first half of the eighteenth century the Protestants had reason to feel complacent—that is, between scares. They had everything their own way: the Catholics could put up little competition, with no political rights and very limited ownership of land. Even so, the overlords naturally did not want to risk stirring up the mob, and their caution had strange consequences at times when they found themselves on the same side as the Catholic clergy. In later years, "the Dublin Government found itself calling on the still proscribed bishops to use their influence to prevent riots" (*Penal Laws,* p. 29), for the officials were in an unenviable position, the classic quandary of forces that occupy a hostile country. They could not trust the people, but they had to live on terms of intimacy with those people nevertheless. The advantage often lay with the underdog because everyone native was secretly on his side. Suppose a magistrate, for example, intended to raid a certain house: more often than not his servants, knowing, warned the inmates of the house well in advance, so that by the time the law arrived everyone there was gone. Like other peoples in subjection, the Irish Catholics became cunning at avoiding trouble. An unregistered priest in ticklish times would say mass with his face veiled or with a curtain between himself and the congregation: later every member of the congregation could truthfully swear that he didn't know who the priest was. Or priests were ordained in a kind of do-it-yourself ceremony in a large group, with a general laying on of hands. No priest could say afterward what prelate had presided. The game was a grim one, but it was a game, and the Catholics usually won it.

For a while high hopes were entertained by the legislators when prizes were offered for discovered priests in the aforementioned act of 1709, but the results of the act proved disappointing. A number of men tried to make their fortunes out of betraying ecclesiastics, but it was a dangerous calling: many suspected priest hunters were murdered. It was a lonely life too: everybody, even Protestants, hated such spies. Mrs. Wall recounts the careers of two outstanding men of this persuasion, Edward Tyrrell and John Garzia. For a time Tyrrell used to go from town to town with a military escort, smelling out priests. Having laid information against Archbishop Byrne of Dublin —one of the Holy See's first appointments—he tried to catch him, but the archbishop, who had been warned, was not in residence at the time. Tyrrell claimed that he once flushed a cardinal in Clonmel, but there is no supporting evidence of this. A notorious liar, he was eventually arrested, tried, convicted, and executed for bigamy. Certainly his was not a success story, nor was that of Garzia, an apostate Spanish priest, though Garzia actually did uncover a good deal of Catholic activity in Dublin, and it was through his efforts that Archbishop Byrne was at last arrested in 1718 and six priests were rounded up. But the archbishop availed himself of his legal right to stay out on bail until his trial, and by the time the case came up—a year later —there was a more favorable climate for Catholicism. The only witness against him, Garzia, did not appear—no doubt on orders from high authority: Mrs. Wall believes that one of the Catholic continental powers had intervened. Everyone knew perfectly well that Byrne was a practicing archbishop, but he was acquitted. Garzia had to write letter after begging letter before he was paid for his priest hunting, and though he got some money at last, he was in perpetual danger from assassins. Having begged a room in the Castle, he did not dare to leave it. The government refused to grant him a pension, the Established Church would not give him a living, and in 1723 he left Ireland for good.

Of course all this does not mean that it was exactly pleasant, even so, to be an ecclesiastic in Ireland in the eighteenth century. The difficulties in keeping the Church strong and united were immense. There was the problem of education for priests—a battle never won though it was not exactly lost either. Standards inevitably became lower, though some young priests were smuggled abroad for a period of schooling. There was also the trouble of finding mass houses enough for the growing population's needs. Chapels had to escape the official eye, so huts were used, and sheds, and movable altars at hedge sites— anywhere would serve and did serve in necessity. Small as these huts were, it was often hard to find spots on which they could stand, since most of the land belonged to Protestants. Mass was sometimes said in the people's houses, or on rocks in the open air. Mrs. Wall tells of a kindhearted Protestant squire of Fermanagh who, on a stormy rainy day, came upon a priest and congregation at mass under a hedge. Instead of reporting the priest and having him hanged, the squire pushed his cows out of their barn and told the priest and congregation to use it for their service. (It is to the eighteenth century with its threats and penalties that Ireland today owes the custom of referring to "chapels" where other people say "churches.") Assemblies of Catholics and holy pilgrimages took place in spite of the law, but whenever anti-papist feeling was running higher than usual the gatherings might be descended upon and dispersed. Probably the worst thing about the laws, as Mrs. Wall says, was their potential: they hung suspended like the sword of Damocles over the heads of the Catholic clergy. The first full outrage of the acts had long since diminished, for example, when in 1757 the governors of the Charter schools of Dublin wrote angrily to a Catholic priest who was trying to keep a child out of the schools that if he or any other priest interfered with them they would use "their utmost endeavours to put into execution... the several laws now in force in this kingdom against popish priests." Conceivably the governors could have implemented this threat, but they too were contravening the acts in writing openly to a priest and accepting the fact that he was actively doing his work. The incident is a good example of how very far the laws had slipped into desuetude. Another significant piece of evidence is that as early as the 1730s local newspapers began as a matter of course to print the obituaries of Catholic priests and bishops, the only observance to convention being that the late prelates were called "titular bishops."

"Letters from Ardagh inform us of the death of Dr. Peter Mulligan, late titular bishop of that see, who departed this life on the 23rd instant," says the Dublin *Daily Post,* as early as 1739. "He was a religious man of the order of the Hermits of St. Augustine...." And this permissiveness increased: says Mrs. Wall, "It is clear from newspaper reports from the late 1740s on, that relations were good between the Catholic clergy and the Government, and that the priests did everything in their power to keep the people from engaging in riots and from causing trouble to the civil authorities. At Easter, 1748, riots were denounced from the altar of every Catholic chapel in Dublin, and it was stated that the sacraments would be denied to anyone taking part in riots" (pp. 61-62). Even more striking is another newspaper story:

"In 1748 we find a butcher before the court in Dublin for assaulting a priest and preventing him from administering the last sacraments to his wife. He was sentenced to be fined and imprisoned, but on the application of the priest in his favour his sentence was reduced to a month's imprisonment" (p. 62). An astonishing turnabout. At the same time the papers began publishing the Pope's ordinances: in Lent 1753 they gave prominence to his dispensation to Catholics from the Lenten fasting on four days of each week because of the high cost of food. They were permitted to eat whatever they could get.

All in all, the Church was well on the way to restitution—a far cry from 1731, when a House of Lords committee instituted an enquiry into the "state of popery" in Ireland, and many houses suspected of harboring religious communities were raided. That year the mayor of Galway reported that his sheriffs had searched a house reputed to be an Augustinian friary, but could not find any of the said friars. "Our faith in his report is rather shaken," says the historian dryly, "when we find an entry in the house-book of the Galway Augustinians for November, 1731, which reads: 'November 9th... a bottle of wine for ye sheriffs... is.id.'" And there is a corresponding entry for about the same date in the account book of the Galway Dominicans, of 2s.2d. spent "for claret to treat ye sheriffs in their search."

But these hole-and-corner games, however amusing they are to read about today, could not have been regretted by the players when the emergency was over. For the Catholic clergy the second half of the century must have been vastly preferable to the first. After years of living like outcasts and fugitives they were permitted, even if only on sufferance, to come out and work in the open. Of course not all was right for Catholics even then. Those of the laity who refused to take the oath of Abjuration were still kept from high office in the state, could not hold commissions in the army, could not practice law, could not vote. They couldn't buy or even lease land. In a score of other and pettier ways as well they were restricted. But when all this has been said, the clergy *was* better off; it had reached a plateau of respectability. If there is such a thing as collective memory—and there is, though we usually call it history—the priests would not forget their years in the wilderness. This is why so many of them, when they had the choice, took the conservative path. After long suffering their Church had been restored to the light and air of liberty, and if many priests later opposed whatever might plunge them once more into the dark, stuffy existence of the underground, it should be no cause for wonder.

CHAPTER

14

IT was natural, considering the situation, that the men who laid the foundations of Ireland's first independence in the eighteenth century should have been Protestant rather than Catholic. The Protestants were the privileged class and had pre-empted the schools, government places, and professions. They had deprived a great number of Catholics of all opportunity. When at last a Catholic leader appeared, he was a man who had got his education abroad, in secret. But the fact that Protestants were in the saddle did not in the end mean that they were less nationalistic than the poorer race, for they too were Irish, and at this time they were beginning to find it out.

One of the strongest Protestant champions of Irish rights was Jonathan Swift. He was born in Dublin in 1667 of English parents settled in Ireland, and was educated in Dublin, at Trinity. In 1689 he went to England, where for ten years he acted as secretary to the diplomat Sir William Temple, attended Oxford, and began writing satire. When Temple died in 1699 Swift returned to Ireland as chaplain to an English nobleman. After that post he held livings in one or another Irish village, visiting England from time to time and remaining in close touch with politics. He resented the trade restrictions imposed on Ireland by the British Parliament through the influence of greedy British tradesmen, and in 1720 he published a paper—anonymous, like all his satirical writings—called *Proposals for the Universal Use of Irish Manufactures*, in which he urged what would now be called a boycott of British goods, suggesting that the Irish burn everything of English origin but their coal.

Swift became dean of St. Patrick's, Dublin, in 1713: the move made no difference in his involvement with political questions. In 1724 he was stirred to fresh indignation by the news of a contract arranged by Sir Robert Walpole, England's first prime minister, with an Englishman named William Wood, who proposed to supply Ireland with copper halfpence and farthings. It was true that Ireland needed copper coins, but not that many: the country would have been flooded. Wood stood to make a 40 per cent profit on the deal, and much of that money was to be passed on to the woman through whose influence he got the patent, the late George I's mistress the duchess of Kendal. It further annoyed Swift and other men of Ireland that the duchess should already be profiting from their country; she drew a pension from the national revenue, a source all too often dipped into to meet the private obligations of the English aristocracy. For instance, George II's sister, the dowager queen of Prussia, drew £800 a year from Ireland, and when she died the pension did not die with her—the duke of Bedford, who was lord lieutenant at the time, appropriated it for his sister-in-law. Swift published a series of papers purporting to be the letters of a linen draper about the new copper coinage. "Do nothing but refuse their half-pence," he advised his readers. "You have a lawful mode of resistance; —adopt it and you succeed." As a result, public outcry did force Parliament to refuse Wood's coins and wipe out the contract.

The dean continued to attack many of Parliament's policies, assailing the custom according to which Englishmen came to Ireland in large numbers to govern the country, even when they had no knowledge of land or people. Again and again he spoke scathingly of the grasping laws that prevented Irish trade with foreign countries. He said that the English legislators framed laws in the spirit of shopkeepers. He was especially bitter when he spoke of Ireland's poverty: "The miserable dress, and diet, and dwelling of the people; the general desolation in most parts of the kingdom; the old seats of the nobility and gentry all in ruins and no new ones in their stead; the families of farmers who pay great rents living in filth and nastiness upon buttermilk and potatoes, without a shoe or stocking to their feet, or a house so convenient as an English hogsty to receive them—" Probably his most celebrated pamphlet is the essay published in 1729, *A Modest Proposal for Preventing the Children of Poor People in Ireland from Being a Burden to Their Parents,* in which it is suggested that superfluous children be fattened up and eaten. Swift died in 1745, but before the end of the century some of his ideas were to be resurrected.

The row over Wood's halfpence had jolted London, and Walpole sent Lord Carteret, who had instigated much of it, to serve in Ireland as the new viceroy. Carteret had a hard time with the men who now controlled Dublin's House of Commons, who were losing patience with their role under the Hanoverian monarchs. Naturally they compared their lot with that of the English legislators, who since 1689 had enjoyed the benefits of a constitution that guaranteed them important powers. The prime minister took the king's place in the cabinet. The ministry was responsible not to the king, but to a majority in Parliament. Parliament, not the king, controlled the army, revenue, and judges. The subject was protected from arbitrary imprisonment by the Habeas Corpus Act. All these privileges were withheld from John Bull's other island, though Ireland's inhabitants were as heavily taxed. It was an added grievance that they had to support an English army of twelve thousand, while in England the corresponding standing army numbered little more than half as many. As elections were not mandatory, what Curtis calls "the shackled and spiritless legislature" of Dublin under George II continued until his death in

1760—a term of thirty-three years—convening every other
year and then only voting money bills: there was no point
in passing acts which, in accordance with Poynings' Law,
must be referred to England for approval. The viceroy was
English; his secretary was English; and, since the viceroy
appointed all ministers, they too were English. One would
not guess, reading such facts, that Ireland was important to
the English economy, but she was.

"Throughout the eighteenth century," writes J. H. Plumb,
"trade to Ireland was the most important branch of English
overseas trade. Three-quarters of Irish land belonged to
Englishmen or to Anglo-Irish Protestant families. By the
middle of the century three-quarters of a million pounds
in rent was leaving Ireland each year for the pockets of
the absentee landlords living in England. No wool was
allowed to be exported except to England: its manufacture
was absolutely forbidden. Irish ships were not allowed to
trade with the colonies, although economically Ireland was
extremely dependent on America"— that is, for flax seed
and potash for bleaching linen (*England in the Eighteenth
Century,* Pelican History, p. 178). Because two products
that the Irish were permitted to sell to the Continent were
wool and beef, they converted most of their farmland to
grazing, and to save space they depended more and more
on the potato, first introduced by Sir Walter Raleigh,
because potatoes need little room. Plumb says that famine
was endemic, but at first potatoes were very helpful: in the
famines of 1730 and 1741, many more would have died
without them. Potatoes and buttermilk made up the diet of
the poor Irish.

Rich and poor, Protestants and Catholics, had much to
complain of, therefore. Some slight relief was afforded them
in the 1740s, thanks to Charles Edward Louis Philip Casimir,
better known as the Young Pretender and best known, no
doubt, as Bonnie Prince Charlie. In 1745 this young man
sailed to Scotland from the Continent, as the Old Pretender
his father had done before him—and as his grandfather
James II had done even earlier. His intentions too were similar.

He meant to get back the crown of England and bestow it on his father. He sailed over the sea to Skye, and there in the Hebrides he collected a large, enthusiastic following of Scottish Highlanders. With this army he marched in triumph to Edinburgh. Scotland was his, and the army then started south, for London. They got as far as Derby, but there they were met and turned back, and the encounter at Culloden settled the war. Bonnie Prince Charlie carried the broken dreams of the Jacobites back to the Continent. From that time on the Stuarts were finished in England, but between the appearance of the Young Pretender in Scotland and his departure, there had been anxious moments for the Hanoverian following, especially in Dublin. The current viceroy, Lord Chesterfield, feared that at any moment he would be called upon to cope with a Jacobite rising. To take the minds of the Catholics off the Young Pretender he even relaxed the Penal Laws, but they were not revoked outright: the threat remained, hanging over Catholic heads.

For all the nominal reform attempted after the Wood affair, the Dublin Castle administration remained corrupt and inefficient. It could hardly be otherwise considering the attitude of the viceroy and his staff, who looked upon their posts as wearisome and their presence in Ireland as unnecessary. A conscientious viceroy came to Ireland every other year and until 1767 spent only a fifth of that in the country: other officials usually stayed away longer than he did. Ireland was provincial, they felt—it was pleasanter to remain in England. Yet in spite of all this, Dublin was slowly becoming a respectable metropolis, with buildings and squares of that excellent design favored during the eighteenth century in English and Scots cities. Lord Chesterfield, for example, landscaped beautiful Phoenix Park. The William Wood affair had a good effect too. Though Ireland still carried a great many parasites on her back, they moderated their demands and took more care with their bookkeeping, until in 1753, to everyone's amazement, the Irish treasury actually showed a surplus for the year. It was the first time in living memory that such a thing had happened, and

parliament proposed that a part of the sum, which was
£77,500, be held back for domestic needs. To the legislators'
indignation, the Privy Council in London demurred. Dublin
had no right to dispose of the money, they said: according
to Poynings' Law, this was a matter for the king to settle.
The Irish could keep the money only if he permitted them
to do so. In fact the king did permit it through an alteration
written into the Money Bill: His Majesty "would be pleased
to condescend that it should be paid towards the liquidation
of the national debt." But Dublin refused to accept the
wording of this alteration. The people had paid the taxes,
said the members, and they had a right to decide what
should be done with their own surplus. The amended bill
was rejected, and after the smoke of battle had cleared away
it was evident to everyone that the same thing had better
not happen again. Nationalism had to be reckoned with in
Ireland as in America.

George II died in 1760 and was succeeded by his grandson
George III, who "commenced his reign with all the frivolity
of a Stuart, and the inelegant obstinacy of a gross Prince
of the House of Hanover," says Henry Grattan the younger
(*Memoirs, etc. of Henry Grattan,* Vol. 1, p. 18). The first
two Georges had been strongly Whiggish as well as German,
but the new English-born king, twenty-two years old, was
Tory in his sympathies, and determined to restore some at
least of the monarchy's power that had been lost. These
aspirations to power did not interest many of Ireland's poor
Catholics, who probably knew little history, but his Toryism
did, because one of the side effects of Toryism in power had
always been an alleviation of their lot. It happened that at
this time a number of Irish Catholics were able to give serious
thoughts to the situation. Despite all the disadvantages
of life in Catholic Ireland, some enterprising men among
them had managed to climb out of the ranks of peasantry
by accumulating capital. These bourgeois gentlemen now
joined forces with a few scions of the ancient aristocracy
to form a group called the Catholic Committee, the aim of

which was to improve the Catholic condition by peaceful means—petitions and appeals to reason. They decided that as a first step in the campaign they must convince authority of Catholic loyalty to both king *and* Pope. It was perfectly possible to entertain both sentiments, they held, and they made several statements to this effect when petitioning for the restoration of at least some civil rights to the Catholic community. For a time these tentative methods did make headway of a sort. Even the most militant of anti-papists had to admit that the Catholics had behaved well for some time, remaining quiet during the Seven Years' War of 1756-63. In earlier times such a war, with its alliance of England and Prussia against Spain, France, and Austria, might well have set off sympathetic repercussions among the Irish Catholics. But there had been none, possibly because Catholic Portugal came into the war on England's side but more probably because the Irish Catholics, now that the Jacobite cause was dead, had no spirit for such adventures. Thus a certain amount of relaxation was permitted: the English allowed a few Irishmen to serve in the war with their Portuguese co-religionists, though only as noncommissioned officers and enlisted men, since the Penal Laws prevented them from holding commissions. But then some of the more timid members took fright at the idea of arming papists, and that put a stop to the enlistment. The same members were further alarmed by a bill inspired by the Committee, proposing to give Catholics the right to mortgage land—for a long time, of course, these unfortunates had been unable to buy, sell, lease, own, or bequeath land—and they had their argument for rejection all ready to hand. In Munster, violence had recently broken out among peasants banded together in a secret society. They called themselves "the Whiteboys" and wore white garments over their ordinary clothes at meetings. The Whiteboys were protesting against tithes, enclosure of common land, rack rents, and forced labor, and Catholicism had nothing to do with the riots. In fact, in the north there were similar risings among members of Presbyterian secret societies, "the Steelboys" and "the Oakboys," protesting against exactly the same grievances. The Presbyterians, in fact, got results: some relief was granted to them. But anti-papists alleged that the Whiteboys of Munster were in collusion with the French in a Catholic plot, and their riots were forcibly suppressed. The new bill was rejected and the tithes remained. Instead of relief measures, 1765 saw a passing of the first Coercion Act into law.

When George III sent Lord Townshend to Dublin in 1767, the new viceroy had orders to stay at his post instead of serving as an absentee official, and do what he could to improve conditions in the Dublin parliament. Under his leadership the beautification of the city continued at an accelerated pace, but the most important change was embodied in a bill, soon passed into law, that provided for a general election every eight years. At least, Curtis says cynically, patronage passed from the hands of the aristocratic groups into those of the viceroy. Corruption remained, but now only the lord lieutenant himself could buy votes and bribe officials, and as the party in power improved in quality, so of course did the Opposition. Until the 1770s the Opposition had scarcely deserved mention, but now more than one respectably intelligent statesman had made his appearance in its ranks, and it became the forcing house of the most nationalistic Irishmen, who until then had had nowhere to go. Such concessions to the Irish as the Octennial Bill, which provided for elections, were not of course granted by England out of sheer benevolence, but because of the nervousness prevailing in London. The English foresaw that they would soon need friendship and willing help from Ireland: the American colonists were showing signs of restlessness, and after the Seven Years' War England's army was seriously under strength. Soon, on orders from Whitehall, Lord Townshend introduced a bill for the augmentation of the army, according to which fifteen thousand men were to be raised in Ireland, of whom twelve thousand would be stationed there for her defense and the rest deployed wherever England needed them. There was strong opposition to this bill. The Irish felt sympathy with the complaining Americans on most points, and would have done so, very likely, even if there had not been many of their own kin among the colonists. However, the bill was forced through and became law. Later the Opposition alleged, with truth, that the conditions of the original bill were ignored time and again: whenever Whitehall panicked, troops earmarked for Ireland's defense were removed and sent to fight abroad.

The year 1776, of overwhelming importance to the American rebels, was also marked by an outburst of complaints in Ireland that centered around restraint of trade. The tight controls imposed by the British on Irish exports had long been a grievance in that country—"the only kingdom I ever heard or read of," as Swift had written, "... which was denied the liberty of exporting their native commodities wherever they pleased." Now, in response to increased clamor from English traders who were feeling the pinch of the war, London's Parliament declared a complete embargo on Irish exports of provisions. This trade was practically all that had been permitted to Ireland, and had long been her mainstay. Soon the country showed evidence of acute depression, which included rapidly mounting unemployment. Grattan cites the figure of ten thousand in Dublin alone. The Opposition leader Henry Flood declared the embargo illegal, and many members from the other side must have agreed, but it was no use protesting to the British while they were being deliberately deaf. At last, however, faced with the fact that they were almost certainly losing the war in America, London began cannily to lift the pressure on the Irish—not much and only here and there, but enough, it was hoped, to discourage rebellious feelings. In achieving these aims they were not wholly successful, since, inevitably, many Irish felt more and more sympathy with the American revolutionaries. Better intelligences in London realized how things were going in Dublin and were concerned. Dublin's parliament at any rate continued to declare loyalty to the Crown, and suited the action to the word by contributing supplies and offering more of their standing army if England should be in need of men, but those who did so had vested interests in the monarchy, and even they might change their attitude if the American war continued to go wrong. English legislators who believed in thinking ahead decided it would be prudent to apply an old, well-tried remedy that had never failed before. They would appease the Catholics for a time.

The Catholic Committee was represented in London by the brilliant Edmund Burke, himself a member of the English Parliament—for it was quite in order for Irishmen to hold such posts. It goes without saying that Burke, a descendant of the ancient De Burgos, was a Protestant, but for that very reason his opinion carried weight when it came to discussing Catholic matters. Soon change made its appearances. The old oath of Abjuration was discarded and replaced by a far milder "declaration," acceptable to the Irish clergy. Then, in 1788, another reform act became law; it provided that Catholics who took an oath of allegiance could lease land for an indefinite period. As a side effect, these relief measures also applied to the Irish Dissenters, who had long suffered many of the disabilities that hampered the Catholics of Ireland: when the Test clause was abolished, Dissenters too became free to hold office. Liberation was academic rather than practical. The Church of Ireland's ascendancy was still ascendant, and there was small chance of any Presbyterian getting into office. Still, the new law made a good impression.

These popularity measures were put through as swiftly as possible, and just in time. General Burgoyne, His Majesty's commander of the troops in America, had made a promising start when he took New York, but on October 17, 1777, he was badly defeated at Saratoga. George Ill's chief secretary of state, Lord North, was now more than ever worried for fear the Irish would see their advantage in such troubled times, and take it. And these worries were not soothed by the creation in 1778 of the Irish Volunteers, the answer to Ireland's fears at what was, admittedly, a tense moment in history. The standing army of Ireland, designed to form the country's defense, had all but vanished overseas, and France was quick to perceive her chance to get at England while George Ill's affairs were going badly. In company with Spain and Holland, the French declared war on their old enemy and announced that they were on the side of the colonists. There was Ireland lying prone before any invader who wished to move in, in her defenselessness a threat to England as she had been since early days, offering to the foe a backdoor entry. Nor was she completely neutral, the Protestant ascendancy reflected with apprehension: surely the Irish Catholics, or many of them, would positively welcome such an invasion and even help it along. When the "Patriot party" of the Opposition announced that they intended to form a corps of volunteers for their island's defense, the English government felt tremendous relief, and fell over themselves offering arms to outfit the new troops. This volunteer corps was tremendously popular, and attracted so many men— most of them Protestant—that at the height of its strength the army numbered eighty thousand. If they had ever been called upon to face the French, they would probably have given a very good account of themselves. As things turned out they were used in another manner, when Flood announced that they were not to be disbanded until Ireland had her rights, beginning with free trade.

To show that he meant what he said, Volunteers, splendidly arrayed, marched through the streets of Dublin, dragging with them a cannon. This weapon, which no doubt had been contributed by the English, bore a placard with the legend, "Free trade or this!" It could not have been difficult to understand the simple message, especially as there were other indications to come. At a meeting in Dublin, the city's "freemen and freeholders" passed a resolution that they were signing a "non-importation agreement," according to which from then on, "until the grievances of this country shall be removed," they would not import or consume anything manufactured in Great Britain. There was a ballad sung in the streets, which the late Swift would have rejoiced to hear:

Ye noblemen, in place or out,
Ye volunteers, so brave and stout,
Ye dames that flaunt at ball or rout,
  Wear Irish manufacture.
Thus shall poor weavers get some pence,
From hunger and from cold to fence
Their wives and infants three months hence,
  By Irish manufacture.

North ignored these protests as long as possible, until the Irish parliament refused to vote more supplies for the war. At last in December 1799 the hated Navigation Acts were amended by the House of Commons, and Ireland was left free—or at least freer—to export her wool, cloth, and glass, as well as to trade with the colonies. Ambiguities existed in the concessions and various unwelcome controls were retained, but they gave relief, and in Ireland some of the more obvious signs of distress vanished. However, if Lord North expected the Volunteers to disband as soon as he surrendered on the Navigation Acts, he was disappointed. The Patriot party now knew exactly how valuable their Volunteers were. Opposition leaders were determined to continue using the corps as a threat to get rid of Poynings' Law and other vexatious conditions.

Henry Flood was away from Parliament for some time, leaving his leadership in 1775 to take up the proffered post of vice-treasurer of Ireland and to occupy a seat in the Irish Privy Council. His move gave rise to considerable resentment on the part of his colleagues. It was said that the king's party had bought Flood—as vice-treasurer he was paid thirty-five hundred pounds a year—but he lost both posts in 1781, and promptly returned to parliament to find the party being led by a newcomer, Henry Grattan. Flood was welcomed back, but Grattan retained a position of equality, and there was sure to be strife between them later on. Grattan was comparatively young—thirty-five—and a brilliant orator, a Trinity graduate who had taken a law degree in England before entering the party in 1775. In fact three outstanding men led the Patriot party between them, at first in complete agreement—Grattan, Flood, and Lord Charlemont. In 1782 these three attended a meeting of Volunteer delegates held at Dungannon, where Hugh O'Neill's ancient fastness had now been transformed into a fairly flourishing linen-manufacturing town. At the meeting a resolution was unanimously voted that Poynings' Law was unconstitutional. Everyone pledged himself to support legislative independence for Ireland, and when Grattan, rendered enthusiastic by so much comradely warmth, went on to propose that "as Irishmen, Christians, and Protestants, we rejoice at the relaxation of the penal laws against our Roman Catholic fellow-subjects," the other Volunteers approved this too. Later, however, when the motion came to the test in parliament, the leaders disagreed. Flood wanted to keep the country and the electorate Protestant, and he argued that the Catholic question was too difficult to handle just then. Why meddle? Lord Charlemont sided with Flood, but Grattan got some part of what he wanted during that year, when more Penal Laws were retracted, leaving Catholics able to lease and buy land and bequeath it to their heirs, as they had long been forbidden to do. They were also declared free to carry arms. Priests were no longer required to register themselves, and Catholic schools were now permitted to exist, though more advanced institutions of learning were still banned to them. In the face of Flood's and Charlemont's attitude Grattan could go no further.

With the other plans outlined in his Dungannon speech he had more success. As he saw things, Ireland could be—would be—independent but not separated from England. For all his reputation as a rebel, Grattan never envisaged separation from the British Empire: he did not see any necessity for such an extreme step. He wanted the Ireland of the future on an equal footing with England, with the right to trade as freely as England did. He saw the two countries sharing the one king, and he saw Ireland making her own laws—but on the English pattern. He was an ardent imperialist, but he was determined that Ireland should have her rights in

that Empire. All three leaders were fully aware that then
if ever was the time to get what they wanted: England was
losing her American colonies and they were determined to
manipulate the situation to their own advantage. None of
them, however, wanted to leave England outright.

The Dungannon meeting was followed shortly afterward
by the news that Cornwallis had surrendered, upon which
tidings Lord North was forced to resign. The English
Whigs who took control after his resignation were in favor
of Ireland's cause, and matters began moving very fast in
her favor. In May the independence of the Irish parliament
was settled and announced. It looked as if everything—
or practically everything—that the Patriot party was
demanding had been won. Poynings' Law, though not
absolutely erased from the books, had disappeared save for
the one point that the Crown retained the right to veto bills.
But privy councils could no longer alter bills in any way, and
Irish judges, whose tenure in office had hitherto depended
on the whim of authority, were now as secure as their
English colleagues. The unpopular Declaratory Act of 1719,
which abolished the appellate jurisdiction of the Irish House
of Lords and affirmed the control of the English Parliament,
was repealed, and another law that had much angered the
Irish, the Perpetual Mutiny Bill, was also canceled.

There was still a lord lieutenant sent over from England,
and he still picked the ministers, and everything depended
on them, thus on him, and thus, in its turn, on London. But
in the first flush of success these facts did not become evident.
When the new lord lieutenant, the duke of Bedford, offered
places in that government to Grattan and Charlemont, the
leaders decided that they should remain with the Opposition
where they could do most good. It was an idealistic gesture
which proved to be ill-advised, but at the moment everything
seemed to have gone so well that Grattan was happy. In a
speech in the House on May 27, 1783, he told the members
that Great Britain was giving up *in toto* every claim to
authority over Ireland, and in a burst of gratitude proposed
that "this newly independent body" contribute £100,000

and five thousand men to the British navy. Carried along on an answering wave of emotion, the House approved the proposal, then went beyond it and voted to give Henry Grattan, leader of his country, a grant of £50,000 for public services.

"Ireland is now a nation," said Grattan.

In the strict sense of the word, of course, she was not. She existed as a parasite, or rather as a sort of Siamese twin with England, and after his first exultation died away Grattan realized this truth as clearly as anyone. Flood too realized it, and so was especially insistent that parliament be reformed, knowing that only by such radical changes in lawmaking would the old ills be eradicated for good and all. As it was, every new bill passed in Dublin, if it could possibly be interpreted as harmful to English interests, was doomed to be killed in London. But even with all his experience Flood could not intimidate the legislature into voting itself out of office. He tried to use the method that had worked so well in the past, and there is a comical if sad story of what happened to the effort. On November 10, 1783, delegates of the Volunteers gathered at the rotunda in full uniform and listened to a fiery speech by Flood. Full of enthusiasm, they drew up a plan for reform, and Flood carried it—in his uniform—into the House of Commons, and there presented it. But the legislators refused to be intimidated, and promptly rejected the plan. This left the Volunteers completely nonplused—high and dry, in fact, without the slightest idea of what to do next. In the end they simply disbanded. Later efforts during that term met with no more success.

Grattan's favorite cause was full emancipation for Catholics, and his most formidable opponent in this was a talented man named Fitzgibbon. Fitzgibbon was firmly on the side of the Protestant ascendancy; he managed to keep emancipation at bay for some years, especially as his rise was rapid and his influence grew. But in spite of such disappointments, for a time all went well in Ireland. Foster's new Corn Law in 1784 had a good effect in halting the tendency toward developing pasture land in lieu of tillage. England was industrializing fast, and needed more and more food from outside. Irish provisions were given preferential treatment over other imports, and her agriculture flourished as a result. Rents went up and the landlords flourished—even the tenants did well, or at any rate better than they had done for a long time. Building was stimulated. Catholics made money at trade. It was not the fault of either Grattan or Fitzgibbon if the very poor did not enjoy a fair share of this prosperity; they kept trying to find some way to bring in these unfortunates. One thing at least was achieved by Grattan in this direction—he managed at last, in 1793, to get a revocation of the old burdensome hearth tax that rendered it impossible for many poor peasants to live in anything but degraded hovels.

The end of 1788 brought shock and dismay to England: King George went crazy. For some time he had been eccentric, but now there could be no doubt about his insanity. Hastily Parliament held a meeting, and after hours of agitated discussion it was decided that the prince of Wales should act as regent for England and Ireland. But this solution, though it seemed obvious and sensible to the English, was resented by Grattan and his associates. Grattan declared that it was not for England to decide a question of such importance on behalf of Ireland. There followed a period of haggling, with the Irish leaders driving a hard bargain, their eyes fixed on reform. In Ireland as in England the House of Commons was full of pensioners and officeholders who depended for their livings on party favor. They were the men who could always be counted on to vote as their masters bade them, and there were many of them: in our parlance, the House was packed. Grattan and company now insisted that these people be weeded out, "purifying" parliament. Flood approved the suggestion as far as it went, but wanted even more purification: he still demanded total reform. Then suddenly the king made a recovery, the prince of Wales was no longer needed as regent, and the Irish leaders had to be satisfied with the gains already made until, a few months later in 1789, France flared into revolution.

CHAPTER
15

DURING the last decade of the eighteenth century Anglo-Irish relations deteriorated at rapidly increasing speed, until the English and their loyal party in Ireland were treating the rest of the nation in much the same spirit as that of the early Norman invaders. Unlike the Normans, however, they had a firm grip on the whole island instead of merely a part of it: there was nowhere for the victims to flee from their overlords, and these went about the business with a spiritual self-assurance that now appears peculiarly unpleasant. To many it seemed so even then. "The truth is, I hate the very name of England," wrote the Anglo-Irish Theobald Wolfe Tone.

The idea of union appeared to the prime minister, Pitt, as a logical way out of the various difficulties he was encountering over Irish parliamentary reform. That recent trouble about the regency, he felt, was a warning of worse to come—only the recovery of George III had saved the situation, and there was almost bound to be a next time. Then the Irish might well set up their own regent, as some had already threatened to do. In trade matters too the Dublin parliament was being awkward. Union between Britain and Ireland, with one parliament serving for both nations in London and the

Irish sending their members, would be tidier altogether.
There would certainly be opposition, but the results would
be worth the trouble, reflected the minister. Then France
erupted and he was beset by more urgent worries.

The oversetting of a monarchy and aristocracy so near
home would have disturbed the English at any time, but
the resulting talk of liberty, equality, and fraternity came
on top of much similar fulmination from the new United
States of America, and all these noisy republican sentiments
together were impossible to dismiss. It remained to be
seen if the fashionable contagion should spread to Ireland:
if it did the situation would be grave indeed. The old fear
of Ireland's offering a back door for an enemy intent on
invading England now haunted Parliament in London, but
for the moment at least the outcome of France's upheaval
remained in doubt, and, as Pitt's informants in Ireland
assured him, public opinion there was divided. On one side
it was undeniable that the French and the Irish Catholics had
much in common because of their religion—a long history
of mutual sympathy, with Irish youth in French schools, the
Irish Brigade in the French armed forces, and France's aid
to the Irish during the Jacobean wars. Now, however, news
began trickling in that the French rebels against monarchy
were also in rebellion against religion, and the Catholic
Church of Ireland, predisposed toward conservatism in any
case, took alarm. Among Ireland's Protestants were some,
like Wolfe Tone, eager to utilize the French Revolution in
the same way they had used the American Revolution, as a
stick with which to beat the British. Grattan, however, was
not in sympathy with this plan. He did not equate a threat
to England from a continental country with the defiance of
Britain's colonists across the Atlantic. One could side with
fellow colonists, he felt, where one could not with foreigners:
the latter alliance looked to him like treason, especially
when in 1790 it seemed that England and Spain, quarreling
over land in America, might go to war with each other. At
this point Grattan hastened to declare that if they did fight,

Ireland and England must get together for the good of the Empire.

This stand infuriated Wolfe Tone, a young barrister of the new Irish breed who did not permit his Protestantism to make him automatically agree with everything England did. In fact he resented practically everything emanating from Britain. He demanded scornfully what Grattan could mean when he talked of "the good of the Empire": what was it, and what had it to do with Ireland in any case? Ireland had no quarrel with Spain, he pointed out. In 1791 he published *An argument on behalf of the Catholics of Ireland,* signed "A Northern Whig," in which he demanded parliamentary reform—the only means, he claimed, by which Ireland might be pulled from British clutches. He advocated a coalition of Irish Catholics and dissenting radicals who might both work for both causes. This idea caught the attention of many members of the public, and Wolfe Tone followed it up with energy and contagious enthusiasm. He went to Belfast, talked it over with some of the leading Presbyterians of Ulster, and joined the Belfast Society of United Irishmen, whose members aimed at wiping out religious differences for the cause of reforming parliament. Later, with the help of a municipal leader, Napper Tandy, another society on the same lines was formed in Dublin.

At first these clubs were exactly what they purported to be—open, aboveboard societies where people could meet and talk about national questions. They were "middle-class debating societies which strove to mould public opinion.... Apparently they still trusted to persuasion, to the pressure of public opinion....They looked forward to the abolition of tithe, a reduction in government expenditure, lower taxation, the encouragement of trade and help for primary education" *(The Course of Irish History,* p. 239). They bore no resemblance to and had no connection with the agrarian secret societies that still flourished over the country: the Whiteboys in the south, still showing how they felt about tithes and rents by burning, robbing, and laying waste the lands of unpopular landlords, and various groups in the north where Catholics and Protestants battled against each other for possession of farms that became scarcer as the population steadily increased. In Ulster Catholics set up a new secret society of this sort, "the Defenders," which attracted many members and quickly spread south. In defiance of this development, northern Presbyterians promptly founded a new society of their own, "the Peep-of-Day Boys."

At the time of the founding of the United Irishmen, Wolfe Tone was still on the side of constitutional reform. He joined the hitherto exclusively Catholic Committee as its secretary, and with the cooperation of strong-minded John Keogh he pushed the Committee's demands more urgently, and revivified the group. The first result of this effort was the Catholic Relief Bill of 1792, introduced by Sir Harold Langrishe. Langrishe once said that the reason Phoenix Park was so swampy was that parliament was busy draining the rest of the kingdom, and his bill, as might be expected, was something less than earth-shaking in its reforms. He did try to do more, but Fitzgibbon, who was now lord chancellor, and others of his mind obstructed most of what might honestly be called relief in the bill. However, a few reforms survived: for instance, Irish Catholics were thenceforth permitted to practice law in the lower courts at least. Then the bill brought an unexpected reaction from London, where, it seemed, it was felt that the legislators who opposed it had actually overdone things. English members were not pleased because they were anxious to appease the Irish Catholics. Following Burke's advice they were willing to give anything—or almost anything—to keep the Irish from aligning with the French. In short, a new climate reigned in Westminster. Wolfe Tone headed a deputation to London and had audience with King George, after which George himself put pressure on Dublin until its parliament passed—with a good majority—the Catholic Relief Bill of 1793. This, a very different document from its predecessor, did away with most of the laws that for years had oppressed the Catholics. They would now be free to bear arms and take degrees at the university, and they could vote—but they were still kept out of parliament and from any government or state office by the old oath. On the credit side for the Patriot party, parliament was at last to be purified to a certain degree at any rate, with some of the pensioners and place holders removed. Grattan was unsatisfied and announced that he was continuing to ask for thorough reform and complete emancipation, but the Catholic Committee considered its work done. It disbanded.

In January 1793 Louis XVI was beheaded: in February the French Republic declared war on England, and stories of other aristocrat executions kept trickling across the Channel to shock and alarm conservatives everywhere in the British Isles. In England the Tories and Whigs considered the danger great enough to merit a coalition. In the division of responsibilities that followed, Ireland was handed over to the Whigs, and in 1795 they appointed as viceroy an Irish friend of Grattan's, Lord Fitzwilliam. Fitzwilliam was an idealist. He wanted to grant full Catholic emancipation as soon as he took office, but this prospect alarmed Fitzgibbon's party. Quickly Fitzgibbon leaped into action to prevent the dreaded Catholic ascendancy by stirring Pitt to wrath against the new lord lieutenant, who, it was alleged, was taking too much on himself and exceeding his instructions. Scarcely a month after his arrival poor Fitzwilliam was recalled. As he made his way to the ship, sorrowing Irishmen dragged his carriage through the Dublin streets.

The affair had a decided effect on Tone, for it made him decide that it was no use and never would be any use trying by constitutional methods to reform parliament and achieve emancipation. For the time at any rate he was right: the conditions brought into being by the war militated against advanced thinking in high places: everyone was frightened by the French Republic and what it symbolized, and repression was looked on as a necessity. On the surface Ireland was offering no cause for alarm in England. Dublin rose to the occasion as she had always done and voted men and money for the war, protesting loyalty all the while. Secretly, however, there were activities of another sort. Tone was busily organizing undercover military preparations, for which he applied to France for help. In answer the French sent an agent with the harmless-sounding name of William Jackson to talk matters over, and Tone gave Jackson a written report on public sentiment, indicating that a French invasion would be popular in Ireland. Soon afterward Jackson, betrayed by an acquaintance, was arrested. He was about to be tried for treason when he killed himself, and Tone, urged by influential friends to make himself scarce, quietly went to Philadelphia and then recrossed the Atlantic to France.

In Ulster, Protestant-Catholic dissension suddenly exploded in "the battle of the Diamond" between Catholic Defenders and various combined Presbyterian groups. Nearly thirty Defenders lost their lives in this engagement, and their triumphant foes formed a new society, the Orange Order, members of which pledged themselves to maintain the Protestant constitution and defend the king and his heirs— against Catholic aggression, as they felt. The Orange Order was to become the strongest of all the religious groups, and many Catholics in Ulster, seeking to escape from its threat, joined the United Irishmen just as that society underwent a radical change. In 1794, because of the war, the government commanded that its meetings cease, and the members had gone underground and transformed their debating club into a secret society. In these conditions it flourished and became better organized, until it was a genuinely revolutionary organ. Against it the government, after the manner of such bodies in wartime, waged persistent battle and altered laws to meet the threat they had themselves created. In 1796 Parliament passed the Insurrection Act, which empowered the lord lieutenant to proclaim any district suspected of harboring United Irishmen, to place it under martial law, and to search buildings and farms, wherever he chose, for caches of arms. Men who administered the society's secret oath were to be punished with death, and those taking such oaths were liable to transportation for life. Suspects could be seized for service in the navy. The Habeas Corpus Act was suspended for the duration.

Wolfe Tone had arrived in Paris early in 1796, and was quickly commissioned as an adjutant general. For nearly a year he conferred closely with French naval officers and other Irish revolutionaries in exile. The project of an invasion tempted the French and they agreed to make a try, but the decision came late in autumn, and preparations wasted more valuable time. The expedition, under the command of a young officer named Hoche, did not get under way until December when the weather was bad and the Channel stormy. If the British navy had been ready the results might have been even worse for Hoche: as it was his fleet was scattered by wind rather than the enemy, and only a few of his ships managed to land in Bantry Bay. Hoche himself was forced to return to France without touching Irish soil, as was Wolfe Tone.

Then Ulster felt the first painful effects of the Insurrection Act, when the lord lieutenant, having heard from informers of arms hidden in the northern counties, instituted a series of searches in 1797. Even he was surprised at the quantity of guns and ammunition his men turned up. A popular leader was convicted of administering the United Irishmen's oath, and was duly executed as the new laws provided. Government troops swarmed over Ulster and behaved more brutally than circumstances seemed to justify: most of them were Protestant, and they pursued their duties against Catholic peasantry with special savagery. Atrocities were unchecked, and the country was devastated.

But in other parts of Ireland the spirit of the United Irishmen was not yet broken, and in 1798, in desperation, they decided to stop waiting for help from France and go it alone. Word was sent around that the great rebellion would take place on May 23. But the timetable was upset by calamity: in March of that year government troops, acting on another tip-off, raided an important meeting that was being held in a Dublin house. They nearly caught Lord Edward Fitzgerald, one of Tone's friends in Paris who had recently slipped into the country, and all the others were apprehended: Fitzgerald was soon tracked down, and received fatal injuries while resisting arrest. Tone was still in France, but the United Irishmen were in no mood to wait for any more leaders, and the rebellion started. Of course it should have begun simultaneously throughout the country, supplies being the most important element in such affairs. But the orders had been hopelessly confused on the way. The first rising took place in the middle of Ireland, in Meath: another followed farther south in Leinster. Then Ulster rose, but the men of the north did not have many resources left, and their effort was doomed from the start. It was Wexford and Water-ford that supplied the real surprises: on May 26, several days late, a large number of poorly armed but determined men followed a Wexford priest, Father John Murphy, into battle and actually took the town of Wexford. By the end of four days, in spite of being equipped only with pikes and courage, they had gained control of the whole county. Other groups nearly succeeded in driving out the government forces occupying New Ross, at the edge of Waterford, and were stopped only when reinforcements arrived to aid the troops. Another priest, Father Michael Murphy, commanded an army that came close to taking Arklow, though like Father John's followers they had no arms but pikes. They would probably have overwhelmed the government soldiers by sheer weight of numbers and enthusiasm if Father Michael had not fallen in battle.

These were glorious victories, but the advantage the insurgents gained could not be followed up and maintained, and the rebellion was crushed when a large number of soldiers arrived from England and met the Irishmen at Vinegar Hill near Enniscorthy. It was a complete rout for the rebels. Father John Murphy was caught and executed. The bitterness of those times is still alive today, generations and nearly two centuries later. A letter from the Honorable Dr. James McGrath of Newfoundland carries a strong echo of it. Dr. McGrath is descended from one of the Vinegar Hill rebels:

"Our rather tenuous knowledge of the family starts in 1799 when Richard McGrath left Carrick-on-Suir in Waterford....He was a blacksmith and, according to family tradition, was implicated in the 1798 rising in Ireland by forging pike-heads for the insurgents and using one himself at the Battle of Vinegar Hill in Wexford. Two popular ballads record this unsuccessful rising.

> "Who fears to speak of '98,
> Who blushes at the name?
> When cowards mock the patriot's fate
> Who hangs his head for shame?
> He's half a knave or all a slave
> Who scorns his country thus,
> But true men—like you, men-
> Will lift your glass with us.
> They rose in dark and evil days
> To free their native land;
> They kindled there a living blaze
> That nothing can withstand.

"It is instructive to remember that the author of this stirring call to arms afterwards gladly accepted a job in the English Customs Service!

"The other ballad (and I suppose there are half a hundred more) is 'The Boys of Wexford.'...

> "Up spoke the Captain's daughter,
> The Captain of the Yeos,
> Saying, 'Brave united men,
> We'll ne'er again be foes.
> A thousand pounds I give thee,
> And come along with me;
> I'll dress myself in man's attire,
> And fight for liberty.

"After this disastrous battle [of Vinegar Hill] the slaughtered Irish were dumped into pits to obliterate any signs of the graves, to prevent any recovery of the bodies which might be taken by friends or relatives and buried elsewhere and their memory perpetuated. This intention of the English authorities was foiled in a most extraordinary and unexpected manner. It seems that when mustering for the rising many of the Irish filled their pockets with their seed corn [i.e. grain, as oats, wheat, or barley, not Indian corn] as a sort of emergency ration, and the following spring this corn germinated and almost every rebel's grave was clearly marked by the green shoots of growing corn....I have always thought of this as one of the most touching episodes in all history."

Afterward only a few scattered bands kept up the resistance. July 17 marked the official end of hostilities, when the new viceroy, Lord Cornwallis, brought in an act of amnesty. On August 22, far too late, help arrived at last from France, when General Humbert at the head of a thousand troops landed at Killala Bay. The new arrivals, marching inland, were quickly joined by a number of Irishmen who even now could not quite give up hope, but these combined forces were soon faced and defeated by Cornwallis's men. Naturally it was impossible for the already landed French to send news of the unfavorable situation to additional French vessels that were on the way at that moment, and head them off. The ship carrying Wolfe Tone was intercepted by the British in consequence. Tone was taken prisoner, court-martialed, and sentenced to death by hanging, but like Jackson he managed to commit suicide before his execution day.

Grattan had continued, as long as his health permitted, to campaign for an independent Ireland. He had protested eloquently against union, but in 1797, disheartened and disgusted, he gave up and retired to England. From there he continued to observe across the Irish Sea, with such dismay as can be imagined, the progress of the United Irishmen's rising and its debacle. With the smoke of battle cleared away and hundreds of Irishmen in flight or transported

for life, Pitt was once more busy about union, which to
him seemed wholly practical, and even necessary. Joining
the two parliaments would assure the Irish Protestants of
ascendancy forever, he reasoned: peace and prosperity were
sure to follow, and everyone would benefit. In fairness to
Pitt it should here be mentioned that this question of union
did not split the country as neatly between Protestants
and Catholics, Irish patriots and English residents as some
writers indicate. There were sincere patriots who were pro-
union, corrupt placemen who opposed the Act of Union
because they wanted to be sure to be on the right horse, and
many people who held views in between these extremes.

In 1799 Pitt came near to attaining his goal when
Parliament rejected Union by the slender majority of five.
Grattan forgot his illness and threw himself back into the
struggle, to argue with all his power on behalf of national
pride and individuality. He was accused of harboring
republican, even Jacobite sentiments, and as a result lost
his place on the Privy Council, but he would not accept
defeat and continued to fight Pitt's men. These were busy
using bribery and cajolery and one promise in particular
that never failed to have its effect—to grant emancipation
to Catholics. Grattan fought gallantly throughout the last
session Dublin's parliament would have, in 1800. Because
he was too ill and weak to stand up and address the House,
he was given special permission to deliver his oration sitting
down.

"I will remain anchored here with fidelity to the fortunes
of my country, faithful to her freedom, faithful to her fall,"
he said. But parliament voted its own death and dissolution
soon afterward, and at the beginning of 1801 Ireland
became—officially—a part of Great Britain. Incidents of
protest continued for a little while, then died away when
the insurgents found more absorbing conspiracies to
concentrate their energies on. In 1802 France and Britain
signed a peace treaty, but it lasted for little more than a
year, after which the two countries were again at war. One
of the United Irish leaders, Thomas Addis Emmet, was in

Paris busily urging Napoleon to invade England by way
of his country: the Emmets were a family of property and
education, but their easy circumstances did not prevent
them from siding with those who wanted an independent
Ireland. In 1775 Thomas had defied the Insurrection Act
by taking the United Irishmen's oath in public. He was
imprisoned in 1802, but got away to Brussels. His younger
brother Robert entered the turbulent world of revolt while
still an undergraduate at Trinity: escaping arrest in 1799,
he went to France. More impetuous than his much older
brother, Robert smuggled himself back into Ireland a few
months after Franco-British hostilities started again, and
organized weapon collecting in Dublin. One of these caches
was discovered by the authorities in May 1803, and Robert
made up his mind to set off a revolt as soon as possible, on
July 23. According to the plan some of the United Irishmen
were to attack the Castle while others attended to various
strong points throughout the city. History repeated itself:
informers were rife, discipline was lacking, and nothing
went according to plan—even Robert Emmet's part of it.
In full daylight, dressed in the forbidden uniform, and not
by premeditation, he led a shambling contingent of eighty
men against the Castle. Bystanders joined in the procession
and excitement ran high. When they encountered a carriage
containing the lord chief justice and his nephew, they
dragged out these unfortunates and killed them.

Emmet fled into hiding nearby: he was reluctant to leave
the country because of his sweetheart who lived there, and
as a result he was captured, tried, and convicted of treason.
He was hanged on September 30, 1803. Robert Emmet's
romantic story and the noble speech he delivered in the
dock have made him one of Ireland's favorite heroes, but
the pride his compatriots felt in him and the excitement of
this last flare-up were poor compensation for the fact that
their country was all but supine.

The government for the new union was arranged according
to a plan that had long since been drawn up. In the "United

Kingdom of Great Britain and Ireland" there were to be one hundred members for Ireland in the Imperial Parliament and thirty-two Irish peers in the House of Lords. The viceroyalty was retained and would continue. The churches of England and Ireland, which were in any case the same, were to be formally united. Between Great Britain, the Empire, and Ireland, with few exceptions, there was to be free trade. Irish members of the House of Commons were required to take the old oath that kept out Catholics, but Catholics in general retained their recently won right to vote. Pitt and Cornwallis, mindful that they had promised complete emancipation to the Roman Catholics of Ireland in 1800, wanted to go ahead with arrangements to carry out the pledge. But George III, now well on the way to permanent insanity, became alarmed by the idea and said that his coronation oath would not permit him to discuss it. Pitt did not press the matter: he said that argument would upset the king and might push him over the edge. So the promise was broken, and Irish Catholics continued to be barred from important state places, judgeships, and high rank in army or navy. Other related promises were also ignored. The Catholic clergy was still unprovided for by the state, and tithes were still collected from Irish Catholics for the benefit of the Protestant Church of Ireland.

Something was happening in Europe and the British Isles that no one has yet been able to explain: it remains for biologists to work out the reason why there occurs, at certain times, what today we call a population explosion. Such a phenomenon occurred in the Western countries at the turn of the century. It was especially noticeable in Ireland, where more than half the population were poor peasants with little or no resources to fall back on. In 1800, with their numbers soaring to four and a half million, the need for farms grew acute, for even potatoes must have some place to grow. There was a constant demand for land, and the more it was sought, the higher, of course, went the rents. Few people realized the danger of the situation. The authorities were only aware that agrarian disturbances were increasing, and they replied with more and more repressive measures. Nothing seemed to be changing: the people demanded the usual things—money for their clergy, the abolition of tithes, lower rent—and Parliament in return postponed action, also as usual. In self-defense the members could have argued that at the time of union the Catholics had had their chance, and turned it down: the legislators had offered to supply money for the clergy if Parliament were permitted to regulate episcopal appointments. If the decision had been left to the Catholic prelates, with their characteristic desire for a quiet life, they would have accepted these conditions, but the laity refused to cede so much power in their own church to a government they heartily mistrusted. A similar arrangement offered to the Presbyterians was quickly agreed to, but the Catholics continued to hold back. That their objections did not weaken with time, but gained in power, was due to a new leader, Daniel O'Connell.

O'Connell, born in 1775, was a Kerry man whose family lived like the country gentry they were in that wild rocky country pounded by the Atlantic. All O'Connells were smugglers, as Sean O'Faolain says cheerfully. Even Daniel's uncle, Count O'Connell, the head of the family, smuggled as a matter of course; it was his chief livelihood, as it was for everyone in the county. The father, Morgan O'Connell, put baby Daniel out to foster with a family of his farm workers. It is not clear why he did this—perhaps the child needed a wet nurse—but there was a family anecdote about the fosterage according to which Morgan, riding by the cottage one day, saw his small son and paused to ask him if he ever got meat to eat. Little Dan answered, "Yes, my father stole one of Morgan O'Connell's sheep, so we had mutton for a while." All the relatives thought that a great joke.

After Daniel moved back into the family home he went to school for a while in Cork, but it did not suffice for long. At that time the Penal Laws still rendered higher education impossible for Catholics. The poorer ones among them were doomed to be "sunk in that state of degradation which compulsory ignorance necessarily produces" (W. E.

H. Lecky, *Leaders of Public Opinion in Ireland,* London, 1791, p. 2), while the richer drew their opinions, with their education, from France. Daniel O'Connell was one of the richer, luckier youths. In January 1791, at the age of sixteen, he and his younger brother were smuggled out of the country by relatives who knew all the best underground routes, to Saint-Omer. There they spent about eighteen months at school, and Dan made a brilliant record before they moved on for what turned out to be only a few months at Douay. The French Revolution was at its height, and religious institutions like Douay were not popular among the insurgents. Several times soldiers passing through the village made trouble for the priests, and at length the boys had to leave in a hurry, on the very day the French king was beheaded. More than once during the flight soldiers noticed the boys and priests in the train, and shouted threats and hammered on the coach roof. Crossing the Channel was an even more frightening experience: two men came into the cabin and proudly displayed a handkerchief which they said was stained with the blood of Louis XVI. Such experiences gave Daniel O'Connell a hatred for violent revolution which he was to retain all his life. A thorough revolutionary, he was opposed to using force to attain revolutionary ends. The conservatism of his religion contributed to his attitude and he saw nothing paradoxical in it even when he called himself, as he was to do, a radical. According to his philosophy, tyrannical authority must be overthrown by peaceful means.

Had the brothers wished to return to Ireland immediately there would have been no need for smuggling themselves in by the same methods they used when they got out. Thanks to the Catholic Relief Bill of 1792, Irish children were now permitted to move back and forth between home and abroad for schooling, but the O'Connell youths stayed on in London to finish their interrupted educations. Again, thanks to that same Relief Bill, it was no longer a waste of time for an Irish Catholic to learn the law, which is what Daniel now elected to do. His brother went home within a year or two, but 1794 found Daniel living in the Temple like many other aspiring barristers, with his name on the Lincoln's Inn rolls. He went back to Ireland in 1796 to take up a practice.

It goes without saying that he joined the United Irishmen, hoping with the other Catholics for emancipation. But when the spirit of the brethren became militant he refused to go along with them: he did not approve of the rebellion of 1798, and had even less use for the conspiracy and rebellion of Robert Emmet. The tragic outcome of these attempts proved for him once more the lesson learned from the French Revolution: "utter disbelief" (as Lecky puts it) in the use of physical force in Irish politics, a distrust of all secret and illegal conspiracy, and an extreme dread of the spirit and tendencies of the French Revolution. All of this, in the light of future events, seems wildly strange: one would think that a man of O'Connell's convictions would be a most unlikely leader of his countrymen. Most Irish took exactly the opposite view and revered, not to say idolized, the martyred Emmet, but Daniel O'Connell had other sources of strength for the revolution he wanted. In another apparent contradiction he set himself against union and for repeal— contradiction because all his closest relatives were Tories. This attitude was a part of their tradition. One O'Connell uncle served in the Irish Brigade in France and remained a stanch royalist until the end. Another was noted for his support of union. So was Count O'Connell, and Daniel's own brother John. After all, the O'Connells were landed aristocrats who would naturally believe in the old order — but Daniel did not.

The maverick took his time getting down to work. No doubt he wanted to feel the country's pulse first. In his journal he writes off 1797-98 as "wasted," but after that he settled down to grueling days, when he studied before sunrise, spent the day in the courts, and went to political meetings in the evening. He had what a lawyer needed above all in that country, an understanding of the national character and of the special situations arising from the harsh Insurrection Acts. English lawyers were often at a loss to deal with the "typical Irish witness," as Lecky too glibly describes him, "with his cunning, dexterity, dislike of simple and straightforward answers, picturesque, diffuse, evasive phraseology..." (p. 8). One might argue that these qualities are always found in the people of subject nations, and one might even ask the meaning of the word typical. But O'Connell could cope with the Irish because he understood them: he was one of them himself. Watching him at work became a favorite local pastime. Among a score of anecdotes about him is one concerning a case about a dead man's will. The point at dispute was whether the testator had been conscious at the time he signed: might his hand not have been guided by some interested party? The principal witnesses seemed to be certain that the man had been conscious, but O'Connell noticed something curiously ritual about their testimony. Each one when talking of the event put it in exactly the same way: "There was life in him." Like parrots they repeated that phrase, until O'Connell suddenly asked one of them, "By virtue of your oath, did you not put a fly into the dead man's mouth, in order that you might swear that there was life in him?" Terrified by what seemed to him supernatural knowledge, the witness admitted that this was the truth.

At another time, thanks to O'Connell's brilliant defense, an almost certainly guilty man was acquitted, and a colleague said to the lawyer, "Do you realize you have freed a wretch unfit to live?" Unabashed, O'Connell retorted, "The poor wretch was more unfit to die!" He always gave a good show. He had, or pretended to have, an uncontrollable temper in court and on the platform at political meetings. He was famous for his violent language, and he explained it by saying that someone had to balance the other Catholics, whose approach he found lamentably weak and poor-spirited. They sounded like beggars, he declared: they were always afraid. They had no idea of their true powers and rights. He wanted to show them that they were strong, so he behaved defiantly and overbearingly. Possibly, however, he really did lose his temper much of the time. It would be no wonder if he did, in frustration at the conditions he

encountered every day in his work. Catholic lawyers, in spite
of the Relief Act, had to put up with humiliating difficulties.
O'Connell could practice but was not permitted to "take
silk": he could never become a judge, or have a chance at the
really good cases. These conditions were not likely to change,
either: the union government was strongly anti-Catholic, as
were the chancellor, the chief justice of common pleas, and
the attorney general, all of whom were solidly installed and
would be for years. Parliament, the rightful ambition of
all good orators, was closed to O'Connell as a career. Yet
within these constricting limits he flourished, as his accounts
show. In 1800, his first year of work, he earned only £200.
By 1804 he had doubled that, and by 1809 the sum was
almost £3000. By 1812 he had more work on circuit than
any other lawyer in the country—more than enough even
for his immense capabilities, and with an income to match.
This success, however, was not what he really wanted from
life.

CHAPTER

16

THE money O'Connell earned and the reputation that accompanied it were both advantageous nevertheless, helping him to win his ambition of power in politics. He realized that this was what he wanted while he was still a struggling beginner, when in 1800, at the age of twenty-five, he heard that the Act of Union had become law. It was a bitter fact, he reflected, that nobody could now put a stop to the process of union, least of all a struggling Catholic barrister who had earned only £200 in the past twelvemonth. The day he got the news, he recalled in his journal in later years, was one of the most depressing he was ever to know.

"I was travelling through the mountains from Killarney to Ken-mare. My heart was heavy, and the day was wild and gloomy. The deserted district was congenial to solemnity and sadness....My soul felt dreary at the loss Ireland had sustained, and I had many wild and Ossianic inspirations."

None of them offered any solution, but O'Connell soon took action of a sort and addressed a public meeting in Dublin to discuss the union. It was a Catholic meeting, and if he actually organized it, as O'Faolain suggests, it was a courageous if not foolhardy thing to do: for good reason Catholics seldom called attention to themselves by acting as an exclusive body. Inevitably, the meeting was raided by Castle troops under Major Sirr, that same officer who had hunted down Lord Edward Fitzgerald, but the major found nothing to act on, no evidence of intrigue or political skulduggery of any sort, and after a hasty inspection he departed with his men, while the meeting proceeded. O'Connell took the podium, and launched into an eloquent speech. He regretted, he said, that they must speak at this meeting as Catholics in particular rather than simply as Irishmen. But this time at least it was necessary to do so: they had been calumniated as Catholics, and must reply as Catholics. They were being accused of having acquiesced in the union, and must deny it. Even worse, it was said that they had abandoned their country in hopes of gaining religious toleration—"and that is a lie!" thundered O'Connell. He asked the meeting to proclaim with him that if the alternatives were offered of union or the re-enactment of the Penal Code, with all its horrors, they would unhesitatingly choose the latter as the more sufferable evil.

But once this had been said and O'Connell's protest was on record, nothing was done during the next nine years, either to weaken the union or to bring about emancipation of Catholicism. O'Connell became better and better known, but his fame was as a brilliant lawyer, not a political leader. He felt that he had made his position clear, and that was enough for the time being: he would have no part of the meek attempts that were made every now and again by Catholic peers and leading Catholic businessmen to improve the situation by means of petitions to London. When the time came O'Connell meant to use stronger means than petitions.

Pitt died in 1806 without having once visited Ireland—a comment of some sort, perhaps, on his attitude toward that country. Still he had done what he could, according to his lights, to keep his promise to the Catholics: it was the king who opposed this effort, and failure could not be helped. So Pitt reasoned, but the upper-class Catholics of Ireland did not agree. They thought that his death offered them fresh hope, and through the aging Grattan they pressed their claims once more. Grattan was of the opinion that they should accept the offer the government had made in 1799, which still held good, of state provision for the Catholic clergy in return for governmental power to veto papal appointments. Once again certain bishops affirmed that they would agree to this arrangement, but nothing further happened for a few years more.

In 1809 O'Connell's long silence on political matters was broken when he addressed a meeting predominantly of Protestants, called together by Robert Hutton of the Dublin Corporation in order to protest against the union. Many of the businessmen's complaints were justified, and O'Connell had plenty of figures ready. He declared that union had already cost Ireland ninety million pounds of revenue, and that absentees were spending more than two million pounds outside of the country every year. Every penny of this money, he said impressively, was wrung from the peasants, and every year as much and more went in interest on their debt, until bankruptcy, famine, and despair were visible in every street in Dublin. Union was a crime to begin with and must continue to be, unless crime, like wine, improves with old age. If these conditions went on, crime would be hereditary and injustice perpetual. The Irish had been robbed of their birthright, said O'Connell.

He went on to make a strong appeal for that old ideal of the United Irishmen, a non-sectarian nation. He decried the religious dissensions which he insisted that the enemies of Ireland had created, and which they deliberately perpetuated, separating the nation into what he called "wretched sections and miserable sub-divisions." The enemy had succeeded in producing "all the madness of party and religious dissension; and while we were lost in the stupor of insanity they plundered us of our country." He implored his hearers to learn discretion from their enemies: "They have crushed your country by fomenting religious discord—serve her by abandoning it forever. Let each man give up his share of the mischief." Before finishing he harked back to his old pledge, made during the year of union: "I trample underfoot the Catholic claims if they can interfere with the Repeal of Union. Nay, were Mr. Perceval to offer me the Repeal tomorrow, upon the terms of re-enacting the entire Penal Code, I declare upon my heart, and in the presence of my God, that I would cheerfully accept the proposal."

After this speech, which might be called an opening salvo, O'Connell got to work in earnest to organize the Catholics into a new body, the Catholic Association. For the first time in the history of such societies this one was not formed around a nucleus of rich, titled personages, for O'Connell had realized the weakness of such supporters: they were the last people in the community to imperil their own security. He reasoned that Catholic emancipation, if it ever came, would come through the poor and oppressed who had little to lose and much to gain by almost any change. O'Connell, being well-known and well-liked, had a wide acquaintance among men of all degrees: now he worked like the adept politician he was to gather them into his organization. The Association met in rooms that he hired at his own expense, and their numbers grew.

In 1793 when the Catholic Relief Act was brought in and a number of pensioners were excluded from the government, the legislators had compensated themselves by passing the Convention Act, ostensibly aimed at safeguarding their position. By this law subjects were forbidden to assemble in groups that were purportedly representative of national interests. On the other hand, groups *were* permitted to assemble for the purpose of petitioning the government. Now O'Connell proposed that the Association set up permanent boards in the main towns of Ireland, a development which to suspicious Protestants looked very like open flouting of the Convention Act. More provocatively, in February 1811 the Association's secretary summoned to Dublin a "General Committee of Delegates" from the outlying groups. Castle troops pounced on one of their meetings and made a few arrests. The excitement soon died down and many Catholics were willing to leave the matter alone, but O'Connell was all for offensive action, and he pressed on. In August, in open disregard of a proclamation by the lord lieutenant, Catholic delegates came from the country once again for a so-called Catholic Committee convention. Six of them were immediately arrested. With all the persuasive power he could muster, O'Connell succeeded even then in holding together his forces, and 150 delegates came to Dublin yet again that October 1811. The meeting was promptly raided, of course, and one of the arrested delegates, Dr. Sheridan, was brought to trial in a test case.

The Crown's argument was that in meeting under false pretense of petitioning, Dr. Sheridan and his companions had contravened the Convention Act. O'Connell for the defense asked just what the act meant. *Had* Dr. Sheridan attended a meeting under false pretense? Cunningly the lawyer wove a mesh of technicalities around the question, with Dr. Sheridan stanchly insisting again and again that he and the others had met "for the sole, legal, and constitutional purpose of petitioning....We are met to petition Parliament." Dr. Sheridan was acquitted. But not all his colleagues escaped so lightly when their turn came at later trials, and in 1812 the Association itself was suppressed.

The year 1813 saw the formal proposal of a new Emancipation Bill that would give the English government not only the right of veto over Church appointments, but the power to appoint commissioners whose duty would be to examine and supervise all documents from Rome. This was submitted for approval to Rome, but the Pope himself did not see it: Pius VII had been imprisoned by Napoleon, and he was not released until the following year. The proposed bill went to Monsignor Quarantotti, who was handling Church affairs during the Pope's absence, and he approved of it. In a letter to the English Catholic bishops he said that he had brought the matter before a special congregation of prelates in Rome and they had decided that Catholics "might with satisfaction and gratitude accept and embrace the Bill." Furthermore, he added, "Since communication with the head of the Church in spiritual and ecclesiastical concerns is not prohibited, but the inspection of the Committee regards only matters of civil polity, this likewise ought to be acquiesced in."

For this somewhat surprising decision there are probably at least two explanations. The prelates of Rome might have felt with the Irish bishops that any arrangement that would achieve emancipation was better than none. More likely, they welcomed the prospect of having votes in the British Parliament, which seemed more important, at the time at least, than the spiritual welfare of the Irish. They may have reasoned that even in such circumstances Ireland's Catholics would be safer than were their co-religionists in France, where Church and state were split and nothing but a man's unsupported conscience stood between him and the damnation of atheism.

Whatever affected their decision, O'Connell would have none of it. He walked about Dublin protesting against it, arguing with fellow Catholics: he stood on what was then Carlisle Bridge—which now, ironically, bears his name—to talk about the matter with passers-by, urging them to attend more and more meetings, until in the end he managed to swing opinion his way not only among the congregations but with the bishops themselves. They agreed that Monsignor Quarantotti had no authority in the question of the veto. For that matter, said the extremists among them, no more had the Pope, and they sent many deputations to Rome to say so in person. One such deputation was led by a priest named Hayes, who was so emphatic, fiery, and intractable in audience with the recently liberated Pius that the pontiff ordered him to leave the city forthwith. But Father Hayes and others made an impression, and Pius began reshaping the veto decision. His alterations did not go far enough to please Daniel O'Connell, and when the Irish bishops read about them in a letter from Cardinal Litta to Pius, dated April 1815, they turned them down. No, they said, they would accept nothing short of a complete wiping out of the veto, and O'Connell declared to the Catholic Board that had taken the place of the defunct Association, "I would as soon take my politics from Constantinople as from Rome."

He had his way without going to Constantinople: the bill was defeated, but the triumph cost him the good will of the Catholic aristocrats of Ireland, and Grattan was very angry indeed. When O'Connell paraded the grievances of Ireland, he said, he left out the greatest grievance: himself. "It is the part of a bad man," he said, "to make use of grievances as instruments of power and render them the means of discontent, without a single honest attempt at redress" (Lecky, *Leaders of Public Opinion in Ireland,* Vol. 2, p. 24).

The Napoleonic wars came to an end. In 1814 Europe became peaceful. Naturally, Napoleon's blockade evaporated, and suddenly Britain's wartime boom in grain was over. Farmers found themselves without a market for their corn (as all grain is called in the United Kingdom) when the buyers who had kept them flourishing for so long disappeared with the armies that had devoured it. Irish landowners had to reconvert farmland to pasture, and were forced to lay off much of their help just when it was hardest for poor people to find other work. Even at the height of the boom it had been a problem for peasant families to house themselves. Now unemployment combined with the soaring birth rate and pushed up rents further and further, so that vast numbers of people, evicted when they couldn't pay their rent, were forced into a life of vagrancy. These conditions naturally led to increased crime, which in turn led the government to take more and more forceful measures.

The fluctuation in grain prices can be said to have had a direct effect on Ireland's population, but not because they used corn for food. The poor Irish scarcely ever tasted corn, but lived on potatoes and milk or buttermilk. Grain cost too much to grow; especially since for more than two centuries the potato had proved to be a far more satisfactory crop in many ways. It needed little land and it was more sustaining, more nourishing than grain. The peasant's existence was completely tied to the potato. He thrived when the crop was good and went hungry when it failed. Now, with the country growing more and more crowded, the potato mattered more than it ever had before. As Cecil Woodham-Smith wrote in *The Great Hunger* (p. 35), "an acre and a half would provide a family of five or six with food for twelve months." Unfortunately the tuber was subject to various ills, or blights, and when one of these struck a neighborhood there was nothing for the people who depended on potatoes for their food but to go hungry until nature relented and let them grow again. During the early part of the nineteenth century blight had appeared here and there, locally, but to us, wise after the event, there were clear warnings in 1817 and again in 1822 with severe attacks of potato disease in wide areas. So many people suffered because of this, especially in 1822, that England subscribed money for Irish relief.

Robert Peel was the secretary for Ireland at the time of the 1817 blight, and he showed great efficiency in his handling of the resulting famine. For his abilities he was admired and honored in England, but to Daniel O'Connell his name was anathema, for Peel, the very essence of the Protestant ascendancy, was firmly opposed to Catholic emancipation. Later, in England, he was to resign in protest against the granting of this emancipation. In Ireland he could not brook even that inoffensive body the Catholic Board, and in 1814 he proclaimed and dissolved it. O'Connell dubbed him "Orange Peel" and said that his smile was like the silver plate on a coffin. It was true that the secretary was of a cold, correct demeanor, but in 1815 O'Connell managed to get under his skin and nearly provoked him into fighting a duel, declaring at a public meeting that Peel wouldn't dare say of O'Connell outside Parliament what he did within its protecting walls. Peel reacted as O'Connell had hoped he would, and challenged him. The challenge was promptly accepted. Friends of both men, scenting disaster, hurried to render the duel impossible on Irish soil at least, and the principals agreed to meet on the Continent instead. But this design was frustrated when O'Connell, on his way to the meeting, was arrested in London and confined until the affair died down.

O'Connell had done his share of dueling in the past, but the Protestants jeered at him after the debacle, saying that he had himself arranged to be arrested in England. From that time on he refused to accept the challenges that so often came his way because of the immoderate language he used in public speaking. Lecky gives examples of his style—"Scorpion Stanley," "bloated buffoon" (this of Alvanley), "stunted corporal" for Wellington, and, of two other victims, "contumelious cur" and "a fellow whose visage would frighten a horse from its oats." Still, it must be admitted that he often got as good as he gave: in that respect it was an uninhibited age.

The old king died in 1820, and the prince regent became George IV. Irish Catholics had great hopes of the new king now that George III was out of the way, for a somewhat complicated reason. In 1787 the prince, as he then was, had secretly married a Catholic widow, Mrs. Fitzherbert, who had steadfastly refused to be his mistress. The marriage ceremony posed a nice problem in law: either the prince in marrying a Catholic had forfeited his right of succession, or the marriage, not having been approved by Parliament, was invalid and Mrs. Fitzherbert was dishonored. The only escape would seem to be a change in the laws that weighed so repressively on Catholics, and the prince had been heard to say more than once that he wanted to change them. But it was not long before the Catholics realized that George IV's ideas in this matter had changed drastically since that long-ago secret ceremony—had changed, no doubt, as swiftly as his bridegroom's ardor wore off. The marriage was ignored, and so were Catholic rights. O'Connell lost no time, but declared that it was no use supporting the Catholic cause until Parliament was reformed. Canning, who took over from Grattan, pursued Grattan's moderate line in pressing for emancipation. On New Year's Day of 1821 he resigned, and William Plunket assumed his duties. Under Plunket's leadership a Relief Bill went to Parliament that seemed at first glance to give the Catholics all they wanted—all even

O'Connell wanted. If it became law, Catholics would be able to occupy parliamentary seats and hold all offices under the Crown except for the lord chancellorship and the lord lieutenancy. But... there was another bill alongside it by which the abhorred veto was to be accepted, in addition to a clause requiring every priest to swear not to take part in the election of any Church dignitary except those the priest conscientiously believed "of unimpeachable loyalty and peaceable conduct." The priest must also promise to have no correspondence with Rome on any matter that might interfere with or affect the civil duty or allegiance due to the sovereign. These two bills were ultimately condensed into one, and it was passed by the Commons and supported by the leading Catholic bishop of England and a petition signed by English Catholics, a group which had always been conservative. But the Irish prelates stood by O'Connell and fought it fiercely. In the end it was defeated in the House of Lords.

In an Ireland suffering grievously from shortage of farming land, overpopulation, and unemployment, O'Connell and his associate Shiel in 1823 formed the Catholic Association of Ireland. This time O'Connell was careful rather than provocative, and made no claim that the Association consisted of delegates representing the nation: he had no wish to bring down more reprisals in the name of the Convention Act. Ostentatiously the society declared itself devoted wholly and solely to constitutional measures such as petitions. Again O'Connell eschewed aristocratic committees and rich Catholics, and devoted his efforts to capturing the support of the masses. To drive the idea home, he conceived of something new; through representatives in every part of the country the poor were invited to join the Association by paying what was called the "Catholic Rent" of a penny apiece, every month; an idea borrowed from the Methodists. The pyschological effect of paying this rent proved enormous. People who had felt helpless all their lives because of poverty experienced a new pride in participating, and new hope of determining their own fate. So many joined that the penny collections added up to a considerable sum—first a hundred, and then a thousand pounds a week. The money paid for printing and other expenses of public relations; it supplied fees for poor men to contest inequity in the courts. News of the Association spread to the coasts of Ireland, and everywhere the poor looked to O'Connell, one of their own kind who had risen up to lead them.

In spite of his growing power and his often intemperate oratory, O'Connell never counseled achieving the ends of the Association by forceful means. He remained consistent in this. Instead he enrolled the clergy in his cause. It was an astute move, and he was the first among his country's politicians to think of it. The village priest wielded a tremendous influence, and O'Connell set out to win him to the larger fold of the Association; most village fathers came willingly into his orbit and cheerfully burdened themselves with the task of collecting the Catholic Rent.

Daniel O'Connell's activities, especially the Catholic Association, were closely watched by the Castle, where people were growing disturbed at the potential of his ragged army. It was O'Connell's custom, as it was Shiel's, to call together great meetings of people in the country and talk to them. These meetings never burst out into disorderly riots, but the Protestants in power could not be sure they would not. Dublin was no stranger to rioting, and the fear of civil war was always with the government. When the news came to Ireland of Bolivar's revolution against Spain in South America, the people greeted it with acclamation that sounded sinister indeed to Plunket, who was then attorney general, and it was even more sinister when one of O'Connell's sons went off with his father's blessing to join the insurgents. In a speech soon afterward, the elder O'Connell said, "Oppression drives the wise man mad. It has not yet had that effect on the Irish people... but if such an event came to pass, may another Bolivar arise to vindicate their rights." The wild applause that greeted this passage moved Plunket to arrest O'Connell and prosecute him, but

there was nothing definite in his speech that could be pinned
down as illegal, and the lawyer went free. However, in 1825
the Association *was* declared illegal, and was duly dissolved.

O'Connell was capable of dealing with such methods: he
had had plenty of practice. Almost before the Association
disappeared a new society was taking its place, with declared
aims that appeared quite innocent and constitutional.
Ostensibly it was nothing but a benevolent association, until
1826 when the ascendancy felt its power. The occasion
was an election in county Waterford. The Relief Act of
1793 had given the vote to those Catholics of Ireland who
held forty-shilling freeholds or more, and by 1826 there
were approximately 100,000 such men. Nobody had ever
thought of 100,000 as a significant number, however, since
a Catholic tenant was expected to vote as his landlord told
him to, under threat of losing his lease. Besides, as Catholics
were not permitted to hold office, there was never a Catholic
contestant. Everything considered, forty-shilling men were
not expected to care one way or the other about elections.
Then Daniel O'Connell showed them the way they could
make a large difference. That year of 1826 there was an
election in Waterford for a parliamentary seat that was
contested by Lord George Beresford, whose family had
vast holdings in the county, and a liberal Protestant named
Villiers Stuart. There was little doubt in the minds of the
ascendancy who would win: Villiers Stuart seemed to have
no chance whatever. It came as a shock to the gentry when
the results showed Villiers Stuart the winner. Those on
Beresford's side were dazed: how could it have happened?
The truth when it came out was even more bewildering.
Villiers Stuart had been elected by the Waterford peasants,
who quietly voted for once as they wished to—or rather, as
O'Connell had told them to—rather than as their landlords
directed them. It took courage, but there were no reprisals:
so many had defied their landlords that it was out of the
question to evict them wholesale.

That was the beginning, but in Catholic eyes the victory
was only a token in comparison with what came next. The

really world-shaking year was 1828. Wellington became prime minister that year, with O'Connell's old enemy Peel as his chief secretary and an Irish M.P., Vesey Fitzgerald, in his new cabinet. Vesey Fitzgerald represented county Clare—ironically enough, he was pro-Catholic himself. According to the law he had to go home and contest a new election so as to ratify his position in the cabinet; this contest was naturally assumed by everyone (but the Catholics) to be a mere formality. But the Catholics saw their chance and quickly collected funds to set up a candidate of their own choice and their own religion. It was to be a symbolic gesture, that was all: everyone knew that Catholics couldn't be members of Parliament, but the society thought the gesture well worth it—if only the right man could be found. Vesey Fitzgerald was a generous, popular landlord, and many Clare people were scandalized at the proposal of playing such a low trick on him. Protestant though he was, they liked him, and wanted no part of the election. It was men from outside, the chief supporters of O'Connell's society, who held out. They sought a suitable candidate in vain, until at last they appealed to O'Connell to come and fight the election himself. It was a brilliant idea: nobody else, probably, would have stood a chance, but O'Connell could swing it if anyone could. And swing it he did: he was elected—at least the sheriff, fearing a riot, announced that O'Connell had won.

This left county Clare for the moment, at least, without a member for Parliament. O'Faolain describes the scene, with Vesey Fitzgerald wandering around town asking his friends, "Where will all this end?" and O'Connell begging the defeated man's pardon for any harsh words he may have used in the heat of battle. The Castle too wanted to know where it would end, and so did London. One English lord wrote to another, "The final success of the Catholics is inevitable. No power under heaven can avert its progress," and most people agreed that if the Catholics did not get their emancipation this time, civil war was inevitable. It remained to convince the king of this, but George IV had

swung around so completely on emancipation that his
words on the subject were too violent for Peel, and had
to be suppressed. It was Wellington's task to show the
situation to the monarch in its true light, which he did
in a series of conversations early in 1829. George IV was
not easy to persuade. He sulked, complained, wailed, and
threatened to abdicate: he tried to get rid of Wellington
and form another ministry, but in the end he gave in, at
the last minute, late at night on March 4. On March 5
an Emancipation Bill was submitted to the Commons: it
was passed in due course and became law on April 13. As
seen from Ireland it had its faults. Peel like George IV had
fought and kicked like a steer, and succeeded in taking
the vote from the forty-shilling freeholders; after that
nothing less than ten-guinea freeholders had the franchise.
The Catholic Society too was dissolved—but the Society
and the voters had already defeated Peel, and if he had his
revenge, so did they. He had to resign, and though for a
time he was reinstated, the government itself fell during
the following year when George IV died. According to
the new act, the only oath now required of members of
Parliament was an inoffensive everyday one of allegiance:
the sacramental test was abolished.

But for O'Connell the government ruled that if he
wanted to occupy his seat he would have to take the
old oath declaring the king head of the Church and the
mass "impious and abominable." This, they said, was
because he had been voted in under the old law, and the
new Emancipation Act was not retroactive. O'Connell
naturally declared that he was not bound to take the oath.
He withdrew, leaving the Commons to debate the matter.
He appeared next day, and was again told he must take
the oath or withdraw. He withdrew. On the third day he
studied the pasteboard on which the oath was printed, and
said, "In this Oath I see one assertion as to a matter of fact
which I know to be false. I see a second assertion as to a
matter of opinion which I do not believe to be true."

He tossed the pasteboard back, bowed, and retired.

Then he returned to Ireland, to Clare, where he was re-elected unopposed, and came back to London to take his seat. He was ready now to wage the next struggle on his agenda, for repeal of the union.

CHAPTER

17

"OTHELLO'S occupation's gone," said a friend jokingly to O'Connell when emancipation was carried.

"Gone!" repeated O'Connell in surprise. "Isn't there a repeal of the union?"

He was more than ready for battle when he took his place in the Commons, but everyone there expected him to make a laughing stock of himself in his maiden speech. They knew or had heard of the manner in which he addressed his Irish audiences—violently, brashly, coarsely. Such a style would never do in the House, they told each other. Members there were accustomed to elegant, subtle, accomplished speakers and much formality: to put O'Connell among such gentlemen was outright cruelty, they felt. As for O'Connell himself, he could hardly have expected a heart-warming welcome. He had had a taste of English hospitality as soon as he arrived, when he was blackballed at the English Catholic club—but then he and the English Catholics had never been fond of each other. They looked on him as a disgrace to the Church and recoiled from his Irishness, whereas he had said in public that one of the emancipation's great defects was in not having excluded them. But O'Connell's first address, when it came, surprised all his critics; it was in entirely different style to his country oratory, with clear, reasoned remarks and no tinge of egotism or "bad taste," to use Lecky's words. He quickly took his rightful place as the respected leader of the Irish contingent.

In 1830 George IV died, and the Whigs, after a long stay in the wilderness, came back to power. For O'Connell this was comparatively comfortable: he could work with Whigs, he felt, and now he began struggling for various reforms while preparing for an all-out fight for repeal. There was much room for reform. The Emancipation Act itself was not satisfactory, having been written in a grudging spirit. All sorts of loose ends remained. Some of these faults were so glaring that they hardly mattered: O'Faolain says that O'Connell dismissed one clause, purporting to suppress all monasteries and Jesuit institutions, as inexecutable, and it was indeed forgotten very soon. What was more vexing were the many petty restrictions that remained: Catholics in office were not permitted to wear official insignia at Catholic ceremonies, so that in 1838 when O'Connell became lord mayor of Dublin he had to leave off his robes at the door of the procathedral. More annoying was the snub administered to him when six Catholic king's counsels were selected—the first ever to practice law in the Inner Bar—and he, of all lawyers in Ireland, was passed over, though his associate Shiel was not. However, such matters were pinpricks in comparison with others, such as the clause disfranchising the forty-shilling freeholders. They had been the backbone of O'Connell's movement, and he felt, with some justification, that he had let them down by not fighting harder for their right to vote. Now that the clause was law he did his best to reverse it, claiming that enormous numbers of people had lost the franchise, and that this was an important matter in Ireland, where only a small percentage had had the vote to begin with. Before the act, in 1829, out of 7,000,000 inhabitants only 300,-000 men could vote. Afterward the number shrank to 26,000.

O'Connell's "tail" of Irish M.P.s were too few to matter

except as a makeweight when the race between the two main parties was close. He hoped that Lord Grey's Reform Bill of 1832 would give him another seventy-two, but it yielded only five. Even this small handful did not always behave as one unit, for they wrangled among themselves, but he did what he could with them, and his voice, at any rate, was listened to in the House.

In Ireland he found that the word "repeal" always got a reaction from people when other less easily understood causes did not. The government passed a temporary Coercion Act giving the lieutenant governor the power to proclaim meetings and "preserve the peace," and it soon proved useful. To further his cause of repeal, O'Connell founded a Friends of Ireland Society, which was immediately suppressed through the agency of the Coercion Act. O'Connell promptly founded the Irish Volunteers for the Repeal of the Union: that too had only a short life before it was quashed. He established so-called "repeal breakfasts," where speeches were made: after some hesitation —for the authorities were not sure just how to apply the act in this case—they were suppressed.

"Curse them," shouted O'Connell, "we'll have Repeal Lunches. If they are suppressed we'll have Repeal Tea and Tracts. If they are suppressed we'll have Repeal Suppers." He established a General Association for Ireland to Prevent Illegal Meetings and to Protect the Sacred Right of Petition: it was suppressed, and Lord Anglesey, the lord lieutenant, wrote from Dublin to London, "Things have now come to that pass that the question is whether O'Connell or I shall govern Ireland." (As a matter of fact Anglesey liked and respected O'Connell, though it worried him to learn, after a long interview, that the latter was still bent on attaining repeal by "desperate agitation.") O'Connell was still busily thinking up new association names when, by a comprehensive proclamation in January 1832, any association under any name whatever was forbidden.

"I'll make myself into an association," he declared, and

held a public breakfast. He was immediately arrested, but the whole fight soon melted away when Parliament dissolved.

In 1835 O'Connell made an alliance with the Liberals, hoping that this move would help him to gain much of what he was after. It helped, but it is a moot point whether or not he paid too dearly for this aid, since the upshot was that he was virtually in bondage for the next three years. However, in the House of Commons many things went better: he won several desired reforms immediately after the alliance, and after Victoria became queen in 1836 and Melbourne headed her government, more reforms passed in the House. Some excluded Irishmen again became eligible to vote. Moreover, the patience-consuming business of integration was pursued, and Protestants in Ireland had to give way at last where they had been grimly holding on to certain places: these were now, at least in theory, open to Catholics. Lecky declares that four years after emancipation there was still not a single Catholic judge or stipendiary magistrate in the whole country: all the high sheriffs except one were Protestant and so were the overwhelming majority of unpaid magistrates and grand jurors, five inspectors general, and all thirty-two police inspectors. Municipal reform was badly needed: the chief towns were in the hands of narrow, corrupt, and intensely bigoted corporations. This reform was achieved in 1838, but it was not easily followed up: one reason Daniel O'Connell was elected mayor of Dublin was that nobody else suitable could be found. Then there was the troublesome matter of tithes. It was Grattan who, before the turn of the century, first tried to lift this very unfair tax from the shoulders of the Irish Catholics, but it remained until Bishop Doyle, an outstanding prelate and sturdy fighter, encouraged the people to "strike," or refuse to pay the tithe. O'Connell was one who struck, and had to appear in court for it. When many of the poor followed Doyle's suggestion and refused to pay, the authorities called in troops of the hated yeomanry, mostly undisciplined Presbyterians from the north, who treated Catholics badly as a matter of conviction. The people fought back. The struggle went on from 1830 to 1836, and it won status in the process, becoming known as the Tithe War—correctly, for it involved outright battles in which a number of men died. At last in 1836 the government passed a Tithe Act which, while not relieving poor Irish in any material way, did at least call the tax by another name. And thenceforth Catholics were no longer called on to support the Protestant Church.

O'Connell didn't confine his efforts in Parliament to Irish affairs alone. He advocated parliamentary reform "of the most radical description" (Lecky), with universal suffrage, secret ballots, and an elective House of Lords. He supported the emancipation of the Jews, being one of the first to propose this measure. He wanted legal reform too, with the simplifying, cheapening, and codifying of the law and the abolition of obsolete forms and phraseology. He ardently advocated the abolition of capital punishment. He was a steady, vehement opponent of slavery, even though his attitude offended Americans who had until then been generous donors to the cause of repeal. When such people stopped sending subscriptions, O'Connell was unrepentant, and spoke in the House of his contempt for a government that could protect slavery, yet pretend to follow the constitutional precept that declared all men born free and equal. When someone remonstrated with him he said, "I would rather have one Irish landed proprietor of weight than all their slave-breeders. It is ourselves alone must work out repeal."

To this end he returned to his old plan to organize his followers at home as he had done for emancipation. In 1843 he set to work much in the same fashion, and the large meetings that had characterized that struggle began again. The technique met with disapproval from his own associates: agitation, as they called the process, had been a good weapon, but they were dubious of bringing it out and using it so soon again. Even Shiel disapproved, but O'Connell continued, and also initiated "tribute," a sort of glorified Catholic Rent on a more ambitious scale. The first tribute was raised by annual subscription, with priests doing the main job of collecting just as they had helped with the Rent in the past. This first subscription, known as the O'Connell Tribute, played the part of a testimonial to the leader: the sum of £50,000 was collected and handed over to O'Connell for his own, to be managed as he liked. After that the money averaged out at about £15,000 a year—astonishing sums for such a poor people. Outsiders stared. There was much snickering at O'Connell, and criticism of him for accepting the money. Stung to self-defense, he answered the critics, declaring that he had earned that money through having worked twenty years for emancipation when, as a struggling young lawyer, he could ill afford the time he gave. For four years, he pointed out, he had borne all the expenses of Catholic agitation without ever getting more than £74 from other workers, and since emancipation he had almost abandoned his practice, though his income for the previous year had been £8000 and would in all likelihood have increased.

"Who shall repay me for the years of my buoyant youth and cheerful manhood?" he demanded, in what was most certainly an un-English way to talk. "Who shall repay me for the lost opportunities of acquiring professional celebrity and for the wealth which such distinctions would ensure?"

These were rhetorical questions, but his people must have promised themselves in their hearts that they would take care of their hero, and their tribute did support him, making him independent of the government, and paid his costs as party leader. Lecky points out that emancipation when it opened Parliament to Catholics immediately increased such costs: most of the tribute money seems to have gone on election expenses—which the historian says were not altogether disinterested, since O'Connell brought into Parliament as many relatives as he could: he used to boast about the number there were in the House. Still, this can hardly be put down to greed. A leader must be sure of his followers, and for such purposes a relative is a better bet than a stranger.

During the lull that preceded the big push, O'Connell may have hesitated once or twice over repeal. At least, O'Faolain thinks he did, and that he asked himself if Ireland might not after all be better off under a reformed English government than in a state of independence. But if he did play with such notions, in the end he always came back to repeal, even in the gentle rain of reforms that pattered down on Ireland during the better years.

"The country had... since 1796 been under a terrorism... in which the normal ascendancy was reinforced by an Orange bigotry which meant to keep the power in Protestant hands in spite of emancipation..." (Curtis, *A History of Ireland*, p. 564). For the first time this terrorism was now broken by Lord Mulgrave, "a noble-minded Viceroy" who discouraged the Orange spirit and saw to it that Catholics got equal treatment with Protestants when they sought places. Mulgrave's policy was naturally unpopular with landlords and other ascendancy men, but his undersecretary Thomas Drummond was another man of the same sort: both wanted justice. As one measure they created a new police force, the Royal Irish Constabulary, whose ranks were filled with native Irishmen. The Constabulary, which Curtis says was more like an army, was highly efficient for keeping order: later, however, it was used for eviction purposes and as the first line for suppressing rebellion. The Orange Order was altogether discredited, and in 1837 it was broken up.

In 1841 the British government was again upset, with the Liberals out and Tories in under O'Connell's old enemy Sir Robert Peel as prime minister. O'Connell "the Liberator" was prepared for this eventuality: a year earlier he had formed the Repeal Association and succeeded in keeping it going without suppression. Now he began calling a series of monster meetings, starting in 1843. The worried authorities dubbed these meetings agitations, though in fact they were peaceful enough, since O'Connell held the people in the palm of his hand and was temperamentally incapable of stirring up active violence, but the English could never feel sure that he wouldn't let slip the leash one day soon. They watched the throngs that came to the meetings in their hundreds and more, silently walking or riding from all corners of the country. The situation was dangerous, they said: it would take little genuine agitation to spark off angry passions in the crowd. One day O'Connell would fail to hold them.

Toward the end of the series O'Connell held a meeting at the hill of Tara, county Meath, selected because of its ancient glory and importance. Today Tara is nothing to see. It is a hill not very far north of Dublin, but not all that much of a hill; of the palace and terraces that once crowned it nothing remains, not even rubble. On the day of the meeting, however, Tara was once more the heart of Ireland, and O'Connell in a leading carriage headed a splendid procession from Dublin. All along the way more vehicles fell in behind him, jaunting cars and farm carts, coaches of every description. Whenever they passed through a small town they were greeted by the population dressed in their best, with buildings decorated with banners and the green branches that were the insignia of O'Connell's people. They picked up local bands and country carts crowded with people, and by the time they reached Tara the crowd was so thick that they couldn't approach the base of the hill; they had to stop three miles off. "The procession... was but as a river discharging itself into an ocean," wrote C. Gavan Duffy of the *Nation* in his book *Young Ireland*. "The whole district was covered with men....The number is supposed to have reached between 500,000 and 750,000 persons. It was ordinarily spoken of as a million, and was certainly a muster of men such as had never before assembled in one place in Ireland, in peace or war." In fact there were probably a quarter of a million souls gathered at Tara, but that was enough and more than enough to worry the Castle.

Behind these great gatherings was O'Connell's firm belief in the efficacy of demonstration. Surely, he felt, if the Irish showed their desire for repeal in this way, Parliament would bow to their wishes. In 1840 he said it: the Repeal Association must persuade four fifths of Ireland's population to join. "When such a combination is complete, the parliament

will naturally yield to the wishes and prayer of an entire
nation. It is not in the nature of things that it should be
otherwise." His confidence was based on experience. Hadn't
the English given in on emancipation after just such a series
of demonstrations![5] All that was needed was to show them
without a doubt how the Irish people felt.

He did not appreciate that the two situations were vastly
different. The battle for emancipation was half won before the
meetings were called. Half or nearly half of the House were
on O'Connell's side to begin with, as were many in the House
of Lords. His chief obstacle then had been the Wellington-
Peel partnership and even they found themselves unable to
withstand the demands of the pro-emancipation group. Once
they were brought round, victory was his. Repeal was a
different matter entirely, for it had few champions among the
English or the Protestant ascendancy at either the beginning
or the end of the agitation. This was not a mere question of
conscience, of being liberal or reactionary: for Ireland to pull
out seemed to the Commons a grave threat to the Victorian
Empire's very existence. Peel expressed the feelings of most
of his colleagues when he said: "There is no influence, no
power, no authority which the prerogatives of the crown
and the existing law give to the government, which shall not
be exercised for the purpose of maintaining the union; the
dissolution of which would involve not merely the repeal of
an act of parliament, but the dismemberment of this great
empire." Much as he would deprecate civil war, he added,
there was no alternative he didn't think preferable to the
dismemberment of the Empire (*Course of Irish History*, p.
260). It was against such fervent faith, pride, and loyalty that
O'Connell hoped to pitch his simple argument of what the
Irish people wanted. He meant to prove to the government
that the only alternatives were repeal or revolution. He hoped
that the sight of these hundreds upon thousands of men would
so convince his opponents. Instead, they girded themselves
up to fight if necessary.

O'Connell planned the last and biggest monster meeting of

the series for October 8, 1843, at Clontarf, where in 1014 the old Irish hero Brian Bora fought his last battle and died after defeating the Ostmen. Many of the Repealers looked forward to October 8 in the happy belief that on that date Dan O'Connell would tell them to go out and take independence for themselves. Certainly O'Connell had no such intentions. He was sure that the meeting itself would be enough to overturn the English, but they and he were never to find out. A few hours before the meeting was scheduled to begin, the government banned it. Parties of Repealers on the road were told the news at the same time that they got O'Connell's orders: turn around and go home. Everyone went home. Obedient to the end, they did exactly what he told them to do.

O'Connell and some of his associates were arrested, accused of conspiracy, and stood trial in Dublin before a jury of Protestants, who found them guilty. They appealed, and the House of Lords reversed the verdict, but O'Connell could not have had heart enough to cheer his small victory. Events had proved him completely wrong in what really mattered, and he had to admit it: it was immaterial how many Irishmen marched to monster meetings or otherwise peacefully demonstrated their wish for repeal: England was determined to keep the union intact. The Clontarf meeting was to have crowned O'Connell's career: instead it marked his first severe defeat, and set him on a downward path. He carried on in the House of Commons, but his health began to trouble him, and in 1847, at the age of seventy-two, he was to die with repeal still out of reach.

A band of younger men had come together around him, however, through the agency of a newspaper called the *Nation* that made its appearance in 1842. At first they supported O'Connell unquestioningly: later their relations with him were not so smooth. The leading spirits of the group, which came to be known as Young Ireland, were Thomas Davis, James Fintan Lalor, Charles Gavan Duffy, and John Mitchel. True to tradition, most of this handful of men, passionately devoted to Ireland's cause, were Protestants. They wanted repeal, or, as they called it, national independence. They sought the true spirit of their country not so much in the annals of modern times as in the ancient land of Gaels and Normans, and they made a conscious effort to learn Gaelic or at least to translate Gaelic legends and spirit into their own tongue. The friction between O'Connell and Young Ireland arose inevitably because he seemed to them too much the Grand Old Man, the patriarch, the bully, and— for they were liberals—they hated his strong pro-Catholic bias: they believed as the early United Irishmen had believed in a sectless nation. The leader was Thomas Davis, who, as befitted a member of the Protestant ascendancy, was educated at Trinity and later became a barrister. James Fintan Lalor lived in the deep countryside and sent in his contributions. A cripple, he was unable to take an active part in farming, but he had a farmer's viewpoint and took the attitude that every peasant had the right to own his land. Gavan Duffy was editor of the *Nation,* a Catholic journalist with theories on the correct Irish parliamentary procedure in the House of Commons. John Mitchel of county Down, a Unitarian solicitor, was in comparison with the others an extremist. He was in favor of Ireland's taking her freedom by any necessary means, even if this meant war. But then none of the Young Irelanders agreed with O'Connell on the necessity of keeping the peace above all, and within a few years these differences brought about a complete break with the old man. By this time England had become aware of Young Ireland, and watched it with some apprehension: at the same time they began to appreciate the fact that O'Connell, however much they had said against him, was a moderate in comparison. At least, as long as he influenced Irish popular sentiment they knew that law and order were safe, whereas if young hotheads took charge there was no telling what might happen.

In 1845 there was plenty of cause for alarm, for the potato crop failed over almost all Ireland, and this meant complete catastrophe for the people, who had learned to live on it exclusively. In an article on the great famine, Dr. E. R. R.

Green (*Course of Irish History*) sums it up: "The figures of the 1841 census reveal the appalling insecurity of Ireland's vast population. Only 7% of holdings were over thirty acres in size. 45% were under five. In Connacht the holdings under five acres went as high as 64%....Over two-thirds of the Irish people were dependent on agriculture for a livelihood in 1841, but the condition of the other third was far from enviable" (pp. 266-67). As for them, British industry was more powerful and efficient: also, there had been severe deflation of Irish money, and steamships and railways, by lowering transport and handling costs, had struck at the livelihood of Irish manufacturers and wholesalers. In short, "The survival of a vast impoverished population depended on the recurring fruitfulness of the potato and on that alone."

In retrospect it may be easy to recognize the danger of this state of affairs, but nothing on the scale of the 1845 potato blight had ever happened in Ireland before, and nobody was prepared for the magnitude of the disaster. Though its nature was unknown at the time, the blight was due to a fungus that spread incredibly swiftly, rendering much of that year's crop completely inedible. Peel, who had had experience in such affairs through earlier, smaller blights, immediately bought about half a million dollars' worth of what the British call Indian corn, to hold ready as a possible disincentive to inflation and soaring grain prices. He appointed a relief commission, and encouraged contributions from the people by promising additional government money in proportion. Relief works were set in motion. But his most important move was responsible for his fall. He repealed the Corn Laws, dear to the English farmer because they protected the selling price of his grain. Peel realized what a ruinous step he was taking, but he was a conscientious official and felt he could not put public money into relief while at the same time retaining artificial means to keep up the price of corn and hinder its importation. As an immediate result he and his party were voted out of power and the Whigs came back. It was the end of June 1846.

On certain principles Tories and Whigs agreed, no matter

what their differences, and one of these principles was the policy of *laissez faire,* the Tightness and inevitability of the laws of economics. One didn't tamper with the law of supply and demand, or buck private enterprise. Even if one did, the law had its way in the end. Peel had come close to meddling thus when he used public money to buy Indian corn; now under the new prime minister, Lord John Russell, the chancellor of the exchequer came to an understanding with the permanent head of the treasury, Charles Edward Trevelyan: no more almost-meddling. Even if the next potato crop was blighted, the food supply must not be augmented by government action: it was to be left exclusively in the care of private enterprise. People would be helped to earn the money with which to buy food from private dealers by means of more relief works—if this was necessary.

The crop failure that took place in 1846 was on a bigger scale than that of 1845, with dreadful results, and conditions were made even worse by government policy. The 1846-47 winter was the harshest the Irish had ever known. Miserable, starving people rapidly fell victim to disease. Most of them were bewildered and helpless, but here and there a ragged crowd summoned up the spirit to protest when they saw ships being loaded with Irish grain for export. The landlords too were caught in a cleft stick: they exported the grain because they were being squeezed for their rates. Many of them evicted tenants who couldn't pay their rent; some evicted paying tenants as well, so that they could sow the land with wheat for export. By February 1847 distress and disease were everywhere. "Famine fever," a combination of typhus and relapsing fever, claimed many, as did scurvy and dysentery. "Famine dropsy," hunger edema, was commonplace. That year saw the migration to America of thousands of terrified poor. In earlier days there had been few emigrants from Ireland. Most of those went no farther than Great Britain, and all of them were sturdy, self-reliant people in search of better chances. These were different—poor, weak, and ill, and many too old or young to do a hard day's work. Both Canada and the United States were angry, and did their best to moderate the flow and discourage the immigrants.

That fall of 1847 brought a remission of the plague in Ireland. Fine crops appeared, but there were not so many landlords with the money to pay men to harvest them; as for potatoes, few had been planted. After two years of maltreatment, the economy of Ireland was in parlous state, and the English, preoccupied with money troubles of their own, did little to help. Lord Clarendon, the viceroy, reported that distress, discontent, and hatred of English rule were increasing everywhere; six landlords were, in fact, shot and killed that winter, as were ten other men who owned land. Believing that a rising was imminent, the viceroy asked London for more powers against emergency. By the end of the year extra troops had been sent to Ireland.

Daniel O'Connell, who had long been ailing, set out for Rome at the beginning of that unhappy year of 1847: he reached Genoa in May, and there died. Young Ireland had not been in touch with him or his Repeal Association since their break with both after the Clontarf debacle, but now he was dead, and they were still alive, alert to take the chance to change Ireland all at once for the better. The only trouble was that the leaders could not agree on how it was to be done, or just what they wanted. That January they formed an Irish Confederation and tried to enlist people in local clubs, through which they hoped to push for repeal, but it was impossible to interest the starving peasantry in anything so abstract. Fintan Lalor proposed an agrarian revolution in which the Irish could take and own their own soil, and most Young Irelanders approved this suggestion: John Mitchel was particularly attracted to it, but he wanted to use violence and the others were unwilling. Mitchel suggested that everyone should refuse to pay rent, for a start, but this action would certainly have put a stop to public relief, which, inadequate as it was, was still something, so the moderate Young Irelanders didn't agree. Mitchel then left the *Nation* to edit a paper of his own, the revolutionary *United Irishman*. For a while he said whatever he liked in print: the Castle had plenty of other worries and paid little attention. Then, in 1848, stirred by news of popular risings in Sicily (January), Paris (February), and Vienna (March), even the moderate Young Irelanders lost their caution and joined Mitchel. Quite openly they advocated insurrection. At a meeting Mitchel told the people to go and get themselves guns. That was too much. Three of the leaders were arrested and tried for sedition: Mitchel was found guilty, sentenced to fourteen years' transportation, and sent away.

As a result, enrollment in Young Ireland clubs suddenly increased, while the government in England hastily completed a new, harsh Treason Felony Act. On the strength of this Gavan Duffy was arrested on July 9 and his associate Meagher was picked up on July 12. Troops moved into the countryside to install themselves near cities. Clarendon insisted on the suspension of habeas corpus, and one of the chief leaders, William Smith O'Brien, a Protestant but also a descendant of Brian Boru, started out to raise the country. In county Wexford he held a meeting with other Young Irelanders and called on the people to join them. There was little response, so the party moved on, to Kilkenny and then Callan. Again, no response. In Cashel, where they next went, they were sure of finding enthusiastic allies waiting, but again they were disappointed. At last in Mullinahone they were welcomed and told that six thousand men wanted to be led against the English, though they had few weapons. In the morning, however, when the volunteers found that no food was to be distributed, they dropped off until only about five hundred were left. Young Ireland had failed to take into account the starvation that pushed all else out of the people's minds.

Even O'Brien's five hundred soon dwindled to fifty, and the only battle that approached his visions of rebellion took place in a Ballingarry farmyard, where he and his handful of peasants attacked a police garrison and were beaten off. He and the other leaders stood their trial and were condemned to death, the sentences later commuted to transportation.

The 1848 potato crop was again blighted, and the winter that followed was as disastrous as that of 1846-47. When at last it was over—though nobody could be sure it was until 1849 was at an end—the toll was counted. In 1845 Ireland's population was more than eight, and probably nine, million. In 1851 it was down to six and a half million, and the next census, in 1881, gave the figure of five million.

CHAPTER
18

MORE than three million Irish, a considerable proportion of the country's population, arrived in America as immigrants between 1846 and 1891. As has been said, they were not always welcomed with glad enthusiasm. They themselves were of course homesick, and tended to cling together in that strange land, even after the newness had rubbed off a little and they had begun to get settled in. It was hardest on the elderly, who longed for home and forgot, or refused to think of, famine or the terrors of eviction. They looked back on a dream place where potatoes did not rot in the ground and fields grew green and wholesome and sweet-smelling: they longed for home, and sang nostalgic ballads about it. Their children, however, were too busy to repine. They worked hard, lived frugally, and sent money back to the old country to help their relatives. Many of these came over in time to join them, when they got the word that there was work in America if you didn't mind plenty of it and could hold off the drink. The majority of news sent home was of that order.

"My dear Father I must only say that this is a good place and a good country for if one place does not suit a man he can go to another and can very easy please himself," wrote a young girl soon after she arrived in New York in 1850.

"I have got along very well since I came here and has saved some money," a young man said, in a letter from Philadelphia dated 1854.

But there was also comment on the effort needed to get along so well, as from a woman living in Denver, who reported in 1884 that she had ten children and helped her husband in his business. She added, "This is a regular driving country. A person with only small means has to keep on all the time."

In 1853 a young lawyer in Washington State reported, "This is a good country for a labouring man....At this time he can earn at least one dollar a day, equal to 4 shillings British. He is in good demand for this sum. He can board himself well—having meat three times a day, for ten dollars a month—two dollars and a half a week, or ten shillings British." But he added a qualification: "Believe me, there is no idle bread to be had here. If you get a dollar a day, you have got to earn it *well*." (All from Arnold Schrier, *Ireland and the American Emigration.*)

In comparison Schrier cites the wages of an agricultural laborer in Ireland in 1850, who, if he was fortunate enough to have work, got less than five shillings a week and rarely ate meat more than two or three times in a year. For all this, a greater surprise for the Irishman newly arrived in America was neither the money nor the food, but the fact that everyone dressed well, and took this luxury for granted. "If you were to see Dennis Reen when Daniel Danihy... dressed him with clothes suitable for this country you would think him to be boss or steward so that we have scarcely words to state to you how happy we feel at present." This came from a young man in Buffalo, writing to his family in Cork in 1850. The classlessness of American society delighted the immigrants. "There are no Gentlemen here," a ranch hand reported approvingly from Washington to his people in Limerick in 1883. "If a farmer in Ireland made 3 or 4 thousand dollars in a year you couldn't walk the road with them. You would have to go inside the fence or they would ride over you" (Ibid., pp. 30-31).

Naturally, in spite of these advantages there were other drawbacks as well as hard work. The immigrant had to be wary of tricksters, especially sharks trying to sell him waterlogged or desert land. He must avoid usurers. He had to face prejudice even among other Irish who had been fortunate enough to precede him—for those already entrenched often disliked meeting immigrants because the newcomers reminded them too painfully of what they had fled from and wanted to forget (though people of other nationalities were worse by far than the Irish snobs). Yet another cause of prejudice was that Americans traditionally detest poverty and seem to look on it as a deliberate state in which people remain from choice rather than a condition visited on the poor by forces beyond their control. The well off were apt to say, "They could perfectly well help themselves if they wanted to," and "Being poor is no excuse for living like animals." Some people resented competition on the labor market. Furthermore, the majority of the new arrivals were Roman Catholics, and in America as in the Old World many people hated the Catholic Church—a sentiment they or their ancestors had brought into the country.

What with so many strains and stresses, explosions often occurred, and the Irish suffered from them. In the early 1850s the Know-Nothing movement was directed specifically at the Irish. Shrier quotes a Philadelphia businessman who wrote in 1855, during the height of the Know-Nothing agitation, to his sister in Ireland to tell her that people had better stay there even if they were poor, because at least they were safe in Ireland from murderers. And prejudice persisted (as we ourselves should know all too well) after the Know-Nothings had subsided, becoming a familiar part of American life. In 1892, in a letter from Iowa, a railroad section foreman told his uncle in Donegal about his new boss, a Norwegian, who had fired every Irish foreman except himself and a Tipperary man: "... he hates the ground an Irishman walks on... and as you are well aware an Irishman is not badly stuck on him either" (Ibid., p. 33).

Yet more and more Irish left home for the United States, in spite of all that churchmen and the government could say to dissuade them. The country, said these worthies, was bleeding to death without her youth, but her youth departed nonetheless, and felt themselves justified. The famine had passed, it was true, but more crop failures were bound to come sooner or later, and even without the famine nobody could claim that Ireland was recovering with much resiliency. Thanks to the Encumbered Estates Act of 1849, ruined landowners were at last permitted to sell their lands, but what good did that do the tenants? The purchasers of these estates were for the most part English or Scottish, the only people in the British Isles who still had money-strangers who were looked on by the locals much as the American carpetbaggers after the Civil War were to be looked on by Southerners. The greatest sufferers from these transactions were those few sturdy tenants who had managed through the thin times to stay on their holdings, for the new owners had no sentimental inhibitions about uprooting and evicting them.

All in all, for a long time Ireland seemed a hopeless place. It would not have reassured the sufferers to be told that in a certain way people were better off than they had been before the famine. No matter what comfort economists took in the picture it was no good telling a ruined tenant who was about to be evicted because be couldn't pay bis lent that there was now more land available, nor did it help an unemployed farm hand to learn that for those who *had* jobs, wages were far better than they had ever been. As always in times of trouble, those rural Irish who stayed at home resorted to secret agrarian societies, groups like the Whiteboys, lumped together in the vernacular as Ribbonism. Ribbonists—dissident agricultural workers— attacked property as a means of expressing protest. They went out in the dark of night, masked, and committed acts of violence against unpopular neighbors such as landowners and oppressive farmer-employers, burning their barns and maiming their cattle, but though such measures afforded them temporary relief and frightened their enemies, nothing was gained. Anger continued to smolder. Seeking someone to blame, the Irish peasants in their misery pointed at Britain and the English landowners in Ireland. They felt that though the English had not actually visited the potato blight on the country they were indirectly responsible for her woes. Had they not conquered old Ireland and destroyed her kings? This rendered them responsible for her, and they had always failed in that responsibility. The famine was only a part of the pattern. Even before, things had always gone wrong. On her own, without the English and the necessity of paying rent to the English, Ireland would have been a happy, solvent country. They, the Irish, had never desired union with tyrant England. Now they wanted to see it dissolved. They wanted a divorce from England.

This, of course, was the sentiment of the Catholic Irish, but in the Protestant north feelings about the union were completely opposite. Almost everyone in Ulster, landowner or textile worker or smallholder, was far more contented than his neighbor in the south. In the industrialized north they were enjoying a boom, with mills working full time to fill the demand for cloth, and tenant farmers, who lived according to "Ulster custom," far better satisfied than southern agricultural workers. The so-called Ulster custom in fact represented all that was left of a system that had prevailed throughout Ireland before the Elizabethan conquest. An Ulster tenant had an interest in his holding, held tenure as long as he paid rent on it, and if or when he wished to leave it could sell his interest. The tenants of the north were reasonably contented, and as a result their landlords, too, were contented.

All in all, Ulstermen decidedly did not want to dissolve the union. It is true that their province was only one of the four that made up Ireland, but though a minority they were very vocal. Disagreement between northern and southern

Irish kept alive old quarrels and prevented the development of a comprehensive nationalism.

Charles Gavan Duffy had been editor of the Young Ireland paper, the *Nation,* and was the only one of his group who stayed on in Ireland after the debacle of 1848. In 1850 he reappeared on the scene as founder of the Tenant Right League, the platform of which was that every tenant in the country had the right of the so-called "three Fs" already embodied in Ulster custom: fair rent, fixity of tenure, free sale of one's interest in one's holding. Members of this league had no desire, or at least no confessed aim, to claim their "rights" by force: they believed they could attain their ends constitutionally, sending to Parliament men who would agitate for the cause in the proper way. In 1852 they made a promising start, for that year, thanks to a new Irish Franchise Act, as many as 103 Irish M.P.s were sent to Westminster, of whom 50, including Gavan Duffy himself, were elected on the Tenant Right League platform. Unfortunately for league hopes, the "Irish Brigade" proved to be a bitter disappointment owing to the quality of some of the members. Two in particular, William Keogh and John Sadlier, were patently self-seeking. Incidentally, they paraded their Catholicism so relentlessly, using it as what in modern speech would be called a political gimmick, that they were mockingly dubbed "the Pope's Brass Band."

An earlier House of Commons had watched maliciously for O'Connell's maiden speech and sniggered in advance, confident that he would never catch "the tone of the House," and would make Ireland ridiculous. In happy-ending style the new member had confounded them and proved master of the situation. But 1852 was different, and the comic Irishmen in the House exhibited all the traits found laughable by the English—funny accents, volubility, and the rest. And they were not only comic, but venal. "They were all pledged not to take any Government office," wrote Desmond Ryan bitterly. "Shortly after, Mr. Keogh became Irish Solicitor-General, and Mr. Sadlier, Lord of the Treasury, in Lord

Aberdeen's ministry. The Tenant-Right movement was split, disillusioned, and wrecked....After it was evident that his movement was broken, Mr. Gavan Duffy said farewell to public life, and went to Australia" (*The Phoenix Flame,* p. 42).

In 1858 men of a different temperament formed a group known as the Fenian Society or the Irish Republican Brotherhood—or, in America, as the Clan-na-Gael. The founders were James Stephens and John O'Mahony, both of whom had been with Smith O'Brien in 1848 and with him fought in the only battle of that rising, in a bedraggled front yard near Ballingarry. During the exchange of shots Stephens had been wounded in the leg and hid in the mountains for several weeks until he recovered. Then he smuggled himself out of Ireland into France, and in Paris met one of his companions in arms, John O'Mahony. The two stayed on in the French city for some time, and had much discussion of revolution with other political refugees. John O'Mahony was a Gaelic scholar, and earned his living by teaching until, in 1853, he went to New York and there joined the Irish Emigrant Aid Society, made up of brother refugees from 1848. One of these, P. M. Haverty, kept a bookshop in town where everyone used to gather, and he set O'Mahony the task of translating Keating's *History of Ireland,* just to keep the intellectual happy. It was from this book that O'Mahony took the word "Fenian," deriving it from the Gaelic *Fiann* or *Fianna* as in *Fianna Eirionn,* "champions of Erin." The original Fianna lived in the late second and early third centuries and attended the heroic Fionn MacCumhail much as the Knights of the Round Table followed King Arthur. O'Mahony liked the idea of using this ancient concept, especially as he felt that the Irish language should be an integral part of his people's struggle for independence. The Gaelic League of later days was to follow him in this. At that time Irish was still a living tongue in the southern and western districts of Ireland and in some places in Ulster, but nothing was done to encourage the saving of it and it was dying out. Exiles, however, clung to the Gaelic nostalgically.

Before they parted O'Mahony and Stephens had made plans to work together to organize the new movement, and in 1857, with his translation finished and being published, O'Mahony sent the all-clear signal to Paris. Stephens immediately returned to Dublin, found a job with a faithful friend from the 1848 insurrection, and on St. Patrick's Day 1858 succeeded in persuading a meeting to join him in forming the Irish Republican Brotherhood. Over in America John O'Mahony was at work on the same project. Soon the American Fenians were sending money to Stephens, and he went on an organizing tour of Ireland with two companions. Ryan says, "... he won over the isolated groups of men inspired by the memory of the Forty-eight rising, but what was even more important than that, he won over the bulk of the younger men in the Ribbon Societies from the idea of secret agrarian conspiracy with a Nationalist tinge to his Fenian conspiracy and leadership" *(The Phoenix Flame,* p. 62). In the Cork town of Skibbereen a secret revolutionary society already existed, bearing the innocent name of the Phoenix National and Literary Society and led by young Jeremiah O'Donovan Rossa. This club was easily talked into joining the Fenians, and soon became a "center"—the conspirators' name for a cell. Someone betrayed the Phoenix and it was raided and dispersed, but fortunately for the movement, the authorities did not realize it was merely part of a much vaster conspiracy.

The original idea of the Fenians was to start their revolution as soon as organization was complete, but in America the Civil War put a temporary stop to these plans.

Fenians had no use for constitutionalism, feeling that it had been tried and found wanting. It was no use Ireland trying to abide by the rules of whatever game was imposed on them, since Britain would not play fair. Clearly she would never release Ireland from the union unless she was forced to do so; therefore the Irish must prepare secretly for all-out war. The Fenians were also opposed to attempting reform in Parliament. They said that campaigning to achieve such halfway ends as land reform merely wasted energy and diluted their sense of purpose. It was better to concentrate on a complete breakaway. There would be time enough for land reform and all other relief afterward, when they had independence.

The Fenian Society, the Irish Republican Brotherhood, or whatever other name the members preferred, was composed of a new sort of man as well as old-style conspirators enlisted from the ranks of Ribbon Societies. The old-style revolutionary was a rustic with a taste for violence, but the new-style man might very well be a city worker: a shopboy, an office clerk, or an artisan. This was a factor of Fenianism that worried many priests, who saw the movement as a manifestation of that new bugaboo Communism and the shopboys as Marx's proletariat. They denounced the Brotherhood and forbade their parishioners to join it, but the Fenians, though most of them were Catholics, ignored such clerical warnings. Already accustomed to the clergy's conservative point of view in politics, they automatically discounted priestly disapproval.

Mutual help was the wellspring of Fenian energy, and American aid poured in to the Brothers in Ireland. This was something new. Irish rebels had always sought help from abroad, but before 1856 most of it came from the Catholic nations of the Continent, usually France. Fenianism, however, asked no favors from Europe and ran up no bills. Fenianism sought independence and represented only Irish sentiment and Irish interests; whether the money came from America, England, Scotland, or Ireland herself, it came from Irish people. The feeling was that wherever Irishmen lived, there was Ireland in spirit, and out of this sentiment came strength. In 1849, in response to a question asked in the House of Lords, Earl Grey, Secretary for War and the Colonies, made investigations and came up with the information that during the 1840s at least £460,000 had been sent from North America to Ireland, mostly from the

United States. His lordship added that this was not the whole story, as it did not include the sum of money sent direct by mail from person to person. Considering that most of the donors were not rich, this was all the more staggering an amount. The Brotherhood alone—contributions to which were of course of later date, and necessarily under cover—received £80,000 from America, all collected from Irish immigrants.

The Civil War ended in 1865 and the conspirators immediately took up their own affairs again. A two-way traffic of secret emissaries kept Atlantic shipping busy; some of the passengers from the United States to Ireland were trained army officers set free by the peace, volunteering to serve the old country, because—as one Encyclopaedia Britannica writer resentfully put it—they were filled with hatred for England. In Ireland all seemed ready for the great revolution, but in America there was a hitch, and by the time it was ironed out, however temporarily, the Irish in Ireland had to postpone operations because some arms they were expecting had not turned up. Again it was America's turn to counsel a halt. One way and another the rising was postponed eighteen months, and the delay was fatal. It was notoriously easy for the English to find out what was going on in Ireland: informers could always be found, and the Fenian rising was no exception. In September 1865 the society's newspaper *The Irish People* was suppressed and some leaders, including O'Donovan Rossa, were arrested. Later the police caught James Stephens too, but he soon escaped again, and those Fenians who were still at large thought he should have rushed ahead with the insurrection, but for some reason he delayed action. Within the following year and a bit more there were only two incidents, an unsuccessful attempt to capture Chester Castle in England and a demonstration in Clare that was quickly stifled.

In the meantime Dublin Castle prepared for the rising they knew was coming because they had been informed. In the usual way they arrested suspects and conducted searches for arms, and suspended habeas corpus. When at last Stephens let slip his leash, on March 5, 1867, the country had been sewed up, and the insurrection, planned to occur simultaneously in Dublin, Kerry, Limerick, and Tipperary, never got a start. Instead the ringleaders still at large were now apprehended, and stood their trial with those captured earlier. Their judge, of all people, was the hated William Keogh, now chief justice, and he gave them brutally heavy sentences. Stephens went back to New York.

With so many Fenians in prison the affair would seem to be finished, but there was one more reverberation that autumn in Manchester, England. On September 18 a police van, carrying two Fenian prisoners back to jail from a court session, was halted in the street by an armed band of young Irishmen who intended to release their fellows. The van door was locked. One of the rescuers shot off the lock, and the bullet ricocheted and killed Sergeant Brett, a policeman. Some of the gang—though not the one who had fired—were caught and stood trial for first-degree murder, and three of these, Allen, Larkin, and O'Brien, were condemned to death for that unpremeditated killing even though none of them were guilty. In court Allen made a statement declaring that he was innocent, and he added, "I do not say this for the sake of mercy. I want no mercy. I'll have no mercy. I'll die as many thousands have died for the sake of the beloved country or in defense of it."

The three Manchester martyrs were hanged on November 23.

Fenianism had been forced underground, but it was not forgotten. Even in England it left memories and unpleasant afterthoughts. Some of the more thoughtful English stepped back, took a long look at Anglo-Irish relations, and wondered uneasily about the reason for such constant upheavals in their oldest colony. Many concluded that the chief cause of Irish discontent must be agriculture, which was still in an unsatisfactory state: tillage had continued to decrease after the famine because there was more money to be made out of grazing, and smallholders with farm laborers suffered accordingly. Others said that such hardships were an old story and did not in themselves supply the answer: the real trouble, they said, was in themselves—the English attitude. Irish complaints against themselves were valid.

This was a novel notion with which the majority fervently, emphatically disagreed, but it was held by a number of people nonetheless, including the Liberal leader William Ewart Gladstone. For years Gladstone had championed the Irish. In 1845 he declared that the Irish situation was the result of "cruel, inveterate, and but half-atoned injustice" administered by Great Britain, and now, in the uneasy climate left by the troubles of 1867, he decided that the English public was ripe for reform legislation. Accordingly, in 1868 he proposed that the Church of Ireland be disestablished. In a way it was amazing that this had not yet been done, for the age of imposing religious beliefs on the Irish was long since dead, but the Protestant clergymen and their supporters of the ascendancy had maintained the status quo. The Church of Ireland served one eighth of the country's population at most, yet it was immensely rich. Once the British were reminded of this state of affairs they were willing to reform it: Gladstone had been right in his estimate of their feelings. To Disraeli's surprise—Disraeli was prime minister at the time—the Commons voted in favor of disestablishment.

Disraeli did not approve, nor did Queen Victoria, and he immediately dissolved Parliament and went to the country, fighting the election in November specifically on disestablishment. Once again he was frustrated: the country voted yes for disestablishment and Disraeli had to resign. In March 1869 Gladstone introduced the Church Act and it became law by the end of May. Its most significant clause was that dealing with disendowment. All Church property was confiscated and, save for provisions for displaced Protestant clergy and a few others, handed over to the commissioners of Maynooth, to be used for the benefit of the people of Ireland.

"Only now," wrote Gladstone to the queen, "by a long, slow and painful process, have we arrived at the conclusion that Ireland is to be dealt with in all respects as a free country, and is to be governed like every other free country according to the sentiments of its majority and not of its minority."

The next matter to which the prime minister turned his attention was land reform in Ireland. From Fortescue, the Irish chief secretary, he heard that the Ulster custom should be taken as the pattern for the landlord-tenant relationship. None of his other ministers ventured opinions on the subject, which they considered ticklish: England's landlords, they told each other, would never stand for such change in Ireland for fear it might spread to themselves. But Fortescue was helpful: he suggested that Ulster custom be extended everywhere in Ireland as it had been in the past, and protected by law, and that tenants who for one reason or another still did not enjoy its benefits should nevertheless be protected in the same way. Gladstone approved, and presented his first Land Act to the Commons on February 15, 1870. Unfortunately, wishing to tread delicately because of English landowners, he had couched his act in terms too vague for practical application. He kept the landlords soothed to be sure, and the bill passed into law, but it made no difference whatever: evictions went on as they had done before. In the end all that can be said for Gladstone's first Land Act was that it did introduce into the Constitution the idea that landowners could be wrong, and that concept, once accepted, could never be wiped out. Someday it would come in useful, but not at that stage.

Nevertheless, for the first time in the memory of the generation, an English prime minister had been seen trying to set things right for Ireland, and Gladstone became the object of fervent admiration in that country—an unusual if not unknown position for an English premier to hold.

The Castle found it troublesome to guard and control their Fenian prisoners; agitation on their behalf, well organized, was rising. For one thing the people of Tipperary insisted on electing O'Donovan Rossa to Parliament, just as if he wasn't in jail. This was bad enough, but it was worse that he should have got news to the outside world—thanks to his journalist friend Richard Pigott, former editor of the defunct *Irish People*—that Rossa was kept in handcuffs throughout the first thirty-five days of his incarceration. Pigott published other stories about mistreatment of the prisoners, and it all furnished ammunition for a group called the Amnesty Association, which was working to get release for them.

Isaac Butt, president of the Amnesty Association, puzzled and exasperated the Castle people because he was so obviously not a revolutionary himself. He was a member of the middle class, solid and respectable as any Englishman—a distinguished barrister, son of a Church of Ireland clergyman, graduate of Trinity. What was such a man doing among the troublemakers? In fact Butt had a long acquaintance with *the* Fenians, having defended many of them in court in the past. Though not a revolutionary, he was Irish and the situation seemed wrong to him. His association was successful in getting a commission of inquiry into prison conditions, and even extracted several of the men, until at last, in 1871, the government declared a general amnesty— or, as they called it, a conditional pardon—for the prisoners, on condition that they go abroad and stay there until the date of what would have been their release. They were to be ticket-of-leave men. The declaration did not settle matters immediately. O'Donovan Rossa, for one, refused to consent to the terms and complained that he was being banished from prison, but at last all were released. Most of them went to New York, where they were given the welcome reserved for heroes. The first five to arrive in January 1871—John Devoy, O'Donovan Rossa, Harry Mulleda, John McClure, and Charles Underwood O'Connell—ran straight into an Irish-American war and were fought over like so many bones as soon as they landed, for there were now *three* Fenian organizations in the United States. The new arrivals sensibly extricated themselves—though John Devoy, for one, made up his mind to unify the factions later if he possibly could—and settled down, if that is the right phrase, to a life of conspiracy among other transplanted revolutionaries.

At home, the uncommitted Irishman might reasonably have asked himself in 1873 what good the IRB all-or-nothing attitude had done his country. Gladstone's efforts might have made an impression on the Irish and restored to them an amount of confidence in parliamentary procedure had it not been for the failure of his third reform attempt, in which he aimed at bringing to Catholic Ireland the means of higher education. Once before, in 1854, a good start had been made toward this end, when the prelates of Ireland set up a Catholic university under Cardinal Newman as rector. But the project was never solidly grounded: the university was not endowed in any way and the government continued to hold out against the bishops' requests for financial help. Gladstone did not want to come to the rescue with money however good the cause: like other Liberals he was opposed on principle to sectarianism in education. Trinity was abandoning religious tests for admission, he pointed out: why then should an exclusively Catholic institution be endowed by the government'? In 1873 he proposed instead the organization of an all-inclusive University of Dublin to take in Trinity, the three queen's colleges, *and* the Catholic university, all as colleges. In such an arrangement, however, the Catholic university would still lack endowments, while the Protestant institutes retained theirs, and the bishops refused to agree to the proposal. Irish M.P.s did as their bishops advised and opposed the bill. Their dissent combined with that of certain Liberal members was enough to kill it by three votes, and Gladstone resigned. Disraeli refused to attempt to lead the House because Tories were in the minority, so Gladstone returned, but it became more and more clear that the Liberals had lost the country's confidence, and he dissolved Parliament in January 1874. (Six years later Disraeli founded the Royal University of Ireland very much along the lines Gladstone had suggested, but with an indirect endowment for the Catholic university.)

Isaac Butt had worked for the Amnesty Association because he thought he should, even though it cut into his practice and lost him much money. But his middle-class background, and perhaps his middle age as well, gave him a far from favorable idea of revolt for revolt's sake. He desired justice, but he was also alarmed to think of the effects a successful Fenian insurrection would have, and he thought this was bound to come unless Ireland was treated with more intelligence. He believed that for the sake of both England and Ireland the right of self-government should be restored to the latter so that things would be as they had been in Grattan's day and until the union. The movement was called "Home Rule" because, as some malicious commentators have suggested, the phrase sounded better, less frightening, than "independence," but no matter what the label the idea found favor among middle-roaders who objected to violence—people from many walks of life and of various religions. They gathered in Dublin one day in May 1870, and formed the Home Rule Association with Isaac Butt as president. True to its origins, the association meant to make its mark constitutionally. Home Rule candidates contested seats in the general election, but their approach was amateurish, and those candidates who won owed their success not so much to the attraction of Home Rule as to other planks in their platforms. The movement did not really come to life until the failure of Gladstone's bill on universities brought down with it the whole Liberal party. Then politicians, looking at the Home Rule concept, suddenly saw its charm. In November 1873 the association was tightened up and changed into the Home Rule League, which announced a definite policy of three aims—denominational education (designed to catch the voters who didn't like Gladstone's bill), land without rent (as Thomas Davis had once demanded), and Home Rule. When the smoke cleared away after the January 1874 election, nobody was more surprised than Isaac Butt to discover that fifty-nine Home Rule candidates had won places: in his wildest hopes he had envisaged only thirty successes. This triumph made the Home Rulers the biggest of any group in the Irish Parliamentary party.

Appearances, however, were flattering. By itself Home Rule would not have stood scrutiny. It fell between two stools, being too radical for the unionists and too censervative for the radicals. But then, the same can be said of most political parties; the true weakness of the league in its early years was embodied in Butt. He was a jolly man, fond of drink and women, but in Parliament he was anything but dynamic: he lacked that quality that inspires hearers. And in spite of the surprising number of seats won on the Home Rule ticket, the leaguers were not numerous enough to carry weight in the Commons, heavily stocked as it was with ruling Tories. Nobody needed the Home Rulers, so nobody listened to them. Even their most moderate demands were ignored. At last some of the Irish became so irritated by repeated failure and by Butt's feebleness that they set out to make their own mark on the indifferent House.

The leader of this intransigent group was Joseph G. Biggar of Belfast, a wealthy provision merchant who was also an important member of IRB. As a grocer in that snobbish age, Biggar had no social standing to lose, but he would not have hesitated to imperil it even if he had possessed it. He worked out efficient ways to drive the league's opponents crazy, at least to force them to pay attention to the Irish. This policy was called "obstruction" because it consisted in holding up the business of the House. For instance, in committee meetings obstructionists insisted on having progress reports made every few minutes. But Biggar's particular technique was that of the filibuster. He first employed it when he was permitted to speak on the Coercion Bill, and began to read aloud, endlessly, from government blue books. He went on and on and on. The House was stunned, helpless. At one time during the four-hour ordeal the Speaker was incautious enough to say that he could not hear. In apologetic tones Biggar replied, "Perhaps I had better begin again"—and did so. He read everything in every blue book he used, including the bit at the end: "London, Printed for Her Majesty's Stationery Office by Eyre and Spottiswood...."

Even this obstructionist tactic was not enough for the determined Biggar. A few days later he saw the prince of Wales in the gallery and said, "I spy strangers." By ancient custom, when this is said by a member everybody in the gallery must leave immediately. The other M.P.s were horrified, but Biggar stood his ground and the prince had to get out. Fortunately for the loyalists in the House, Disraeli quickly proposed a suspension of the rules, the House overwhelmingly agreed, and the prince was allowed to come back. Biggar, never the toast of the Commons, became their villain from that time on. Even his own party apologized for him over the prince affair. In one of the newspapers he was decried in the most insulting terms: "When he rose to address the House, which he did at least ten times tonight, a whiff of salt pork seemed to float upon the gale and the air is heavy with the odor of peppered herring." None of this disturbed Biggar—it probably pleased him. He wanted to put Ireland on the map and he had done so: he might have reflected that in this way he was giving English M.P.s, a strong desire to grant Ireland Home Rule if only to get himself and his adherents out of Westminster. But the majority of Irish M.P.s, a poor-spirited lot, were ashamed of the grocer, and even Isaac Butt, whose spirit was sturdy enough, did not approve of his methods. One man among them, however, who came on the scene in 1875, realized the value of what Biggar was doing. Two years later he joined Biggar's little band—there were now seven obstructionists— and signified his intention of helping. This volunteer was Charles Stewart Parnell.

CHAPTER

19

PARNELL was born in 1846, the second son of a Wicklow family of English Protestant origin, distinguished people who had been in Ireland for generations. Sir John Parnell, chancellor of the exchequer under Grattan, was his great-grandfather. His mother was American, a violently anti-English woman who took it for granted, nevertheless, that her children should be educated in England. In appearance and manners Parnell was a thoroughly English gentleman, tall and good-looking—at any rate everyone said he was good-looking, though in most of his portraits he wears a luxuriant beard, and one can hardly tell. He appeared reserved, cold, and unemotional. These are traits we do not usually associate with the Irish, but in Parnell's social class people did not wish to seem emotional. Nevertheless it was with a sort of passion that Parnell approached his work in Parliament, and when disaster overtook his career it was through another passion.

His father died when he was a schoolboy of thirteen, in 1859, when Fenianism was new. Mrs. Parnell was a sore trial to her son because she embraced this cause. For the next few years, whenever she was in residence in the family's Dublin house, Charles ran the danger of encountering in the drawing-room youths who were obviously from the working class, and burning with revolutionary fervor. He disapproved heartily of his mother's keeping open house for such characters, but they had the ardent support of his favorite sister Fanny, three years younger than himself. At fourteen Fanny was writing poems in praise of liberty, and publishing them in the Fenian Society's journal *The Irish People*. When the paper was suppressed in 1865 and the first lot of Fenians were arrested, the sixteen-year-old girl attended their trial every day. She wept when the defendants were sentenced, whereas Charles was unmoved. To put it plainly he was a young prig, typically snobbish.

Years passed. Charles fell in love and was rejected, and went on a "wanderyear" in the United States. He came home to enter into his inheritance, the Wicklow estate of Avondale, where he lived as a country squire. Then one day he surprised everyone by going into politics. His attention had been caught by the Home Rule League and he applied to Isaac Butt for help in finding a seat. Butt was delighted with Parnell: the young man was attractive and well-mannered and would lend tone to the party: besides, he seemed to have money and could pay his own election expenses. The new recruit knew nothing about public speaking and his first campaign was a failure, but he soon caught on and developed excellent style. In 1875, at the age of twenty-nine, he won a by-election for a seat in Meath and was sent to Westminster. For two years after that he maintained the silent, respectful attitude proper to a beginner. He watched Butt, a master of well-mannered inaction, and he observed the bumptious Biggar with his noisy crew. Parnell was percipient enough to realize that Butt's group was approved by the English because it offered no trouble. Such gentility had no place in the cut and thrust of parliamentary life, he felt, and he made his decision. At the beginning of the 1877 session the country gentleman joined the rowdy, low-class obstructionists.

Late one night the House was discussing the Mutiny Bill, which had to be renewed every year. The minister for war had the floor. Parnell, aiding Biggar, kept interrupting him with amendments, questions, and demands for progress reports—the usual obstructionist tactics. Somebody went to fetch Butt from the smoking room and asked him to control his young hoodlums, and Butt hurried into the House. The minute he got there he apologized for Parnell, saying "I am not responsible for the member for Meath and cannot control him. I have, however, a duty to discharge to the great nation of Ireland, and I think I should discharge it best when I say I disapprove entirely of the conduct of the honorable member for Meath." This was the way Isaac Butt always talked, but he had been surprised by his protégé's behavior, and was probably hurt as well.

Parnell replied, comparatively simply: "The honorable and learned gentleman was not in the House when I attempted to explain why I was putting down notice of my amendments." This implied that Butt had administered his rebuke too readily and without waiting to find out the facts, merely because English members had asked him to. Parnell was justified, but his statement amounted to a declaration of war, and war followed, inside and outside the House of Commons. Outside, the dispute was carried on in letters to the press, Butt arguing that nobody could damage the authority of the House of Commons without damaging the cause of freedom, Parnell retorting that the English insisted on "the artificial maintenance of an antiquated institution." Militant Irish members were enthralled by their new champion.

In September that year there was a routine annual meeting of the Home Rule League. Hitherto Isaac Butt had always been elected president, but this time he was not even mentioned. Charles Stewart Parnell alone was nominated and duly elected. Poor Butt's heart was broken. In May 1879 he died, poor and forgotten, and when Parnell heard the news he showed no signs of emotion—but then, he seldom did.

Michael Davitt, just Parnell's age, became a Fenian when

he was nineteen. His parents had emigrated from Mayo to England when he was a small child. He was one of the conspirators in the abortive attack on Chester Castle, and later became organizing secretary for the society in Britain. His chief occupation was smuggling firearms into Ireland. Caught in the act in 1870, in Paddington Station, London, he was convicted and sentenced to fifteen years' imprisonment. He served seven years of this in English jails, in conditions of revolting cruelty. By the time he was released on parole, in 1877, the Fenian cause had come to grief in Ireland and most ringleaders were in America. Davitt of course was aware of all this and had even heard of Parnell, whose sudden rise interested him. In Dublin his friends soon introduced him to the bright new star, and Davitt and Parnell became friends. The Fenian had had time in prison to think deeply, and he had come to certain conclusions. There was no point any more in the secret-conspiracy game, he decided: the Brotherhood would do better to work for land reform first, and worry about repealing the union later. This philosophy was in direct opposition to IRB policy, which was to get independence first and reform land ownership later, but Davitt's thinking corresponded with that of other Fenians such as Biggar and young John O'Connor Power, who was also an M.P. Orthodox Fenians felt that both these men were in error in the very fact that they were in Parliament, since in order to occupy their seats they had had to take the oath of allegiance to the British Crown, but Davitt considered this objection a quibble. If a man could work better for the cause within the House than without, more power to him. That was why Parnell interested him: he thought it might be possible to recruit him.

Other Fenians too were showing an interest in Parnell. John Devoy, now an editor on the New York *Herald,* heard about him from another *Herald* man, O'Kelly, in Europe as a correspondent: "I had a long chat with Parnell... a man of promise. I think he ought to be supported. He has the idea I held at the starting of the Home Rule organisation—that is the creation of a political link between the conservative and the radical nationalists." In another letter he said, "I am not sure he knows exactly where he is going, but he is the best of the Parliamentary lot."

As a result, in 1878 a visiting Clan-na-Gael official, Dr. William Carroll of Philadelphia, had a meeting with Parnell. With Carroll was John O'Leary, for whom Fanny Parnell had wept in 1865, and Parnell was accompanied by the journalist Frank Hugh O'Donnell. O'Leary voiced the scornful objection of many Fenians: "I might as well warn you gentlemen that I have never been able to see how Ireland is to be freed by keeping the Speaker of the English House of Commons out of bed." To this Parnell made no reply, but O'Donnell retorted that the nationalists were at least doing *something,* whereas the Fenians merely waited for another insurrection, and had not fired a shot for ten years. After the interview Parnell said to O'Donnell, "They want to catch us but they are not going to. Purely physical force movements have always failed in Ireland."

Davitt did not despair of Parnell's eventually coming to some agreement with the Fenians, and when he went to America that autumn he talked a good deal of his new friend's ideas for land reform. These theories impressed two editors, Patrick Ford of the *Irish World* in New York and the remarkable John Boyle O'Reilly of the Boston *Pilot*. Both men had large audiences and were able to spread the word. They adopted each his own plan of action, but were agreed that land reform of some kind was what Ireland needed.

On October 25, 1878, John Devoy sent a cable to Parnell, signed by a number of associates, including Carroll, along with him. This was an open message, and read: "Nationalists here will support you on the following conditions: First—Abandonment of the federal demand and substitution of a general declaration in favour of self-government. Second—Vigorous agitation of the land question on the basis of a peasant proprietary, while accepting concessions tending to abolish literary eviction. Third—Exclusion of all sectarian issues from the platform. Fourth—Irish members to vote together on all Imperial and Home Rule questions, adopt an aggressive policy and energetically resist coercive legislation. Fifth—Advocacy of all struggling nationalities in the British Empire and elsewhere."

The compromise principle embodied in Clause Two was later known as the New Departure. Parnell did not reply directly and made no promise in any form, but in his speeches afterward he supported peasant proprietorship.

The IRB in Ireland, however, did not accept Devoy's suggestion, and stood their ground on the subject of participation in Parliament like the old-style Fenians they were. Ultimately they expelled Biggar and O'Connor Power for having gone to Westminster, but Davitt beat them to the post and resigned.

For several years Britain had felt the pinch as American farm produce moved into the Old World market and undercut the farmers' profits. When English farmers suffered, Irish farmers suffered that much more, and so did migratory Irish laborers who depended on seasonal work in England. The country was already in distress before the end of 1878, and the winter of 1878-79 was unusually cold and harsh. In the early spring the tilled land in the western counties showed the ominous, dreadfully familiar signs of potato blight. It was possible that 1879 might reproduce the horrors of 1845, with hunger, eviction, and death.

Michael Davitt returned from America in March and went to the worst-hit county, his native Mayo, to put his theories into practice and organize the tenants. In April he arranged a meeting at Irishtown to protest against the extortionate rents that were being demanded by a local clergyman landlord, and more than ten thousand people attended, a number that surprised everyone and worried some. Davitt got John O'Connor Power to talk to the protesters about ways and means to avert disaster at this meeting, the first of a series of agrarian demonstrations that he organized. But on June 1 he interrupted his work to attend a private conference in the Morison Hotel, Dublin, with Parnell and John Devoy: Devoy had risked arrest by breaking his parole and returning to Ireland especially for the occasion. That day Parnell agreed to lead Davitt's land movement. Devoy later claimed that he had agreed to more than that and had promised firmly that neither Home Rule nor land reform should get in the way, when the time came, of the Fenians' cherished armed insurrection. But Parnell always denied this and Davitt agreed that he had not gone so far. Probably Devoy took Parnell's long silences for assent. Parnell did promise to visit Davitt's next and biggest monster meeting out at Westport, Mayo, a week later. Excitement ran high when the news was broadcast, and the thousands of people who came to hear him were not disappointed. Parnell gave explicit advice: "You must show the landlords that you intend to hold a firm grip on your homesteads and lands. You must not allow yourselves to be dispossessed as your fathers were dispossessed in 1857."

Your homesteads? *Your* lands? Though a landlord himself, Parnell was talking in the spirit of Thomas Davis, and his words were to become the keystone of the National Land League of Ireland. Later, at a Dublin meeting, he repeated the message: "Show your power and make them feel it."

Parnell inspired an extraordinary loyalty in his diverse followers, and held them together as if by magic. It was not the magic of oratory— Parnell was no demagogue—nor that of the common touch like O'Connell's. O'Connell had always been available, and could talk to the people in their own idiom, but Parnell never tried, and his spell was exerted from a distance. Often he was not even to be seen. He was an intensely private person, but his guarded mystery was as effective as O'Connell's matey approach to people. There are questions that have never been answered. For instance, how did he achieve his skill so suddenly? What changed the Anglicized prig to the people's darling? Many could not understand why a landowner should declare war on his own class, but this is a question easier to answer: he was not the first nor the last to do so. No doubt he felt, however belatedly, something of the spirit that possessed his mother and his talented sister Fanny. There is no question, either, as to why the Irish wanted him. Conor Cruise O'Brien wrote, "The House of Commons in the eighties was still an aristocratic assembly and it was a great advantage to the Irish to have a leader who would neither 'misunderstand its tone' nor let himself be overawed by it" *(Parnell and His Party, p. 6).* Another advantage: his status kept him at a distance from his working partners, and his advancement did not cause the resentment they would have felt if any of them had been in a similar position. "'They wanted a county gintleman,' sneered a disgruntled co-member of the party. They did, and for good reason" (Ibid.). A Fenian named Mat Harris said much the same thing to O'Donnell: "We are a nation of Catholics and we want a Protestant. It looks well. We are a nation of peasants and we want a landlord to head us. It looks well. You are neither a Protestant nor a landlord. Parnell is both."

The strangest element in Parnell's standing and the enthusiasm he engendered is that it was all a tremendous effort for him. He was never in rude health. He was fastidious. He liked privacy. There was nothing genuinely extrovert about him, but as a politician in quest of power he had to be hail-fellow-well-met with everyone, and he hated every minute of it. Only his mistress Katherine O'Shea knew this. Alone with her in the later years, when his health was failing, he would refer to his admiring henchmen and companions as rabble, scum, and gutter sparrows. He spoke of Healy as a chimney sweep. But he carried on, did his job, and rose steadily.

The National League of Ireland was founded on October 21, 1879. Parnell was elected president and Davitt was one of the secretaries. Its aim was, first, to relieve the tenants and reduce rack rents, and then to abolish landlordism and hand over the land to its workers. The people soon felt great confidence in the league: they learned from Davitt and his companions how to exert strength they had not realized they possessed. When Davitt was arrested after a meeting in Sligo for having used provocative language, so many people demonstrated that the authorities were intimidated and dropped the case. Early in November the countryside learned of a tenant farmer of Balla who was to be evicted. The league called a protest meeting, and Pamell and Davitt added a caution in advance that the demonstrators must be "dignified, peaceful and orderly." They were. Eight thousand men marched through Balla to the farmer's hut and around it in two columns, one led by Parnell, until the farmer came out and told them the eviction had been postponed. Triumphant speeches ended the affair. After that, whenever an eviction was pending people blocked the road ahead of the process server and cut any bridges he might have to cross; and he was unable to get food or drink in the neighboring villages. In 1880 a crowd stoned certain process servers—although they had brought with them a strong police guard for protection—who meant to serve a hundred warrants in one village: by the end of the day only four of those warrants had been delivered. When the people took to stripping process servers naked, landlords could not find anyone to take on the job.

This success was encouraging but expensive for the league, and in December Parnell went to America to collect money. John Dillon, son of the Young Irelander John Blake Dillon, accompanied him. They had a hearteningly profitable time, collecting $200,000 in two months. Parnell had to argue endlessly with Clan-na-Gael members opposed to the New Departure, especially as he continued to assert that he didn't want armed revolt in Ireland. After one of his talks an old man came up and handed him thirty dollars, saying, "Here are five dollars for bread and twenty-five dollars for lead." But the Clan-na-Gael helped him greatly, not only with generous contributions but by organizing his meetings. The visitors found themselves so busy with details that Parnell sent home for a twenty-four-year-old journalist, Timothy M. Healy, to work as their secretary on the tour: Healy had been reporting on proceedings in Parliament for the *Nation,* and always gave Parnell good notices. "Healy used Parnell to climb the ladder of success," wrote Jules Abels. "He might have reached it by another route, but he owed everything to Parnell—for which he possibly never forgave him. At any rate, Parnell's reward was that in the end Healy turned on his master and led the fight to crush him. When Parnell had been dead twenty-five years, Healy, in his memoirs, spattered mud on the name of the departed leader" *(The Parnell Tragedy,* pp. 83-84). In those early days, however, Healy was still an admirer. It was he who dubbed Parnell, at a wildly enthusiastic reception in Montreal, "the Uncrowned King of Ireland."

The tour was brought to a sudden end when Biggar cabled that Parliament was being dissolved, and Parnell and Dillon returned at once.

In the general election of 1880 Gladstone's campaign was based on other matters than Ireland, but Parnell won more places from the Old Guard for his candidates. Ireland sent sixty Home Rulers to Westminster, the number almost evenly split between Parnellites and 'Whigs," which was the somewhat confusing name applied to members who imitated the English and sought personal advancement by what we would call apple polishing. One of these untroublesome characters, William Shaw, was now head of the Home Rule party, but on May 17 Parnell challenged him and won the leadership by a large majority.

Customarily, at the opening of each parliamentary session a speech from the throne outlines the government's future program. It is an announcement of intent, and for this reason the queen's speech for the 1880 session shocked the Irish members; for in spite of their country's critical plight it dealt with many far-flung corners of the Empire but made no mention whatever of Ireland. Parnell, as the head of a group that wished to demand a relief bill immediately, was soon at loggerheads with William Shaw, who, true to his Whiggish policy, wanted to follow the advice of Chief Secretary Forster and say nothing. A noisy clash would have followed if Gladstone had not produced a bill approved by Forster, providing that evicted tenants be paid compensation for improvements they had made on the property, the money to come from the disestablished Church fund. This bill went up to the Lords, who delayed action on it for a month and then turned it down. Ireland was unrelieved, and the countryside seethed with discontent and violent agrarian action. After that session Parnell stumped the country with Michael Davitt, exhorting the people to join the Land League. They did, in thousands.

One day when Parnell was addressing a meeting at Ennis he described a type they all knew and hated, the "gombeen man"—a scavenger who bought farms from which tenants had just been evicted. "What would you do to such a man?" he asked. In the outcry of angry suggestions that answered him he heard "Shoot him!" Parnell replied to this: No, he should not be shot. There was a more Christian, charitable way to deal with him. He should be shunned, treated as if he did not exist, isolated. If one met him on the road, in the street, in market, or in church, one must give no sign of seeing him. Parnell assured his hearers that no man could withstand such treatment. And that was the origin of the boycott, though, as it happens, the genuine Captain Boycott was not a farm buyer but that even less popular creature, the rent collector; estate agent for Lord Erne of Lough Mask House, county Mayo. Boycott, a hard man, refused to accept rents at the "fair figure" fixed by the tenants and evicted them wholesale. One day, just when his fields were ready for the harvest, he discovered that all his hired help had vanished from fields and house together. His animals went untended. He could buy nothing in the village, and soon ran short of supplies. His mail wasn't delivered. Captain Boycott was completely cut off from his fellow men, and in the end, just as Parnell had predicted, he couldn't take it. He retreated to England, while the Leaguers joyfully adopted his name as a verb for their new protest strategy. (Boycott did ultimately come back to Ireland, to an out-of-the-way village a long way from Lough Mask where he ended his days quietly.)

Parnell never came as close as Davitt wanted to complete

acceptance of Fenianism, but he went to lengths extreme enough to win IRB approval, and money continued to come from the Clan-na-Gael coffers across the sea. In the period 1879-82 Ireland produced so many agrarian outrages that this time became known as the Land War. Ten thousand evictions took place in those years, with two thousand incidents in 1880 alone. The Land League exerted tremendous influence, working by means of secret meetings and word-of-mouth directions. During the summer and fall of 1880, when it looked as if the harvest would be good, farmers were quietly told not to give their crops to their landlords, and Davitt proudly carried around a letter from a man in Mayo to show to friends: "To the Honourable Land League.

Gintlmen in a monint of wakeness i pade me rent, i did not no there was a law aginst it or i wud not do it. The people pass mi as if the small pox was in the house, i hear ye do be givin pardons to min that do rong, and if ye will send mi a pardon to put in the windy for evryone to rede it, as God is mi judge, i will never komit the crime agin" (C. C. O'Brien, *Parnell and His Party*").

Not all landlords and agents got off with a mere boycotting: many outraged tenants preferred the satisfaction of sniping. Of course the Land League did not go unremarked by the English. Parnell was accused of being the moving spirit of all this lawlessness, and on the second of November 1880 a determined attempt was made to down him. With Patrick Egan and Thomas Brennan of the Land League, and with Biggar, Dillon, and two other M.P.s, he was taken into court in Dublin to answer charges of conspiracy to prevent evictions and payment of rents. The accused, confident that no Irish jury would dare to convict them, sat patiently through twenty days of trial while outside the Four Courts police battled mobs of Parnell champions. The defendants were acquitted.

Anti-Irish feeling rose to fever pitch in England, in spite of a few voices that spoke of England's duty to relieve the distress of the starving, and the government reacted in time-honored manner. On March 2 a new Coercion Act became law, followed by a "Peace Preservation" bill. Thus reassured, landlords promptly increased evictions. But very shortly afterward, on April 7, Gladstone presented his Land Bill, a surprisingly good offer to the Irish tenantry, containing everything the old Tenant Right League had demanded in 1850. The prime minister had worked hard on his bill, while refusing to consult Parnell on any point whatsoever (he did not approve of Parnell). He considered it his swan song. Once before he had tried to retire but had been called back, but now, he was sure, the end of his career was close at hand.

Privately, Parnell admitted the virtues of the bill, though he could see that there were grave omissions, most notably any provision for leaseholders or tenants in arrears. For a while he was undetermined as to what public attitude to take. The bill did not please his radicals, so though he could appreciate its many virtues he decided not to express approval. In debate he refrained from interference or obstruction, and objected only to the clauses providing that "fair rent" should be fixed by land commission courts. It was clear that the bill would pass in spite of this; among others, some of Parnell's own party supported it, and he settled the problem at last by leading his firmest supporters out of the House when the vote was being taken after the second reading. Neatly, he had saved his name without spoiling the bill's chances. After it became law he and the league continued to oppose the clauses they did not like. They advised tenants not to go to court to have their rents fixed, but to wait on league decisions. Long afterward Gladstone paid tribute of a sort to league activity when he said, "I must make one admission and that is that without the Land League, the Act of 1881 would not be on the statute books." At the time, however, he was enraged when the organization continued to interfere with the working of the new law.

He attacked Parnell by name when speaking at Leeds, and Parnell replied in a speech in Wexford, on October 10, and gave back as good as he got. Among other things he called the prime minister "a masquerading knight-errant." Three days later, not at all to his surprise, he was arrested under the Coercion Act and put into Kilmainham jail to await trial, with a number of other Leaguers, on charges of having abetted various recent agitations. (Michael Davitt, however, was jailed in England, in Portland prison.) The prisoners immediately drew up a paper calling for a general strike against the payment of rent—the "No-Rent Manifesto"—and circulated it. This manifesto was deprecated by the Catholic clergy. Others too, though they were usually on Parnell's side, thought he had gone too far. The Land League was promptly suppressed, and tenants, left without its reassurance (or its threats), went in throngs to the land courts and paid their rents according to court decisions. But the league rose like a phoenix, re-embodied as the Ladies' Land League, headed by Anna, one of Parnell's sisters, a determined woman who saw to it that agrarian outrage continued. Almost forty-five hundred incidents were chalked up in 1881. The women Leaguers were even more relentless than the men had been, and were also more practical. They put up huts for evicted tenant families and cared for them.

Parnell in prison became even more popular than Parnell free. Confinement was bad for his health, but his companions took good care of him. Probably the worst of the imprisonment, to his mind, was the strain it imposed on his relations with Katherine O'Shea, at this time pregnant with his child. The love story had begun in July 1880. Mrs. O'Shea was born Katherine Wood, daughter of an English baronet who went into the Church. She was a sister of the noted General Evelyn Wood. At twenty-one she had married the Irish Captain William Henry O'Shea, or "Willie," then of the 18th Hussars, because she was fascinated by his charm and good looks. Her father had died poor and the bride brought no dowry, but she had useful relatives, and was the favorite niece of her widowed aunt Mrs. Benjamin Wood, "Aunt Ben," who had a lot of money and was always good for a loan. This was fortunate for Katherine, as Willie was something less than a financial wizard. He had quitted the regiment when he married. Under his happy-go-lucky

management project after project failed, and Aunt Ben had
to come to the rescue repeatedly. The O'Shea marriage soon
ran short of honeymoon fervor. In 1875 Aunt Ben bought a
house for the twenty-nine-year-old Katherine near her own
house at Eltham, southeast of London, and settled a regular
income on her, in return for which the niece agreed to be
the old lady's companion for the rest of her life. Aunt Ben
was then eighty-three, and there seemed little doubt that she
would leave her fortune to Katherine O'Shea.

Five years later Aunt Ben was still alive. Willie, father of
three, had inherited land in county Clare and now suddenly
took a notion to enter the general election and try for
Parliament. He won the seat and one of his first acts as a
member of Parliament was to cast a vote for Parnell when
the latter was struggling with William Shaw for leadership
of the Home Rule party. Willie's action puzzled those
who knew him as a Whig; but he had decided to back the
winning horse. As an M.P.s wife Katherine came often to
London to give or attend parties, and so she met Parnell. He
had had little to do with women, but he fell in love with her
as soon as they met, and by the autumn of 1880 they had,
as the novelists put it, consummated their love. The rank
and file of the party did not suspect the affair and there was
no reason why they should: Parnell had always maintained
such aloofness that unexplained absences on his part were
only to be expected. As for O'Shea, his wife later insisted
that he knew everything from the start and was willing,
even eager, to profit from the situation. But it is difficult
to be sure—O'Shea may simply have been too conceited to
face the truth. Certainly Parnell visited the O'Shea house
with perfect freedom. When he felt ill Katherine nursed him
and the lovers were much together. More than once O'Shea
showed signs of bad temper: once he flew into a rage with his
wife for setting spies on him—as he claimed—in an attempt
to catch him out in some infidelity. (It should not have been
difficult to do this.) He marched into his house, found a
portmanteau belonging to Parnell, sent it off to London,
and departed. Parnell wrote calmly to Katherine, asking her

to find out from Willie where he had left the luggage: he had asked, he said, at the parcel office, the House of Commons cloakroom, and his hotel, without success. Another time O'Shea tried, though not very hard, to fight a duel with Parnell, but Katherine's sister patched things up.

But there were other complications. In those days, when lovely woman stooped to folly she was very likely, unless she happened to be barren, to be caught out. Katherine's pregnancy could have been very awkward, but neither she nor Parnell, sequestered in Kilmainham jail while she gave birth, seems to have been perturbed about Willie. Parnell was anxious, to be sure, and wrote at great length to his "dear little wifie" expressing his worry for her health and their child's, but when the little girl was born on February 16, 1882, Katherine wrote reassuringly to the father that Willie had no suspicion of the truth, and had only stipulated that the child—which was weakly—be baptized at once. To this she had assented, though if the truth had been known— that is, that both parents were Protestant—little Sophie Claude would not have been baptized a Catholic, as were Katherine's other children. Parnell saw his tiny daughter before she died: he was released on parole in April to attend a nephew's funeral, and he went straight to Eltham.

At this time the government had begun to soften toward Ireland. Some ministers were ready to entertain the idea that Parnell's objections to the Land Act were well founded. William Forster, chief secretary for Ireland, had stood in the way of mediation, but he was no longer trusted by Gladstone. The land commission courts were indeed reducing rents, but landlords were evicting more and more people for arrears, just as Parnell had prophesied.

For his part, Parnell would have been glad to talk it out, but there could be no question of a public meeting with the prime minister as long as he was in prison. He suggested to Willie that the latter act as intermediary and make an approach. O'Shea was happy to do so, as the task added to his feeling of self-importance, and he wrote to Gladstone and Joseph Chamberlain, the president of the Board of Trade, to suggest an interview between the premier and Parnell. A side effect of this correspondence was that O'Shea and Chamberlain got acquainted and O'Shea continued to run errands for Chamberlain, often boasting of the friendship. After a good deal of intrigue and secret communication, when Parnell was back in jail, the agreement known as the Kilmainham treaty was hammered out. Parnell and the others were to be released; evictions would cease; rents would be settled by a new Arrears Bill; tenants in arrears would benefit from the Land Act; coercion was to end. In return Parnell promised that the work of the Ladies' League would cease: there would be no more agrarian outrages. Everyone was pleased except Forster. He resigned.

Parnell and Dillon, free and back in England, went to greet Michael Davitt when he was released from Portland prison, and traveled up to London with him. During the journey Parnell talked in a manner that surprised Davitt. He criticized the Ladies' League for having gone to extremes and even complained of "anarchy." He would not listen when Davitt praised Anna Parnell's work. No doubt he was feeling apprehensive about the reactions of the radicals in the movement; he knew that they would not be happy about the treaty, since if they had things their way nothing short of independence would bring an end to agrarian action and general violence. If so, his uneasiness was justified: the Clan-na-Gael when they heard the news overwhelmed him with reproaches, and the flow of American money dwindled sharply.

Davitt's release and the conversation about Anna Parnell took place on May 6, 1882. That same day, the newly appointed chief secretary for Ireland, Lord Frederick Cavendish, husband of Gladstone's niece, arrived in Dublin to launch the auspicious new order. In the evening he walked through Phoenix Park—it was a fine day— with the undersecretary, Thomas Henry Burke, toward their next appointment. Burke had been selected for murder by a terrorist group of Dublin, the Invincibles, who aimed at settling Ireland's troubles by assassinating important English officials. One of their number was a former Fenian named James Carey. The Invincibles had intended to kill Forster just before he left, but there was a slip-up in the plans, and they decided that Burke would do just as well. True, he was Irish, but he worked with the English. The assassins were waiting for him in the park. The fact that he was walking arm in arm with some stranger did not deter them: at the planned moment they set on him with surgical knives, and when Cavendish tried to defend him they killed him as well, still without the slightest idea of his identity.

Parnell was aghast at the news, and with reason, for the public was sure to blame him for this act as they blamed him for all violence in Ireland. So it developed. Few believed that he knew nothing of it and could not name the assassins. Even when black-edged cards were sent to all the Dublin newspapers with the message "The deed was done by the Irish Invincibles" Parnell remained under suspicion. Instead of revoking the Coercion Act as had been promised in the Kilmainham treaty, the government on May 11 brought in a new and much harsher Crimes Bill, and though Parnell fought it with all his might, it became law. During the stages of the bill he tried to get into secret communication with Gladstone through Katherine O'Shea's offices: she wrote to the prime minister begging him to see her, and on three occasions he granted interviews to her. His advisers warned him that she was Parnell's mistress, but that was not the real reason she did not make headway: Gladstone could not hold back the Crimes Bill in the face of public opinion, whatever he wished. But he managed to keep his promise in another respect: three days after the Crimes Bill was introduced he brought in an Arrears Bill by which arrears of rent on all properties worth less than £30 were canceled, and he succeeded in pushing it through.

The Dublin police caught James Carey on another charge in 1882. Already on the trail of the Invincibles, they tricked him, saying that his accomplices had accused him of committing the murders: he then admitted everything. All the members of the gang except Carey were executed;

he was pardoned because he had turned queen's evidence. Under a different name he sailed out to South Africa with his family to start a new life, but before he arrived a fellow passenger, Patrick O'Donnell, discovered his identity and shot him dead. O'Donnell was brought back, convicted, and sentenced to death. A lot of people pleaded for his life. John Devoy solemnly declared that he had shot Carey in self-defense, a theory "hard to reconcile with the evidence that O'Donnell fired several shots while in pursuit of Carey" (O'Brien and Ryan, eds., *Devoy's Post-Bag,* Vol. 2, p. 229). The Clan-na-Gael even formed an O'Donnell Committee, but none of these efforts sufficed, and the prisoner was executed. Money raised in New York paid for a monument to his memory in Glasnevin cemetery in Dublin.

With most, if not all, suspicion of complicity in this affair removed from Parnell's name, he enjoyed more popularity than ever among his followers, and at the end of 1882 they were dismayed to see that he was advertising his home, Avondale, for sale. Parnell was never much good in money matters. He had mortgaged the estate for £12,000, and now felt that he had to let it go. T. D. Sullivan promptly wrote an article in the *Nation* saying that people should contribute to a testimonial fund for the chief, so that he could pay off his mortgage and start all over again. Sullivan thought that £17,000 would do it. But contributions were slow in coming, and the Parnell Tribute would probably have been a failure if Gladstone had not interfered. Heartily disapproving of the idea, Gladstone asked himself why Catholics should give their money to a Protestant in any case. Then he made one of the most glaring mistakes of his life and sent word to the Pope by way of an Irish Catholic M.P., indicating his misgivings. The Pope was no more intelligent about the matter than Gladstone, and he acted. On May 11, on his orders, a cardinal in Rome sent a rescript to the bishops of Ireland on the subject of Parnell's affairs, saying that it was the duty of the Irish clergy, especially the bishops, "to curb the excited feelings of the multitude."

The Irish bishops were galvanized into action. They led

the way, immediately sending contributions to the Parnell Tribute—big contributions, too—and the multitude followed their example. Six months after the cardinal's rescript the Tribute amounted to £37,000, and by the end of the year it was an even £40,000. Strictly speaking, this reaction was not so much a tribute to Parnell as a sign of anger that the Pope had submitted to English pressure, but the effect was the same.

In 1866 a Swedish scientist, Alfred Nobel, invented dynamite and thus unwittingly exerted a considerable effect on Irish affairs. Irish terrorists really took to dynamite. The Crimes Act of 1882 was due to expire in 1885 and Gladstone would have been happy to see the last of it, but dynamite made this impossible. Terrorists grew more fierce and audacious as the time of the law's demise approached, outdoing themselves in January 1885, when three explosions were set off all at the same moment, in the Tower of London, Westminster Hall, and the House of Commons. Naturally, when the bill came up for consideration it was not dropped, but renewed. Parnell's party fought this action. During the second reading of the reconstituted bill, forty Parnellites joined the Tories and made it possible for them to defeat the government. Gladstone resigned, leaving the Conservatives in office for a few months before the general election: during that time they dropped the Crimes Bill and introduced into Ireland a new scheme of land purchase, the Ashbourne Act, that proved to be one of the most successful ever tried. A grant was made of £5,000,000, out of which a tenant could borrow the whole sum needed to buy his holding, paying it back over forty-nine years at a reasonable rate of interest— 4 per cent. As things worked out it was actually cheaper for a tenant to buy his farm than pay rent on it. The tenants were not long in realizing this, and the act was so successful that the original grant had to be renewed within three years.

The general election, by which the Liberals came back to power, was affected by the Franchise Act of 1884. Many

more men in Ireland as in England now had the vote, and
Parnell's party was strengthened, with all but two Irish
members—one from Ulster, the other from Dublin—
committed to Home Rule. Gladstone interpreted these
results as a clear mandate to carry Home Rule through, and
in the spring, on April 8, 1886, he introduced a bill providing
that Ireland should have her own parliament which would
rule the country in all domestic matters. But no mention
was made of compensation for unionists or Protestants,
for which reason the Conservatives sharply attacked it.
Undeterred, on April 16 Gladstone brought in a Land Bill
for Ireland far more radical than any yet proposed by an
English prime minister. It was really a land nationalization
instrument, providing that the land should be handed over
to the tenants and the landlords bought out. Two members
of his own cabinet resigned rather than support Gladstone
in this venture, but the seventy-four-year-old premier
was not dismayed by this nor by the Opposition's violent
reaction. The bill got as far as the second reading on June
8, and was then rejected by a majority of thirty. Gladstone
thereupon proposed to dissolve Parliament. Queen Victoria
protested against this, arguing that there had recently been
far too many elections, but he had his way, and on June 26
he went to the country to fight yet one more election on the
Irish question. The Liberals lost, but Gladstone continued
to struggle for Home Rule from the Opposition benches. As
has been seen, Gladstone was already something of a hero
to the Irish. Now he was acclaimed, and his picture hung in
many Irish houses.

Parnell maintained stiff discipline over his party, but they
disciplined themselves as well. On entering Parliament all
members took a pledge of fidelity. Until 1885 the pledge
taking was voluntary, but then they changed the rules and
the pledge. From then on the new version was *required*
of candidates, not voluntary, and was to be taken before
instead of after the election. That same year, for reasons best
known to himself, Willie O'Shea announced that he would
not take any pledge at all, and he continued to say so even

when told that he wouldn't be allowed to contest the Clare seat if he did not. To resolve the difficulty the campaign manager suggested that he try for a Liberal seat instead of a Nationalist one, in Ulster or England. Parnell, appealed to, got him a chance at Liverpool, but the captain didn't win the nomination there. He became upset, and made wild threats about what he would do to that blackguard Parnell if he didn't get a Nationalist seat.

Knowing the facts, we can see why Parnell took the next step, but party members were staggered when he said that O'Shea must have the safe seat of Galway. When O'Shea was defying the rules, too! It didn't make sense. Biggar, who understood the situation, telegraphed Parnell, "The O'Sheas will be your ruin." Healy fulminated. The voters of Galway were up in arms, but when O'Shea sent for Parnell to come out there and help him, Parnell went. Biggar and Healy defied him, but Healy was intimidated by his master's icy glare, and Biggar too subsided. Parnell pushed ahead, O'Shea got his seat, and the bulk of the party, strengthened by priests who supported Parnell, rebuked the rebels for having imperiled the cause over such a little thing. Now the leader was in an unassailable position, and even the members of the Irish National League of America, which had succeeded to the American Land League in 1883, changed their tune. In August 1886 they published a statement expressing their hearty approval of him.

The activists thought that it was time for some new form of agitation, arguing that Gladstone's Land Bill had failed in its main purpose and tenants were finding it impossible to pay even the fixed rents. Parnell, however, was reluctant to take the risk of another Coercion Act or of disenchanting the Liberals with Home Rule. During the first days of the autumn parliamentary session he tried to bring in relief for the tenants by staying evictions, but the attempt was unsuccessful, and on September 24 he appealed to the Irish National League of America, asking its members to subscribe to an anti-eviction fund. He made a similar appeal in Ireland. Then in the party journal, *United Ireland*,

an article appeared—"A Plan of Campaign" was its title—
which outlined a program nicely calculated to fall short of
alarming the Liberals but which yet supported the tenants.
According to the formula suggested, the tenants of each
estate were to get together and decide how much rent they
could afford to pay, as distinct from the amount fixed by the
land court. Then they were to offer this approved sum to the
landlord. If he accepted it, well and good. If he refused, the
money would be given instead to a committee elected by the
tenants, and used to help those evicted for non-payment of
rent. The beauty of the plan was that everything would be
carried out by the tenants themselves, not the league: the
league's part was merely organization of the tenants. Thus
it could not be again suppressed under the Coercion Act
that was bound to be passed as soon as Parliament could go
through the necessary motions.

Through the winter of 1886-87 the plan had a marked
effect on the eviction rate, lowering it appreciably. Of
course the Tories disbelieved Parnell when he denied having
any connection with it, and toward the end of March 1887
the expected Crimes Bill was introduced. But before it
could be given a second reading, the whole Parnell story
took a different turn. *The Times,* in what must be the most
disgraceful period of its varied career, started publishing
a series of articles under the general title "Parnellism and
Crime." In these, grave accusations were made against the
head of the party, one of them being that he encouraged
the murder of landlords. The climax was reached in the
issue of April 18, when *The Times* printed a facsimile letter,
purportedly from Parnell, admitting that his public attitude
of dismay toward the Phoenix Park murders had been
pretense, and making excuses for the assassination of Burke.

Parnell indignantly denied having written the letter.
He said it was a forgery published by *The Times* at that
particular moment to help along the Crimes Bill. Undeniably
it did help the bill, which soon passed its second reading. A
long lawsuit followed, until at last, in February 1889, it was
proved beyond a doubt that the letter had been forged by the

Irish journalist Richard Pigott, the same man who exposed the harsh treatment given to O'Donovan Rossa in prison years before. Pigott had slipped badly since those days: now he would do anything for money, and it was made clear that this was exactly what he had done when he forged the letter. After being humiliated in court he fled to Madrid, and there blew out his brains. Parnell sued *The Times* for damages: in February the following year he was awarded £5000.

Now he enjoyed tremendous popularity. The very people who had welcomed the scandal hurried to join in the chorus of praise. He and Gladstone worked together for Home Rule and treated each other with courtesy. Neither doubted that Home Rule would be a fact after the next general election.... But none of this mattered as much to the Irish leader as the fact that Katherine O'Shea was hopeful that she could at last buy Willie off, for Aunt Ben had died and left her fortune to her niece.

Mrs. O'Shea moved to Brighton with her household— since the death of Sophie Claude she had borne two more children to her lover. Parnell took the house next door. Everything seemed to be going well for both of them. Then the Woods, Katherine's relatives, decided to contest Aunt Ben's will on grounds of "undue influence." Willie O'Shea joined them. And then on December 30, 1889, the newspapers carried a staggering story: Captain O'Shea was suing his wife for divorce, and had named Charles Stewart Parnell as corespondent.

The eccentric O'Shea could have precipitated a scandal at any time in the preceding three years, ever since he had been sure of his wife's infidelity. There are many theories as to why he chose the time he did. In after years Katherine declared he had waited all that time for Aunt Ben to die, since until her demise there was always hope of extracting just a bit more from the old lady. Possibly he joined in the will contest in order to discredit his wife and thus strengthen his case for divorce. Possibly it was vice versa: his divorce might help him get the money, but it is most likely that Joseph Chamberlain influenced him to destroy Parnell and his work.

At first Parnell's people refused to hear a word against him. When Davitt asked him what the charges might mean, Parnell told him—at least so Davitt reported—that he would emerge from the whole trouble without a stain on his reputation. Parnell later denied having used exactly those words. We might dismiss this discrepancy as a semantic difficulty. Conor Cruise O'Brien sums it up: "This statement... would hardly have reassured those who, like Healy and Biggar, had realized as early as 1886, at the time of the Galway election, how matters stood between Parnell and the O'Sheas. The ambiguity here was that to Davitt, as to other Catholic Irishmen, the statement conveyed that the charge of adultery was false; Parnell, however, seems to have meant to say no more than that he had not infringed on the code of honour of a gentleman, and that Captain O'Shea had not been deceived—matters of indifference to most of Catholic Ireland, which was interested only in the truth or falsity of the adultery charge" *(Parnell and His Party,* p. 280). Later, infuriated by what he considered double-dealing, Davitt became Parnell's bitter enemy. When the case came up for trial on November 15, 1890, Parnell and Mrs. O'Shea made no attempt to defend it, and the verdict automatically went against them. Afterward there was little the most loyal could say.

Parnell seemed to look on the whole thing as a private matter, assuming that anyone with pretensions to decency would ignore it. He married Katherine O'Shea in a registry office—"Get up, get up, it's time to get married!" he called cheerfully that morning as he rapped at her bedroom door. What disconcerted his people more than anything else was that he made no gesture toward resigning his chairmanship, but continued in his customary way with the chores of a political leader. The world did not know how to react.

Slowly, anger rose against him and made itself felt. It originated in England, not Ireland. It was Manning who urged the Irish prelates to show their disapproval, but throughout the affair the Catholic Church was to follow rather than lead the outcry. Parnell's severest critics were the lower middle class of England, the great "nonconformist conscience" of that country. Gladstone knew them well, and he said Parnell must go. For the good of the party, he told Parnell, he should resign, even if only temporarily.

"The bishops and priests of Ireland have left it to the sturdy dissenters of Great Britain to make their protest," wrote Davitt, and it was then that the hounds began to bay at home. A meeting of Irish prelates announced that Parnell was "unworthy of the confidence of Catholics." Members of the party began to speak out. Healy was especially violent, though Davitt was not far behind him: it was Davitt who called Parnell a "cold sensualist." This seems unnecessarily harsh and not at all accurate, for Parnell had one and only one love, but Davitt felt betrayed. The party became disorganized. Parnell defied Gladstone and his Liberals and the party became less organized than ever, most of them longing for him to resign. He would not resign.

His outstanding genius had always been what seemed an unerring judgment of people and their reactions. Even now he very nearly pulled it off, but... from America came angry messages that his continued leadership was impossible. Dillon and O'Brien were against him and could not be discounted. At last on Monday, December 1, seventy-three members met in their usual room in the House of Commons, Committee Room 15, to fight it out. The anti-Parnellites had planned to vote their leader out of the chair, but found this impossible because Parnell was in the chair and would not relinquish it. Whatever was to be said had to be said in his presence, and he sat there stubbornly, through attack and counterattack. Several days were spent in argument that got nowhere: the anti-Parnell group tried to talk things over with Gladstone, but he refused to enter any dialogue until the question of leadership was settled. The deadlock was broken when members retired to the room next door to vote, and emerged to say that Parnell was out. The group had split. Each portion claimed to represent the true party, but the true party had ceased to exist.

Twenty-four out of the seventy-three stood by Parnell, the chief of these being John Redmond. Parnell tried to carry on working as if he could not believe what had happened, but the pretense could not survive the next general election, when he lost his seat. He stood as candidate three times for re-election, but was beaten every time. His health had been getting worse for years past. In the autumn of 1891 he caught a chill, and on October 6 he died at Brighton.

Few men who were in the final struggle ever forgot the bitterness of those days. Whatever Parnell's magic was, it faded and left in most of his comrades only a violent resentment. Yet in 1898, when the fury had cooled, no less a person than Gladstone, talking with Parnell's biographer Barry O'Brien, paid him a striking tribute: "Parnell was the most remarkable man I have ever met. I do not say the ablest. I say the most remarkable and the most interesting. He was an intellectual phenomenon." And the old man added, "Had Parnell lived and had there been no divorce proceedings, I do solemnly believe there would be a Parliament in Ireland now....A wonderful man, a terrible fall."

CHAPTER

20

THE Liberals replaced the Conservatives at the end of 1892 and entered on what was to be their last term of office for some years to come, and Gladstone took the opportunity to introduce one more Home Rule Bill in February the following year. The Lords promptly rejected it, after which honorable failure the old man gave up and nothing more was heard of the Irish question in Westminster for a time. In Ulster it was different: unionists there had consolidated their strength during the Parnell crisis and were now in formidable mood, watchful of their interests and ready to oppose the slightest sign of Home Rule agitation. The new Ulster Defense Union even made plans to form a Protestant army, collecting funds toward this end, but the Tories who soon supplanted the Liberals thought the unionists might as well spare themselves the trouble and expense, holding that the Irish only asked for Home Rule because they were discontented with the way the British governed them. Take away the reasons for their discontent, said the Conservatives, and they would soon simmer down and forget Home Rule.

To achieve this goal Tory ministers were willing to be more liberal than the Liberals. The chief secretary for Ireland, Arthur Balfour, amended the Ashbourne Act for land purchase by increasing the government's financial guarantee and making what he considered better terms. Unfortunately his new arrangements were so complicated that the change had the opposite effect, and land purchase lagged. Then Balfour became prime minister, and in 1903 the next chief secretary, George Wyndham, produced a Land Purchase Act that made the sale of estates compulsory throughout Ireland. This did it: at last the land question was really settled. When the act became law there were still more than 500,000 tenant farmers in the country, but by 1904 the tenant farmer had become a rarity. The large landowner, who had held power in Ireland for generations, disappeared within a decade, and in 1914 Ireland was a nation of smallholders.

For nine years after Parnell's death the Irish Parliamentary party remained split into two Home Rule groups. John Redmond had to withstand a determined effort by John Dillon to unseat him: possibly the fact that Dillon was himself challenged by Tim Healy saved Redmond, but the unedifying squabble, like several others, displeased the Clan-na-Gael, as reduced subscriptions plainly indicated. Finally in 1900 the members took warning, made up their differences and reunited, with Redmond still the leader. It was high time for harmony. Ireland like her neighbors was trying desperately to meet the challenge of competition from overseas agriculturalists and marketers, which had been growing for years and was now a grave problem. New methods of transport made it possible for the Americans to undersell Irish and British produce and still earn a profit. In Ireland the only people who could hold out against these conditions were rich graziers. The small dairy and mixed-farm owners were inexperienced and had no chance in world marketing: they badly needed education. Horace Plunkett, seeing the approach of this crisis, had written in 1888: "When the land question is settled Ireland may be quieted, but no one thinks she will be prosperous. Foreign competition has ruined her agriculture."

Plunkett knew what he was talking about. At thirty-four, when he wrote this, he had already spent ten years in Wyoming at various jobs that ranged from that of ranch manager down through cowhand to cook. An extraordinary man, younger son of Lord Dunsany of Meath, he read history at Oxford, but even as an undergraduate he thought more about contemporary social problems than his elected studies, and in 1878 he formed the "Dunsany Co-operative Society," which comprised his father's tenants, the steward, and himself. He worked hard at this project, taking his turn at selling in the shop. Then he went off to the wild West, but when his father needed him at home and he returned to Dunsany, he found the co-operative still running and making a small profit. Plunkett acted ably as agent for old Lord Dunsany, and when the old man died he carried on in the same capacity for the heir, his sickly elder brother, but the work did not take up all his energy. Soon he was teaching dairy farmers to organize co-operative creameries, and though the movement was opposed by shopkeepers the idea took on. In 1894 he launched the Irish Industrial (or Agricultural) Organization Society, which spread the co-op movement through all agricultural Ireland and took in the manufacture of butter and bacon, marketing, and the supplying of farm equipment.

In 1891, as part of the new policy to "kill Home Rule with kindness" and while Balfour was still chief secretary, the government set up a Congested Districts Board, financed with money from the disestablished Church fund, to administer the poverty-stricken areas of the nine western counties where need was greatest. Balfour asked Plunkett to become a member, and he accepted. (He tried to interest John Dillon in the board and in creamery co-ops as well, but Dillon, who owned a shop himself, snubbed him.) The board was just the sort of thing Plunkett liked: it got results. Harbors were built, fishing methods improved, cottage industries supported, and advice given on the latest agricultural methods. Thanks to a new act of 1903, board members were enabled to acquire more acreage from big estates and add it to holdings too small to be viable: two million acres were thus bought and redistributed.

"The Board is really doing good work and improving the houses of the people," wrote Plunkett in 1913. Two years later he noted: "An interesting illustration of the rising standard of living in Congested Districts. When the Board gave out windows 2 ft. 10 in. X 2 ft. 2 in. the people complained that they were too large. Now they complain that they are too small."

Another product of the "be kind to Ireland" policy was the new light railway system that was introduced to open up the remote districts of the west, and yet another was the county council system, in which new councils, wielding a certain amount of local authority and containing some elected members, took the place of the earlier groups that were all appointed judicially. But of all such reforms the most significant was embodied in the Universities Act of 1908, when Augustine Birrell was chief secretary. The Royal University was abolished and replaced by two others, the National University—centered in Dublin, though with colleges in Cork and Galway as well—and the Queen's University in Belfast. Officially the National University was non-sectarian: in practice, however, it was managed by Roman Catholics, whereas the Queen's University was "independent," i.e. Protestant. This sop to Ulster sentiment did not satisfy the unionists, who opposed the Universities Bill as a matter for the record, though they could not put a stop to it. The one exception was Horace Plunkett, one unionist M.P. who was temperamentally unfitted for the position, though it took him years to face this fact.

These were all important reforms, but—with the possible exception of the Universities Bill—they failed to capture the good will of the country's youth, or touch the imagination. Under O'Connell and Parnell the Irish had embarked on a search for their own identity. Now, though less hungry, they were dissatisfied. To be sure, they had made great gains. A peasant could bring up his family under his own roof with reasonable certainty of enough to eat. These were prizes nobody decried, but the Irish still wanted pride of self, and in the absence of independence there was no chance of gaining it. Politics had proved disappointing, dry, and—where Parnell was concerned—painful. The once sweet rallying call to Home Rule no longer tempted young men: they were out of temper with parliamentary games, and, though they loved the English no better than they had before, they were tired of the fight. Writers and painters, at least, found it more rewarding to the spirit to look back on the golden age of legend than forward to district boards and co-operatives.

Among these one of the leading spirits was William Butler Yeats, poet and dramatist of Sligo. In 1889 when he was twenty-four he published a book of poems titled *The Wanderings of Oisin,* and his native country continued to inspire much of his work—*Fairy and Folk Tales* in 1890, and a few years later another collection, *Irish Representative Tales.* The year 1893 saw the appearance of his essay *The Celtic Twilight.* With Lady Gregory he sponsored the movement that produced the Abbey Theatre, opened in 1904, and encouraged Irish literature and drama.

"Drove to Coole Park to spy out the land for I.A.O.S.," wrote Plunkett in 1896. Coole Park was Lady Gregory's house. "... W. B. Yeats, the young poet, a rebel, a mystic and an ass, but really a genius in a queer way, I believe, and Edward Martyn, a clever writer of the more imaginative kind, were fellow guests. It was interesting and by no means a waste of time." But Yeats, Lady Gregory, and their associates J. M. Synge, T. W. Rolleston, and George Moore, were for the most part English speakers writing in English with what one might call an Irish accent: young Douglas Hyde, another Irishman, wanted a truer Irish rebirth, of and through the use of the Gaelic language. As an undergraduate at Trinity Hyde was an active member of the Society for the Preservation of the Irish Language, and became adept enough in the tongue to write poems in it. He visited New York in 1891 and gave a lecture there in Irish, urging the audience to hold on to that language because it was their strongest bond

of unity and the best way to preserve the nation. Returned
to Dublin, he accepted the presidency of a new National
Literary Society, and in his inaugural lecture in November
1892, entitled "The Necessity for De-Anglicizing the Irish
Nation," he elaborated on the theme. Abroad as at home
this lecture, which was published, attracted the attention
of Irishmen. Hyde declared that the Irish relinquished their
strongest claim to nationality when they abandoned their
culture—their language, dress, and customs. Such Irish
claimed to hate the English, yet imitated the English in
everything. But they could save themselves even at this late
date if they halted the slide, renounced all imitation of the
English, and worked to preserve their language. The lecturer
described with enthusiasm how this preservation could be
accomplished by house-to-house visiting and exhortation of
Irish people—*really* Irish people, not middle-class imitation
English, but descendants of the workers.

John MacNeill, for one, was deeply impressed by such
ideas. He was born in 1867 in the north, the Glens of
Antrim, and had been educated at a Protestant school in
Belfast before coming to Dublin to work as a junior clerk in
the Four Courts and attend law lectures at Trinity. He had
already become interested enough in the Gaelic language
to learn it well, and that interest had led him to study Irish
history. To Hyde he now proposed founding a Gaelic League.
Hyde liked the idea and agreed to be president, so the league
was founded on July 31, 1893. As a sign of his passion for
all things Gaelic MacNeill changed his first name to the
Irish form of Eoin. In the beginning, the league's chief and
only aim was to preserve the Irish language. That Hyde
had found enough Irish speakers in New York to fill a
lecture hall was probably attributable to the law of culture
dissemination, which holds that old fashions endure longest
on the outer fringes of a culture, but now members in Ireland
sought out the old people still at home who had the Gaelic.
Leaguers followed MacNeill's example too and examined
the archives in quest of Irish poems, songs, and traditional
material generally. This led them more than once across the

trail of an earlier group, the Gaelic Athletic Association, founded in 1884, in which young people were encouraged to play national games, mainly curling, and urged to eschew "such foreign and fantastic field-sports as lawn tennis, polo, croquet, cricket and the like" (as Archbishop Croke of Cashel put it). To this day cricket is frowned on in Ireland, but the most ardent nationalism has not vanquished football.

It was the league that made St. Patrick's Day a national holiday— and also closed the pubs on the same date. But the Leaguers' greatest success was in the educational field; in 1903 they could announce with pride that within one year the Irish language had been introduced into thirteen hundred national schools where it was being taught to the children, and that after the National University opened, all candidates for places had to pass an examination in the language, which inevitably became known as "compulsory Irish."

The London-based journalist and editor of the influential paper *The Leader*, D. P. Moran, was one of the league's ardent supporters. It was thanks in large part to his advocacy that it waxed in popularity and power. Moran did not subscribe to the founders' idea that it should be non-political as well as non-sectarian, but he did his best for "Irish Ireland" by praising its work nevertheless. He instituted a "Buy Irish" campaign to protect national industry, and readers who did not always agree with his more extreme ideas were interested in the organization in spite of this. The journalist was always provocative. He said that the cause of Irish civilization had been thrown overboard in Grattan's time, and since then every political leader, without exception, had hoodwinked the people. He said Wolfe Tone was not Irish but a Frenchman born in Ireland of English parents. Of the Irish Parliamentary party of his own time he said, "I deny that [the party] is composed of real Irishmen....their education, literature and social surroundings are either English or, what is far worse, imitation English." He poked fun at the Abbey dramatists and players much as Gilbert scouted the aesthetes of England in *Patience,* saying that the poetic youths heard lake water lapping even when stirring their punch.

Douglas Hyde sincerely disclaimed political aims for the league, but the organization was bound to take on a certain amount of politically tinged nationalism sooner or later. Those Leaguers who did, ultimately, become political were not connected in any way with John Redmond and the seventy-nine other M.P.s in Westminster, which they looked on as a backwater. They turned instead to Arthur Griffith, a Dublin printer who had supported Parnell in his final campaign. After Parnell's death he went to South Africa and came home when the Boer War broke out. (This was the last English war in which there was no serious resistance against the conscription of Irishmen.) In 1899, in Dublin, Griffith started a lively weekly paper called *The United Irishman* in memory of John Mitchel's journal of 1848, and in its columns he asked an old Fenian question which was to be the basic principle of Sinn Fein: Why did Ireland send M.P.s to Westminster at all? Griffith argued that the union was an illegality, and every Irishman who acted as a member of the English Parliament was compounding that illegality: therefore all Irish members should be withdrawn from Westminster, and Ireland should set up her own government at home. He did not advocate complete separation from England, though he really wanted it: he felt that such a move would split the country into factions, unionist versus nationalist. In this respect Sinn Fein was to differ from the Irish Republican Brotherhood, which advocated separation at all costs even if it meant using force. Griffith proposed that England and Ireland remain together under the Crown, as they had been in Grattan's time when there was a parliament in Dublin.

Hungary had just established its independence of Austria by the use of bloodless methods like those Griffith advised for Ireland—passive resistance, abstaining from the Austrian parliament, and self-reliance. He published a number of articles on this subject first in the *Irishman* and then in a pamphlet entitled "The Resurrection of Hungary." Even more strongly than Moran he advocated a "Buy Irish" policy, declaring that Ireland must support her own industries and commerce. He approved of the drive to preserve the Gaelic language, but did not share Moran's scorn of the Abbey group. On the contrary, it was through his efforts that the National Council was formed in 1903, numbering among its members Yeats, Edward Martyn, George Russell, and Maud Gonne—English writers every one. He had already encouraged the foundation of the nationalist club Cumann na nGaedheal. These different elements finally came together in Sinn Fein, which means "Ourselves Alone." A wit has defined the Sinn Fein movement as "Christian Science in politics."

Unlike the Gaelic League, the Sinn Fein League was not a formal society but an organization to which you belonged if you decided you did, without ceremony. It was non-sectarian. Griffith wound up *The United Irishman* in 1906 and began to publish a journal named *Sinn Fein* instead, explaining Sinn Fein in the first issue: "It is the declaration of the Irish Protestant Parliament and Protestant Volunteers of 1782, it is the declaration of the Irish Catholic Parliament and Catholic army of 1689, and the meaning and justification of every Nationalist movement in Ireland since 1172." It was born, as a matter of fact, at the National Council's first annual convention on November 28, 1905, at the Rotunda in Dublin—a small meeting, but attended by those whose names were to be heard again and again. Patrick Pearse was there, and Dr. Pat McCartan, just back from five years in America where he had joined the Clan-na-Gael. Pearse was the son of an English stonemason and his Irish wife, both keen Home Rulers: until Parnell's fall the elder Pearse had admired the leader intensely. Born in Dublin in 1879, Patrick was a scholarly boy who showed an aptitude for Gaelic. While waiting for a place at the Royal University, at the age of seventeen, he taught at his school, the Christian Brothers' College, and as an undergraduate he founded the New Ireland Society. He gave lectures at this society on such topics as "Gaelic Prose Literature." He read law, took his B.A. in 1901, and was duly called to the bar, but after a few years he turned back to his preoccupations, Gaelic and education. From first to last he was a poet. In 1908 he founded St. Enda's College, where boys were taught in both Irish and English, and, two years later, St. Ita's, a girls' school run on the same lines.

At the convention Griffith proposed a "Council of Three Hundred" to serve as a *de facto* parliament in Ireland, and the meeting approved. Delegates of various organizations then joined together in the name of Sinn Fein: these organizations were the National Council itself, Cumann na nGaedheal, Inghinidhe na hEireann (the Daughters of Erin), and the Dungannon Clubs of Ulster. The Daughters of Erin was founded in 1900 by Maud Gonne in protest against the exclusion of women from Ireland's nationalist societies, and was a sort of successor to the Ladies' Land League. Maud Gonne was English, the daughter of a former assistant adjutant general at the Castle. She had rebelled against her parents' world and devoted her life to the Irish cause. The Daughters' first campaign had been to snub Queen Victoria—the Famine Queen, as Maud Gonne called her—on her visit to Ireland in 1900. They did it simply enough by giving a children's party on the day Victoria was giving *her* children's party at the Viceregal Lodge. Fifteen thousand children went to look at the queen that day, but twenty thousand attended the Daughters' party.

The Dungannon Clubs represented active republican elements in Ulster and had been founded by Bulmer Hobson and Denis McCullough of the IRB in Belfast. Both of them were keen, active organizers and ardent separatists.

That year, 1905, witnessed the failure of another attempt in England to put through a Home Rule Bill in spite of a number of influential Tories who were in favor of it. One was George Wyndham of Wyndham's Act, and another was his undersecretary, Sir Anthony MacDonnell. For two years Wyndham had worked, through an Irish Reform Association, for limited self-government for Ireland by means of a council with some elected members. Even that changeable monarch Edward VII was believed to be in favor of this compromise, but the Irish unionists heard of the plan in advance and took alarm. They stirred up their colleagues, the English unionists, and in the ensuing quarrel Wyndham had to resign. A general election in January 1906 brought the Liberals back.

By this time some Irish M.P.s had begun to lose faith in the traditional pattern of politics. In 1908 one of them contested a by-election in North Leitrim on a Sinn Fein ticket and very nearly got in. Redmond took alarm, but even then did not go to great lengths on the matter; he merely requested action on Home Rule yet again. It never occurred to him, at least, that he might be doing no good in Westminster. The cold fact was that the Liberals did not then need Irish votes and saw no reason to pay for them. But in 1908 Campbell-Bannerman died and Asquith became prime minister, and in 1909 the House of Lords exasperated the government by rejecting Lloyd George's Land Taxation Bill. The government determined to remove this stumbling block once and for all, but before they could take action the general election of 1910 proved that the palmy days were over. The Liberals got in again, but with a majority so reduced that Redmond and his party were once more necessary, which meant that the old Home Rule pledge had to be kept as soon as possible. In 1911, with Redmond's help, the House passed the Parliament Act, which took away the Lords' power of veto by restricting it to three successive actions: thereafter a bill sent to the Upper House could be rejected no more than twice, and it automatically became law when it went up for the third time. The next Home Rule Bill sent to the Lords would become law in, if not before, 1914.

The prospect dismayed Tories with vested interests in Ireland. They foresaw the irredeemable loss of power and property as soon as the Irish had Home Rule, for Belfast and all the industrialized area around it were very much part of Britain's economy. Father F. X. Martin says: "How intimately the interests of the Ulster industrialists were

identified with the Orange agitation is seen in the fact
that when the Indemnity Guarantee Fund for the Ulster
Volunteer Force was opened in September 1913 the twelve
members of the Ulster Unionist Council each subscribed
£10,000, the first contributions to a fund which rapidly rose
to £1,000,000" (1916—*Myth, Vact, and Mystery,* pp. 54,
55). The Ulster Protestants had, for added reason, the fear of
being engulfed by Roman Catholicism. Of course, fighting
for their rights was no new idea: it had started with Hugh
O'Neill if not earlier, perhaps even before Malachy defied
Brian Boru, back in the tenth century. In 1886, when Lord
Randolph Churchill, wishing to annoy Gladstone, went
to Belfast and addressed a meeting there on the subject of
Home Rule, he had pleased them vastly by giving them the
slogan "Ulster will fight, and Ulster will be right." Now the
unionists had another tag line: "Home Rule means Rome
rule."

The Ulster Unionist Council needed a new chief. After
some discussion the members decided on the brilliant
barrister Sir Edward Carson, a good choice, they felt, even
though he was no northerner: he came from Dublin. Carson
had served as solicitor general in both Ireland and England,
and was an outstanding M.P. for the Conservatives. He
accepted the invitation and crossed over to Belfast in 1911
to meet the council in person and be viewed by his followers.
The Ulster unionist M.P. for East Down, James Craig, who
owned an estate, Craigavon outside Belfast, arranged an
Orange and unionist demonstration for Carson's benefit: on
September 23, fifty thousand men from the Orange Order
and the unionist clubs marched from the city center to
Craigavon, where Carson was waiting to greet them. In a
strong speech, heartily cheered, he told them to be prepared
to be responsible for the government of "the Protestant
province of Ulster" the minute Home Rule became law.
"We will yet defeat the most nefarious conspiracy that has
ever been hatched against a free people," he cried. Carson
was sincere in his horror of Home Rule: he was passionately
determined to save the union, with which he felt Ireland's

whole fate was bound up. "It is only for Ireland that I'm in politics," he had told Balfour two years earlier. There were more great demonstrations, and groups of Orangemen began meeting regularly for military drill.

On April 11, 1912, Asquith introduced the Home Rule Bill that seemed certain to pass in spite of the House of Lords. For such a momentous instrument it was not particularly revolutionary, retaining as it did many powers for the British Parliament, even direct control of the police force. Certainly it did not meet with the approval of the Sinn Fein: Griffith said, "If this is liberty the lexicographers have deceived us," but most nationalists were willing to accept it as a start in the right direction. It was the unionists who would not have it at any price, and contested it as stubbornly as if it had offered complete independence.

The whole House was now split on Irish Home Rule, with Conservative lined up with unionist and Liberal with nationalist. After the third reading in January 1913 the Lords rejected the bill as a matter of form, but it was now only a question of time before it became law, and the Ulster Unionist Council, in readiness for that day, turned itself into a provisional government. In September 1912 thousands of Ulster unionists had already signed a "covenant" to the accompaniment of Protestant churchly blessings: the covenant was, however, a warlike, threatening document. When the Home Rule Bill had its third reading the council decided to recruit an "Ulster Volunteer Force" of up to a hundred thousand men. Carson had no religious bigotry, but he thought the force a good idea since it would enable Orangemen to blow off steam without attacking the local Catholics. His associates had more ambitious projects for it. Men signed on in great numbers; by the end of February 1914 there were ninety thousand Ulster Volunteers, each of whom, as soon as he was inducted, entered on a period of training and marching, and the council appointed the retired English General Richardson to command the troops. At first they had only makeshift arms—broom handles or wooden army rifles—and they complained about this until an aging unionist firebrand, Major Fred Crawford, announced that he happened to have collected a cache of arms in England. Now, with the aid of a few associates, he moved these things into northern Ireland. In December 1913 the government somewhat tardily clamped down on gunrunning. Crawford's hoard did not go far, and the Volunteers went on complaining until the major proposed buying a whole shipload of arms in Germany and bringing the lot direct to Ireland. This was done, the guns being shipped through Larne.

These actions convinced the authorities that Ulster would indeed fight, and that its cause was thoroughly popular with all sections of the Protestant community. Their determination also impressed the Liberals—it was a Liberal who first suggested that part of Ulster might be excluded from the Home Rule Bill, though nobody else at that time would consider such action. Redmond thought of the Irish concept of nationhood and the nationalists of Ulster and replied, "For us Ireland is an entity." Carson too wanted a complete Ireland within the union. He did at one time bring forward an amendment for the exclusion of Ulster, but he was bluffing and trying to wreck the Home Rule Bill when he did it: he believed Home Rule would be impossible without the north. And the Ulster Unionist Council feared the effect on themselves of exclusion, because "Though they commonly spoke as if the province of Ulster were solidly protestant and unionist, they knew very well that Roman Catholics formed almost half the total population, that in three of the nine counties they were overwhelmingly predominant, and that in two more (Fermanagh and Tyrone) they had a small, but distinct, majority" (Beckett, *The Making of Modern Ireland*, p. 249).

Asquith went ahead with his preparations. In March 1914 the Crown's naval and military forces in Ulster were strengthened in case of trouble, but the government had reason to doubt that the troops would move against Ulster even if ordered to do so, and the War Office directed the commander in chief in Ireland, Sir Arthur Paget, to find out how the men felt on this point. Paget asked his officers outright what they would do if they were called on to fight Ulstermen, at the same time reminding them that refusal would mean dismissal from the force. In equally forthright fashion fifty-eight cavalry officers at Curragh military headquarters replied that they would not take aggressive action against the Ulster Volunteers, orders or no orders, dismissal or no. It was very embarrassing for the War Office and the affair had to be kept quiet. Nobody was dismissed.

All this drilling and gunrunning in the north was observed with great attention by the other Irish, whose reaction is perhaps difficult for outsiders to understand, but then again perhaps it is not. They approved of, even envied the Ulster Volunteers, especially after the arrival of the German arms ship. As Patrick Pearse wrote, the Orangeman with a rifle was a much less ridiculous figure than the nationalist without a rifle. On November 1, 1913, Eoin MacNeill, who was now professor of early and medieval history at University College, published an article entitled (in Gaelic) "The North Began," in which he called for an "Irish Volunteer" movement for the nationalists, invoking as a model the old volunteer movement of Grattan's time. The idea rapidly caught on, the fact that Redmond was not enthusiastic being a help rather than a hindrance—though later he was to accept the *fait accompli*. The IRB quickly moved in on the project, seeing the advantages such a force would offer when they were ready to push for separation. MacNeill was not a separatist: he wanted Home Rule, but there was no showdown on this difference of outlook at the beginning, and the Irish Volunteer Force was established by the end of November, with MacNeill elected president and four IRB men, Patrick Pearse, Sean MacDermott, Eamonn Ceannt, and Joseph Plunkett on the Volunteer Committee. Like their counterparts in the north the Irish Volunteers marched and drilled and camped out, and complained of having no guns. As a result smuggling was organized and carried through— not by the IRB, but by a group that was overwhelmingly

Anglo-Irish and Protestant, including Erskine and Mrs.
Childers, Alice Stopford Green, and Sir Roger Casement.
The Childers' yacht *Asgard* ran part of the only available
rifle supply into Howth, where a British regiment opened
fire on the crowd that had gathered to help and killed three
people. The rest were brought in by two smaller yachts to
Kilcoole, county Wicklow, without accident. In all there
were only fifteen hundred rifles. The Howth affair showed
that gunrunning was not as easy for the Irish Volunteers as
it had been for the Ulstermen: obviously the authorities did
not maintain the same benevolent indifference south of the
border.

At the end of July the government's attention was diverted
to trouble on the Continent, in Serbia, and by the end of a
few days more the Great War had burst on the world. Irish
matters, including Home Rule, would have to be shelved,
said the English. Both Carson and Redmond agreed to a
postponement of Home Rule: it became a law, but remained
in suspension. The nationalists on the Volunteer Committee
resented Redmond's action in pledging them to patience and
alliance with England when he had never put the question
to the people, especially as on July 8 the Lords had passed
an amending bill, overlooked by most people in the swelling
excitement, providing that the six counties of the northeast
be excluded from the workings of the Home Rule Act. The
nationalists were even angrier when Redmond addressed a
group of Volunteers who were parading near his country
home and urged them to go out and fight the Germans. The
committee called a convention to talk it over, and in the
resulting argument, which became very fierce, the force
came apart. Most of the men elected to follow Redmond.
The rest, a mere fraction of the total number, stayed with
O'Neill.

There is no doubt that most Irishmen were willing to
accept the agreement made by Redmond and Carson:
many enlisted for service against the Germans, long before
conscription in Ireland was even mentioned. Today, because
we have been instilled with the idea that the Irish were

in constant rebellion against British rule, it comes as a
surprise to look at the statistics, but there they are. In April
1916, just before the balloon went up, there were 150,000
Irish serving in the British army and a further 115,000 in
various other services—the RIC (Royal Irish Constabulary),
the DMP (Dublin Metropolitan Police), and Redmond's
National Volunteers, as opposed to the at most 16,000
Irish Volunteers under MacNeill. "For every Irishman with
MacNeill there were over sixteen with the British" (F. X.
Martin, 1916—*Myth, Fact, and Mystery,* p. 108). Moreover,
as Father Martin courageously points out, the Easter Rising
cannot in any way be said to have enjoyed popular support:
not even the 16,000 Irish Volunteers as a body were in
favor of it, and half their headquarters staff, including the
commander in chief, MacNeill, opposed it.

The Irish Volunteers, then, were comparatively few, but
their number was augmented by a small, tough body of men,
the Irish Citizen Army, whose organization anticipated
theirs. The army was founded in 1913 through the efforts
of the labor leaders James Larkin and James Connolly.
Both of these men were born abroad of immigrant Irish
parents, Larkin in Liverpool, Connolly in Edinburgh. Both
were experienced in labor relations when they arrived in
Ireland. In the early years of the century conditions in the
Irish countryside were better than they had been in years,
but city slums were as bad as any in the Western world,
so bad that Marx and Lenin considered Dublin a likely
spot for the great proletarian revolution to begin. "How
can people bear to live in such places?" wrote Connolly's
daughter Nora after an electioneering campaign. "Why
don't they burn them down? I went up pitch black stairs,
my feet slipping and squelching in the filth on them....And
the smell—the smell...." Connolly, who founded the Irish
Socialist Republican party, would have agreed with Marx
as to Dublin. As a militant he had little use for the Gaelic
League approach: "You cannot teach starving men Gaelic,"
he said. He and Larkin organized the Irish Transport and
General Workers' Union (ITGWU) in 1909. Four years later,

in 1913, union and owners met in a violent confrontation that continued for eight months. The memory of the Dublin lockout and the misery accompanying it lived on for years, and many union members were bitter with the IRB for refusing to back them at that time. It was during the lockout that the leaders established the Citizen Army, to protect the workers and their families, and at first it numbered less than three hundred, but was well trained even then. Connolly, a confirmed nationalist, finally agreed that the army should go with the Volunteers in spite of the fact that the corps was full of IRB members. Larkin opposed this decision.

As all this indicates, the IRB, at least those members who started out as Gaelic Leaguers, had changed dramatically in outlook and was now thoroughly saturated with the idea of revolution by force. Many of them were poets, and they were the most activist of all. It is impossible to devote space to all the leaders who played a part in the Easter Rising, but some should be mentioned. Of course there was the chief actor Patrick Pearse, and Eoin MacNeill, though he did not want the rising. There were Denis MacCullough and Bulmer Hobson, Ulster nationalists like the crippled Tom Clarke, a Fenian who served fifteen years in English jails for dynamiting and had come to Dublin from New York. Clarke opened a tobacco shop in Parnell Street that became a meeting place for the rebels, and he served as go-between for the Clan-na-Gael and the IRB. His closest friend was young Sean MacDermott, another Ulsterman, who managed the Fenian newspaper *Irish Freedom* and was national organizer for the IRB. Then there was The O'Rahilly from Kerry, a well-off man who had spent some years in America.

As fervor increased among the politicos, intramural feuds also gained heat. Sean O'Casey, an early member of the Citizen Army, was bitterly prejudiced against the IRB and the Volunteers because of the Dublin lockout grievance. When Countess Markievicz wanted to join the army he objected because she was closely associated with the Volunteers, and when the army voted to let her in anyway he resigned. Which brings us to the subject of "Madame," the countess. In spite of her exotic title she was Anglo-Irish: Constance Gore-Booth from Sligo, who married the Polish Count Casimir Dunin-Markievicz. She was born in 1868 and brought up, like Maud Gonne, as a privileged member of the upper classes. She was beautiful, intelligent—and restless. She met "Cassie" in Paris, where both were studying art. In 1903 they went to live in Dublin. No doubt in other times Constance would still have been much the same: she is a familiar enough type in England, rebellious against conventional life, impulsive, and sure enough of herself not to mind being considered eccentric. In fact she enjoyed the spotlight. In 1908 she joined the Daughters of Erin and then moved on, by way of Bulmer Hobson, to the Sinn Fein. Connolly so impressed her that she helped to organize woman workers. One day she was irritated by the news that the viceroy had introduced the Boy Scout system into Ireland. Nothing could be sadder, she said, than to see Irish boys saluting "the flag that flew in triumph over every defeat their nation has known." Some years earlier Bulmer Hobson had organized Na Fianna Eireann (those ancient Fenians again, but in another context) in Belfast—classes where young boys and girls studied Gaelic subjects and played at hurling. He dropped the project when he moved to Dublin, but Madame now started it up again as Ireland's answer to the Boy Scouts. Under her leadership the Fianna took on a military aspect. She enlisted adolescent boys and arranged that they should learn to drill. She took them on camping trips. The movement grew, though Cassie complained to cronies that the young devils drank his whisky, and after Madame met and made friends with James Larkin, Fianna shared headquarters with the ITGWU. Later the boys became messengers for the revolutionaries, and did important work in this respect.

One man who was closely connected with the rising was not in the end able to participate. This was Roger Casement, another Ulster-man. He was born in 1864. At seventeen he went to work for the Elder Dempster Shipping Company in Liverpool, and three years later shipped out as purser in one of the company vessels sailing to the west coast of Africa. There the Civil Service took him on, and he remained. Little by little he was promoted until he had reached a position of trust. Then the Foreign Office gave him the undercover job of investigating rumors of atrocities in the Congo, where Leopold, king of the Belgians, held a monopoly on practically everything and was making a fortune out of rubber. As consul, Casement was able to get into the country and see things for himself. Afterward he sent a full report home. The rumors were true, he said: disgusting cruelties were being perpetrated. The grim story was published in the press, and when Casement came back to England in 1904 he was the man of the hour. In London he met fifty-seven-year-old Alice Stopford Green, born in Ireland, daughter of a Protestant archbishop of Meath and widow of the English historian J. R. Green. Mrs. Green too wrote on historical subjects; after considerable thought she had come to the conclusion that the English had no right to be in Ireland and her work was propaganda disguised as history. Casement was only too glad to agree with her—he happened to be in a particularly anti-English mood at the time, smoldering with the suspicion that the Foreign Office did not believe what he said about the Congo, but he was always touchy, as men who spend their lives in the tropics tend to be. Even after a special commission bore him out and he no longer resented the Foreign Office he agreed with Mrs. Green's ideas, and when he visited Ireland he looked up her friends—Bulmer Hobson, Eoin MacNeill, the English novelist Erskine Childers, and others of like political convictions. That summer he was made a Companion of the Order of St. Michael and St. George.

In 1910-11 Casement completed another mission that was very like the first one, though this time it was in South America, where he was sent as consul general to Rio. Once more he was told to investigate conditions among rubber workers, this time in country along the Putumayo River in the northwest. In spite of great hardship and ill health he got the information that was needed: his ensuing report described conditions even worse than those he had found in the Congo. He returned to England late in 1911, and was knighted.

Londoners thought of the honored, honorable Sir Roger Casement as being completely Anglicized. Tall and good-looking, with great charm of manner, he was admired by everyone he met. There was regret but sympathetic understanding when in 1913 he retired from the Service on the grounds of ill health, and it seemed natural that he should then go back to live in Ireland: after all, they said to one another, he was Irish, though one tended to forget it. During the next year he visited England once or twice, possibly to keep his hand in, for though nobody there suspected it the old intelligence expert was again busy with a cause, immersed in the affairs of the Irish Volunteer Corps and their plans to bring those fifteen hundred Hamburg guns to Howth. The Volunteers needed money for these and other arms they hoped to get later on, so they looked, as always, toward America, where gallant old Devoy still reigned over the faithful, keeping in touch with other Irish-Americans throughout the country, telling them where to send their money and for what. In ordinary times it would have been possible simply to write to Devoy, who would see that the funds were sent, but these were not ordinary times and one could not trust the post office. Roger Casement offered to go in person to see Devoy and take care of these matters, and on July 4, 1914, he sailed for New York.

CHAPTER
21

IT is probably true to say that the Volunteer Committee was split from the beginning, also that almost to the end Eoin MacNeill was unaware of the split. With Bulmer Hobson and one or two others he was kept outside of the circle around Tom Clarke and Patrick Pearse, the Clarke-Pearse party growing more and more secretive as they completed their plans for insurrection. They were so careful that even Connolly and The O'Rahilly, though they were fairly close to Pearse, did not know until late in the day what was going on. The O'Rahilly was excluded because it was common knowledge that he favored peaceful settlements of political disputes, whereas Connolly could not be trusted for the opposite reason: he was too militant, and they feared that if they let him in on the secret he might jump the gun before they were ready. As for MacNeill and Bulmer Hobson, in Pearse's estimation they were hopeless. Both of them had declared in favor of waiting until the end of the war before making new demands for independence. MacNeill believed that any other action would inspire punitive measures against the Volunteers and might well hasten conscription legislation: he said that the government was too strong to defy, and without the prospect of success the leaders were not morally justified in chancing their hand. As late as February 1916 he declared, "To enter deliberately on a course of action which is morally wrong is to incur the guilt not only of that action itself but of all its direct consequences. For example, to kill any person in carrying out such a course of action is murder." And he added that a hopeless insurrection could not be justified by the prospect of some future or political advantage which might be hoped for as the result of non-success—a statement that ran directly counter to the reasoning of Clarke and Pearse, who saw the projected rising as almost certain to fail but as a beacon in its very failure. Pearse thought of it as a bugle call, an inspiration that would sweep future generations to the goal he and his could not achieve.

Augustine Birrell, chief secretary for Ireland, afterward said with anger that the Easter Rising never had a chance, but its leaders knew this as well as he did. Success was not their first and only aim. "[The rising] was imaginatively planned with artistic vision and with exceptional military incompetence," writes Father F. X. Martin dryly. "... The revolt was staged consciously as a drama by its principal actors. It is not without significance that Pearse, Plunkett and MacDonagh had all directed plays in their time" (1916—Myth, Fact, and Mystery, pp. 9, 10). In an important respect it was unlike Irish rebellions of the past; the leaders were not Anglo-Irish Protestants but Irish Catholics, many of them poets, at that. If Pearse had not been a poet, one is tempted to say, his attitude would have been more rational. In his daily life before the rising he was one of the gentlest of souls: nevertheless he wrote: "Bloodshed is a cleansing and sanctifying thing and the nation which regards it as the final horror has lost its manhood. There are many things more horrible than bloodshed; and slavery is one of them"—this from a man who had seldom if ever seen the shedding of blood. He spoke enviously of the war that had broken out on the Continent in 1914: the exhilaration of war, he said wistfully, was something Ireland had not known for over a hundred years. "The last sixteen months have been the most glorious in the history of Europe. Heroism has come back to the earth," he wrote. "... It is good for the world that such things should be done. The old heart of the earth needed to be warmed with the red wine of the battlefields." Upon reading this his friend Connolly, militant though he was, lost patience and retorted by way of his paper *The Irish Worker,* "No, we do not think that the old heart of the earth needs to be warmed with the red wine of millions of lives. We think anyone who does is a blithering idiot."

On the whole, however, Pearse swept his companions along with him, never more than on the occasion of O'Donovan Rossa's funeral. The old Fenian died in 1915 in New York, and his body was sent back to be buried in Glasnevin cemetery, where Patrick Pearse delivered the graveside oration. His words in the peroration are memorable:

"They think that they have pacified Ireland. They think that they have foreseen everything, they think that they have provided against everything; but the fools, the fools!—they have left us our Fenian Dead, and while Ireland holds these graves, Ireland unfree will never be at peace."

The Castle may have marked this speech, but there was a war going on in Europe, and besides, as they probably reflected, the Irish always talked like that: it didn't mean anything. Possibly the only people seriously disadvantaged by such outbursts were the southern Irish in the British forces abroad, where the War Office held them in suspicion and behaved accordingly. They were not permitted to form their own regiments, for example, as the northern Irish did, and John Redmond's son—of all people—was refused a commission. At home, however, the Castle authorities contented themselves with watching for what they considered provocative speeches and articles. Whenever they saw something they did not like in a nationalist newspaper they would pounce and close it down. Connolly grew agile at evading such raids. The Coalition Cabinet, formed in May 1915, was heavily weighted in favor of Ulster, including as it did both Carson and Bonar Law, like Carson a Conservative

opposed to Home Rule, and *The Worker's Republic,* one of
Connolly's papers, in November ran a taunting little verse:

> Full steam ahead John Redmond said
> that everything was well chum;
> home rule will come when we are dead
> and buried out in Belgium.

In January 1916 the IRB's Supreme Council decided that
an insurrection should take place on Easter Sunday of that
year, April 23. They appointed a Military Council that
included MacDermott, Pearse, Plunkett, and Tom Clarke.
Jim Connolly was to be kept in the dark, as has been said,
for fear that he might throw his Citizen Army into the
breach ahead of time, and, of course, Eoin MacNeill was
not informed either. The council started at once to work
on a plan for all of Ireland. Center of the action, naturally,
would be Dublin, but there were Volunteer actions planned
for many places in the provinces as well—north of county
Dublin, Wexford, Connacht, Tyrone, Meath, Limerick,
Cork, and Kerry. For a while they contemplated the taking
over of Ulster at the same time, but it was undeniable to
the most enthusiastic member of the council that Volunteer
forces were already being spread very thin, and common
sense, if the phrase does not seem completely out of place
in this context, prevailed: the Ulster idea was dropped. The
first necessity for the rest of the country was arms for the
troops, which brings us back to Sir Roger Casement.

Casement was in America when the Great War started,
and he greeted the news with delight: all the Irish rebels
thought it a good thing that Britain should be distracted.
Soon he evolved a plan to contribute to the cause, and talked
it over with the German ambassador, Count von Bernstorff.
He proposed going to Germany and there recruiting Irish
prisoners of war for an "Irish Brigade," which would fight
against the British. Von Bernstorff thought the thing worth
trying, and recommended it to his Foreign Office at home.
They consented. Casement then got in touch with his friends

in Ireland to tell them what he was going to do, and they suggested that if their rebellion should break out while he was in Germany, he could help expedite the delivery of the arms being held there in reserve. There is evidence that John Devoy, "the old man," took a dislike to "Rory," as Casement was called in Irish-American code, but the Clan-na-Gael came up with the money for his expenses nevertheless. Casement seems to have entertained hopes that Germany would contribute manpower of her own to the Irish cause if need should arise, though it is difficult to find where he got the idea from. He sailed from New York on October 15, 1914.

The IRB and Clan-na-Gael would have sided with any nation that went to war with England, and Casement had the highest regard for Germany—at least until he found himself forced to stay there. But Patrick Pearse and his colleague and fellow poet Joseph Plunkett, the son of Count Plunkett, went a good deal further than Casement: for a while they entertained the notion of enthroning a German, Prince Joachim, as Ireland's king as soon as the war was won. It was an idea inconsistent, to put it mildly, for republicans to have. Perhaps they were inspired by the example of the thirteenth-century Irish chiefs who invited King Haakon of Norway to be their ruler and lead them against the Anglo-Norman invaders. If so, second thoughts of Dermot MacMurrough and his invitation to Henry II, the acceptance of which led to such unfortunate results, might well have given them pause. In any case, no more was heard in Ireland of Prince Joachim.

Casement had a poor time of it in Germany. Ill health plagued him, and, which was worse, the Irish prisoners in overwhelming numbers rebuffed his proposition. In vain he offered freedom, regular pay, even an ensured escape to America after the war if things went wrong and Germany did not win. Only a handful of men took him up and volunteered for the brigade, and they had to be protected from their fellow prisoners afterward. High-ranking German officers jibbed at the notion of arming renegades: after a while the officers' suspicion of Casement himself began to infect the whole Foreign Office. As the months went on he was treated with an indifference that bordered on contempt. When, on February 16, 1916, the General Staff heard from New York that the date of "general uprising" in Ireland had been decided as Easter Sunday, nobody bothered to tell Casement about it, nor did any word reach him of the cable that arrived next day at the Foreign Office from the embassy in Washington: "The Irish leader John Devoy informs me that revolution in Ireland due to start on Easter Sunday. Requests arms to be sent to Limerick, west coast of Ireland, between Good Friday and Easter Sunday. Further delay impossible..."

The British were intercepting all wires between Washington and the German Foreign Office, and they duly read this one, but Casement did not know about the plans for the rising until March 7, when he found out from a fellow Irishman, Monteith. Hurriedly he engaged in last-minute arrangements for the arms ship, but he became more and more discouraged as he learned that the Germans—who, after all, had other things on their minds—did not intend to send troops along with the twenty thousand obsolete rifles and ten machine guns that had been purchased by the Irish conspirators.

There now occurred one of the many ham-fisted or at least amateurish rearrangements that contributed to the failure of the rising. Pearse and his companions, after having alerted America and all the Irish Volunteers (not to mention Germany), and having divulged the date as Easter Sunday, now decided to change their plans. The rising would stand a better chance, they reasoned, on April 24, Easter Monday, because it was a bank holiday and all the garrison except for a skeleton staff would probably be at the Fairyhouse Races, a regular fixture for Easter Monday. By the time word of this change had been sent out to the various interested parties, the German arms ship *Aud*, disguised as a Norwegian trawler, had sailed with her load of rifles from Lübeck for Fenit on the Kerry coast, where according to her first instructions she was to be met by Volunteer emissaries sometime between April 20 and 22. The second instructions, that the *Aud* was to arrive later, on the twenty-third, were not received by the ship because she had no wireless. The British, better equipped, got both messages and were on the watch.

On April 11 Casement, with Monteith and a member of the German Irish Brigade, Daniel Bailey, set out for Ireland. It was a troubled, roundabout voyage that entailed travel in not one but two U-boats—the first one they embarked in broke down and had to return to port. Casement was very anxious about the rising, which he was sure would not succeed: he was eager to get to Ireland in time to put a stop to it. He seems to have been confident that he could, that his news of Germany's refusal to contribute manpower to the struggle would turn the scales.

Tom Clarke had been elected president of the provisional government of the Irish Republic, but for some reason he declined the post in favor of Patrick Pearse, and so it came about that Pearse appears as the chief actor in the events of Easter Week. Before the date of the rising was changed it was Pearse, as director of operations in the Volunteers, who ordered that the corps should ostensibly begin routine field maneuvers on Easter Sunday. Such exercises were familiar to the public and no explanation would be needed for gray-green uniforms and parades on Easter Day. It was MacNeill who grew suspicious and began to ask questions when he heard of the maneuvers order, but he was answered with convincing lies, and subsided. Connolly, however, was finally let in on the secret, his colleagues no doubt feeling that there was hardly time now for him to anticipate proceedings and spoil the plan.

On April 20, Maundy Thursday, two events on the Kerry coast had an important bearing on the rising, and one of them was disastrous. This was the capture of the *Aud* by a British warship, which picked her up as she hovered about offshore waiting in vain for the expected reception. She was taken under guard to Queenstown Harbor, the skipper managed at the last minute to scuttle her, and she sank with her cargo, taking with her all hope of an effective rising in the Irish provinces. Early in the morning of the same day Roger Casement and his two companions debarked from their submarine into a small boat and rowed over to Banna Strand, close to Tralee, capsizing once on the way and landing soaked to the skin. Casement sent the other men to look for friendly Volunteers, and waited for them in a ruined fort. A farmer came upon the abandoned boat and reported it to the local constabulary, who promptly searched the strand and found Casement. He was arrested and sent to jail, there to await trial for treason.

In Dublin, meantime, MacNeill had been led astray by the so-called Castle Document, which is now generally believed to be a forgery perpetrated by the Military Council to stir up laggard Volunteers and egg on MacNeill himself to action. Written in an easily deciphered code, it purported to carry directions from the Castle Military Council to the constabulary to arrest the IRB leaders and "isolate" certain buildings, including Pearse's St. Enda's School. Eoin MacNeill fell for it, though his reaction was not as extreme as the conspirators had hoped: he merely ordered the Volunteers to be on the alert, and the whole matter was forgotten when genuine crises overtook the corps.

The events of Easter Week were so crowded that it seems best to sort them out in a list, as follows:

1. Connolly alerted the officers of the Citizen Army and told them that zero hour was to be the evening of Easter Sunday, at six-thirty in Dublin, seven in the provinces.
2. Late at night on Maundy Thursday Bulmer Hobson learned accidentally of the risings and hurried to tell Eoin MacNeill. MacNeill, horrified, confronted the leaders and declared that he would do everything in his power to stop it—everything, that is, but inform the Castle. The others argued with him until, by

Friday afternoon, they had convinced him that it was
too late to halt the rising; that if they did so the Castle
would certainly find out all about it and would take
punitive action against the Volunteers. MacNeill was
persuaded until

3. O'Rahilly in his turn discovered the plans and
   endeavored to change MacNeill's mind yet again. At
   this juncture the news arrived that the *Aud* was on
   the sea bottom with all her cargo and that Casement
   had been apprehended. The loss of the rifles put
   paid to any hope that the rising could succeed in the
   provinces, and their failure would inevitably mean
   doom for the Dublin part of the venture.

4. MacNeill immediately countermanded the orders that
   had already gone out to the Volunteers, so that those
   in the country would know and act accordingly. To
   make sure that there might be no mistake within the
   city he published an announcement in the *Sunday
   Independent*: "Owing to the very critical position,
   all orders given to the Irish Volunteers for tomorrow,
   Easter Sunday, are hereby rescinded and the parades,
   marches, or other movement of the Irish Volunteers
   will not take place. Each individual Volunteer will
   obey this order strictly in every particular."

5. Reading this notice, the Castle authorities were
   reassured and put aside their worries. They had read
   all incoming and outgoing cables, and the officers
   had gloomily accepted the fact that they could not go
   on holiday junkets with their families and watch the
   Fairyhouse Races on Monday. Now they cheered up
   and made plans for the races after all. It should be
   mentioned, by the way, that there were only twelve
   hundred troops in Dublin, all told.

6. The Dublin Volunteers, on the other hand, had been
   keyed up and were eager for excitement. MacNeill's
   orders, therefore, left them disappointed and bitter.
   On Easter Sunday the Volunteer Military Council
   held an emergency meeting to talk over the situation.

It was obvious that from the common-sense viewpoint
MacNeill was right: without the *Aud's* cargo the
provincial Volunteers could not possibly put up a
fight, and without them the Dublin effort was almost
certainly ruined. Nevertheless the council elected to
ignore MacNeill, brush aside his orders, and forget
that a second contradictory order could not reach
the provinces in time. They voted unanimously to
carry on with the rising. It was what Coogan calls "a
democratic vote in favor of death." MacNeill and The
O'Rahilly, bowing to the will of the majority, joined in,
and Pearse once more issued orders for mobilization.

Next morning, Easter Monday, those Volunteers and
army men who had received the message assembled at the
ITGWU headquarters, Liberty Hall, ready for action. There
were not quite two thousand in all. They received their
separate orders to seize various strong points of the city, and
started out at noon, led by their officers. One party of a
hundred marched toward the Westland Row station, south
of the city, under the command of a mathematics teacher
named Eamon de Valera who held the rank of brigade
adjutant. De Valera had known nothing of the conspiracy
and did not like it now that he had been told, but he did his
job for all that, and so did all the others.

Dublin was sunk in typical bank holiday somnolence,
and for some minutes the marching men did not attract
attention at all as they made their way among the citizens
in the streets. One party, detailed to capture the Castle,
made an attempt and was turned back, but the others took
and occupied five other points—the GPO or General Post
Office, the Four Courts, Jacob's biscuit factory, part of the
South Dublin Union Hospital, and—after De Valera's men
had moved up from Westland Row station—Boland's Mills
at Mount Street Bridge. Those who moved into the GPO
included Connolly, Pearse, Clarke, Plunkett, and a stalwart
young staff captain named Michael Collins, Plunkett's ADC.
It was a quick, smooth operation: they took the guard by

surprise, pushed out the post-office workers, and barricaded the windows. A few Lancers who galloped down the street to the attack were driven off with shots from the windows. The republican tricolor was raised over the building, greeted by a sardonic cheer or two from the small crowd of curious spectators who had gathered. Then Pearse, Clarke, and Plunkett came out on the front steps, where Pearse, white with emotion and in a voice at first uncertain, read aloud the Proclamation of the Irish Republic.

POBLACHT NA H EIREANN

THE PROVISIONAL GOVERNMENT
OF THE
IRISH REPUBLIC
TO THE PEOPLE OF IRELAND

Irishmen and Irishwomen: In the name of God and of the dead generations from which she receives her old tradition of nationhood, Ireland, through us, summons her children to her flag and strikes for her freedom.

Having organised and trained her manhood through her secret revolutionary organisation, the Irish Republican Brotherhood, and through her open military organisations, the Irish Volunteers and the Irish Citizen Army, having patiently perfected her discipline, having resolutely waited for the right moment to reveal itself, she now seizes that moment, and, supported by her exiled children in America and by gallant allies in Europe, but relying in the first on her own strength, she strikes in full confidence of victory.

We declare the right of the people of Ireland to the ownership of Ireland, and to the unfettered control of Irish destinies, to be sovereign and indefeasible. The long usurpation of that right by a foreign people and government has not extinguished the right, nor can it ever be extinguished except by the destruction of the Irish people. In every generation the Irish people have asserted their right to national freedom and sovereignty; six times during the past three hundred years they have asserted it in arms. Standing on that fundamental right and again asserting it in arms in the face of the world, we hereby proclaim the Irish Republic as a Sovereign Independent State, and we pledge our lives and the lives of our comrades-in-arms to the cause of its freedom, of its welfare, and of its exaltation among the nations.

The Irish Republic is entitled to, and hereby claims, the allegiance of every Irishman and Irishwoman. The Republic guarantees religious and civil liberty, equal rights and equal opportunities to all its citizens, and declares its resolve to pursue the happiness and prosperity of the whole nation and of all its parts, cherishing all the children of the nation equally, and oblivious of the differences carefully fostered by an alien government, which have divided a minority from the majority in the past.

Until our arms have brought the opportune moment for the establishment of a permanent National Government, representative of the whole people of Ireland and elected by the suffrages of all her men and women, the Provisional Government, hereby constituted, will administer the civil and military affairs of the Republic in trust for the people.

We place the cause of the Irish Republic under the protection of the Most High God, Whose blessing we invoke upon our arms, and we pray that no one who serves that cause will dishonor it by cowardice, inhumanity, or rapine. In this supreme hour the Irish nation must, by its valour and discipline and by the readiness of its children to sacrifice themselves for the common good, prove itself worthy of the august destiny to which it is called.

Signed on Behalf of the Provisional Government,

THOMAS J. CLARKE

SEAN MACDIARMADA	THOMAS MAC DONAGH
P. H. PEARSE	EAMONN CEANNT
JAMES CONNOLLY	JOSEPH PLUNKETT

The details of what followed have been written up in scores of books and articles: for lack of space the story is here telescoped and only a few outstanding points are mentioned. The people at first paid little attention to the Proclamation, though it was hung on the GPO wall for them to read and digest at leisure after Pearse had read it to them. Many turned their attention instead to looting, smashing shopwindows and taking what they liked, a side effect of revolution that much distressed the idealistic Pearse. Fires were started, and those Dubliners who had more to lose than the rabble did became more than ever indignant at what was happening. It was bad enough to be ordered about and herded out of such places as St, Stephen's Green and the better-class hotels, but this was sheer anarchy, they felt. People were being shot.... Why didn't the Castle do something about it?

The Castle did, but it took time for reinforcements to arrive. Not until Wednesday did retribution descend on the insurgents, as troops with heavy artillery, under the command of General Sir John Maxwell, began to attack their strong points. The insurgents took what comfort they could from a rumor that the Germans were coming to their rescue, but conditions worsened: O'Rahilly was killed and Connolly was badly wounded in the thigh. Pearse wandered about, now and then making a speech or issuing a communique. About that time the men in the GPO heard from Arthur Griffith, who through an oversight had been left out of the hostilities. The leaders had promised to give him a signal when the rising was about to start, but had not done so. Now he got a message in to them, reprimanding them for their forgetfulness and asking if he could join them. Sean MacDermott, realizing that the fight was lost, replied telling Griffith to stay out of it: he could go on fighting with his pen afterward, MacDermott said.

Out in the country little was happening. Only in county Meath Thomas Ashe, at the head of the 5th Battalion, Dublin Brigade, captured some police barracks near Ashbourne and ambushed a motorcar column of RIC reinforcements, and in Wexford three hundred Volunteers occupied Enniscorthy, Gorey, and Ferns. They gathered a number of recruits and were all set to march on Dublin, but then they got orders to wait, and when next they heard it was all over.

Within the city the insurgents resisted and fought with tremendous bravery. They held out against great odds for nearly a week, but by Friday it was obvious that the end was near, and on Saturday Pearse, thinking of the suffering imposed on the citizens, surrendered unconditionally, at two o'clock in the afternoon. The commanding officers in the other parts of Dublin did the same, except for De Valera at Boland's Mills, who did not get the news until the next day. Then, as his disgusted men marched past the staring crowd, De Valera said to the onlookers, "If only you would have come out with knives or forks!" He did not yet understand that the populace were in a fury with him as with all the insurgents, that some of them had helped the troops, that some Irish Volunteers had actually fought against the rebels.

One can hardly wonder. Sixty-four rebels and 130 British had been killed, but the civilians suffered most. From April 27 to July 11 there were 250 dead buried in Glasnevin cemetery, all of them victims of the rising. Total casualties added up to 3000. The once lovely city had lost a third of her buildings, and smoked for a week after the surrender. All this happened to them, said the civilians, though they had taken no part in the rising: they had not even been asked if they wanted a rising. They were furiously indignant—until the executions began.

An enraged officer walked up and down among the men who had surrendered, striking out at them with fists and feet. He pulled the old cripple Tom Clarke out of the crowd and stripped off his clothes. He beat up Michael Collins. This officer, an embodiment of unleashed vengefulness, was fairly representative of the victorious troops for the first few days after the surrender, when ninety rebels were hastily court-martialed and condemned to death, and the spirit of revenge endured until fifteen of the ninety had been executed. On May 3 Pearse, MacDonagh, and Clarke were shot. The next day brought the execution of Plunkett and others, including Patrick Pearse's younger brother Willie—though Willie had had little to do with the rising and scarcely deserved martyrdom. Sean MacDermott and Connolly died on May 12. It was probably the manner of Connolly's death that at last nauseated the public: his wound had gangrened, and he was in such a bad way that soldiers had to carry him out on a stretcher and prop him up to receive the bullets.

The rest of the ninety escaped death and were committed to prison instead. The pacifist Sheehy Skeffington, who had stayed out of the rising altogether, was shot without trial by an officer later proved to be insane. But nobody was particularly sane for a while—more people were arrested, it was said, than ever took part in the rising.

"They are shooting the leaders of the Rebellion, some 8 so far," wrote Horace Plunkett in his journal, "and Con Gore-Booth of long ago—the Countess Markievicz for 18 years— has been condemned to death. She is deeply dyed in blood but her motives were as noble as her methods foul. I met Powerscourt and he was, he told me, begging the authorities to shoot her....I shall urge her reprieve." Lord Powerscourt was an old friend of the Gore-Booth family. Madame was not executed; with De Valera and seventy-three others she found her sentence commuted to life imprisonment, a mercy for which she was not grateful. She had wanted to die with Connolly, and mourned him deeply.

In general, Dubliners after the executions came to mourn Connolly with the Countess: already many had changed their minds altogether about the whole rising. When in the House of Commons Redmond spoke of "the insanity of a small section of people," he was unaware that the insanity, if such it was, had begun to spread through Ireland's rank and file.

"The Military executions will be a black chapter in Irish history," wrote Horace Plunkett. Admittedly, he said, a few ring leaders should have been executed: it was not "politically possible" to avoid such action. "But three wrong things were done: too many were shot; the executions were too long delayed, and the disproportion between the punishment

and the crime was given the worst possible appearance...."
His friend Bernard Shaw wrote in a letter to the *Irish Times:*
"My own view is that the men who were shot in cold blood, after their capture or surrender, were prisoners of war, and it is therefore entirely incorrect to slaughter them....An Irishman resorting to arms to achieve the independence of his country is only doing what Englishmen will do if it be their misfortune to be invaded and conquered by the Germans in the course of the present war." It was a fight for Irish independence, he added, against the British government—a fair fight in everything except the enormous odds his countrymen had to face. The letter was published on May 10, two days before the shooting of Connolly. On May 11 John Dillon, ignoring Redmond's lead, spoke furiously in Parliament:
"You are letting loose a river of blood, and make no mistake about it, between two races who, after three hundred years of hatred and strife, we had nearly succeeded in bringing together. Is that nothing? It is the fruit of our life-work... you are washing out our whole life-work in a sea of blood." In spite of angry boos he went on: "... I am not ashamed to say in the House of Commons that I am proud of these men....I say I am proud of their courage and if you were not so obtuse and stupid... you could have these men fighting for you....it is the insurgents who have fought a clean fight, a brave fight, however misguided, and it would have been a damned good thing for you if your soldiers were able to put up as good a fight as did these men in Dublin—3000 men against 20,000 with machine-guns and artillery."

Thomas MacDonagh had left behind him a letter exonerating Eoin MacNeill, so MacNeill escaped execution but went to prison.
Roger Casement's trial was held June 26-29. He wanted to use the line of defense suggested by Shaw, who wrote it out for him: "I am an Irishman. I deny England's right to rule our country and I submit that as an Irishman I owe no allegiance to England and I claim the right to go where I

choose and appeal to whom I like for aid against England. I took the course I did with my eyes open and if England claims my life let her hang me, and be damned to her."

However, Casement was talked out of this approach, and his trial was a conventional one at Bow Street. Horace Plunkett was there for the opening, noting afterward, "The fool was guilty of High Treason without a doubt....He is, I think, mad." The prisoner was found guilty. On August 3 he went to the scaffold.

CHAPTER

22

INEVITABLY the executions stirred up wrath among Irish-Americans, and soon United States officials talked gravely to their opposite numbers in London, saying that the State Department could not afford to ignore the Irish element among American voters. If Britain wanted United States help in the war, they said—and she needed it—she was going about getting it in a very odd way. Caught between the Americans and the Ulster-Tory unionist bloc, Lloyd George's government could not afford to hesitate. Just before Christmas they made up their minds and released the small fry who had been interned since April without trial in British concentration camps. Among those sent home to Ireland was Michael Collins, who had spent much of his time in captivity studying the background of the IRB. At twenty-six Collins was a splendid physical specimen who also had an excellent brain. As a boy in West Cork he had passed a Civil Service examination, and had worked as clerk in the London Post Office until he returned to Dublin just in time for the rising. Back once more from England, he was eager to start rebuilding the Volunteer structure and the IRB. The wholesale executions had left the field wide open, and Collins stepped straight onto the Supreme Council. He also became secretary of the National Aid Association for collecting and administering relief to victims of the rising, a post that gave him good cover.

Like many of its members, the old Sinn Fein had undergone a change, and was now composed of people holding widely varied ideologies, though the organization's creator, Arthur Griffith, still clung to his original aims and held to the concept of incomplete independence for the nation rather than complete separation. Collins was not in sympathy with this idea, but he did not declare open disagreement. At a by-election at Roscommon in February 1917 the younger man worked for the Sinn Fein candidate Count Plunkett, father of the dead poet. Plunkett won easily over the Parliamentary candidate—a purely symbolic victory, since Sinn Fein winners were sworn not to go to Westminster, but considered themselves members of a kind of shadow parliament at home.

All the nationalist organizations—Sinn Fein, the Gaelic League, the Labour party, Cumann na mBann—met together on April 19 to form a National Council. As such they declared Ireland a separate nation, and announced that she would seek representation at the peace conference that was sure to be held soon, since the United States was at last entering the war.

In May another Sinn Fein candidate, Joseph McGuinness, ran in a by-election in Longford, and though he could not campaign in person—he was still in Lewes jail—the voters elected him.

June 16 brought about the release from British prisons of all the rest of those Irish who had been incarcerated after the rising. Among them was Eamon de Valera, who had maintained his hero status in jail by organizing and leading the other prisoners. The only top-rank rebel to survive, he had escaped execution because he was born in New York and the English didn't want to annoy the United States by shooting him—not that he considered himself American. His mother was an Irishwoman, nee Coll, who in New York married Vivian de Valera, a Basque or perhaps a Spaniard—

nobody seems sure which—from Cuba. Eamon was born in 1882. Vivian de Valera died in 1884, and an uncle, Edmund Coll, brought little Eamon to Ireland, where he grew up in the Coll family in the Limerick countryside. He was a clever youth who won scholarships and taught school to get through college. In 1904 he got his degree in mathematical science from the Royal University. He learned Irish well enough to teach it in a Gaelic League class, and was committed early to the IRB cause. One of the first of the Volunteers, he was not, as has been said, among the policy makers who planned the rising, but he fell in with it nevertheless. Extremely tall, thin, dark, and somber-looking, he resembled the popular idea of Don Quixote—an unusual type in Ireland. "The leader in Bolands is a fine looking man called The Mexican," wrote an Anglo-Irish woman in her journal soon after the surrender, "he is educated and speaks like a gentleman."

As soon as he was free De Valera was invited to stand as Sinn Fein candidate for the approaching by-election at East Clare, and he accepted. The campaign began at once, and he won by a two-to-one majority. A month later another Sinn Fein candidate was elected at Kilkenny. In spite of the moderate ideas of Griffith and some others, Sinn Fein in its new form favored an Irish republic rather than the proposed partition; this spirit alarmed the authorities and they retorted in time-honored manner, stepping up the pressure and arresting those who flew the tricolor or made speeches considered seditious. One of the arrested men was Thomas Ashe of the Ashbourne incident of Meath. The police threw him into prison with several of his associates, and the young men all went on hunger strike. After the brutal custom of the time they were subjugated to forcible feeding. During this operation a prison official manhandled Ashe, with the result that the prisoner died. The Irish public mourned Ashe and grew more and more mutinous, so the authorities made yet more arrests. Michael Collins was jailed for three months in Sligo. In reaction the Volunteers were besieged by recruits, and expanded rapidly.

All this worried Lloyd George, and he set out to make peace.

He had already made offers to this end, but it was necessary to placate the unionists in his cabinet, so he promised that Ulster need not be included in whatever Home Rule arrangement might result from the discussions proposed. As to the rest of Ireland, they could have their parliament, and the two portions of the country might participate in a council, without authority, at which delegates from each side of the border could make suggestions and talk them over peacefully.

Somehow neither the unionists nor the nationalists cared for this idea, so the prime minister proposed a convention of all the parties instead, and this opened in July 1917, with Horace Plunkett in the chair. Sinn Fein and Labour refused any part of it, and Ulster nearly did the same, reminding Lloyd George that the unionists had been promised they would never be compelled to attend an all-Ireland parliament. However, in the end northern unionists did send delegates, if only to ascertain how many counties they might expect to be awarded —six or nine. The southern unionists too attended, and battled forlornly against a partition that would leave them outnumbered and swamped in a Catholic Ireland.

Instead of taking part in Lloyd George's convention, Sinn Fein called one of their own in Dublin in October, the Ard-Fheis, at which De Valera was elected president and a great variety of questions were discussed. In 1917 Sinn Fein was anything but exclusive: its members represented practically every point of view except Britain's, but on one point they all stood firmly together—conscription. It was agreed that every member would resist, by force if necessary, any attempt made by the British to draft the Irish.

April 1918 marked the end of months of discussion, and Plunkett's convention produced the Home Rule proposal Lloyd George had been waiting for. Now he felt that he could no longer delay the passing of a Conscription Act— for the country after four years of war was in dire need of manpower. His new act provided for the conscription of older men, and for the first time empowered the government to extend the operation to Ireland. This was too much even for Redmond's Home Rule party, as it was still called although Redmond himself had recently died. The members walked out of the House and returned to Dublin, there to join with the other nationalists in protest. The lord mayor of Dublin called the new law a declaration of war, and the M.P.s joined De Valera in getting the bishops to bless an anti-conscription campaign. All Ireland except Ulster observed a one-day strike. Collins organized from morning till night, and thousands of men lined up at their local chapel doors to sign the pledge against conscription. Westminster at last gave in and withdrew the offensive portion of the act, but by that time the Volunteers had been built up into a formidable army, and Sinn Fein was stronger than it had ever been.

Suddenly the government struck back, rounded up nearly all the Sinn Fein leaders including De Valera and Griffith, and put them in jail, where they were to remain for nearly a year. The reason given for the arrests was vague; something about a German conspiracy, constructed around the rumor that a man shipwrecked on an Irish beach claimed to have been a member of Casement's original Irish Brigade. Collins escaped the dragnet. On the night of the arrests, with the daring simplicity that marked his methods, he moved into a house that had already been raided and slept there quietly. Afterward he teamed up with Harry Boland, another Sinn Feiner who had escaped the attention of the authorities, and between them they looked after the affairs of the absent leaders, Boland organizing for the Sinn Fein and Collins for the Volunteers.

The armistice was declared in November 1918. In a general election that December Sinn Fein had a landslide victory and won 75 out of 105 seats, the old Redmondite party getting only 6 and the unionists 26. Thirty-six elected Sinn Feiners were in jail, and none of the others, of course, went to Westminster to claim their seats: instead they met at the Mansion House in Dublin on January 21, 1919, to proclaim themselves the First Dail Eireann—the Assembly of Ireland. In the chair was Cathal Brugha (Charles Burgess) of Carlow, a man of great courage, who had played an important part in the resistance to conscription. All the proceedings were in Irish. Only twenty-seven of the elected members were actually present: when the roll was called the clerk replied at appropriate moments, "Imprisoned by the English." Then the assembly declared for a republic and a provisional constitution was read aloud, followed by a declaration of independence. Delegates were selected for the approaching peace conference in Paris. At the Dail's second meeting De Valera, *in absentia,* was elected president.

The English professed to find all this procedure funny and meaningless, but they did not laugh when they heard of an ambush that was carried out at the same time by Volunteers in Tipperary. Working independently of the central authority, these men commandeered a supply of gelignite, shooting dead two armed policemen in the process. Collins and Boland were not implicated; they were in England at the time, engineering the escape from Lincoln prison of De Valera. The tale of the escape is a great favorite among the Irish, and no wonder; it offers all the excitement of a *Boys' Own* adventure story. It begins where De Valera, while lighting candles for mass, managed to make a wax impression of the key to a gate in the outer prison wall. The bit of wax was then smuggled out to Collins and Boland, who had a key made to the pattern and smuggled it back into jail, baked in a cake. Unfortunately it didn't work, so they had another key made, and that didn't work either. Then they smuggled in to the prisoners a blank key, along with the tools to cut it—that day's cake must have been especially heavy—and at last, on the night of February 3, De Valera and two associates slipped out. Collins had planned that De Valera should be hurried off to safety in America, but he was still in Ireland when the English, having discovered the escape, forestalled mockery in a new and clever way by suddenly announcing that *all* their Irish prisoners could go free. The authorities had known all along that De Valera was escaping, they said, and had deliberately permitted him to go.

The new president came back to Dublin on March 22 and stayed only long enough to select his cabinet: Brugha (Defense), Griffith (Home Affairs), Plunkett (Foreign Affairs), Cosgrave (Local Government) , MacNeill (Industry), and Countess Markievicz (Labor), with Collins as minister of finance. Then, disguised as an ordinary seaman, he departed for America. In June President Wilson told the Irish delegates in Paris that they could not be accepted for the peace conference. That same month De Valera disembarked in New York. For the next eighteen months he traveled around the country, covering at least ten thousand miles, giving lectures as his predecessors had done, and taking up collections for the Irish cause. He was not seeking only money: he wanted the Irish-Americans to exert pressure on Washington to recognize the Irish Republic and his own presidency, and he found this mission harder going, for in international matters the Irish-Americans now tended to feel themselves more American than Irish. It was a natural development—the Great War had intervened, a new generation had grown up, and time had diluted the bitterness left by the immigrant fathers. Even Devoy was reluctant to co-operate with De Valera: he was now sharing his authority with Judge Daniel S. Cohalan, one of the new type who used the Irish question primarily to advance the Irish-American cause. Both Devoy and the judge advocated something less than outright independence for the Old Country—something they called self-determination. In spite of this disappointment De Valera collected money, for whatever their sentiments, Irish-Americans were incurably generous.

The British got around to proclaiming the Dail Eireann as illegal in September 1919. Before the end of the year Lloyd George introduced the Government of Ireland Act— sometimes called the Better Government of Ireland Act, sometimes called the Partition Plan—which provided for two separate parliaments in Ireland and embodied many of the proposals of the Home Rule Bill of 1914. Each side was

to have a House of Commons and a Senate, and each was to
send members to Westminster. Some of the Senate members
were to be nominated by the Crown; it was this clause
above all that the Dail would not accept. The 1919 act is
important because of the way things turned out. At the time
Lloyd George constructed it, everyone—except, perhaps,
the nationalists and the unionists of Ulster—expected it to
be a stopgap until Ireland should once more be united, after
differences on religion and economy were smoothed out.

In southern Ireland Michael Collins shouldered the lion's
share of the responsibility, which in theory was distributed
throughout the cabinet. The Tipperary incident introduced
the era of the Troubles, and they were now in full swing,
with Collins in his element. He had a genius for organizing
undercover activities, and he took virtual command of the
Volunteers. Cathal Brugha resented this, feeling that as
minister of defense he himself should be managing the corps.
He had to submit to necessity, but his grievance created a
permanent break between the men, though in the past they
had been good friends. In the saga of the Troubles Collins
has the stature of such folk heroes as Paul Bunyan, or, if
the name had not been pre-empted for another Irish saga,
we could call him Ulysses. Certainly he was as crafty as
the Greek. Over and over he outwitted the authorities, who
never knew when or where he might strike, and through
it all he remained in Dublin, unrecognized by the police.
He attacked in many ways and for various reasons. For the
sake of vengeance he decreed death for the officer who had
mocked Tom Clarke after the surrender in 1916. Spies and
informers had long been useful to the Castle, so Collins
moved to eradicate them: many suspects were shot down
without mercy.

In spite of the situation, municipal and urban elections
were held in January 1920, and again Sinn Fein candidates
won almost everywhere. Sinn Fein set up its own courts of
law, rather as the Land League had done in earlier years,
and the people applied to Sinn Fein courts for justice rather
than going to the Crown courts.

Most of the Volunteers were now members of the Irish Republican Army and had become a redoubtable guerrilla force, moving in ordinary clothing and undetected among the civilians. At times they gathered in bands for engagements, but usually they worked in small groups in hit-and-run operations. Under Collins himself was a special unit of twelve, "the Squad," who carried out his orders to kill within the city limits. IRA members infiltrated sensitive areas of government such as the Post Office, where they intercepted mail and kept the leaders advised, as did other Civil Service clerks and shipping-company employees.

The British maintained fifty thousand troops in Ireland, armed with up-to-date equipment from the battlefields of the Great War-artillery, tanks, machine guns. Yet they could not cope with Collins' IRA, which numbered only fifteen thousand in all and whose fighting force, limited by lack of arms, was usually about three thousand. The Royal Irish Constabulary felt the effects of the unremitting harassment, and many of their men resigned. In March 1920 the English raised a new class of auxiliary troops in Britain from among the ex-soldiers and ex-officers who were at loose ends after the armistice. Because there was a shortage of uniforms in Britain, the noncommissioned men were clothed in policemen's khaki tunics, caps, and belts worn with ordinary dark trousers. In Ireland this costume won them the soubriquet "Black and Tans," after a certain breed of foxhounds. They were paid ten shillings a day. The officers' division was simply called the Auxiliaries: they got a pound a day. In "the Tan War" that followed their introduction, a period of sixteen months, the country was subjected to ever mounting violence. Whenever a Black and Tan or Auxiliary was killed, the village or neighborhood where he met his end was burned out in reprisal, and if the villagers operated a creamery, that too was destroyed. For their part the IRA burned houses belonging to people suspected of unionist sympathies or of helping the Black and Tans generally. These suspects were usually Protestant and prosperous, whereas the villagers were Catholic and poor, so the Tan War, in following ancient lines of cleavage, rapidly took on a sectarian aspect. Violence led to atrocities of which both sides were guilty, and Ireland was racked with hatred.

Feelings rose to white heat over the case of Terence MacSwiney, a man with the face of an ascetic saint, who nevertheless believed in violence in warfare. Taken prisoner and confined, he went on hunger strike. Days passed, and still MacSwiney would not eat. More days passed. MacSwiney grew weaker, but he did not eat. His fame spread through Ireland, to the Continent and to America, where newspaper headlines kept the public informed every day. After seventy-four days of self-starvation MacSwiney died, and took his place among the martyrs.

In May 1920, after the Government of Ireland Act became law, a general election was held. The southern Irish simply treated the proceedings as if they were electing their Second Dail, voting for Dail members but not the new senators. It was a quiet campaign. One hundred twenty-four Sinn Fein candidates were returned unopposed, and nobody else ran except four non-nationalist candidates (unopposed) for Trinity. The Trinity members and the senators appointed by the Crown dutifully met on June 28, the day the new parliament was to have opened. But nobody else turned up, so they went home. In Ulster things were different. A riot-torn campaign produced forty unionist members and ten nationalists, with Sir James Craig as prime minister, but the end of the campaign did not bring peace. Mobs, organized by the Ulster Volunteers, attacked Catholics, destroyed their property, and drove them out of their jobs. In Belfast, in the two years of July 1920–June 1922, 445 people were killed: 267 Catholics and 185 Protestants. Two thousand people were wounded, and five thousand Catholics were forced out of the shipyards.

November 21, 1920, ten days after the second anniversary of the armistice, was marked in Dublin by the goriest incident of the Tan War, and is still referred to as Bloody Sunday. That morning, before most people were awake, armed IRA members suddenly made simultaneous assaults on more than thirty households in an attempt to wipe out all the informers in Dublin. Collins' Squad had previously named them. The intruders shot fourteen men in this way, but for various reasons the rest escaped. That afternoon a number of Black and Tans, bent on retaliation, irrupted into a football match at Croke Park in search, as they later said, of the guilty IRA men. They fired into the crowd and killed twelve innocent people, including a player, and wounded sixty. Then, having failed to get the men they sought, they retired. That night they had better luck and captured three men, who were taken to the Castle and immediately killed.

By the end of the year both sides had had enough and were looking for a way out. Michael Collins knew that he could do no more than maintain the status quo, and some of his people were getting tired, whereas the British saw no other way than to mount an all-out campaign to subdue the country, an idea most of them did not like even though the unionist Sir Henry Wilson, chief of the imperial staff, was all in favor of it. Lloyd George dropped hints suggesting that it was time to negotiate. Roger Sweetman, a pacifist Sinn Feiner who was a long-time adherent of Griffith's, came forward with a priest, Father O'Flanagan, to represent the Irish, and for some time they bargained with Lloyd George's representative without coming to any conclusion.

On the day before Christmas De Valera came back from America. As one who had been wielding supreme authority and must now relinquish it, Collins was irritated by the situation, especially by the president's ignorance of how the battle was going and his suggestions. Besides, the split had widened between Collins and Cathal Brugha, who was now joined on his side by Austin Stack, and though De Valera made a few gestures toward reconciling the angry men they remained at odds. Winter and spring passed. On June 22 King George V, who had come to Belfast for the opening of the northern parliament, made an appeal—"to

all Irishmen to pause, to stretch out the hand of forbearance
and conciliation, and to join in making for the land which
they love a new era of peace, contentment, and goodwill."
Two days later Lloyd George invited De Valera and Craig to
a conference; both accepted, and after a few conversations
in London a truce was declared on July 10. The following
day, in accordance with its terms, British troops in Ireland
began moving out. But De Valera objected to so many of the
proposals made to him in London that the conference was
suspended for weeks on end. After he returned to Dublin
the Volunteers trained and prepared and imported arms
against the possibility that hostilities might be renewed.

There were two conditions in the British proposals on
which their authors held firm and which they refused to
consider withdrawing. Northern Ireland was to make her
own decisions, they said, and national Ireland, no matter
how independent she might be in other respects, must
remain within the Empire. De Valera boggled at both these
terms. One of his chief characteristics at any time was great
deliberation in coming to conclusions—what Coogan has
brilliantly described as "indecisive intransigeance"—and
this acted as a brake on all negotiations. Progress was slowed
down even further, if possible, because the Dail members
could not agree among themselves on just what to settle for.
From August 10, when everything ground to a standstill,
until early in October, they had plenty of time to discuss
it. Griffith thought they should not hold out against this
condition or that; the important thing was to attain peace
in which to talk matters over; later they could learn to live
with compromise. Brugha and Stack, on the contrary, were
all for rejecting the British terms and going back to war if
they had to. Collins, who had a better notion of Ireland's
chances in a renewed war, sided with Griffith. De Valera,
though he never quite committed himself, probably inclined
toward Brugha's ideas.

At last word came from Lloyd George inviting De Valera
to London to start a second conference on October 11.
Somewhat to everyone's surprise De Valera refused to go

in person, but sent a delegation headed by Griffith and Collins. George Gavan Duffy, Robert Barton (who was a brother-in-law of Erskine Childers), and Eamon Duggan went along as representatives; among the secretaries was Erskine Childers. De Valera gave two reasons for refusing: his place was at home, he said, because he was the head of state, and anyway he had already turned down the British conditions, so somebody else would have more room to maneuver. The delegates were invested with plenipotentiary powers, but the cabinet did not seem to realize what the word plenipotentiary meant, as they also told the men they must not sign any treaty without first clearing it with Dublin. In addition, De Valera instructed them to advocate a plan he called "External Association," according to which Ireland would not come under the Crown but would not be completely cut off from the Empire: she would be a republic and at the same time enjoy dominion status.

In London the talks entered another period of slow motion. External Association got nowhere with the British, who continued to insist that Ireland recognize the king, and Griffith, feeling that the point had little intrinsic importance, was willing to concede it. Collins swung back and forth between exasperation and his more normal tendency to agree with Griffith, until a letter arrived from De Valera saying, "There is no question of our asking the Irish people to enter into an arrangement which would make them subject to the Crown, or demand of them allegiance to the King. If war is the alternative we can only face it." Griffith was naturally angry at such belated interference, and it is possible that the argument that followed had the effect of shelving the other and far more important condition relating to Ulster, whereas if the delegates had made a determined stand on that point they might have got somewhere.

At last on December 6 the treaty—though according to Dublin's directions it was as yet only a provisional one—was signed. It proposed that the Irish Free State should be a self-governing dominion of the Empire, like Canada and Australia. Crown representatives would be appointed as were dominion governors general. Members of the Irish parliament were to take an oath of allegiance to the Crown. Britain would be responsible for coastal defense and would maintain naval establishments in Ireland. Northern Ireland could if she wished withdraw from Irish Free State authority and retain the constitutional status within the UK given her by the act of 1920. If she did decide to retain this status—and this was a foregone conclusion—there would be a readjustment of the boundary line between south and north, decided on by a commission representing Northern Ireland, the Irish Free State, and Great Britain. The Irish delegates were led to believe that such a readjustment would take from Northern Ireland's jurisdiction those border counties inhabited by a Catholic majority, "returning" them to the Irish Free State. Such an operation would have practically obviated partition as far as the Free State was concerned, but in the event it never happened. The commission was not even appointed until 1924, its report was never acted upon, and the three parties signed an agreement in 1925 that confirmed the status quo.

"Think—what have I got for Ireland?" asked Collins in a letter he wrote just after the petition was signed. "Something which she has wanted these past seven hundred years. Will anyone be satisfied at the bargain? Will anyone? I tell you this—early this morning I signed my death warrant."

In Dublin the treaty had a mixed reception. The majority were in favor of it, but the clause about the English king stuck in the craws of others. De Valera was so angry that he refused to accept the affirmative vote of the cabinet, insisting on a longer debate and another vote from the whole Dail. The exercise gained him nothing, since on January 7, at the end of a wearisome debate, the Dail too voted to ratify the treaty, sixty-four to fifty-seven. De Valera immediately resigned, and Griffith was elected president of the Republic—but this was the *old* legislature, whereas according to the treaty there was to be a new provisional government as well: a confusing arrangement. A stormy scene in the Dail ended on an even more dramatic note as De Valera left the room, with Collins shouting after him, "Deserters all to the Irish nation in her hour of trial!" This was quite a shout, but Constance Markievicz topped it by shouting back, "Oath breakers and cowards!" "Foreigners! Americans! English!" retorted Collins, to which the Countess flung back the last words: "Lloyd Georgites!"

On January 14, 1922, the provisional government of the treaty was formed with Collins at the head and William T. Cosgrave and Kevin O'Higgins to support him. The Dail continued to function at the same time, but it was Collins' duty to take over power from the British viceroy, Viscount Fitzalan of Derwent, last of his breed, who handed over all the appurtenances, the Castle and the army barracks and depots. Overnight the IRA had become respectable and was now the national army of the Irish Free State, with uniform and regular pay, but some of the soldiers were discontented with the treaty nevertheless: about half of them thought it should never have been signed. Collins' defenders maintained that this unrest in the ranks was due to his protracted absence, and it is true that he had gone reluctantly to London for this reason. Brugha and Stack, said the Collins defenders, didn't know how to handle the men, but one must admit that it was no new problem. When war is over, armies are often difficult to keep in order. Whatever the reason, after the ratification a number of officers in Limerick, anti-treatyites, came to blows with other members of the forces who were pro-treatyites. The antis seized some of the barracks left empty by the departing British and the pros seized the rest. Collins was still trying to settle their differences when on April 13 a group of Republicans (as the anti-treaty people had begun to call themselves), led by one of De Valera's supporters named Rory O'Connor, seized the Four Courts and settled in. Then they sent letters to the Dail stating their terms and aims, and urged the Dail to take the matter of the treaty out of cabinet control and save the country "from Civil War now threatened by those who have abandoned the Republic."

From the shelter of the Four Courts they directed a

number of military operations; they imposed a new boycott on Belfast after an earlier one had been suspended, and sent out armed men who held up trains from Ulster and, whenever their masters were pinched for funds, raided banks. For a while nothing was done to dislodge them, while Griffith and Collins tried to settle things at a higher level. They proposed an election to resolve the treaty question, but De Valera refused, saying that the electoral register was out of date. Anyway, he added, even if the vote was held and the voters supported the treaty, the anti-treaty Republicans would repudiate the result. Violence increased, with a sinister rise in sectarian incidents, until at the end of May De Valera and Collins compromised and agreed on a general election by the results of which the will of the people could be seen. If pro-treaty Sinn Feiners outnumbered anti-treaty Sinn Feiners, that would be that. The election, on June 16, gave the pro-treaty Sinn Feiners a large majority—but their victory had come too late to avert war.

The precipitant was Northern Ireland. During the Free State's struggles to consolidate her new status, Ulster too was undergoing troubled times. In 1920, to avenge their Catholic brothers north of the border, the IRA had imposed the aforesaid boycott on Belfast, and this hurt Northern Ireland in the pocket as well as making the Protestants—if possible—more than ever anti-Catholic. For their part the Catholics accused Sir James Craig and his government of showing bias, especially after the government raised and armed a force of special constabulary to maintain law and order. Ulster Catholics who had seen these men before in an earlier incarnation, as the Ulster Volunteer Force, were not deceived, and indeed the constables—all Protestant —still carried the same rifles that were run into Larne in 1914. For law-and-order men the constabulary acted remarkably like gangsters, and Craig's government found it impossible to keep them under firm control. In March 1922 Craig and Collins met in London to discuss the matter, and came to an agreement: Collins would call off the Belfast boycott and make the IRA behave if Craig saw to it that Ulster's

Catholics got fair treatment. Admittedly, Collins' control over the IRA was just about as shaky as Craig's over the special constabulary, but both men did their best, and law and order actually began to appear in Northern Ireland. Then on June 22 everything was changed.

The hawkish Sir Henry Wilson, who had opposed the truce, in his capacity of military adviser to Northern Ireland abetted Orangemen when they committed atrocities against the Ulster Catholics. On that day, June 22, while standing before his own door in London, he was set upon and killed by two Irishmen, veterans of the Great War, in which they had fought with the British forces: they were now acting for Rory O'Connor. The British government protested strongly to Dublin, threatening to attack the Four Courts themselves if nobody else would. The discussion was still proceeding when a Four Courts convoy of cars on its way to Belfast was intercepted by Free State troops who arrested the officer in charge. His followers promptly kidnapped the Free State's deputy chief of staff. Next day, June 27, the provisional government ordered the insurgents in the Four Courts to surrender, and when they refused, on June 28 the building was shelled, stormed, and cleared out. The leaders were taken into custody, but not before their men mined and fired the building, destroying all the papers in the Public Record Office. The civil war was on.

It was a bloody struggle, with cruelty mounting on both sides as it continued. De Valera and his party combined with the Irregulars— those of the IRA who were anti-treaty— and announced that they were the only original Irish Republic. On October 25 De Valera was elected president of the Republic, but the expected surge of the nation to his standard never materialized. The people could no longer be stirred: they had had enough. The Church, too, opposed De Valera and backed the Free State government. Only those who had already entered the battle went on fighting as if automatically, each side trying with more and more outrageous methods to stamp out the other. Liam Lynch, commander of the Irregulars, told his men to shoot every

Free State officer above the rank of lieutenant and any deputy who had voted for the treaty, so they killed a deputy and the deputy president of the Dail. On hearing this news Free State officers shot Rory O'Connor and three other Four Courts prisoners.

The deadly game went on because there was no way to stop it, until most of the leaders had been stamped out. Cathal Brugha died in character, with his boots on, shooting it out at the door of the Gresham Hotel during the Four Courts battle. Harry Boland was wounded and died. Erskine Childers was shot by a Free State firing squad. Griffith died of a heart attack on August 12, and on August 22 Michael Collins was killed in ambush, in his own county Cork. Liam Lynch died in battle at the end of April 1923. The loss of the Republican commander emphasized the unfavorable position now occupied by the anti-treatyites and convinced De Valera that his cause was hopeless. He asked the provisional government to negotiate, but they refused, and he was forced to proclaim an unconditional cease-fire on May 24.

So the civil war ended at last, too late for most of the chief figures in the struggle. De Valera and more than twelve thousand of his Republicans went to jail for a while, and W. T. Cosgrave became prime minister. De Valera succeeded him in 1932. But with these facts, as with all others pertaining to the story of Ireland after the civil war, we must leave the almost-certainties of history to move into the controversial region of journalism.

CHAPTER

23

1923: De Valera's new opposition party, Fianna Fail, won the general election and he became prime minister, a post he held until 1948.

1939: The Second World War broke out. The Irish Free State decided to remain neutral, but Northern Ireland stood by Great Britain.

1957: De Valera, having been in and out of the wilderness, returned as prime minister, a tide now rendered in Irish as Taoiseach.

1959: Sean Lemass became Taoiseach and De Valera was moved over to the presidency, which he still occupies at this date of writing, 1969.

1960: Irish troops went to the Congo with other U.N. nationals on a peace-keeping expedition. The Republic of Ireland had been a member of the United Nations since 1946.

1965: With much fanfare Captain Terence O'Neill, prime minister of Northern Ireland, met Taoiseach Sean Lemass in Belfast for a friendly visit.

1969

There has never been a chance for any party but the

Unionists to rule in Northern Ireland. This is a sectarian matter as well as a political one, with one million Protestants to half a million Catholics. Ulster has preserved the Protestant ascendancy, and up until yesterday the Unionists did not worry much about the minority third of the population. However, the Irish Republic has maintained a consistent policy of opposition to the whole idea of partition, claiming that it is, or ought to be, merely a temporary expedient. Republican statesmen seldom miss a chance to express their calm belief that the six counties of Northern Ireland— Antrim, Down, Armagh, Deny, Tyrone and Fermanagh— will inevitably revert one day to the Republic where they belong. In the meantime Republicans keep up a lively interest in what goes on up there, now and then making remarks in public that, with their proprietary flavor, have a most irritating effect on the government of Northern Ireland. There are also hotheads in the IRA, which still exists as a quasi-secret order, who maintain nuisance activity on the border.

The Catholics of Northern Ireland are of a divided mind. In franchise, education, housing, and jobs they complain, with justice, that they are victims of discrimination. Still, the poorest among them get more help from the British welfare state than the poor of the Republic receive from Dublin. To take one example: butter is cheaper in Ulster than in the Republic even though it probably comes from Republican cows and creameries, because the British government subsidizes dairy farmers and the butter itself, and Dublin does not. (As a result a lot of butter is smuggled back into the Republic from Ulster. There is no denying that the whole partition question is complicated.) Pulled in one direction by a natural sympathy with their co-religionists in the south and in the other by a Protestant government that hands out welfare relief no matter what else it holds back, the average Ulster Catholic has a right to be neurotic, and he was ripe for the crisis that broke on the country on October 5, 1968, at Londonderry. That was the date chosen by a new organization, the Northern Civil Rights

Association, to demonstrate in protest against limited franchise for the Catholic poor, alleged gerrymandering in local government elections, and discrimination in allocation of houses and employment. Most of those who rallied to the call were young people. The demonstration was broken up by the Royal Ulster Constabulary, and—in the language of Republican commentators, then as always keeping an anxious, avuncular eye on Northern Ireland happenings— violence ensued. Complaints were also violent, and Captain Terence O'Neill replied to them with the announcement that he was setting up a Commission of Enquiry into the course of events that had led to the affair, and a promise that legitimate grievances would be remedied. More trouble followed in January.

In the election of the week of April 13, 1969, a new note was sounded in Ulster's political history when a twenty-two-year-old undergraduate of Queen's University, a Catholic girl named Bernadette Devlin, became M.P. from Mid-Ulster for the British House of Commons. This was not the same thing, of course, as winning a seat in Stormont, Northern Ireland's parliament, but it was startling nevertheless, and newspapers on both sides of the water made a great fuss about Miss Devlin. April 19, a few days later, had been chosen by the Civil Rights Association as a good day for a five-mile protest march in Londonderry—or Derry, as Republicans and headline writers prefer to call the town. The authorities banned the march, the civil rights people tried to march anyway, and violence again ensued, this time producing three hundred casualties. An emergency debate was held on the matter in Westminster on April 23, during which Miss Bernadette Devlin declared that none of Captain O'Neill's promises had yet been kept. Altogether Miss Devlin bade fair to become one of the most vocal of Ulster's Catholics: for months she had the lion's share of headlines both in Ireland and Britain, though she was run a close second by an Ulster fire-eater named Ian Paisley, the self-styled moderator of the Free Presbyterian Church of Northern Ireland. Reverend Paisley, who is dedicated to

the confounding of the Pope and all his works, has been to
London on purpose to demonstrate against an ecumenical
gesture made by Cardinal Heenan when the cardinal
delivered a sermon in St. Paul's. He also went to Switzerland
to protest against the Pope's visit there, but the Swiss held
him incommunicado at the airfield.

The civil rights protestors have no love for the RUC, but their
sentiments toward the B Specials are even less affectionate.
The B Specials are a volunteer special constabulary in Ulster
who stand ready to help when the ordinary police cannot
handle matters by themselves. There are eighty-four hundred
of these volunteers, and they are all Protestant. In a manner
of speaking they are no strangers to us, though their name
has been altered: we last saw them in 1920, brandishing
the Larne rifles of 1914. By 1969, however, they were better
armed.

As Bernadette Devlin said, the government neglected to
carry out Captain O'Neill's promises. Furthermore, they
not only continued their inactivity in this respect, but
jettisoned the captain himself. After a violent internecine
battle he resigned, to be replaced by the more conservative
Major Chichester-Clark. Then came August 12, which is
a special date for Londonderry. Every year the Protestants
of the town commemorate 1689, when the inhabitants,
most of whom were stanchly for William of Orange, were
besieged by James II's troops. For three months they held
out, stoically resisting the pangs of hunger. At one moment,
when the mayor tried to surrender and opened a gate in the
wall that still surrounds the town, thirteen heroic apprentice
boys prevented the disgrace by closing and barricading the
gap. At last on August 12 William's men broke through the
boom on the river and lifted the siege, and Londonderry
was saved. On every anniversary of the twelfth, therefore,
members of a Protestant club called the Apprentice Boys (or
'Prentice Boys, if one has a taste for whimsey) of Londonderry
circumambulate the town along a broad flat pathway on the
wall, which at one point runs high alongside a Catholic slum

called the Bogside. It is a gay affair: in William III uniform the so-called Boys parade to stirring music, their women dancing along with them. In the general excitement these marchers and their girls have been known to make rude, mocking gestures at the denizens of the Bogside, singing songs calculated to annoy with such words as these:

> Up the long ladder and down the short rope:
> Three cheers for King William, to hell with the Pope;
> And if that won't do
> We'll cut them in two
> And bury them under the Orange and Blue.

In 1969, as August 12 drew near, it was suggested to the gentlemen who govern Northern Ireland that the march of the Apprentice Boys, considering everything, might be canceled just for once. The suggestion was overruled, the gentlemen deciding that as the Apprentice Boys always enjoyed the march and as it was good clean fun, there was no reason to impose a ban.

This is journalism, so let us now turn to the journals. Headlines and text from *The Times,* London:

August 12: N. Ireland police hurt in clash.
August 13: 80 policemen hurt, tear gas used in Derry rioting. ... Police action followed a day and night of the worst violence the city has known, sparked by the traditional march of the Protestant organization the Apprentice Boys of Derry... Petrol stock seized from GPO depot.
August 14: Mobs attack Ulster police stations. Eire urges U.N. intervention.
August 15: (Armagh:) Man dead in new rioting. (Derry:) Police armoured cars open fire. 400 troops bring peace to devastated Bogside.
August 16: Belfast rioters use machine guns. (Dublin:) IRA "may intervene in Ulster."
August 18: Chichester-Clark accuses Eire of hooliganism.

August 19: Arms threat from IRA shocks Dublin. Anger
and tears at funeral of Belfast victims.
August 20: British Army takes over control of Ulster police.
B Special force to be phased out.
August 21: Northern Ireland leaders face political crisis.
Police specials will stay—Faulkner [minister of
development] .
August 23: B Specials' guns are called in. (Belfast, Aug.
22:) Lieutenant-General Sir Ian Free-land,
G.O.C. Northern Ireland, today asked Mr.
Anthony Peacocke, Inspector-General of the
Royal Ulster Constabulary, to start putting
arms issued to B Special forces at Belfast and
Londonderry under central control.

More or less secretly, by way of Dublin and then transatlantic
plane, Bernadette Devlin slipped away to the United States,
her avowed intention to collect a million dollars for the relief
of riot victims in Derry and Belfast.
Summing up in both towns, Catholics pointed out that
their people had suffered far more casualties than had the
Protestants, and that many more Catholic than Protestant
houses were burned out.
From Dublin the Taoiseach, Mr. Jack Lynch, continued
to proffer advice and encouragement to Ulster Catholics,
while a member of his government went to New York to ask
the United Nations personally to intervene. This request, as
Mr. Lynch cheerfully admitted, got the brush-off. Stormont
told the Taoiseach to stop talking about matters that were
not his concern, and Mr. Lynch brushed off Stormont.

From the *Daily Express*

August 23: Row over Ulster arms curb B-Specials 'May
Quit' if Guns Go Troops of the 2nd Battn.
of the Grenadier Guards will land in Ulster
today, making the build-up of British troops
there almost 1,000 more than the 6,000 asked

for by Sir Ian [Sir Ian Freeland]. New York: Miss Bernadette Devlin who said in New York today that the ultimate hope for peace in Ulster is reunion with the Irish Republic added: "My Parliamentary salary (£3,250) has been used to buy petrol and barbed wire."

From *The Observer*

August 24: What hope for peace in Ulster? ... At first, when it seemed that Mr. Wilson was imposing a strongish hand on Stormont, the Catholics were cautiously optimistic, the Protestants close to angry despair. Then, when Major Chichester-Clark returned home and he and Mr. Faulkner set about reassuring the Protestants on the fate of the "B Specials," their mood swung to relief, and the Catholics retreated behind their spiritual barricades, muttering that they had not been represented at the talks and the results were nothing to do with them. Now that Westminster has cleared some of the confusion surrounding the exercise of law and order, the Catholics are slowly edging forward again, and the Rev. Ian Paisley is talking about a new Ulster Covenant, presumably to be signed by Protestants in their own blood as it was in 1912....

ET CETERA.

RULERS OF ENGLAND AND (AFTER 1603) GREAT BRITAIN, FROM HENRY II.

MONARCH (OR PROTECTOR)	REIGN BEGAN	DIED	AGE	YEARS REIGNED
Henry II	1154	1189	56	35
Richard I	1189	1199	42	10
(Coeur de Lion)				
John	1199	1216	5o	17
Henry III	1216	1272	65	56
Edward I	1272	1307	68	35
Edward II	1307	1327	43	20
Edward III	1327	1377	65	50
Richard II	1377	1400	34	22
Henry IV	1399	1413	47	13
Henry V	1413	1422	34	9
Henry VI	1422	1471	49	39
Edward IV	1461	1483	41	22
Edward V	1483	1483	13	0
Richard III	1483	1485	35	2
Henry VII	1485	1509	53	24
Henry VIII	1509	1547	56	38
Edward VI	1547	1553	16	6
Mary I	1553	1558	43	5
Elizabeth I	1558	1603	69	44
James I	1603	1625	59	22
Charles I	1625	1649	48	24
Oliver Cromwell	1653	1658	59	5
Richard Cromwell	1658	1712	86	1
	(Resigned 1659)			
Charles II	1660	1685	55	25
James II	1685	1701	68	3
	(Deposed 1688)			
	Interregnum Dec. 11, 1688 to Feb. 13, 1689			
William III	1689	1702	51	13
and Mary II	1689	1694	33	6
Anne	1702	1714	49	12
George I	1714	1727	67	13
George II	1727	1760	77	33
George III	1760	1820	81	59
George IV	1820	1830	67	10
William IV	1830	1837	71	7
Victoria	1837	1901	81	63
Edward VII	1901	1910	68	9
George V	1910	1936	70	25
Edward VIII	1936	(Abdicated)		1
George VI	1936	1952	56	15¾
Elizabeth II	1952			

BIBLIOGRAPHY

Abels, Jules: *The Parnell Tragedy.* London, 1966.

Barrington: *The Ireland of Sir Jonah Barrington,* ed. Hugh B. Staples. Seattle, 1967.

Beckett, J. C.: *The Making of Modern Ireland 1603-1903.* London, 1966.

Bieler, Ludwig: *Ireland, Harbinger of the Middle Ages.* Oxford, 1963.

Binchy, D. A.: *Linguistic and Historical Value of the Irish Law Tracts.* London, 1943.

Brown, Thomas N.: *Irish-American Nationalism, 1870-1890.* Philadelphia, 1966.

Chadwick, Norah (and Myles Dillon) : *The Celtic Realms.* New York, 1967.

Coogan, Timothy Patrick: *Ireland Since the Rising,* London, 1966.

Curtis, Edmund: *A History of Ireland.* London, 1936.

Curtis, Edmund: *A History of Mediaeval Ireland.* Dublin, 1923.

Danaher, Kevin: *Ireland Long Ago.* Cork, 1962.

Digby, Margaret: *Horace Plunkett: An Anglo-American Irishman.* Oxford, 1949.

Dillon, Myles (and Norah Chadwick) : *The Celtic Realms.* New York, 1967.

Duffy, C. Gavan: *Young Ireland, A Fragment of Irish History, 1840-1845.* Dublin, 1884.

Girodias, Maurice (with P. Singleton-Gates): *The Black Diaries of Roger Casement.* New York, 1959.

Hanson, R. P. C: *Saint Patrick: His Origins and Career.* Oxford, 1968.

Inglis, Brian: *The Story of Ireland.* London, 1966.

Lecky, W. E. H.: *Leaders of Public Opinion in Ireland.* London, 1871.

Mac Coll, Rene: *Roger Casement: A New Judgment.* London, 1956.

McCoy, Hedley: *Padraic Pearse, a New Biography.* Cork, 1966.

MacManus, Francis (editor): *The Years of the Great Test.* Cork, 1967.

Marreco, Anne: *The Rebel Countess: The Life and Times of Countess Markievicz.* London, 1967. Martin, F. X.: *1916—Myth, Fact, and Mystery. Studia Hibernica* 7, 1967-68. Martin, F. X. (editor): *Leaders and Men of the Easter Rising; Dublin 1916.* London, 1967. Martin, F. X., and T. W. Moody (eds.): *The Course of Irish History.* Cork, 1967. Mathew, David: *The Celtic Peoples and Renaissance Europe.* London and New York, 1933. Noyes, Alfred: *The Accusing Ghost or Justice for Casement.* London, 1957.

O'Brien, Conor Cruise: *Parnell and His Party, 1880-90.* London, 1957.

O'Brien, William, and Desmond Ryan (eds.): *Devoy's Post Bag; 1871-1928.* Dublin, 1953.

O'Connor, Frank: *The Big Fellow: Michael Collins and the Irish Revolution.* (Revised edition.) Dublin, 1965.

O'Faolain, Sean: *De Valera.* London, 1939.

O'Faolain, Sean: *The Great O'Neill; His Origins and Career.* London, 1942.

O'Faolain, Sean: *King of the Beggars; a Life of Daniel O'Connell.* London, 1938.

Orpen, Goddard Henry: *Ireland Under the Normans.* England, 1911.

Otway-Ruthven, A. J.: *A History of Medieval Ireland.* London, 1968.

Phillips, W. Alison: *The Revolution in Ireland 1906-23.* England, 1926.

Quinn, David Beers: *The Elizabethans and the Irish.* Ithaca, 1966.

Ryan, Desmond: *The Phoenix Flame—A Study of Fenianism and John Devoy.* London, 1937.

Ryan, Desmond, and William O'Brien (eds.): *Devoy's Post Bag;* 1871-1928. Dublin, 1953.

Schrier, Arnold: *Ireland and the American Emigration.* Minneapolis,

1958. Singleton-Gates, Peter (with Maurice Girodias): *The Black Diaries*

of Roger Casement. New York, 1959. de Tocqueville, Alexis (ed. by E. J. M. Mayer): *Journeys to England and Ireland.* London, 1958.

Wall, Maureen: *The Penal Laws, 1691-1760.* Dundalk, 1967.

Wedgwood, C. V.: *Thomas Wentworth, First Earl of Strafford 15931641. A Revaluation.* London, 1964. Woodham-Smith, Cecil: *The Great Hunger: Ireland 1845-9.* London,

1962.

About the Author

A revolutionary woman for her time and an enormously creative writer, Emily Hahn broke all of the rules of the 1920s, including by traveling the country dressed as a boy, working for the Red Cross in Belgium, being the concubine to a Shanghai poet, using opium, and having a child out of wedlock. Hahn kept on fighting against the stereotype of female docility that characterized the Victorian era and was an advocate for the environment until her death at age ninety-two.

Emily Hahn (1905–1997) was the author of fifty-two books, as well as one hundred eighty-one articles and short stories for the *New Yorker* from 1929 to 1996. She was a staff writer for the magazine for forty-seven years. She wrote novels, short stories, personal essays, reportage, poetry, history and biography, natural history and zoology, cookbooks, humor, travel, children's books, and four autobiographical narratives: *China to Me* (1944), a literary exploration of her trip to China; *Hong Kong Holiday* (1946); *England to Me* (1949); and *Kissing Cousins* (1958).

The fifth of six children, she was born in St. Louis, Missouri, and later became the first woman to earn a degree in mining engineering at the University of Wisconsin. She did graduate work at both Columbia and Oxford before leaving for Shanghai. She lived in China for eight years. Her wartime affair with Charles Boxer, Britain's chief spy in pre–World War II Hong Kong, evolved into a loving and unconventional marriage that lasted fifty-two years and produced two daughters. Emily Hahn's final published piece in the *New Yorker* appeared in 1996, shortly before her death.

www.ingramcontent.com/pod-product-compliance
Lightning Source LLC
Chambersburg PA
CBHW021212090426
42740CB00006B/192